MY HERO ACADEMIA

SHONEN JUMP COMICS

VOL. 15

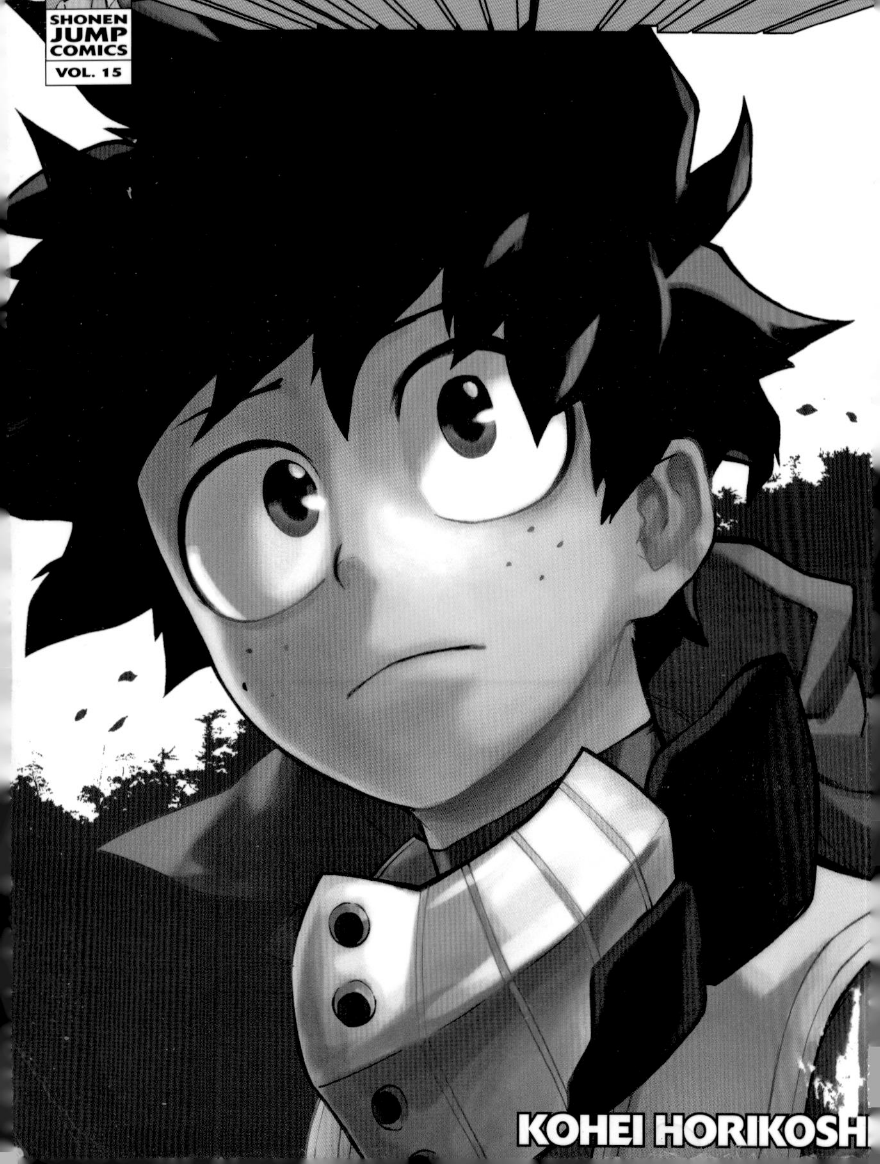

KOHEI HORIKOSHI

MY HERO ACADEMIA

15

SHONEN JUMP Manga Edition

STORY & ART **KOHEI HORIKOSHI**

TRANSLATION & ENGLISH ADAPTATION **Caleb Cook**
TOUCH-UP ART & LETTERING **John Hunt**
DESIGNER **Julian [JR] Robinson**
SHONEN JUMP SERIES EDITOR **John Bae**
GRAPHIC NOVEL EDITOR **Mike Montesa**

BOKU NO HERO ACADEMIA © 2014 by Kohei Horikoshi
All rights reserved.
First published in Japan in 2014 by SHUEISHA Inc., Tokyo.
English translation rights arranged by SHUEISHA Inc.

The stories, characters and incidents mentioned in this publication are entirely fictional.

Printed in Canada

Published by VIZ Media, LLC
P.O. Box 77010
San Francisco, CA 94107

10 9 8 7 6 5 4
First printing, October 2018
Fourth printing, December 2020

PARENTAL ADVISORY
MY HERO ACADEMIA is rated T for Teen
and is recommended for ages 13 and up.
This volume contains fantasy violence.

Volume 15!! Thanks for picking it up. Lately, I've started
sunbathing. Sunlight's the best.

KOHEI HORIKOSHI

CHARACTERS

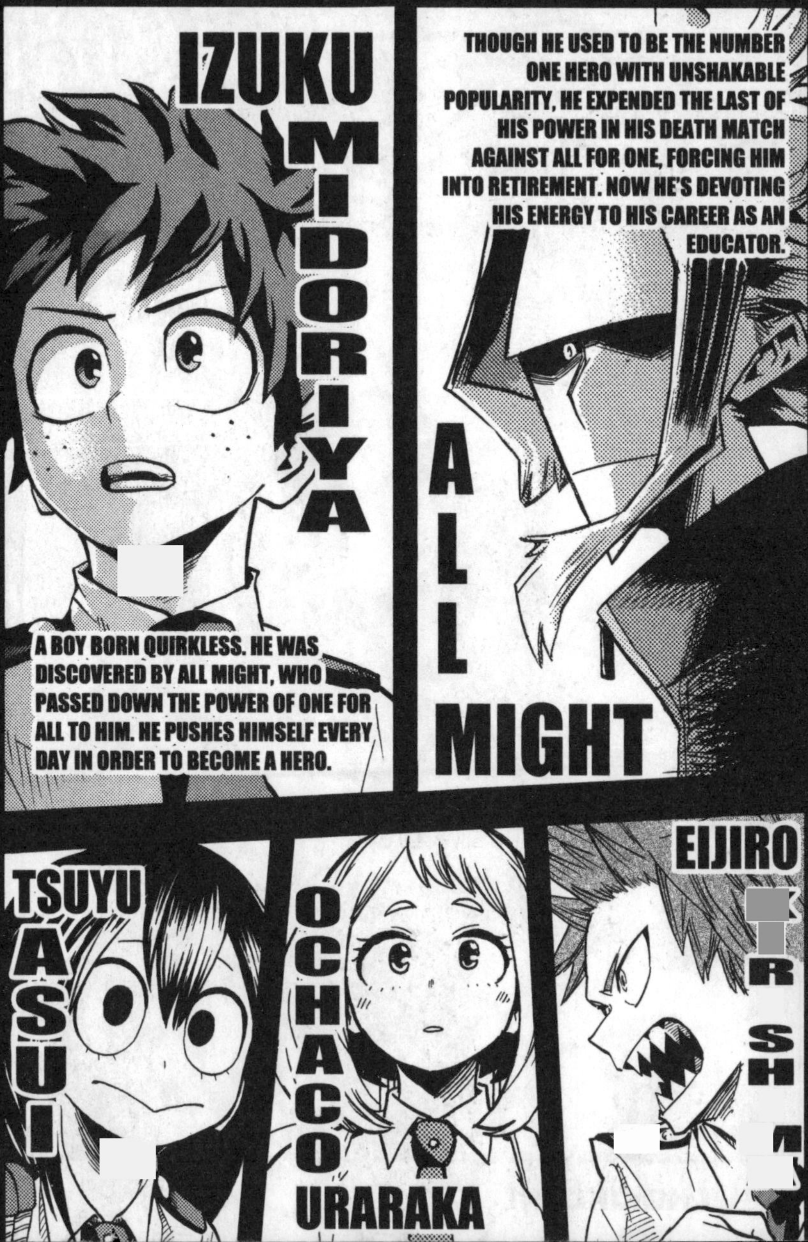
ALL MIGHT
THOUGH HE USED TO BE THE NUMBER ONE HERO WITH UNSHAKABLE POPULARITY, HE EXPENDED THE LAST OF HIS POWER IN HIS DEATH MATCH AGAINST ALL FOR ONE, FORCING HIM INTO RETIREMENT. NOW HE'S DEVOTING HIS ENERGY TO HIS CAREER AS AN EDUCATOR.
IZUKU MIDORIYA
A BOY BORN QUIRKLESS. HE WAS DISCOVERED BY ALL MIGHT, WHO PASSED DOWN THE POWER OF ONE FOR ALL TO HIM. HE PUSHES HIMSELF EVERY DAY IN ORDER TO BECOME A HERO.
EIJIRO
OCHACO URARAKA
TSUYU ASUI

MY HERO ACADEMIA

Fighting Fate

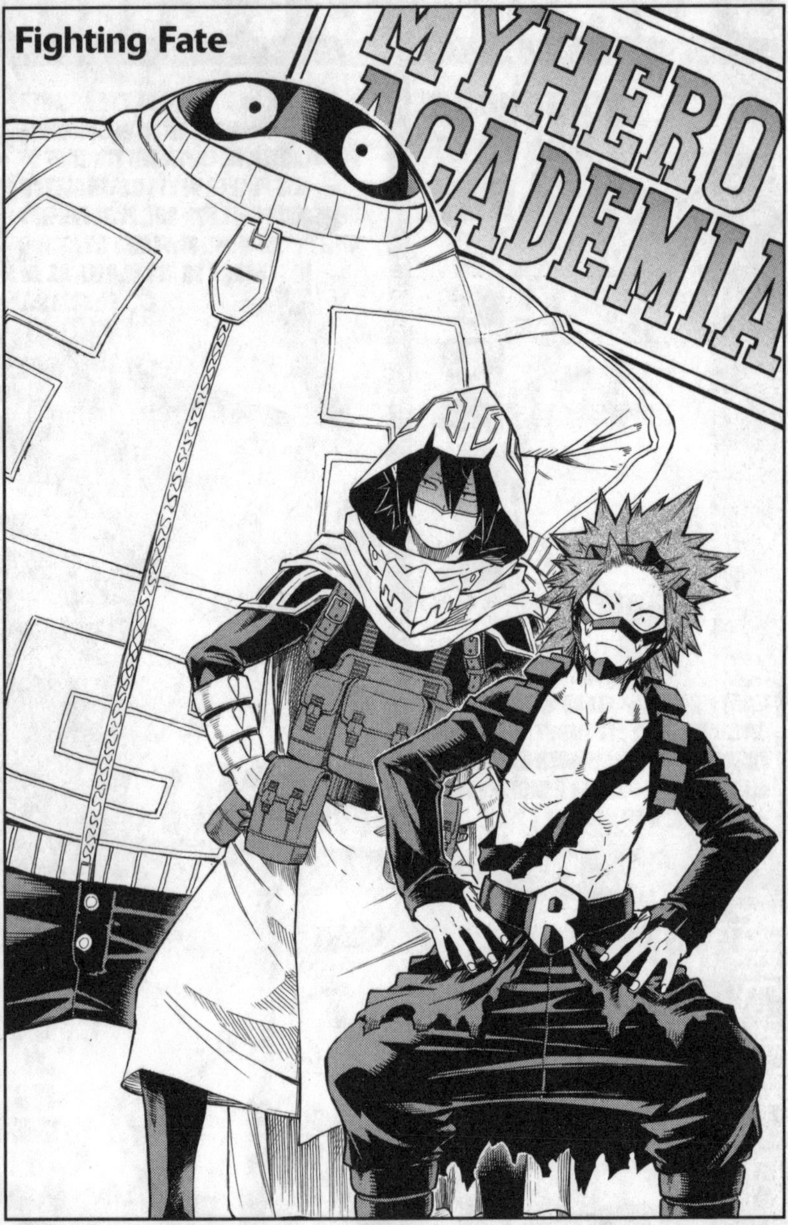
MY HERO ACADEMIA
R

KOHEI HORIKOSHI

One day, people began manifesting special abilities that came to be known as "Quirks," and before long, the world was full of superpowered humans. But with the advent of these exceptional individuals came an increase in crime, and governments alone were unable to deal with the situation. At the same time, others emerged to oppose the spread of evil! As if straight from the comic books, these heroes keep the peace and are even officially authorized to fight crime. Our story begins when a certain Quirkless boy and lifelong hero fan meets the world's number one hero, starting him on his path to becoming the greatest hero ever!

STORY

U.A.'S "BIG THREE"

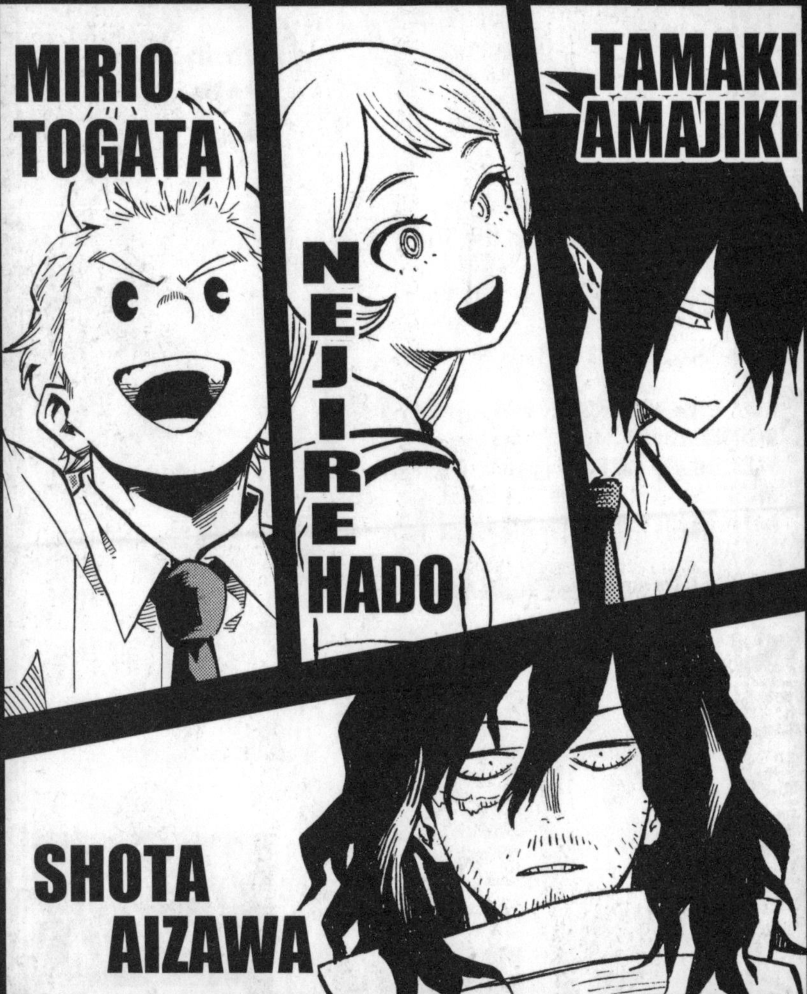
TAMAKI AMAJIKI
NEJIRE HADO
MIRIO TOGATA
SHOTA AIZAWA

MY HERO ACADEMIA

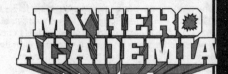

Vol. 15

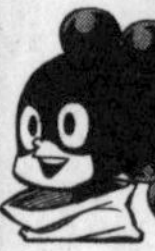

CONTENTS

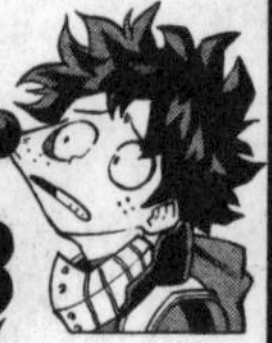

Fighting Fate

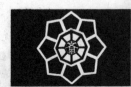

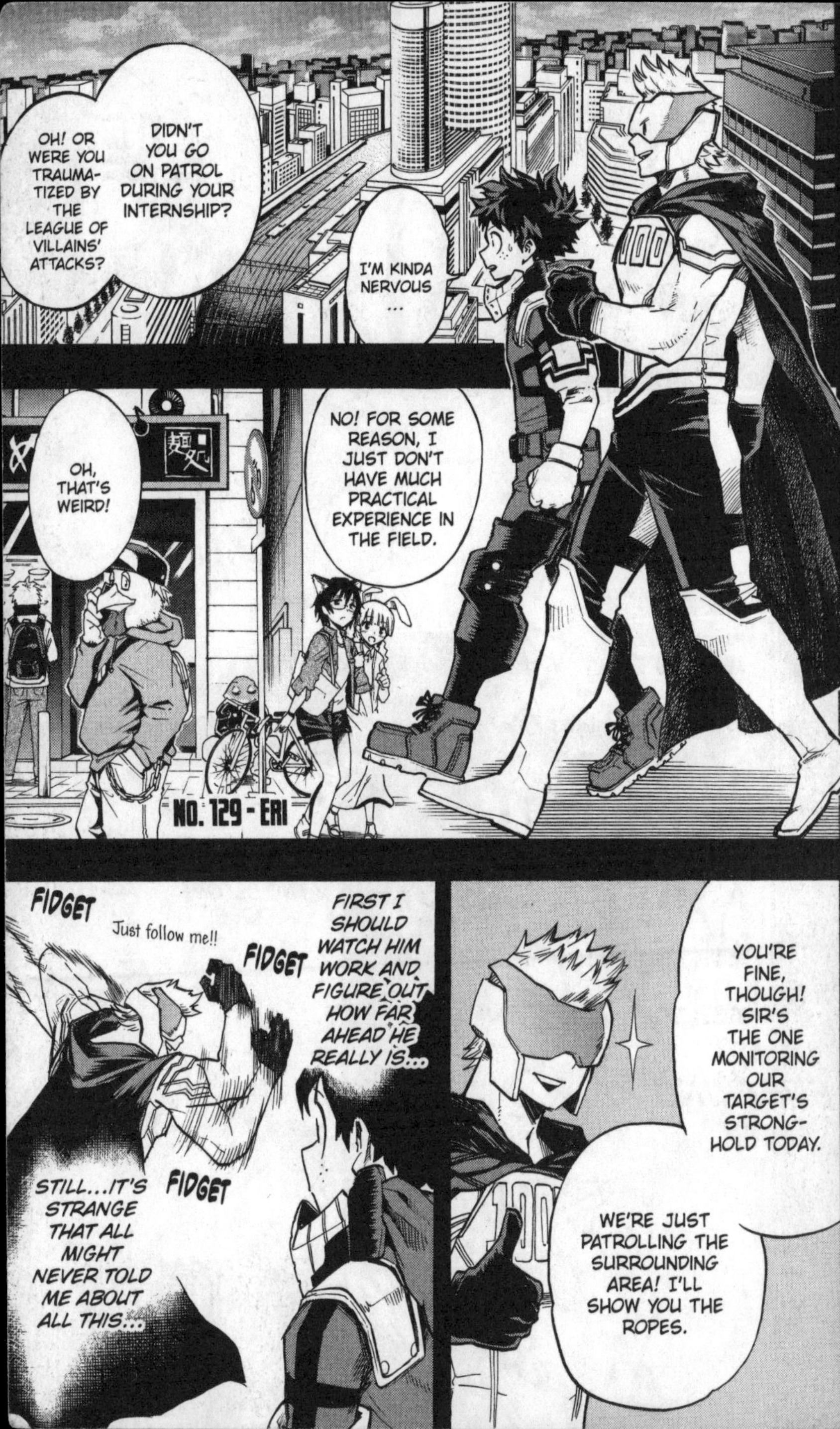
I'M KINDA NERVOUS...
DIDN'T YOU GO ON PATROL DURING YOUR INTERNSHIP?
OH! OR WERE YOU TRAUMATIZED BY THE LEAGUE OF VILLAINS' ATTACKS?
NO! FOR SOME REASON, I JUST DON'T HAVE MUCH PRACTICAL EXPERIENCE IN THE FIELD.
OH, THAT'S WEIRD!
NO. 129 - ERI
YOU'RE FINE, THOUGH! SIR'S THE ONE MONITORING OUR TARGET'S STRONGHOLD TODAY.
WE'RE JUST PATROLLING THE SURROUNDING AREA! I'LL SHOW YOU THE ROPES.
FIRST I SHOULD WATCH HIM WORK AND FIGURE OUT HOW FAR AHEAD HE REALLY IS...
FIDGET
Just follow me!!
FIDGET
STILL...IT'S STRANGE THAT ALL MIGHT NEVER TOLD ME ABOUT ALL THIS...
FIDGET

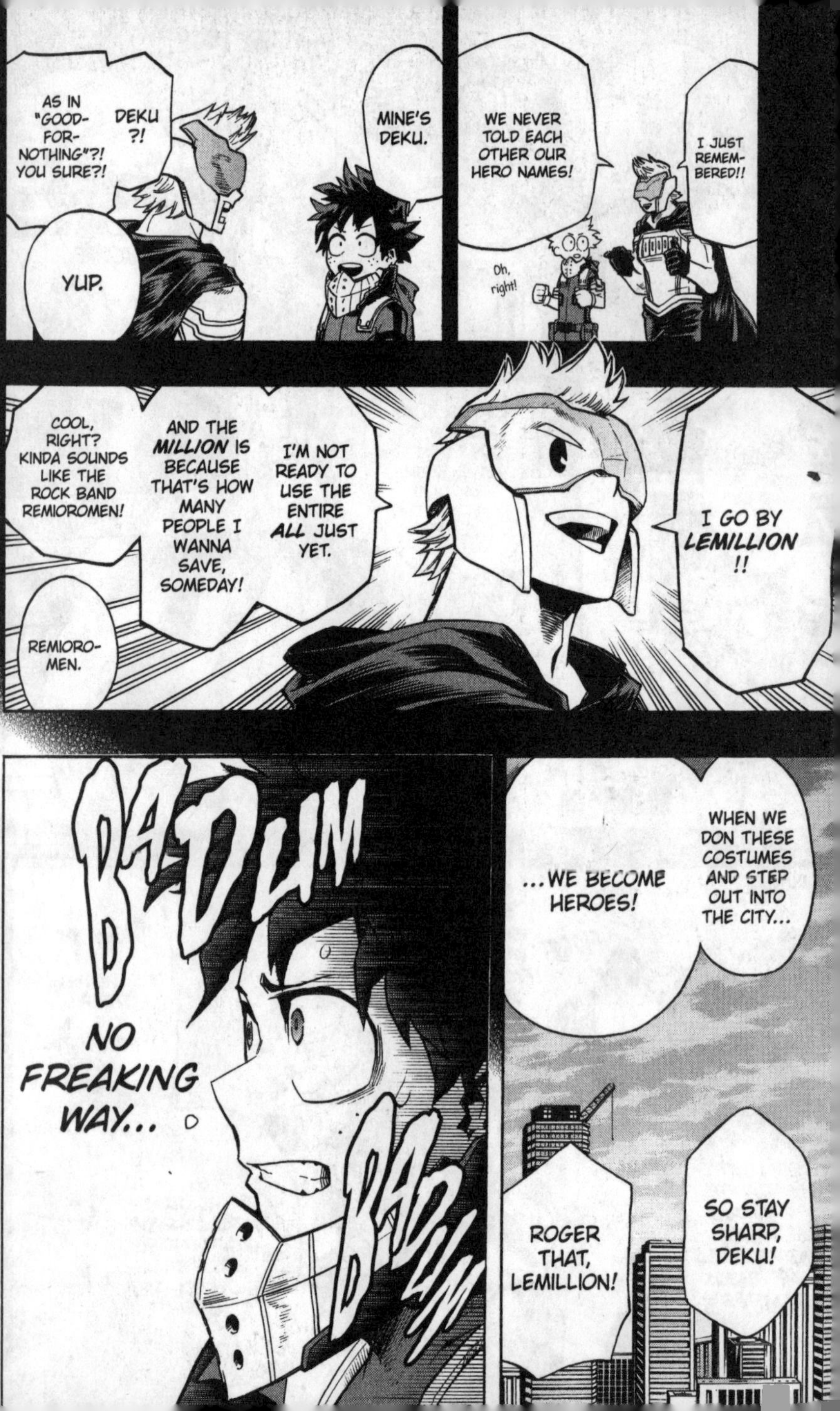
I JUST REMEMBERED!!
WE NEVER TOLD EACH OTHER OUR HERO NAMES!
Oh, right!
MINE'S DEKU.
DEKU ?!
AS IN "GOOD-FOR-NOTHING"?! YOU SURE?!
YUP.
I GO BY LEMILLION !!
I'M NOT READY TO USE THE ENTIRE ALL JUST YET.
AND THE MILLION IS BECAUSE THAT'S HOW MANY PEOPLE I WANNA SAVE, SOMEDAY!
COOL, RIGHT? KINDA SOUNDS LIKE THE ROCK BAND REMIOROMEN!
REMIORO-MEN.
WHEN WE DON THESE COSTUMES AND STEP OUT INTO THE CITY...
...WE BECOME HEROES!
SO STAY SHARP, DEKU!
ROGER THAT, LEMILLION!
BADUM
NO FREAKING WAY...
BADUM

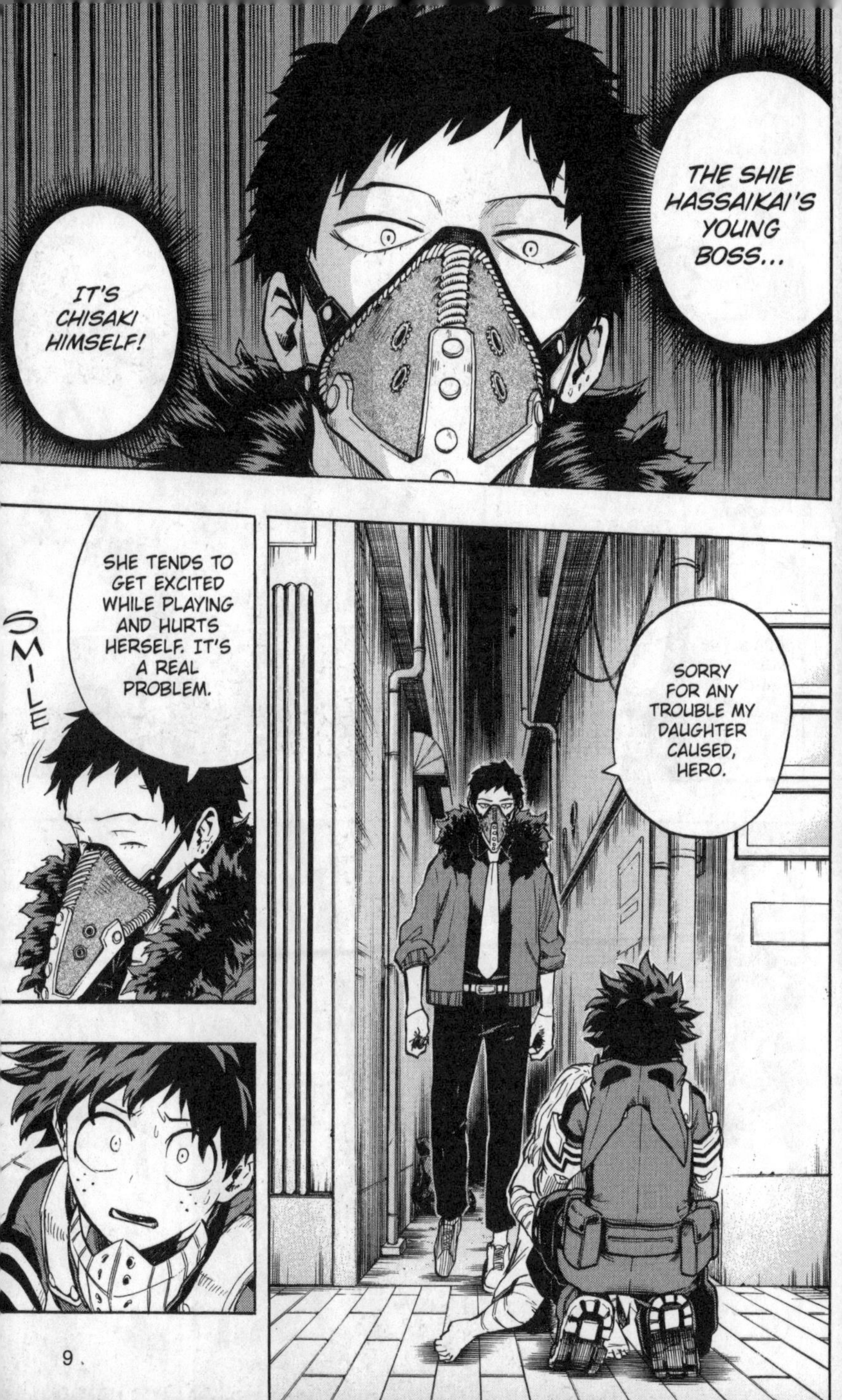

THE SHIE HASSAIKAI'S YOUNG BOSS...
IT'S CHISAKI HIMSELF!
SORRY FOR ANY TROUBLE MY DAUGHTER CAUSED, HERO.
SMILE
SHE TENDS TO GET EXCITED WHILE PLAYING AND HURTS HERSELF. IT'S A REAL PROBLEM.

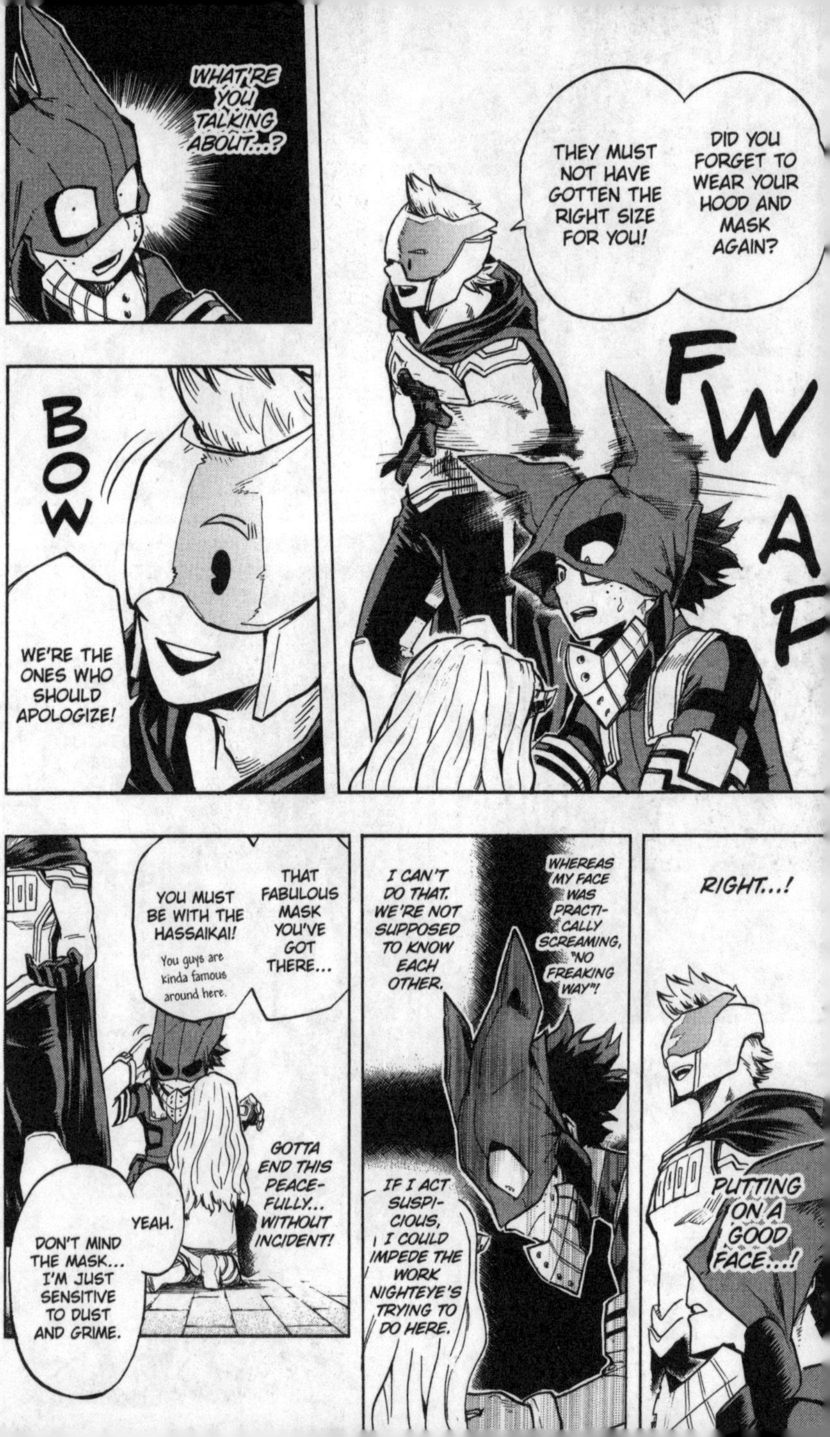
DID YOU FORGET TO WEAR YOUR HOOD AND MASK AGAIN?
THEY MUST NOT HAVE GOTTEN THE RIGHT SIZE FOR YOU!
FWAP
WHAT'RE YOU TALKING ABOUT...?
BOW
WE'RE THE ONES WHO SHOULD APOLOGIZE!
RIGHT...!
PUTTING ON A GOOD FACE...!
WHEREAS MY FACE WAS PRACTI-CALLY SCREAMING, "NO FREAKING WAY"!
I CAN'T DO THAT. WE'RE NOT SUPPOSED TO KNOW EACH OTHER.
IF I ACT SUSPI-CIOUS, I COULD IMPEDE THE WORK NIGHTEYE'S TRYING TO DO HERE.
THAT FABULOUS MASK YOU'VE GOT THERE...
YOU MUST BE WITH THE HASSAIKAI!
You guys are kinda famous around here.
GOTTA END THIS PEACE-FULLY... WITHOUT INCIDENT!
YEAH.
DON'T MIND THE MASK... I'M JUST SENSITIVE TO DUST AND GRIME.

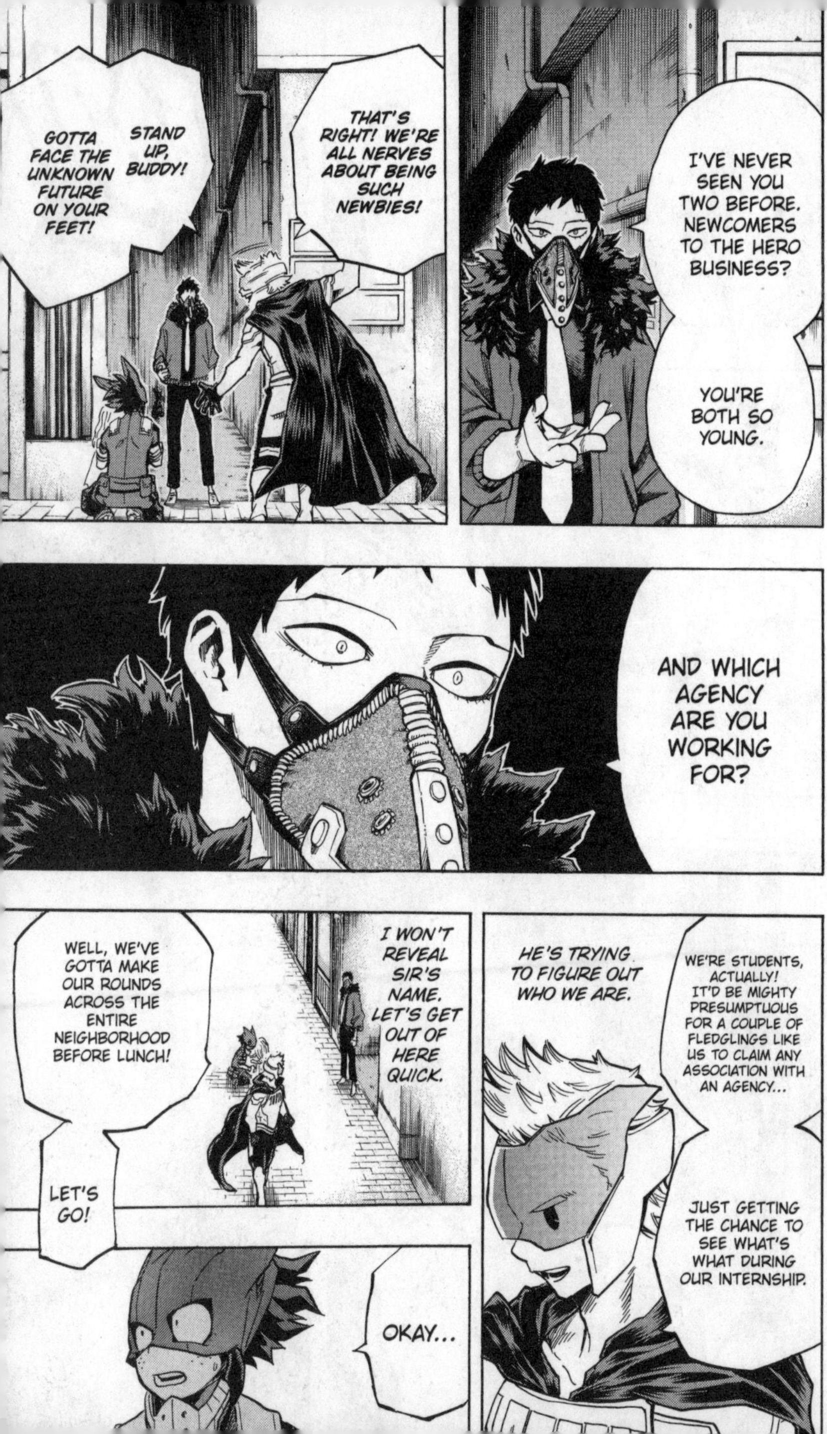
I'VE NEVER SEEN YOU TWO BEFORE. NEWCOMERS TO THE HERO BUSINESS?
YOU'RE BOTH SO YOUNG.
THAT'S RIGHT! WE'RE ALL NERVES ABOUT BEING SUCH NEWBIES!
STAND UP, BUDDY!
GOTTA FACE THE UNKNOWN FUTURE ON YOUR FEET!
AND WHICH AGENCY ARE YOU WORKING FOR?
WE'RE STUDENTS, ACTUALLY! IT'D BE MIGHTY PRESUMPTUOUS FOR A COUPLE OF FLEDGLINGS LIKE US TO CLAIM ANY ASSOCIATION WITH AN AGENCY...
HE'S TRYING TO FIGURE OUT WHO WE ARE.
JUST GETTING THE CHANCE TO SEE WHAT'S WHAT DURING OUR INTERNSHIP.
I WON'T REVEAL SIR'S NAME. LET'S GET OUT OF HERE QUICK.
WELL, WE'VE GOTTA MAKE OUR ROUNDS ACROSS THE ENTIRE NEIGHBORHOOD BEFORE LUNCH!
LET'S GO!
OKAY...

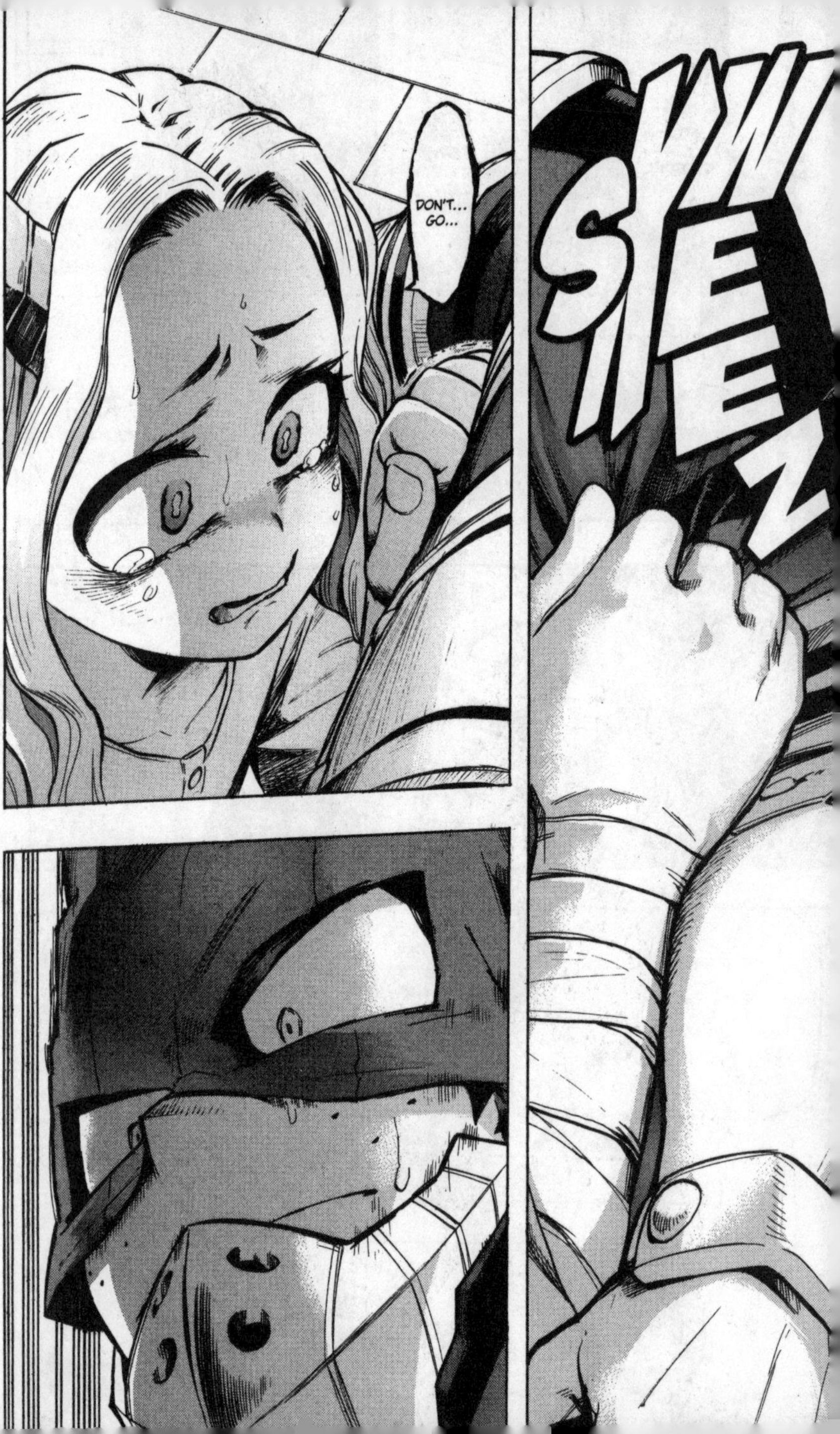
DON'T... GO...

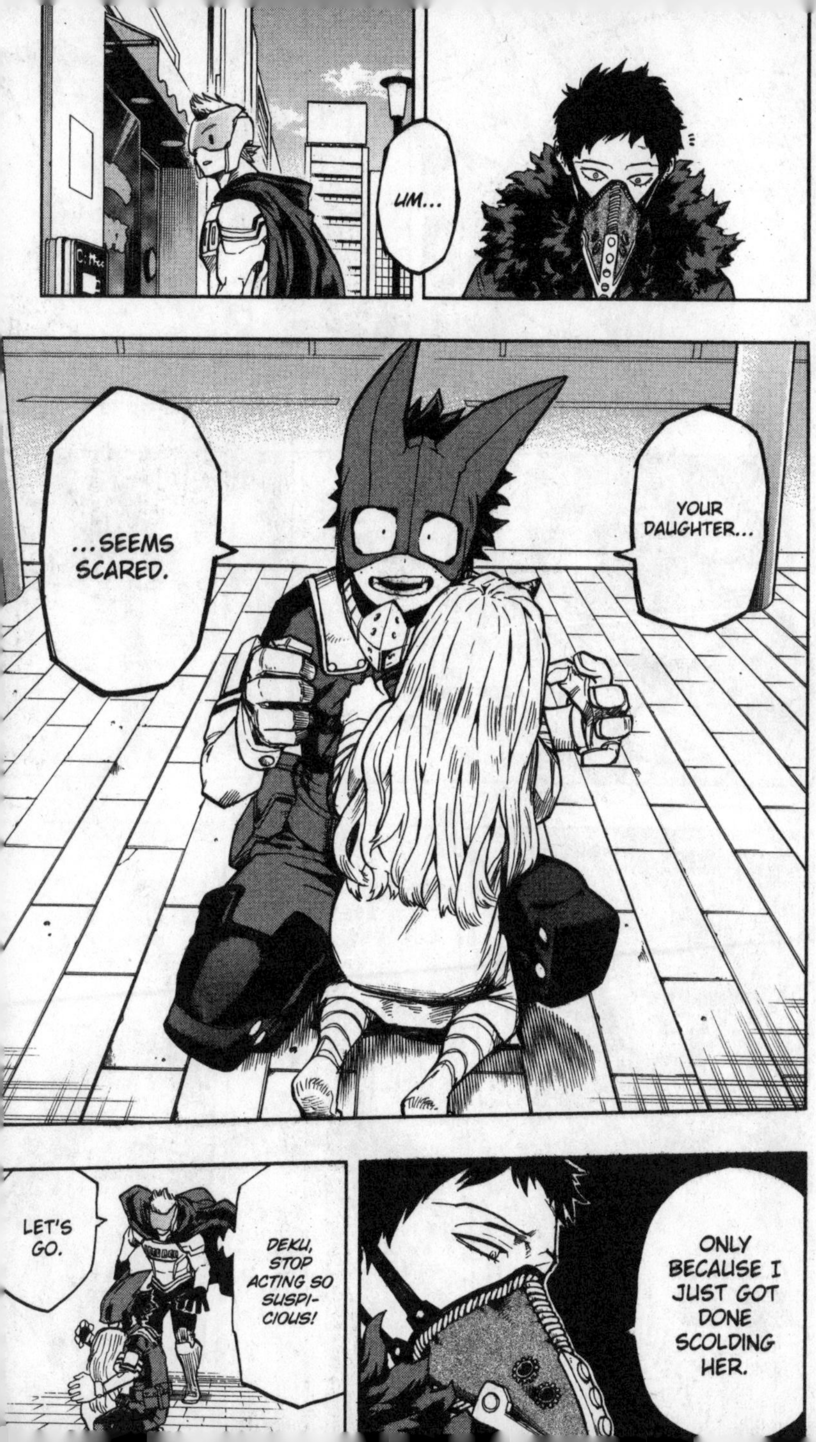
UM...
YOUR DAUGHTER...
...SEEMS SCARED.
ONLY BECAUSE I JUST GOT DONE SCOLDING HER.
LET'S GO.
DEKU, STOP ACTING SO SUSPI-CIOUS!

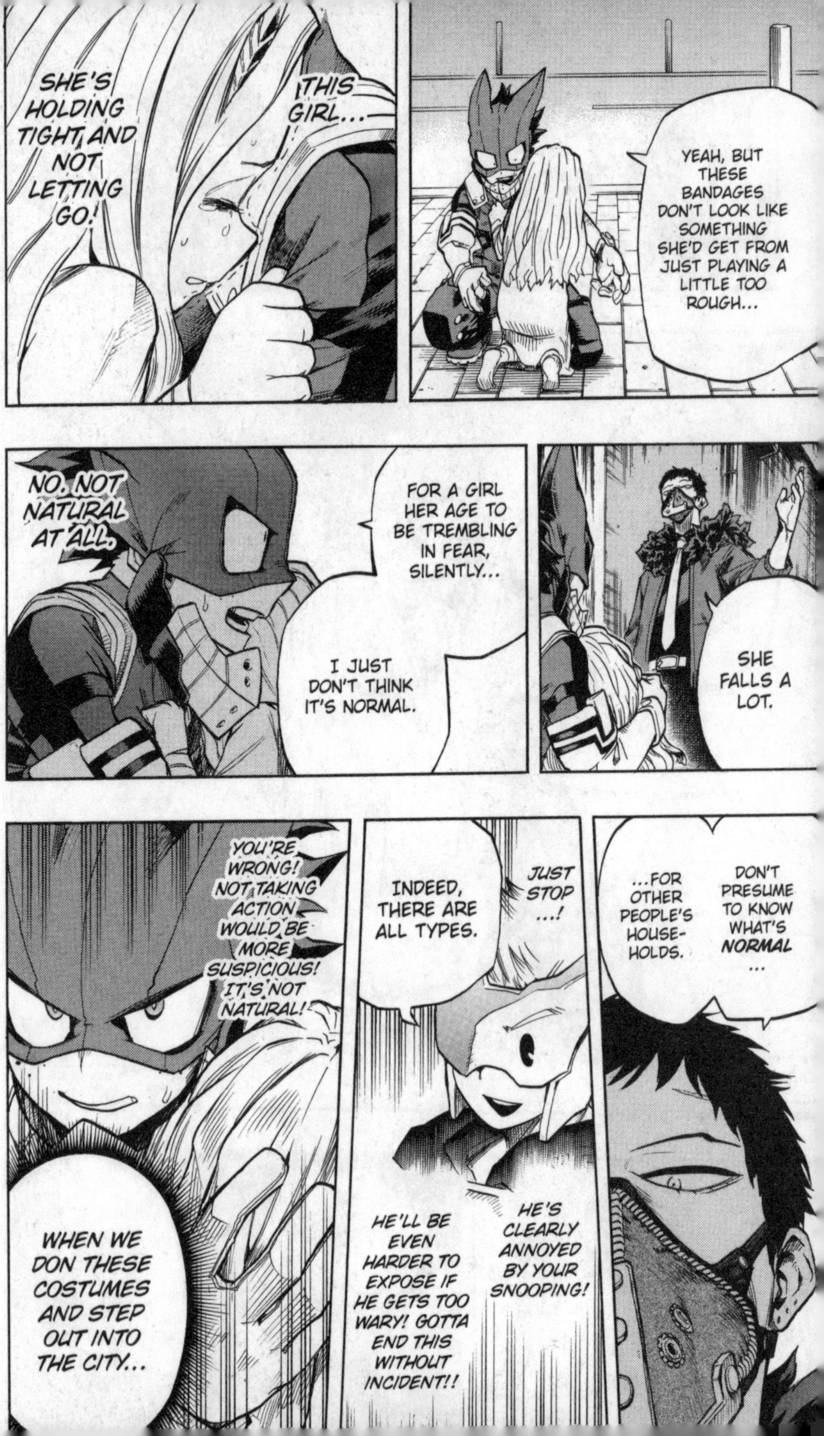
YEAH, BUT THESE BANDAGES DON'T LOOK LIKE SOMETHING SHE'D GET FROM JUST PLAYING A LITTLE TOO ROUGH...
THIS GIRL...
SHE'S HOLDING TIGHT, AND NOT LETTING GO!
SHE FALLS A LOT.
FOR A GIRL HER AGE TO BE TREMBLING IN FEAR, SILENTLY...
I JUST DON'T THINK IT'S NORMAL.
NO. NOT NATURAL AT ALL.
DON'T PRESUME TO KNOW WHAT'S **NORMAL**...
...FOR OTHER PEOPLE'S HOUSE-HOLDS.
JUST STOP...!
INDEED, THERE ARE ALL TYPES.
HE'S CLEARLY ANNOYED BY YOUR SNOOPING!
HE'LL BE EVEN HARDER TO EXPOSE IF HE GETS TOO WARY! GOTTA END THIS WITHOUT INCIDENT!!
YOU'RE WRONG! NOT TAKING ACTION WOULD BE MORE SUSPICIOUS! IT'S NOT NATURAL!
WHEN WE DON THESE COSTUMES AND STEP OUT INTO THE CITY...

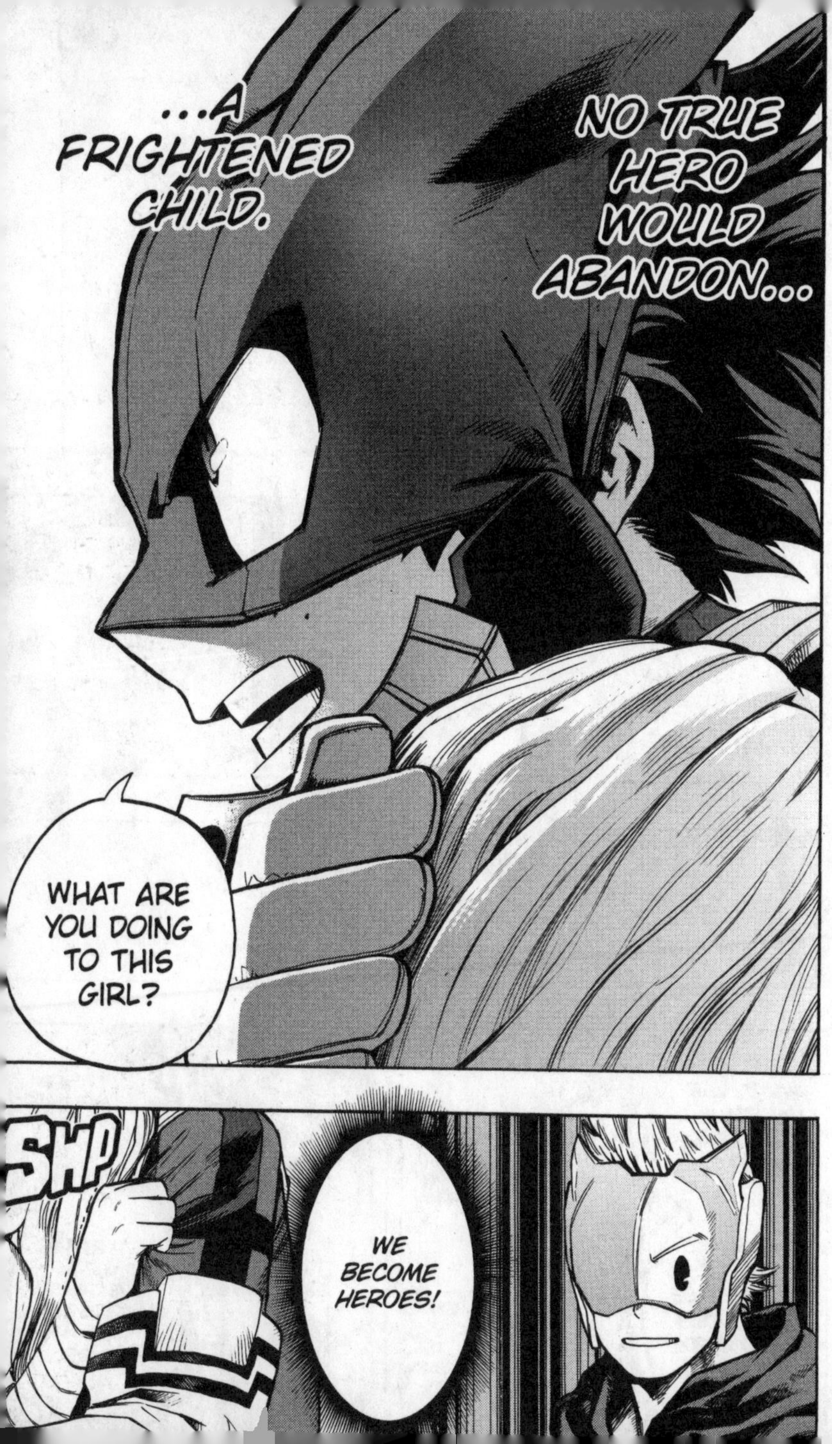
NO TRUE HERO WOULD ABANDON...
...A FRIGHTENED CHILD.
WHAT ARE YOU DOING TO THIS GIRL?
WE BECOME HEROES!
SHP

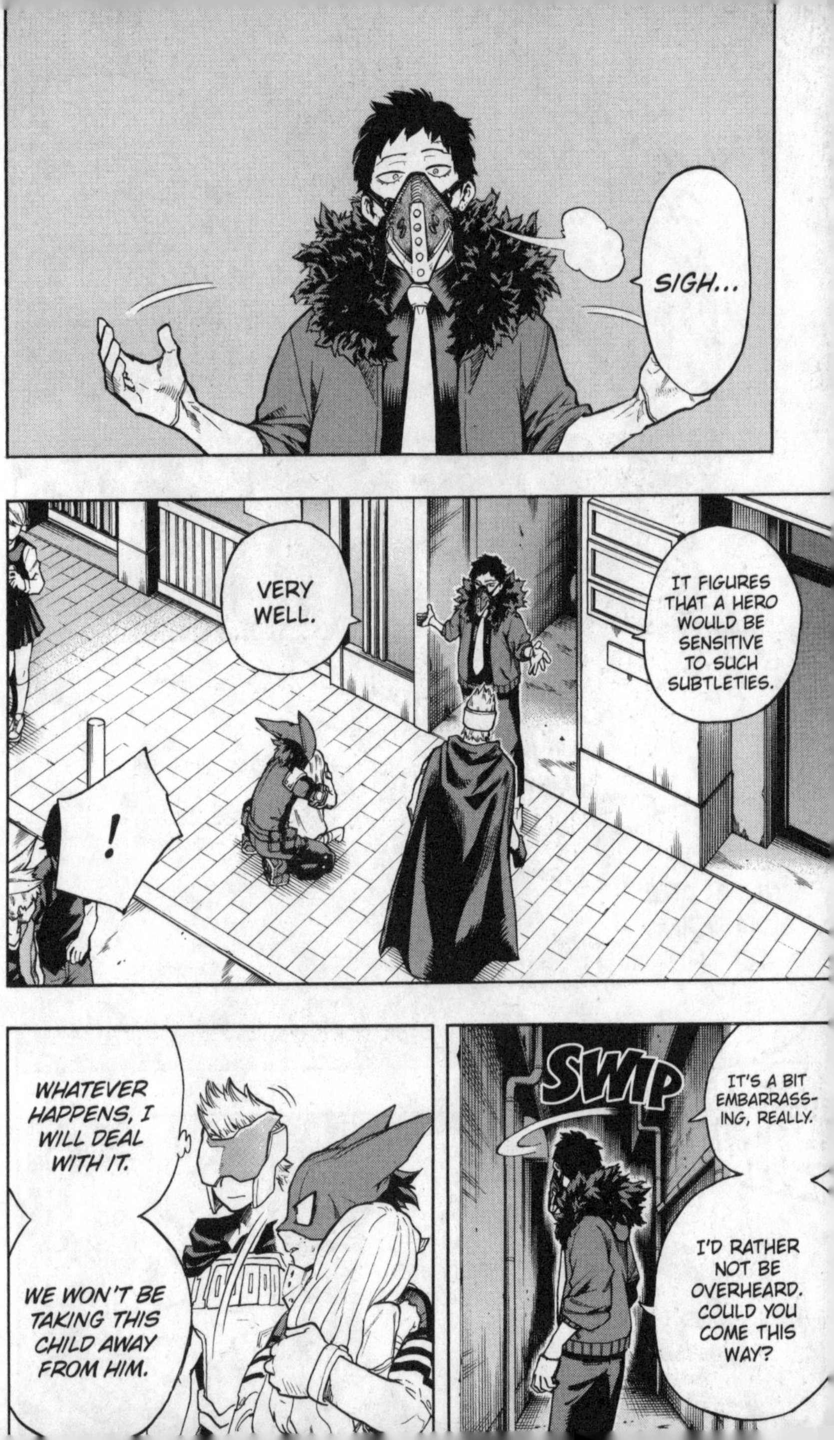
SIGH...
IT FIGURES THAT A HERO WOULD BE SENSITIVE TO SUCH SUBTLETIES.
VERY WELL.
!
SWIP
IT'S A BIT EMBARRASS-ING, REALLY.
I'D RATHER NOT BE OVERHEARD. COULD YOU COME THIS WAY?
WHATEVER HAPPENS, I WILL DEAL WITH IT.
WE WON'T BE TAKING THIS CHILD AWAY FROM HIM.

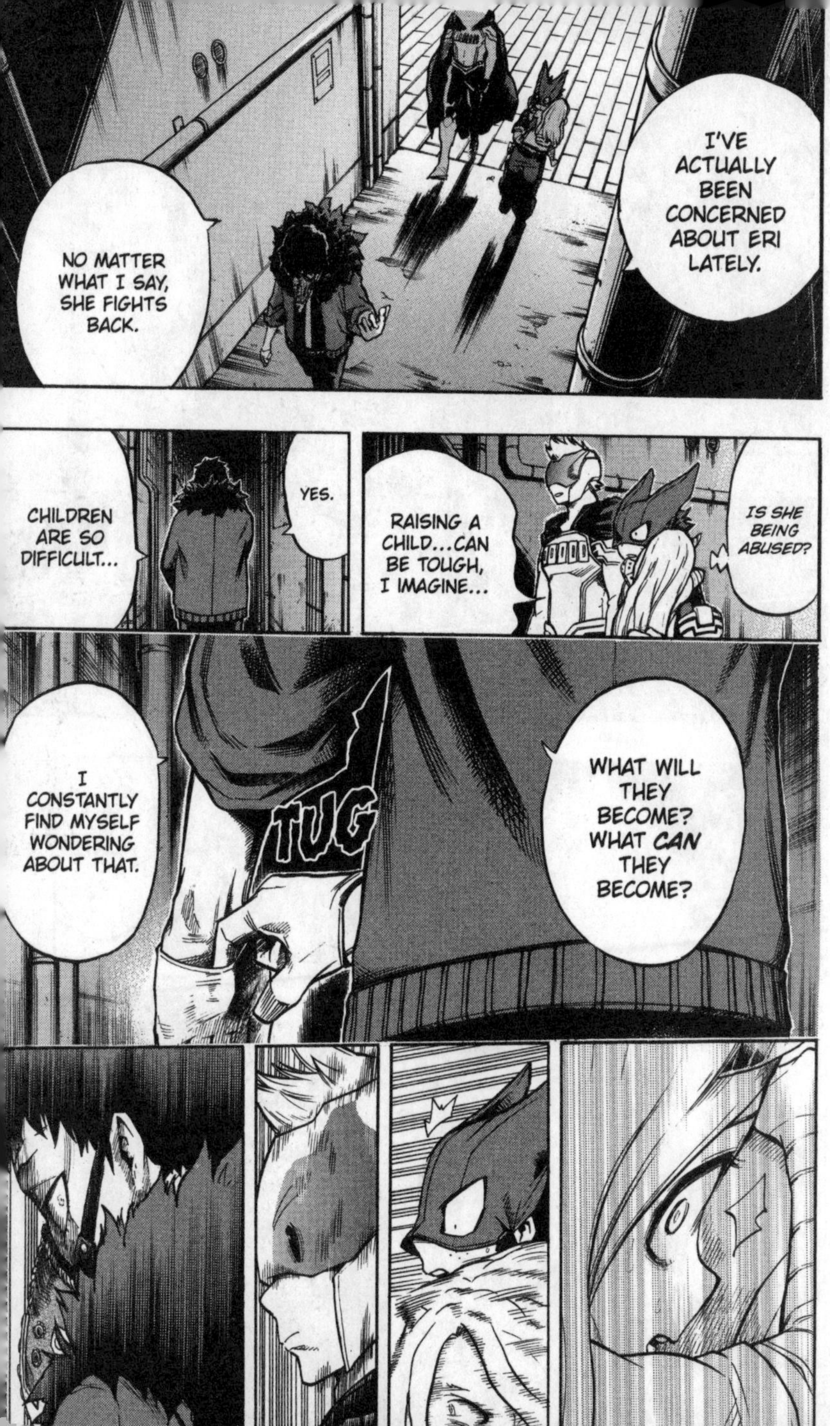
I'VE ACTUALLY BEEN CONCERNED ABOUT ERI LATELY.
NO MATTER WHAT I SAY, SHE FIGHTS BACK.
IS SHE BEING ABUSED?
RAISING A CHILD...CAN BE TOUGH, I IMAGINE...
YES.
CHILDREN ARE SO DIFFICULT...
WHAT WILL THEY BECOME? WHAT *CAN* THEY BECOME?
TUG
I CONSTANTLY FIND MYSELF WONDERING ABOUT THAT.

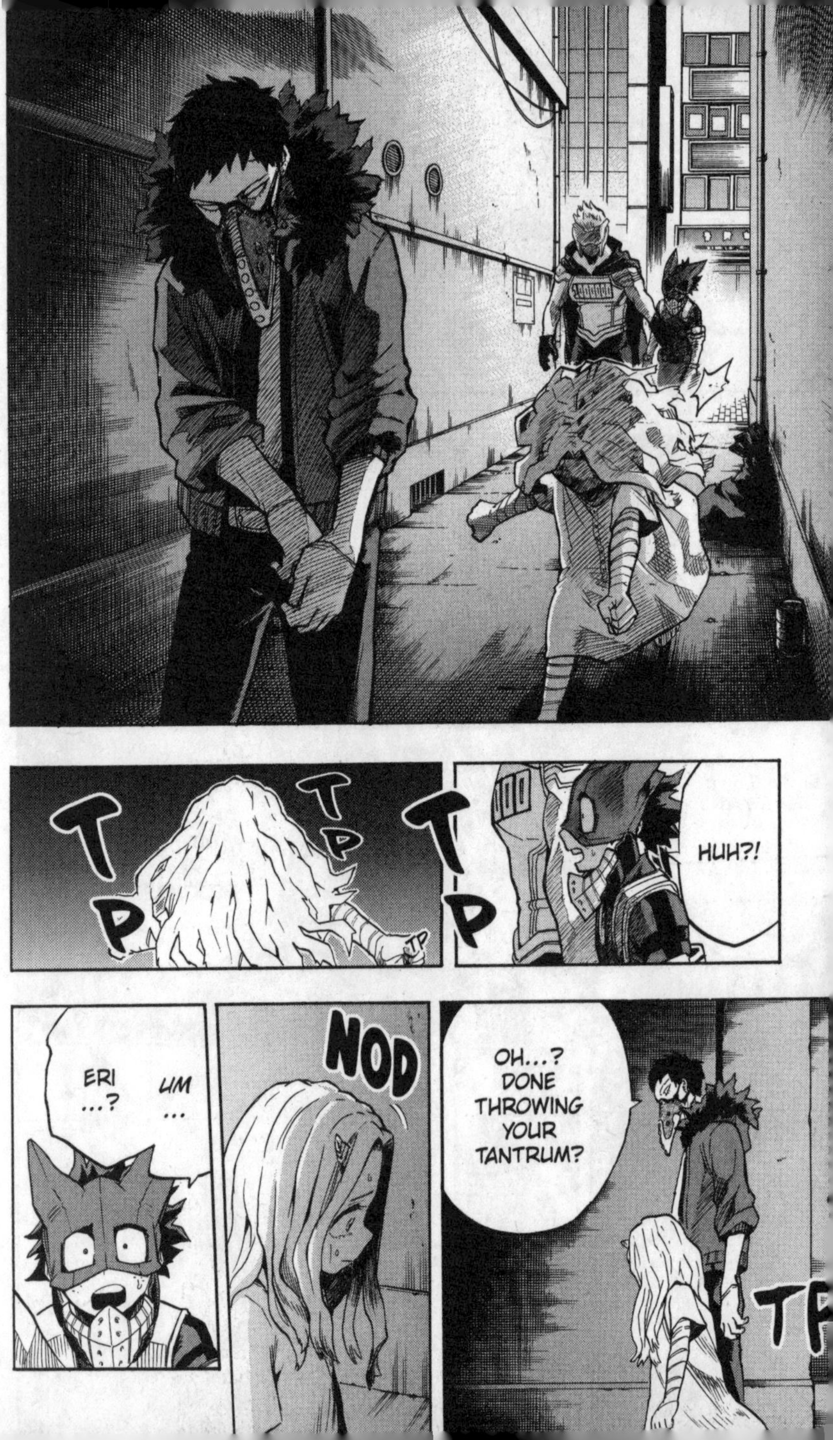
HUH?!
TP
TP
TP
OH...? DONE THROWING YOUR TANTRUM?
TP
NOD
UM ...
ERI ...?

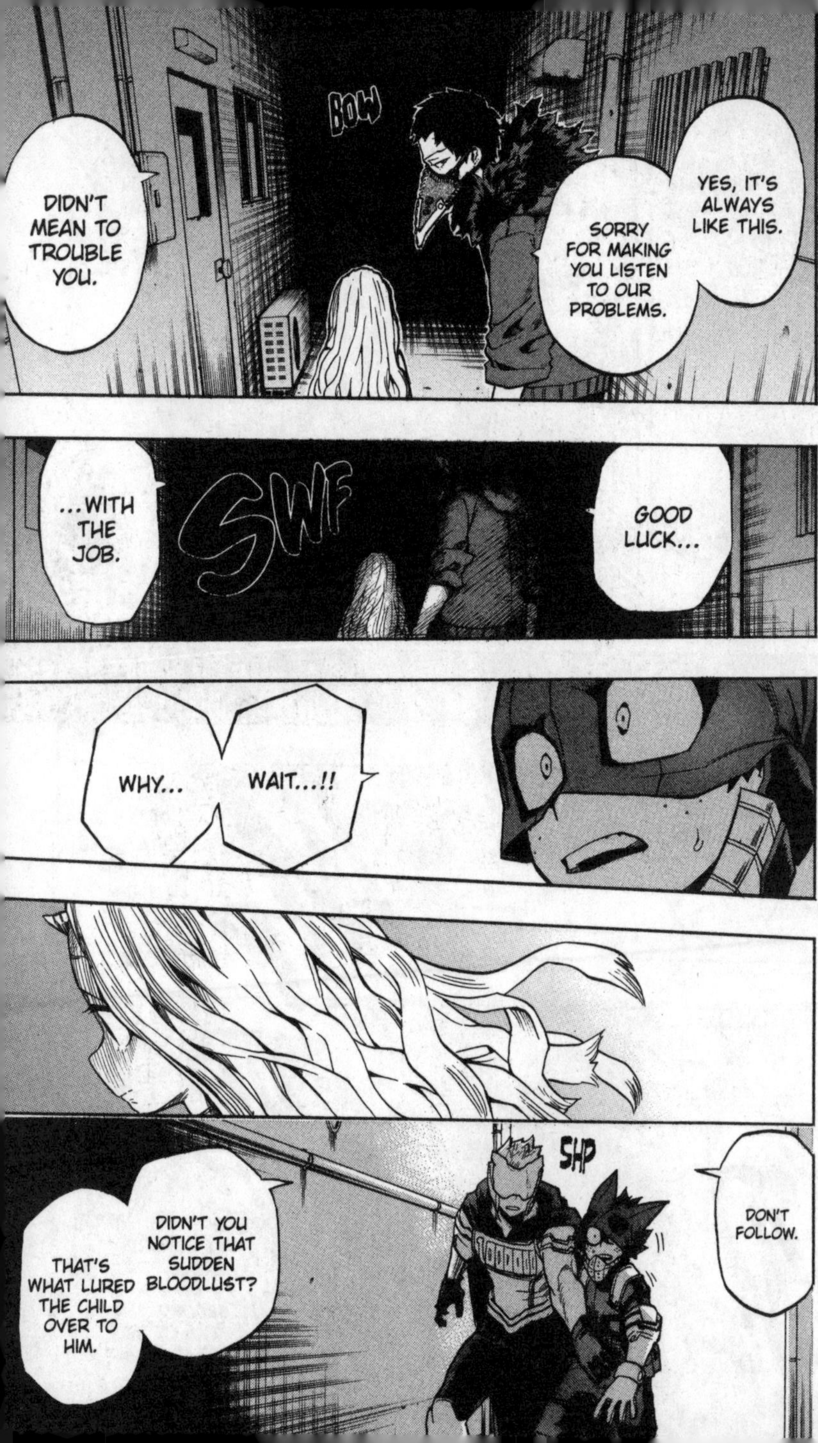
YES, IT'S ALWAYS LIKE THIS.
SORRY FOR MAKING YOU LISTEN TO OUR PROBLEMS.
BOW
DIDN'T MEAN TO TROUBLE YOU.
GOOD LUCK...
SWF
...WITH THE JOB.
WAIT...!!
WHY...
DON'T FOLLOW.
SHP
DIDN'T YOU NOTICE THAT SUDDEN BLOODLUST?
THAT'S WHAT LURED THE CHILD OVER TO HIM.

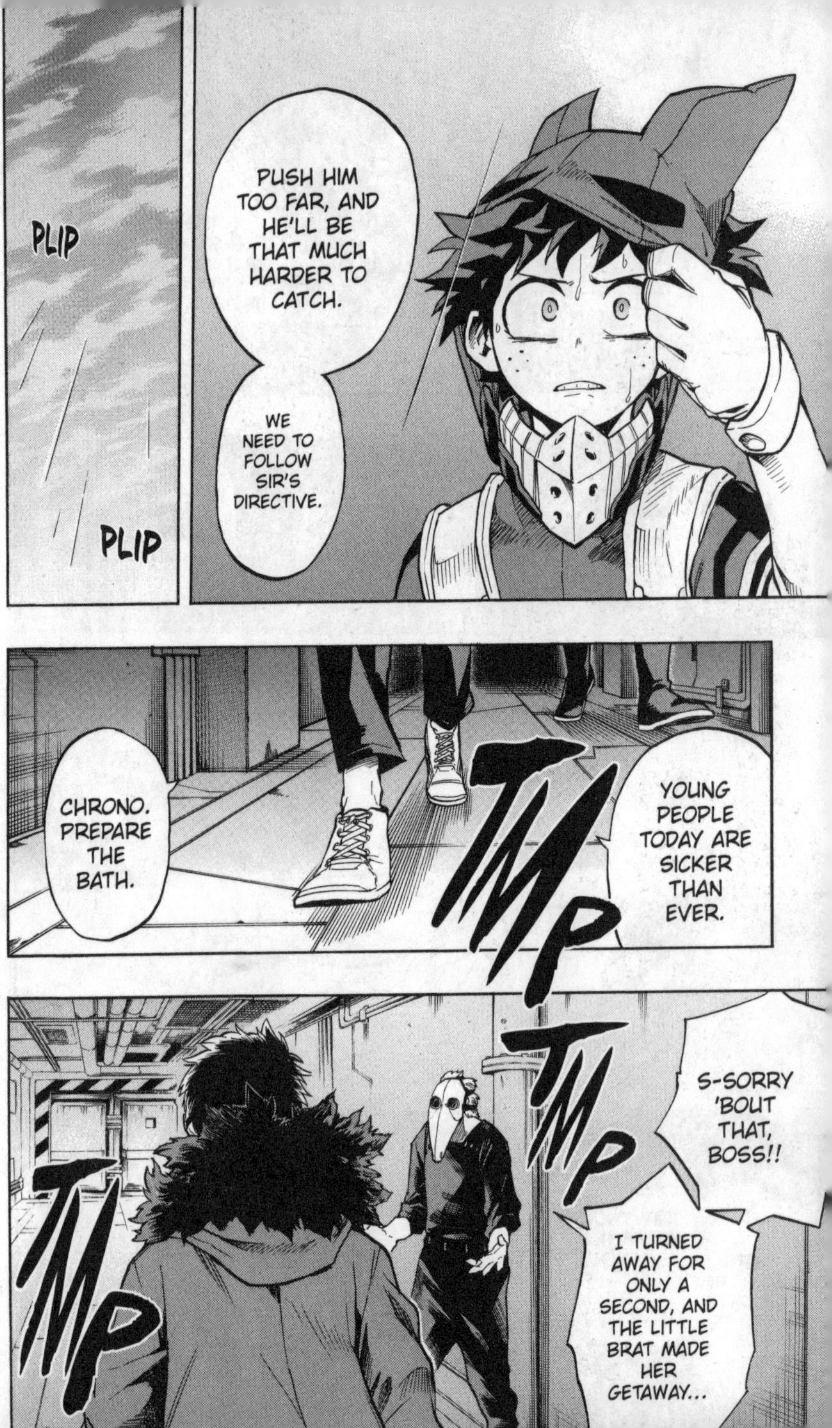
PUSH HIM TOO FAR, AND HE'LL BE THAT MUCH HARDER TO CATCH.
WE NEED TO FOLLOW SIR'S DIRECTIVE.
PLIP
PLIP
YOUNG PEOPLE TODAY ARE SICKER THAN EVER.
TMP
CHRONO. PREPARE THE BATH.
TMP
S-SORRY 'BOUT THAT, BOSS!!
I TURNED AWAY FOR ONLY A SECOND, AND THE LITTLE BRAT MADE HER GETAWAY...
TMP

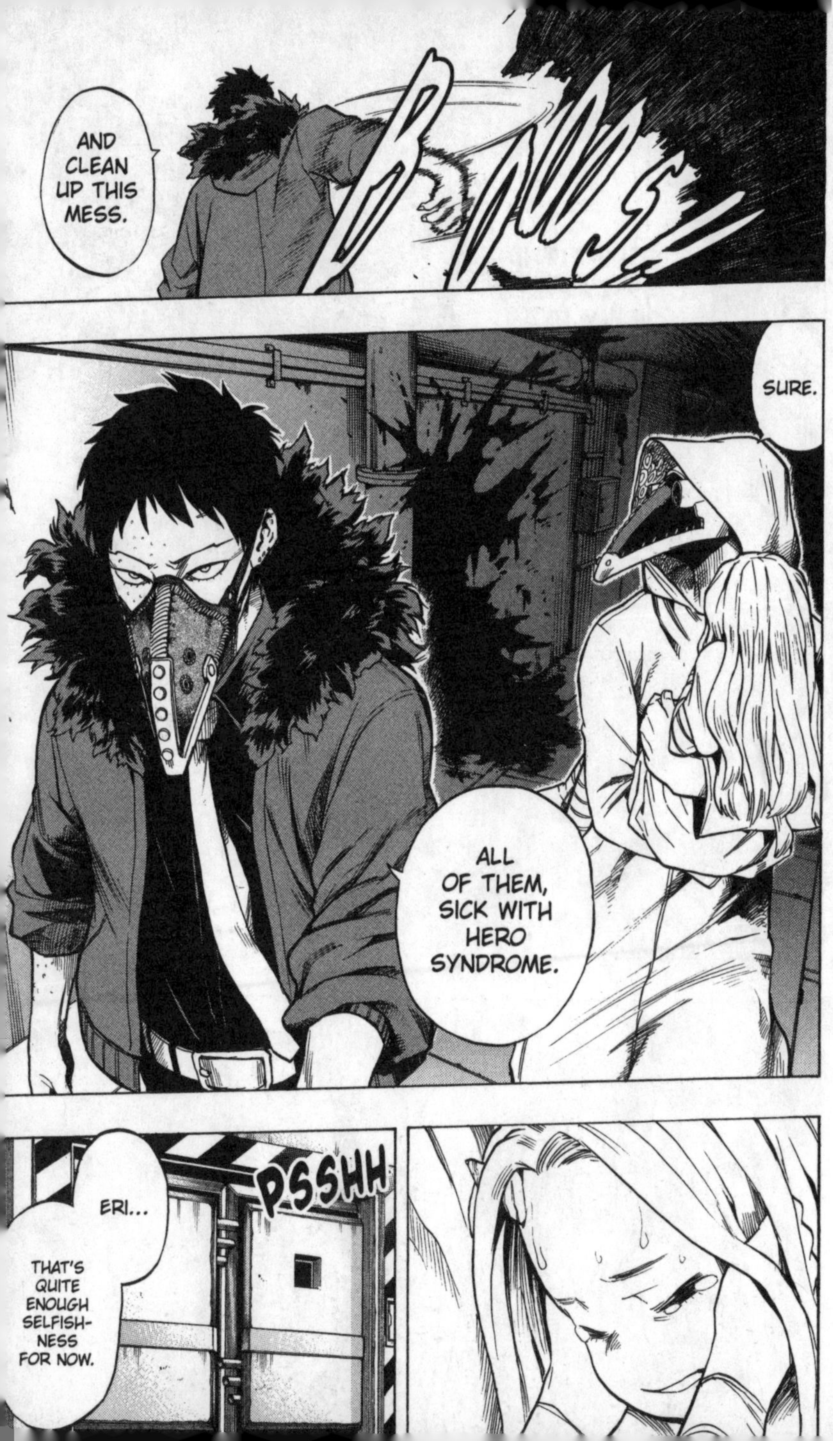
AND CLEAN UP THIS MESS.
SURE.
ALL OF THEM, SICK WITH HERO SYNDROME.
PSSHH
ERI...
THAT'S QUITE ENOUGH SELFISH-NESS FOR NOW.

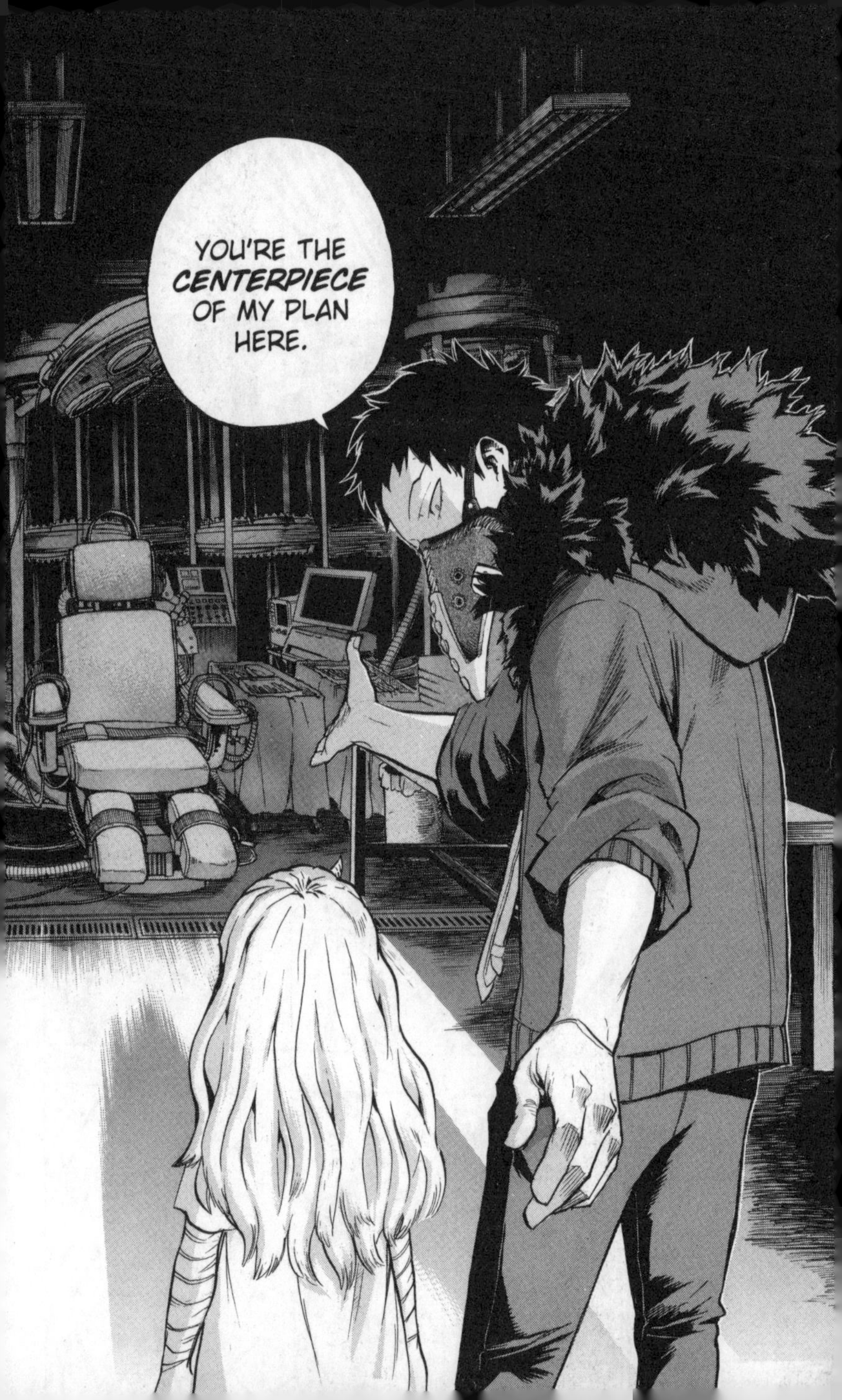
YOU'RE THE *CENTERPIECE* OF MY PLAN HERE.

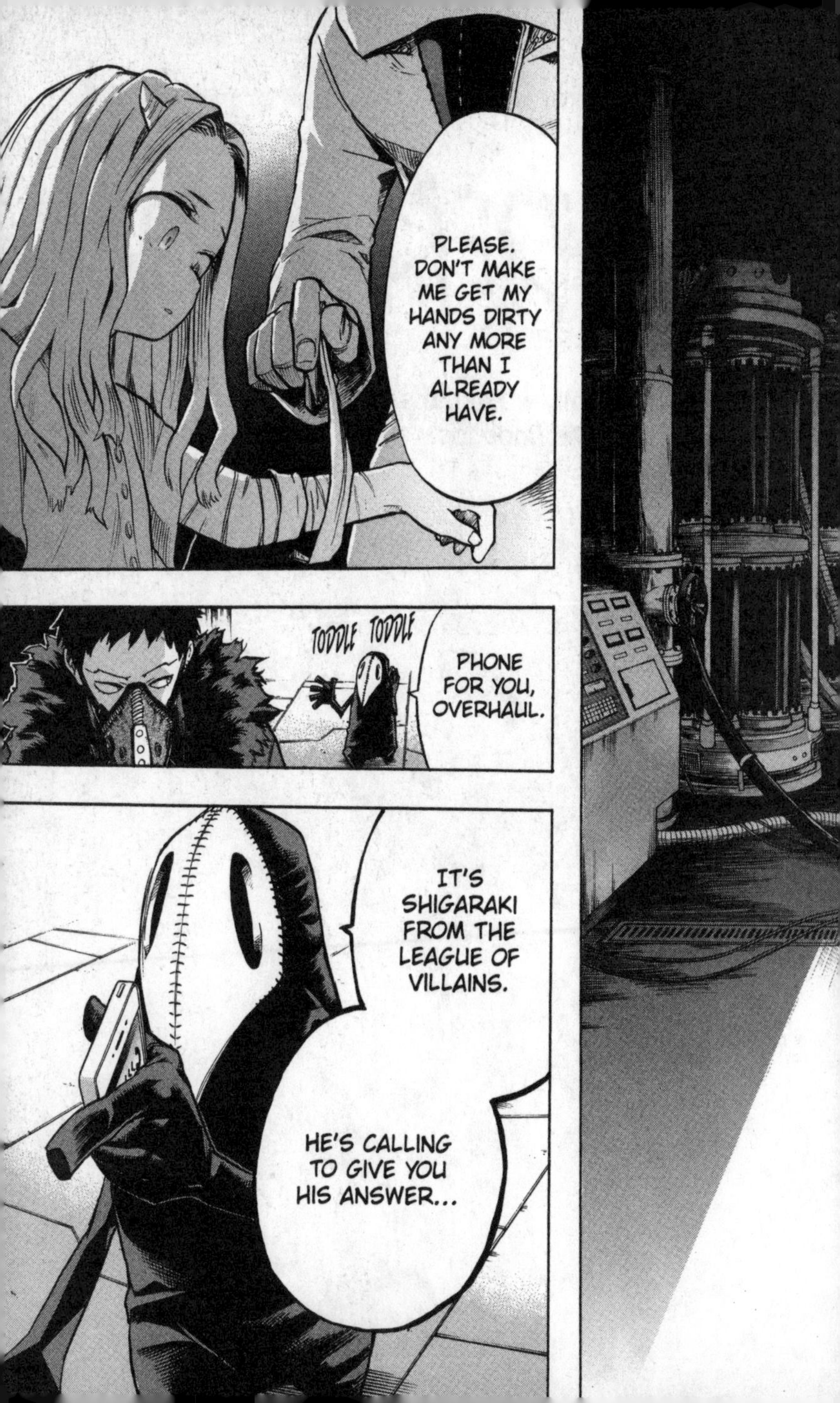
PLEASE. DON'T MAKE ME GET MY HANDS DIRTY ANY MORE THAN I ALREADY HAVE.
TODDLE TODDLE
PHONE FOR YOU, OVERHAUL.
IT'S SHIGARAKI FROM THE LEAGUE OF VILLAINS.
HE'S CALLING TO GIVE YOU HIS ANSWER...

THE DEKU MASK

- Fiiiiiinally we get to see this.
  With the hood too.

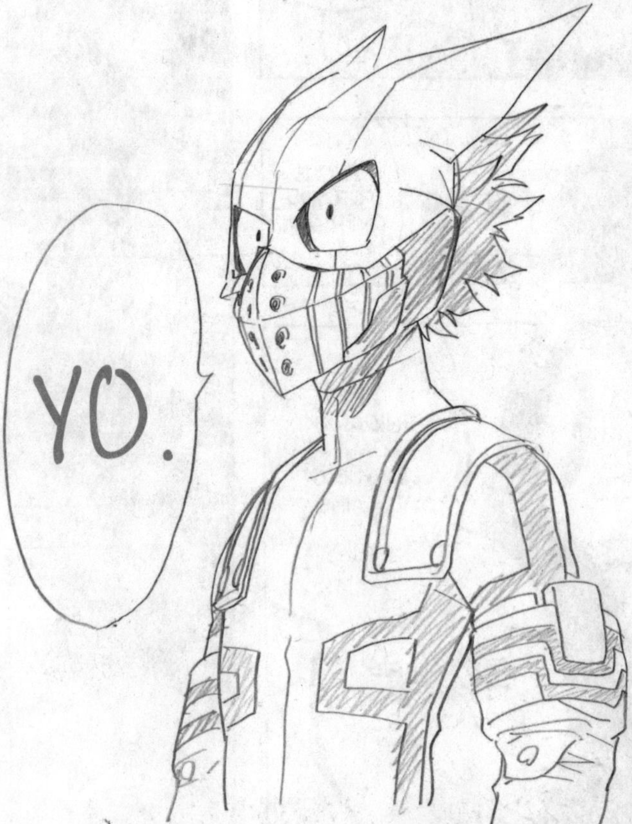
YO.

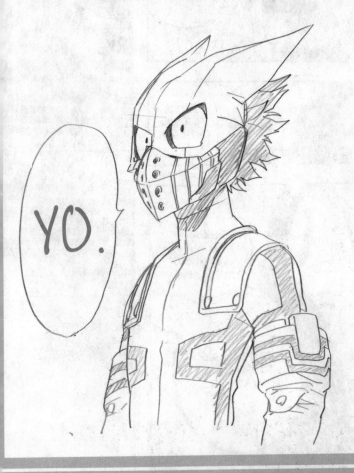

No. 130 - Listen to the Truth

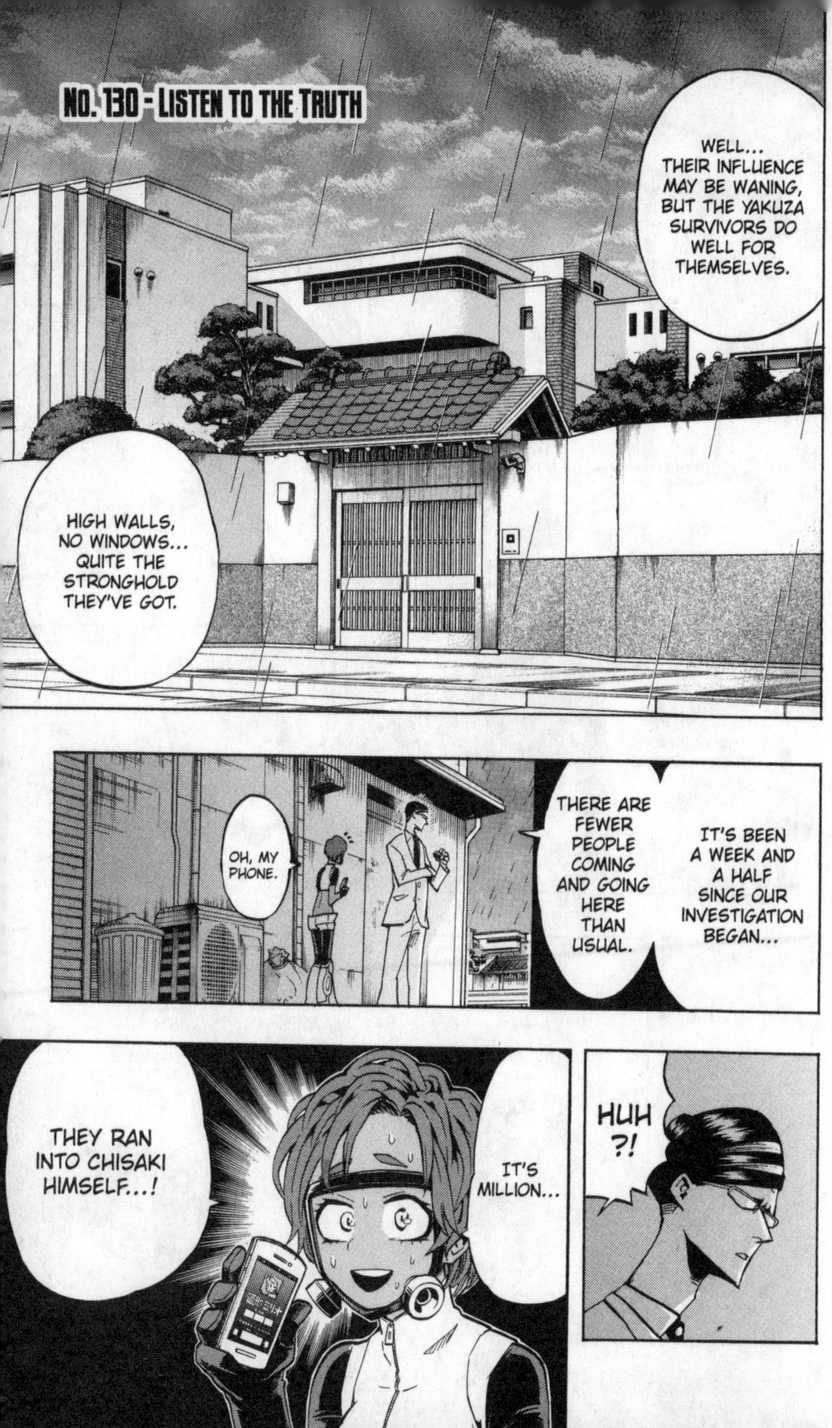
WELL... THEIR INFLUENCE MAY BE WANING, BUT THE YAKUZA SURVIVORS DO WELL FOR THEMSELVES.
HIGH WALLS, NO WINDOWS... QUITE THE STRONGHOLD THEY'VE GOT.
IT'S BEEN A WEEK AND A HALF SINCE OUR INVESTIGATION BEGAN...
THERE ARE FEWER PEOPLE COMING AND GOING HERE THAN USUAL.
OH, MY PHONE.
HUH ?!
IT'S MILLION...
THEY RAN INTO CHISAKI HIMSELF...!

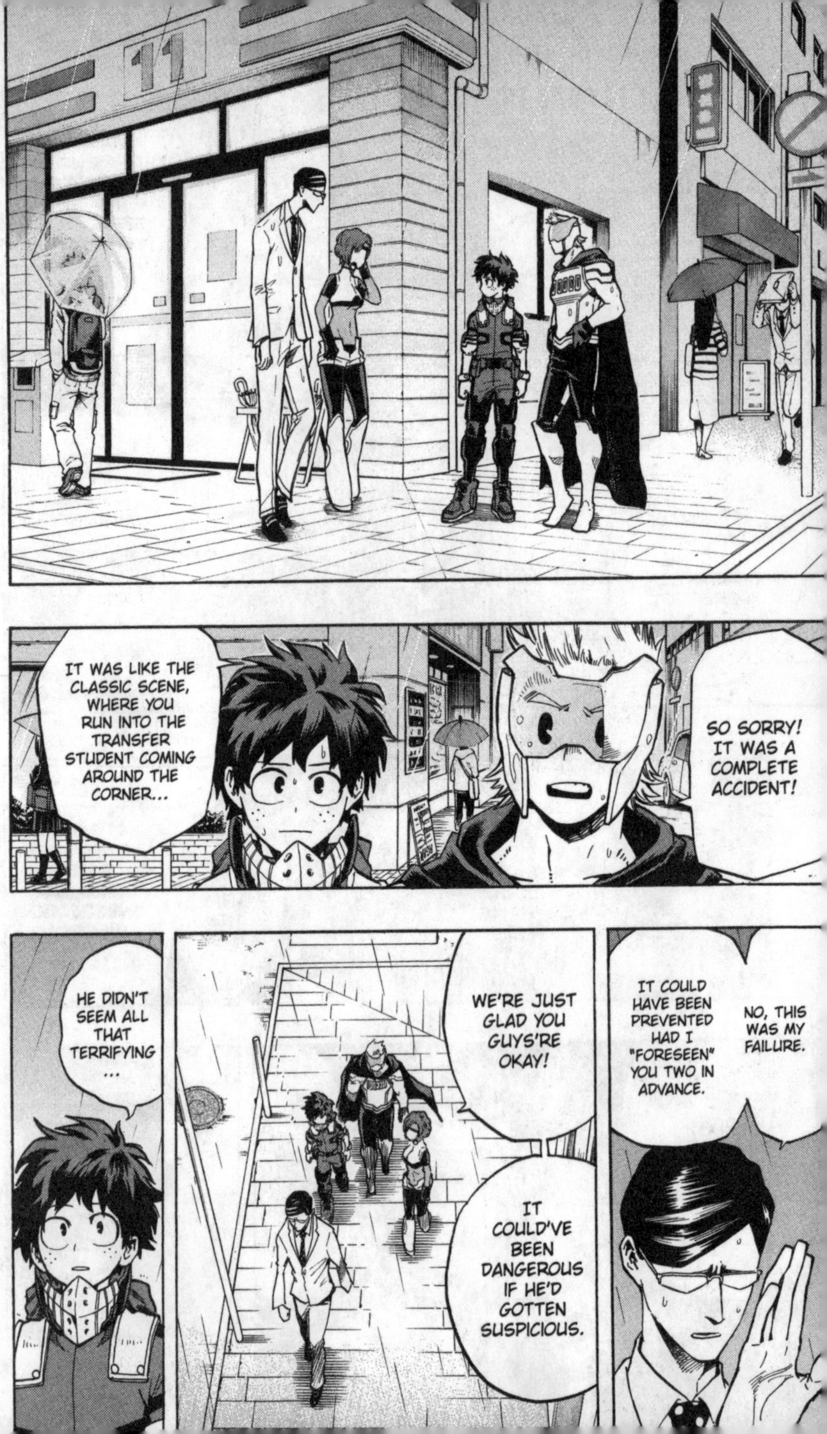
SO SORRY! IT WAS A COMPLETE ACCIDENT!
IT WAS LIKE THE CLASSIC SCENE, WHERE YOU RUN INTO THE TRANSFER STUDENT COMING AROUND THE CORNER...
NO, THIS WAS MY FAILURE.
IT COULD HAVE BEEN PREVENTED HAD I "FORESEEN" YOU TWO IN ADVANCE.
WE'RE JUST GLAD YOU GUYS'RE OKAY!
IT COULD'VE BEEN DANGEROUS IF HE'D GOTTEN SUSPICIOUS.
HE DIDN'T SEEM ALL THAT TERRIFYING ...

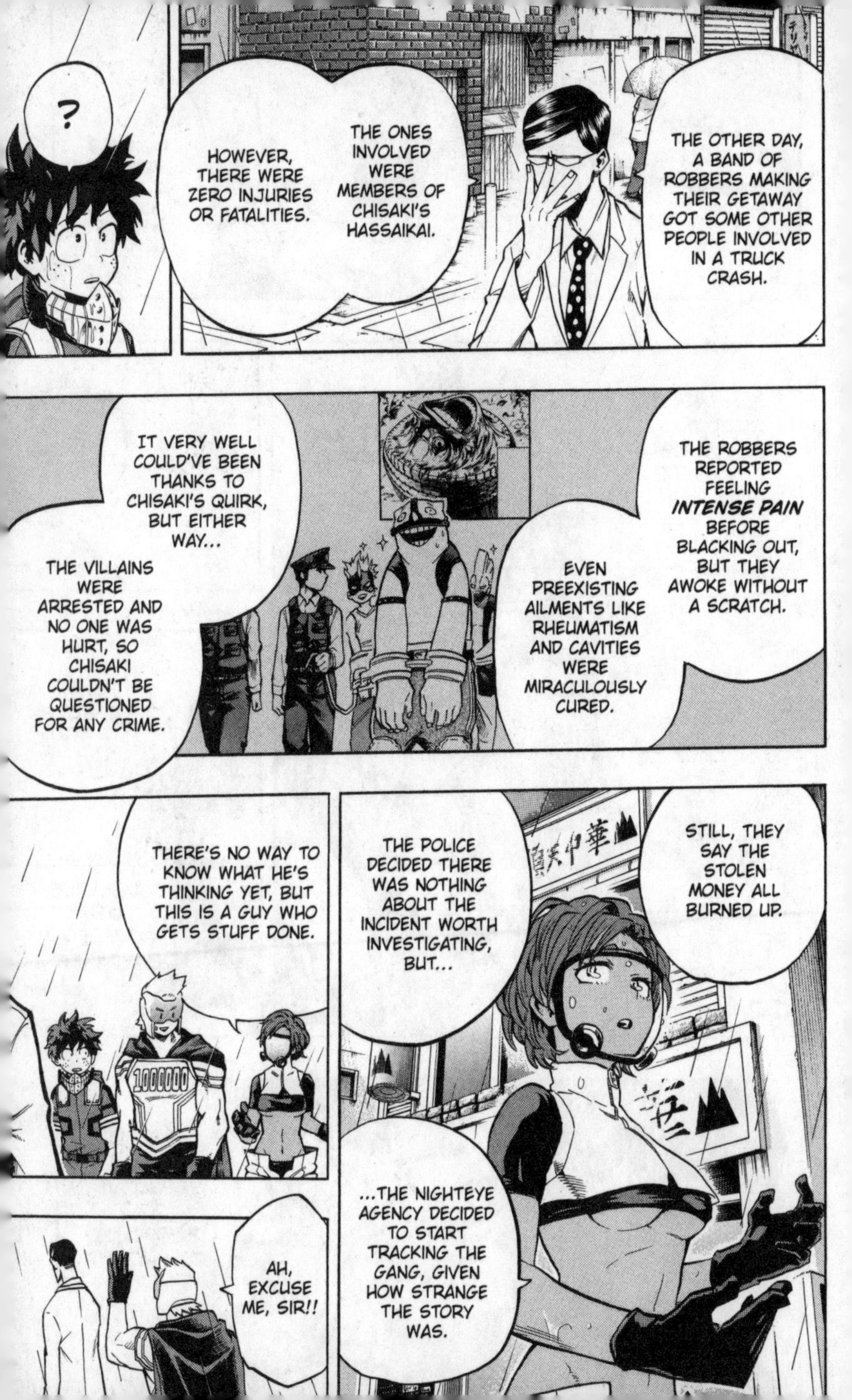
THE OTHER DAY, A BAND OF ROBBERS MAKING THEIR GETAWAY GOT SOME OTHER PEOPLE INVOLVED IN A TRUCK CRASH.
THE ONES INVOLVED WERE MEMBERS OF CHISAKI'S HASSAIKAI.
HOWEVER, THERE WERE ZERO INJURIES OR FATALITIES.
?
THE ROBBERS REPORTED FEELING ***INTENSE PAIN*** BEFORE BLACKING OUT, BUT THEY AWOKE WITHOUT A SCRATCH.
EVEN PREEXISTING AILMENTS LIKE RHEUMATISM AND CAVITIES WERE MIRACULOUSLY CURED.
IT VERY WELL COULD'VE BEEN THANKS TO CHISAKI'S QUIRK, BUT EITHER WAY...
THE VILLAINS WERE ARRESTED AND NO ONE WAS HURT, SO CHISAKI COULDN'T BE QUESTIONED FOR ANY CRIME.
STILL, THEY SAY THE STOLEN MONEY ALL BURNED UP.
THE POLICE DECIDED THERE WAS NOTHING ABOUT THE INCIDENT WORTH INVESTIGATING, BUT...
...THE NIGHTEYE AGENCY DECIDED TO START TRACKING THE GANG, GIVEN HOW STRANGE THE STORY WAS.
THERE'S NO WAY TO KNOW WHAT HE'S THINKING YET, BUT THIS IS A GUY WHO GETS STUFF DONE.
1000000
AH, EXCUSE ME, SIR!!

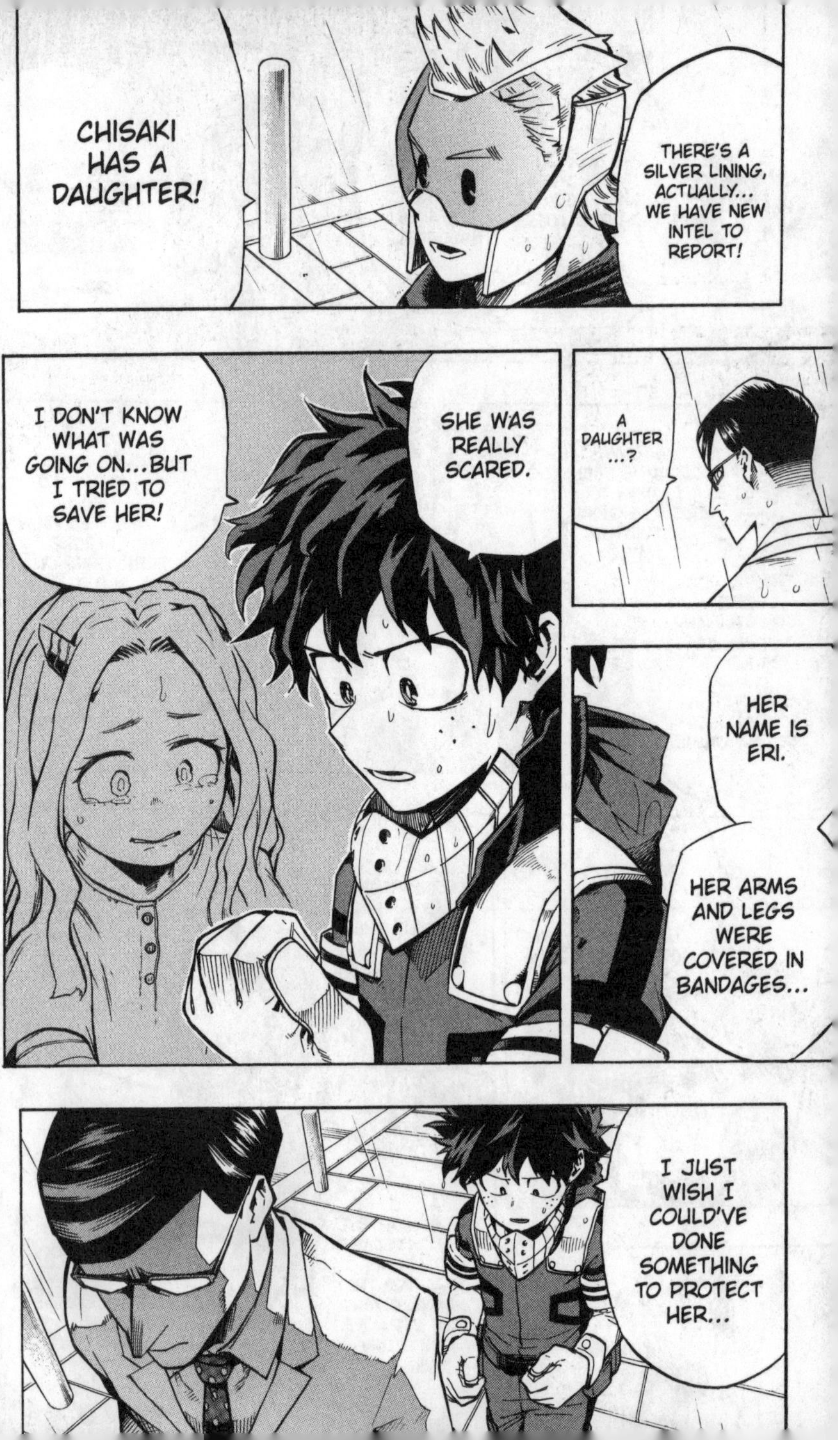
THERE'S A SILVER LINING, ACTUALLY... WE HAVE NEW INTEL TO REPORT!
CHISAKI HAS A DAUGHTER!
A DAUGHTER ...?
HER NAME IS ERI.
HER ARMS AND LEGS WERE COVERED IN BANDAGES...
SHE WAS REALLY SCARED.
I DON'T KNOW WHAT WAS GOING ON...BUT I TRIED TO SAVE HER!
I JUST WISH I COULD'VE DONE SOMETHING TO PROTECT HER...

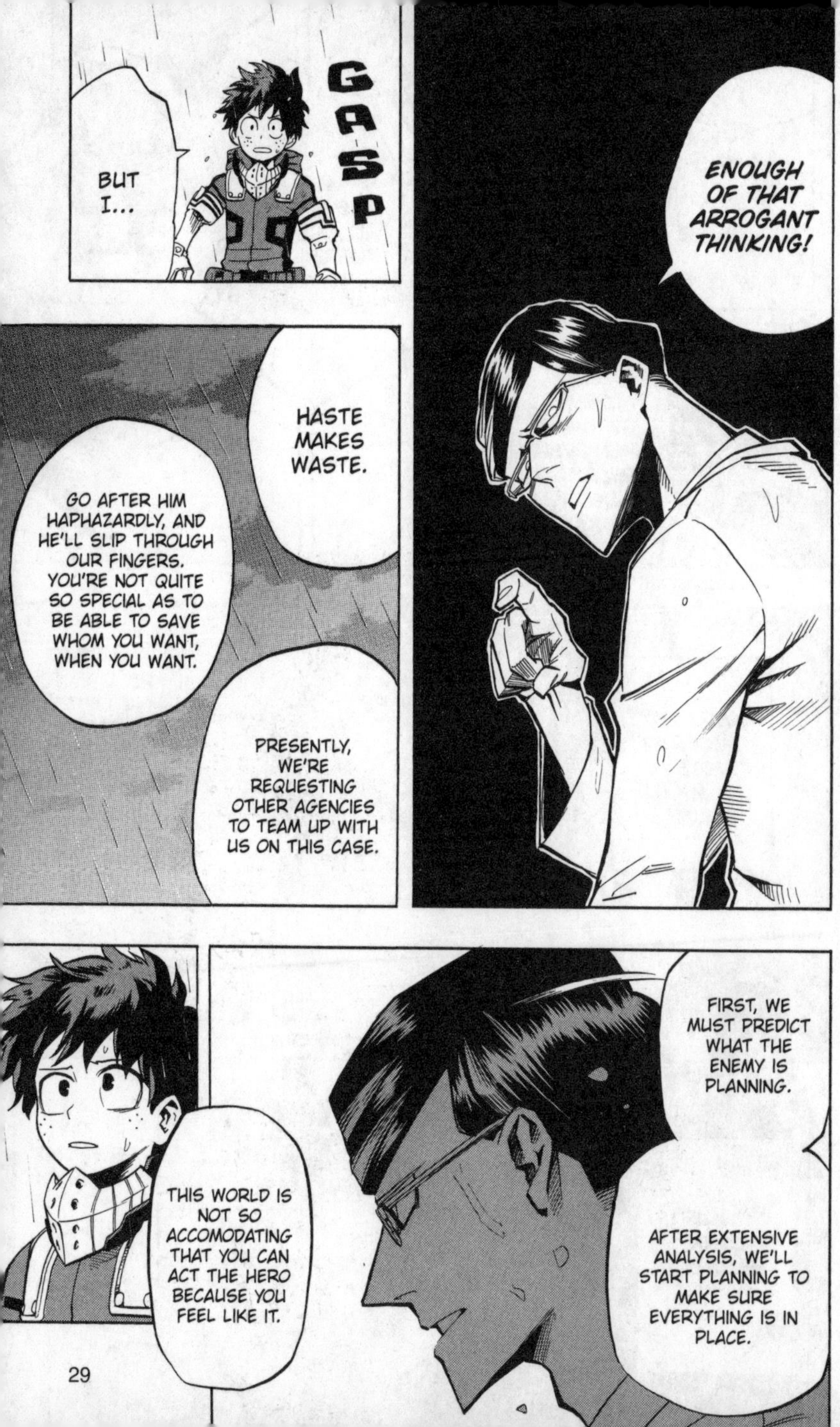
ENOUGH OF THAT ARROGANT THINKING!
GASP
BUT I...
HASTE MAKES WASTE.
GO AFTER HIM HAPHAZARDLY, AND HE'LL SLIP THROUGH OUR FINGERS. YOU'RE NOT QUITE SO SPECIAL AS TO BE ABLE TO SAVE WHOM YOU WANT, WHEN YOU WANT.
PRESENTLY, WE'RE REQUESTING OTHER AGENCIES TO TEAM UP WITH US ON THIS CASE.
FIRST, WE MUST PREDICT WHAT THE ENEMY IS PLANNING.
AFTER EXTENSIVE ANALYSIS, WE'LL START PLANNING TO MAKE SURE EVERYTHING IS IN PLACE.
THIS WORLD IS NOT SO ACCOMODATING THAT YOU CAN ACT THE HERO BECAUSE YOU FEEL LIKE IT.

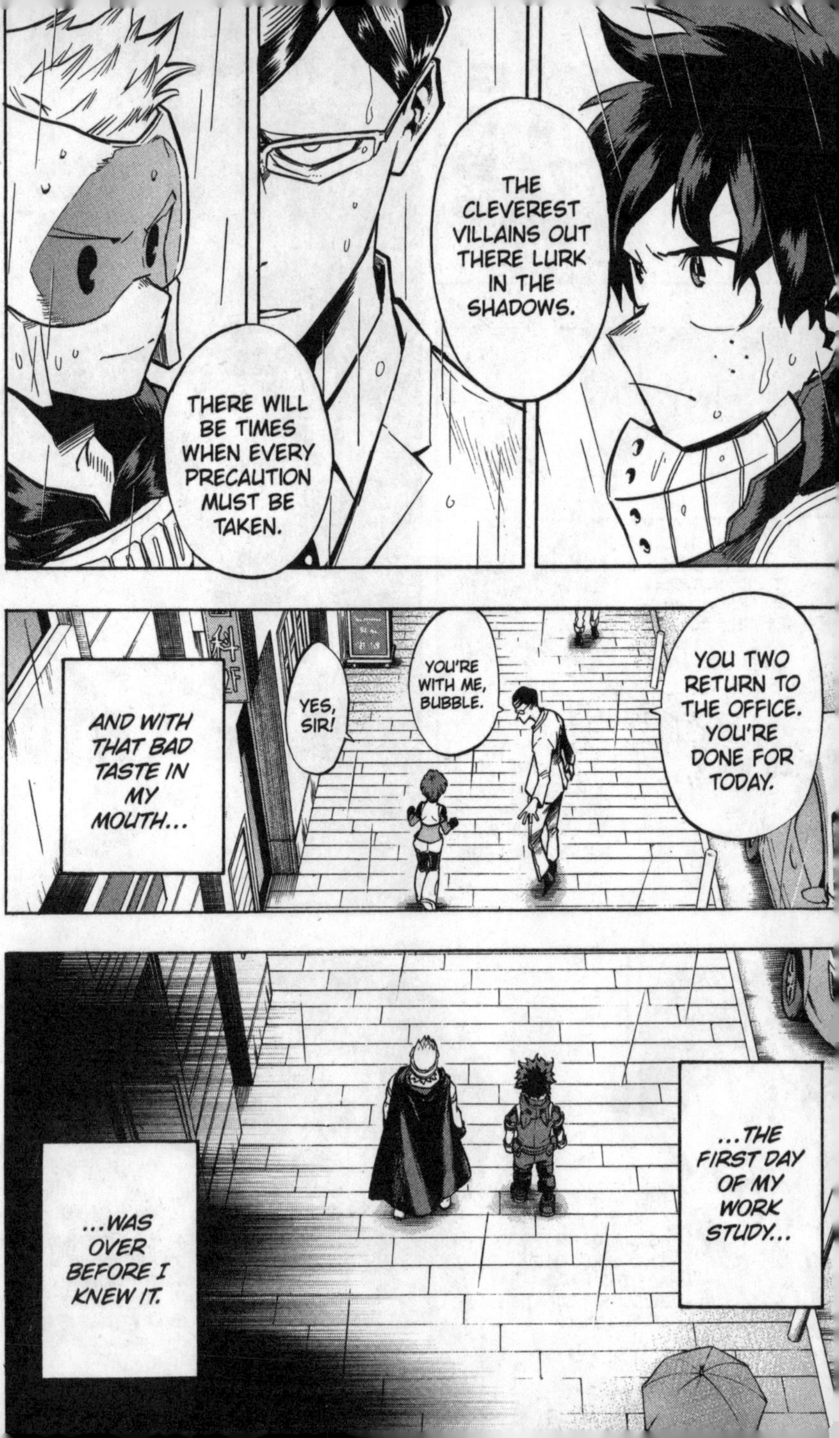
THE CLEVEREST VILLAINS OUT THERE LURK IN THE SHADOWS.
THERE WILL BE TIMES WHEN EVERY PRECAUTION MUST BE TAKEN.
YOU TWO RETURN TO THE OFFICE. YOU'RE DONE FOR TODAY.
YOU'RE WITH ME, BUBBLE.
YES, SIR!
AND WITH THAT BAD TASTE IN MY MOUTH...
...THE FIRST DAY OF MY WORK STUDY...
...WAS OVER BEFORE I KNEW IT.

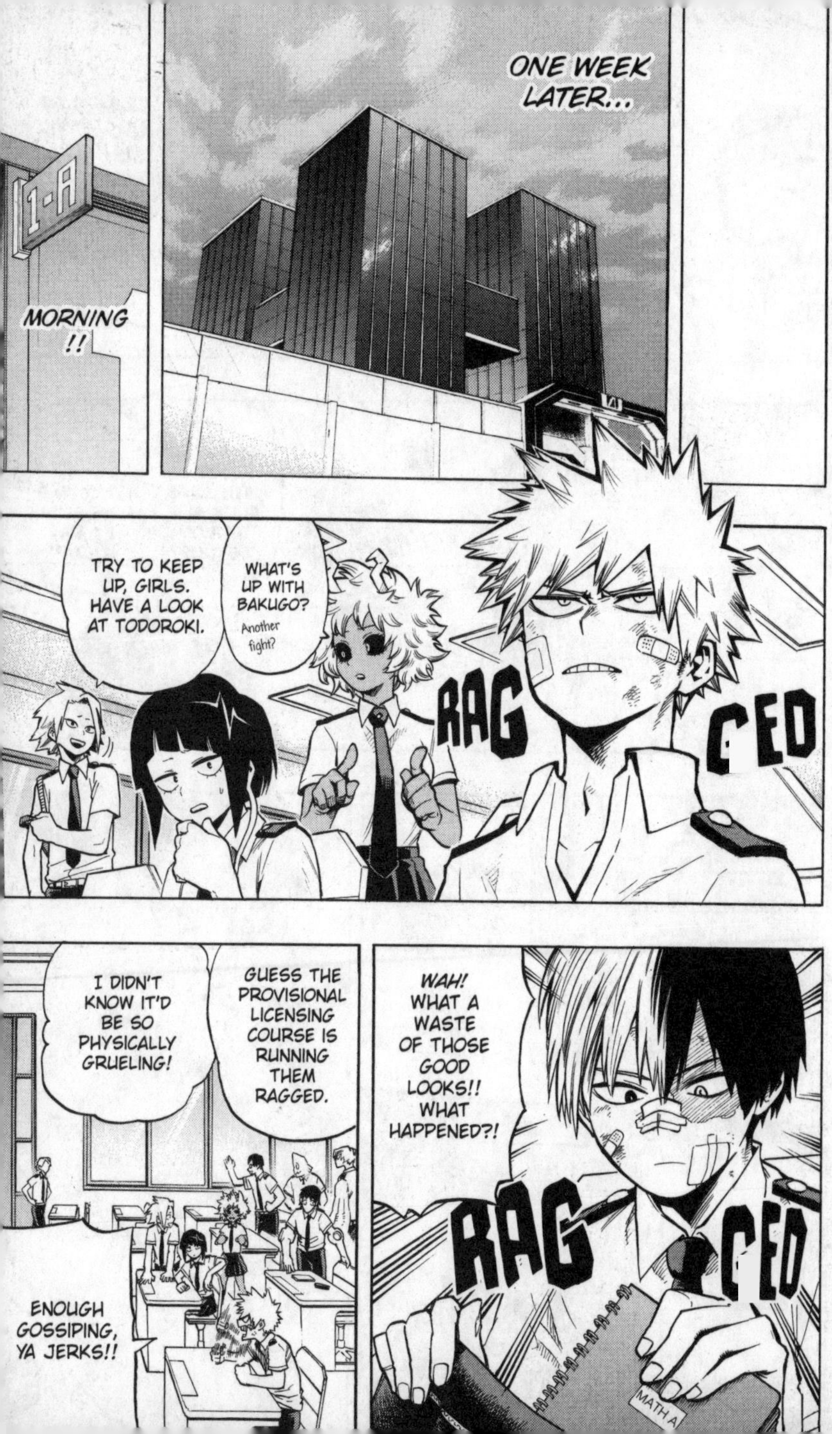

ONE WEEK LATER...
MORNING !!
RAG
GED
WHAT'S UP WITH BAKUGO? Another fight?
TRY TO KEEP UP, GIRLS. HAVE A LOOK AT TODOROKI.
WAH! WHAT A WASTE OF THOSE GOOD LOOKS!! WHAT HAPPENED?!
RAG
GED
MATH A
GUESS THE PROVISIONAL LICENSING COURSE IS RUNNING THEM RAGGED.
I DIDN'T KNOW IT'D BE SO PHYSICALLY GRUELING!
ENOUGH GOSSIPING, YA JERKS!!

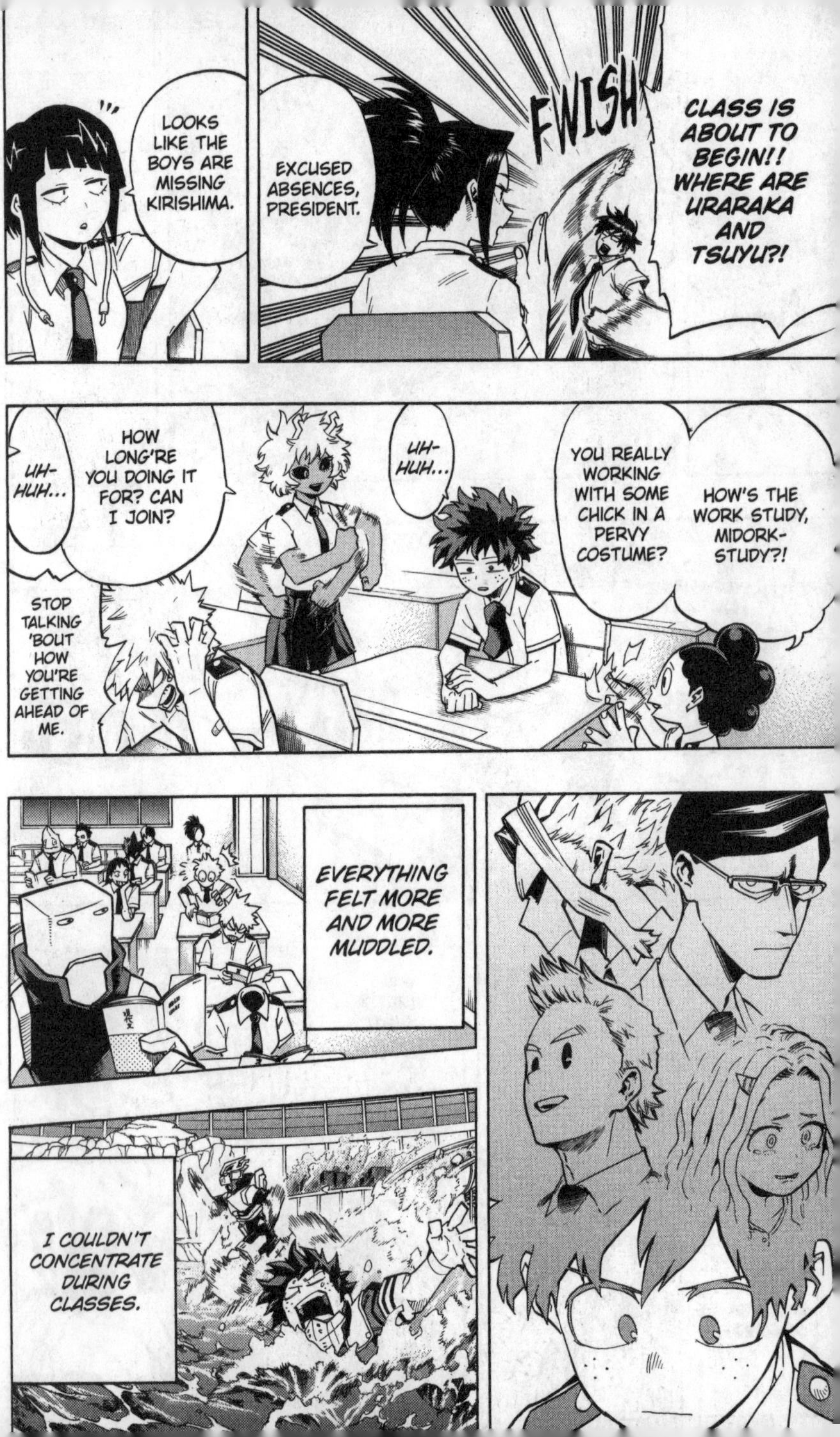
FWISH
CLASS IS ABOUT TO BEGIN!! WHERE ARE URARAKA AND TSUYU?!
EXCUSED ABSENCES, PRESIDENT.
LOOKS LIKE THE BOYS ARE MISSING KIRISHIMA.
HOW'S THE WORK STUDY, MIDORK-STUDY?!
YOU REALLY WORKING WITH SOME CHICK IN A PERVY COSTUME?
UH-HUH...
HOW LONG'RE YOU DOING IT FOR? CAN I JOIN?
UH-HUH...
STOP TALKING 'BOUT HOW YOU'RE GETTING AHEAD OF ME.
EVERYTHING FELT MORE AND MORE MUDDLED.
I COULDN'T CONCENTRATE DURING CLASSES.

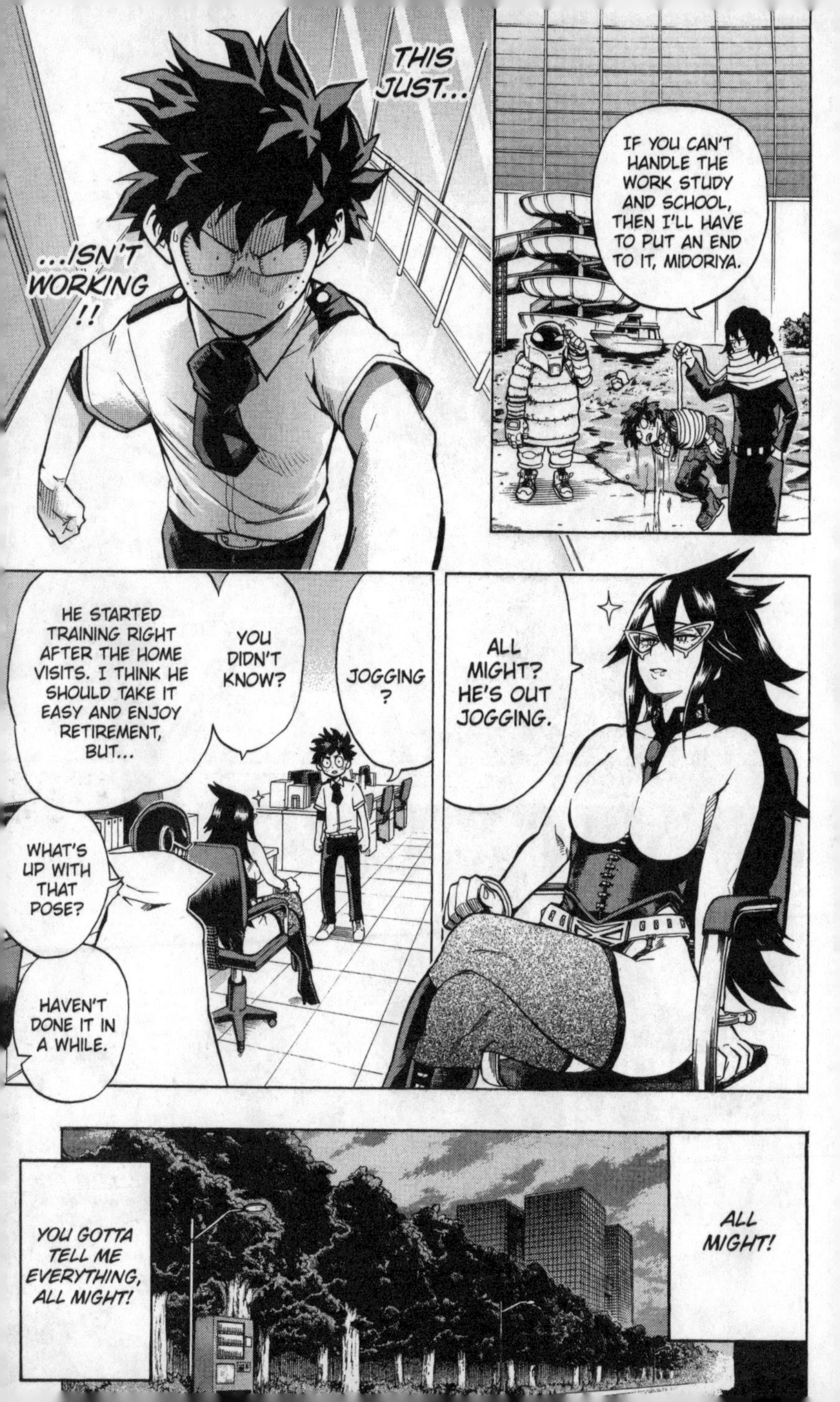
IF YOU CAN'T HANDLE THE WORK STUDY AND SCHOOL, THEN I'LL HAVE TO PUT AN END TO IT, MIDORIYA.
THIS JUST...
...ISN'T WORKING !!
ALL MIGHT? HE'S OUT JOGGING.
JOGGING ?
YOU DIDN'T KNOW?
HE STARTED TRAINING RIGHT AFTER THE HOME VISITS. I THINK HE SHOULD TAKE IT EASY AND ENJOY RETIREMENT, BUT...
WHAT'S UP WITH THAT POSE?
HAVEN'T DONE IT IN A WHILE.
ALL MIGHT!
YOU GOTTA TELL ME EVERYTHING, ALL MIGHT!

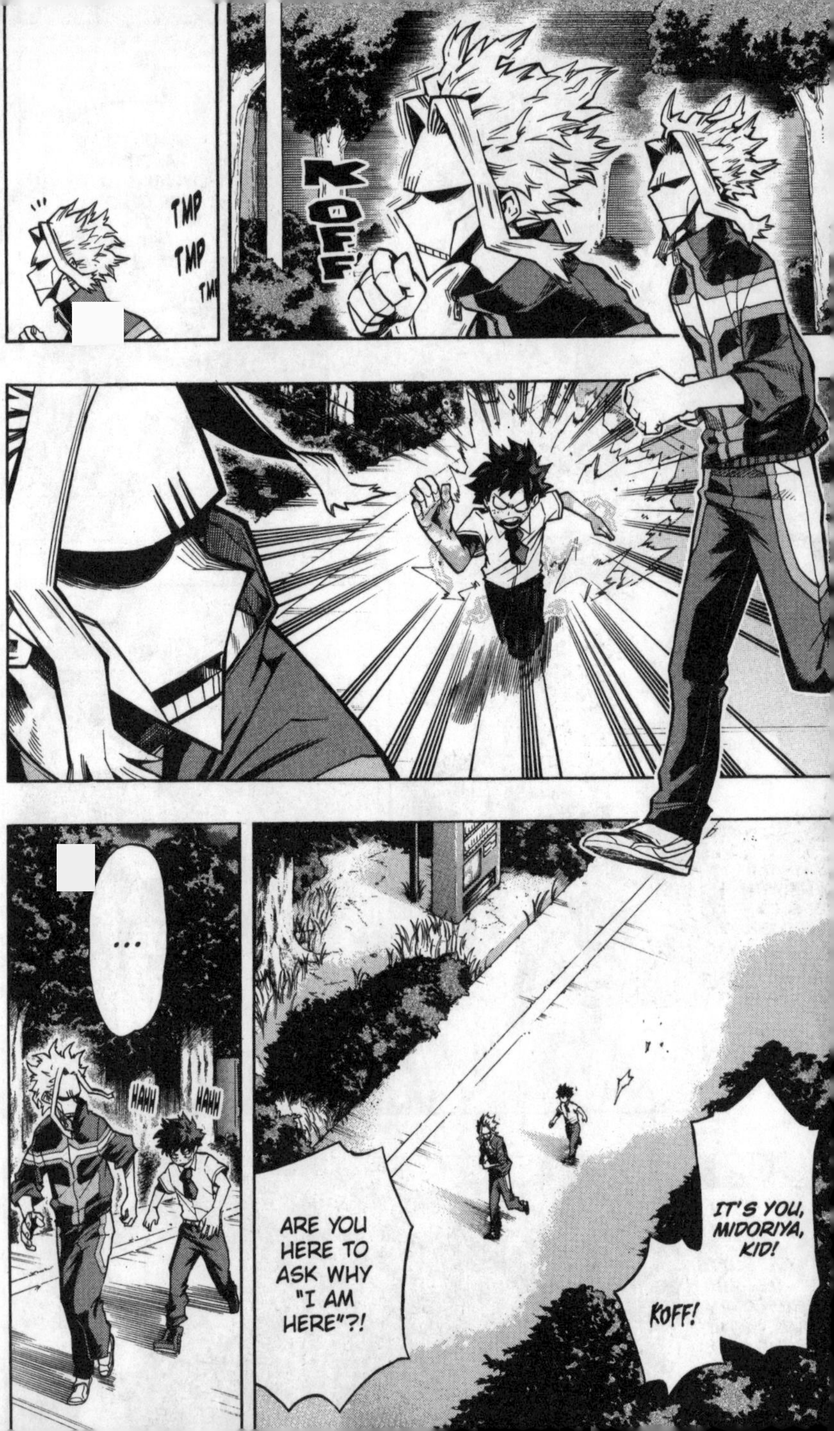
KOFF
TMP TMP TMP
IT'S YOU, MIDORIYA, KID!
KOFF!
ARE YOU HERE TO ASK WHY "I AM HERE"?!
...
HAHH HAHH

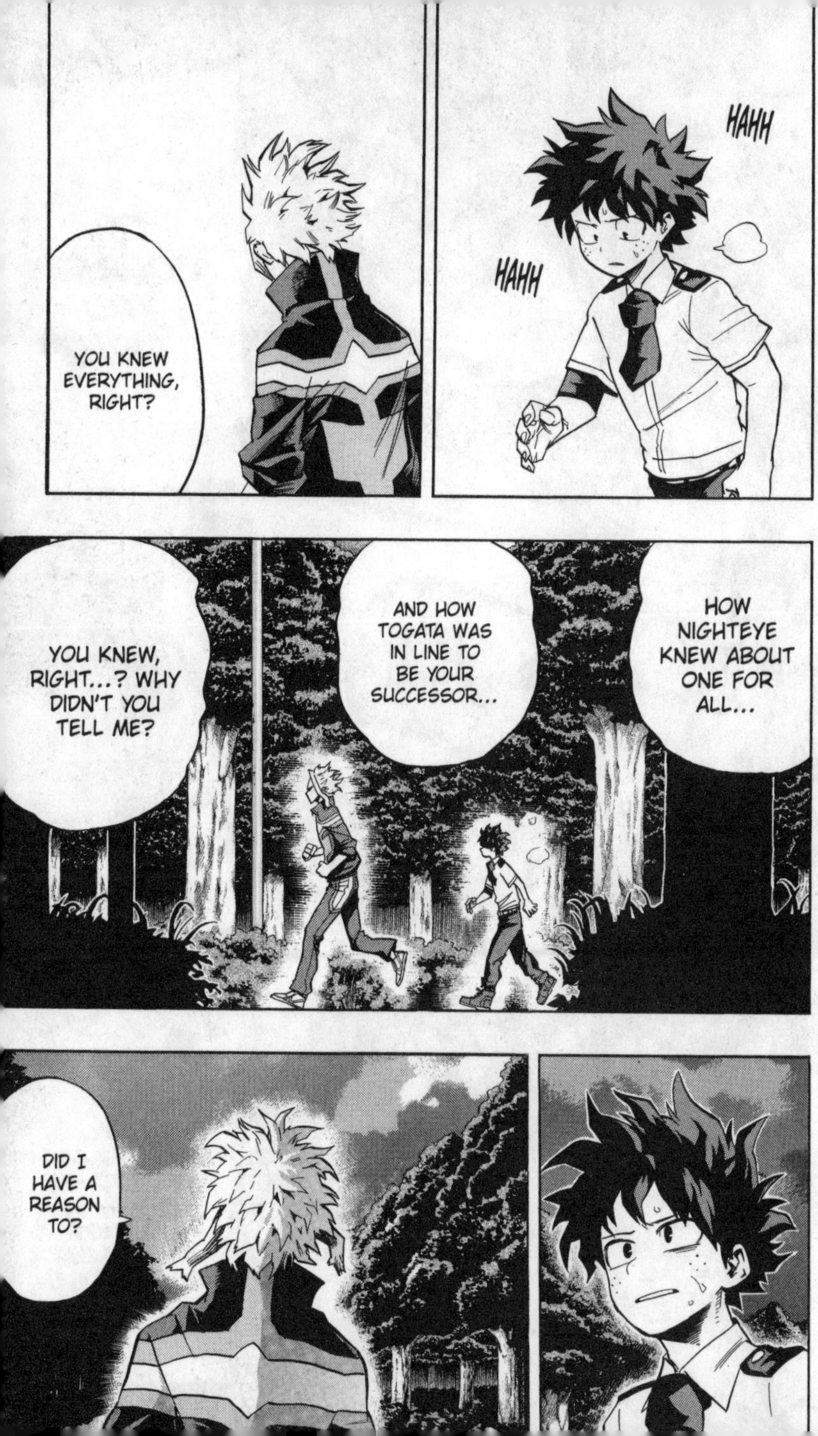
HAHH
HAHH
YOU KNEW EVERYTHING, RIGHT?
HOW NIGHTEYE KNEW ABOUT ONE FOR ALL...
AND HOW TOGATA WAS IN LINE TO BE YOUR SUCCESSOR...
YOU KNEW, RIGHT...? WHY DIDN'T YOU TELL ME?
DID I HAVE A REASON TO?

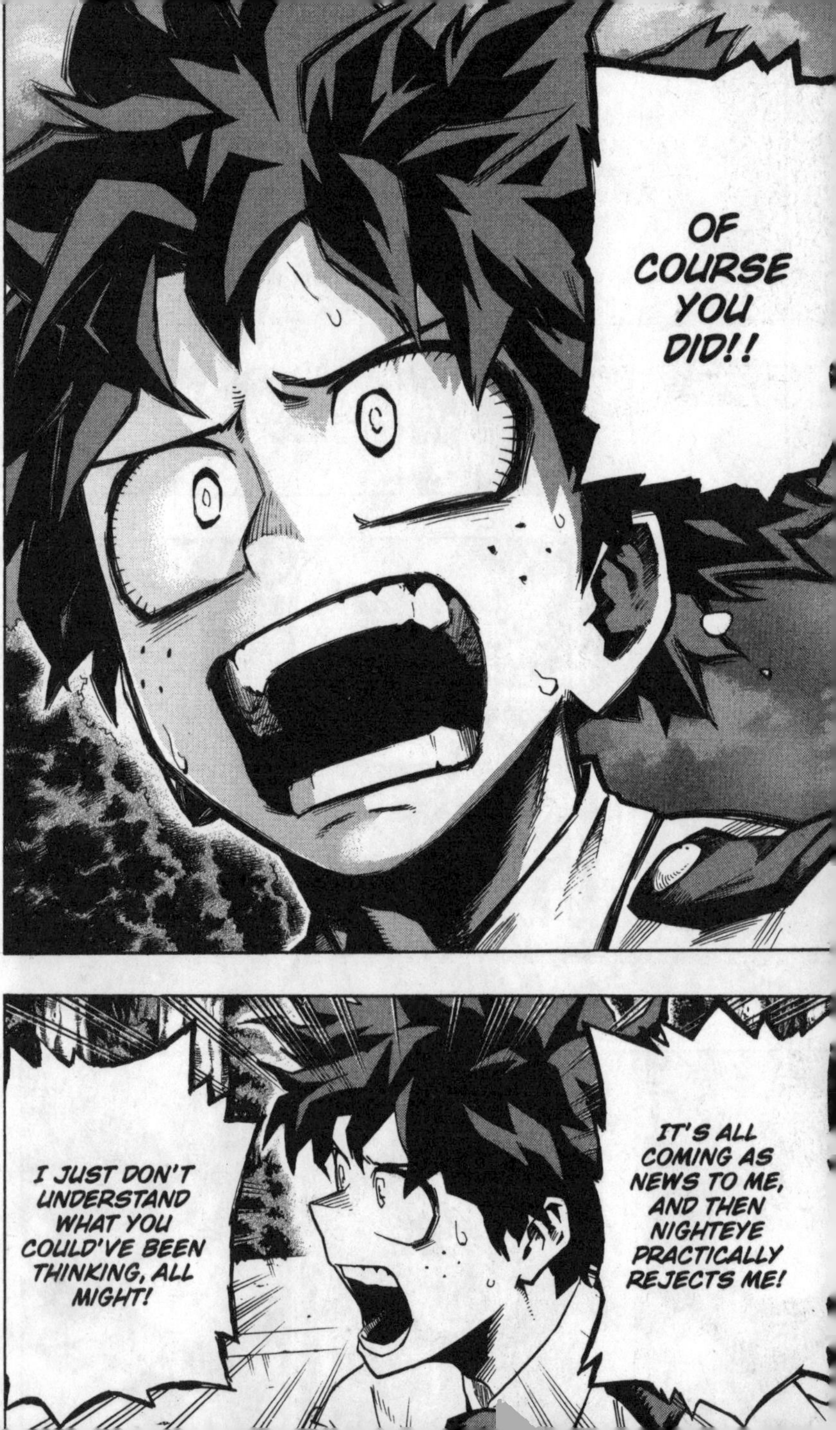
OF COURSE YOU DID!!
IT'S ALL COMING AS NEWS TO ME, AND THEN NIGHTEYE PRACTICALLY REJECTS ME!
I JUST DON'T UNDERSTAND WHAT YOU COULD'VE BEEN THINKING, ALL MIGHT!

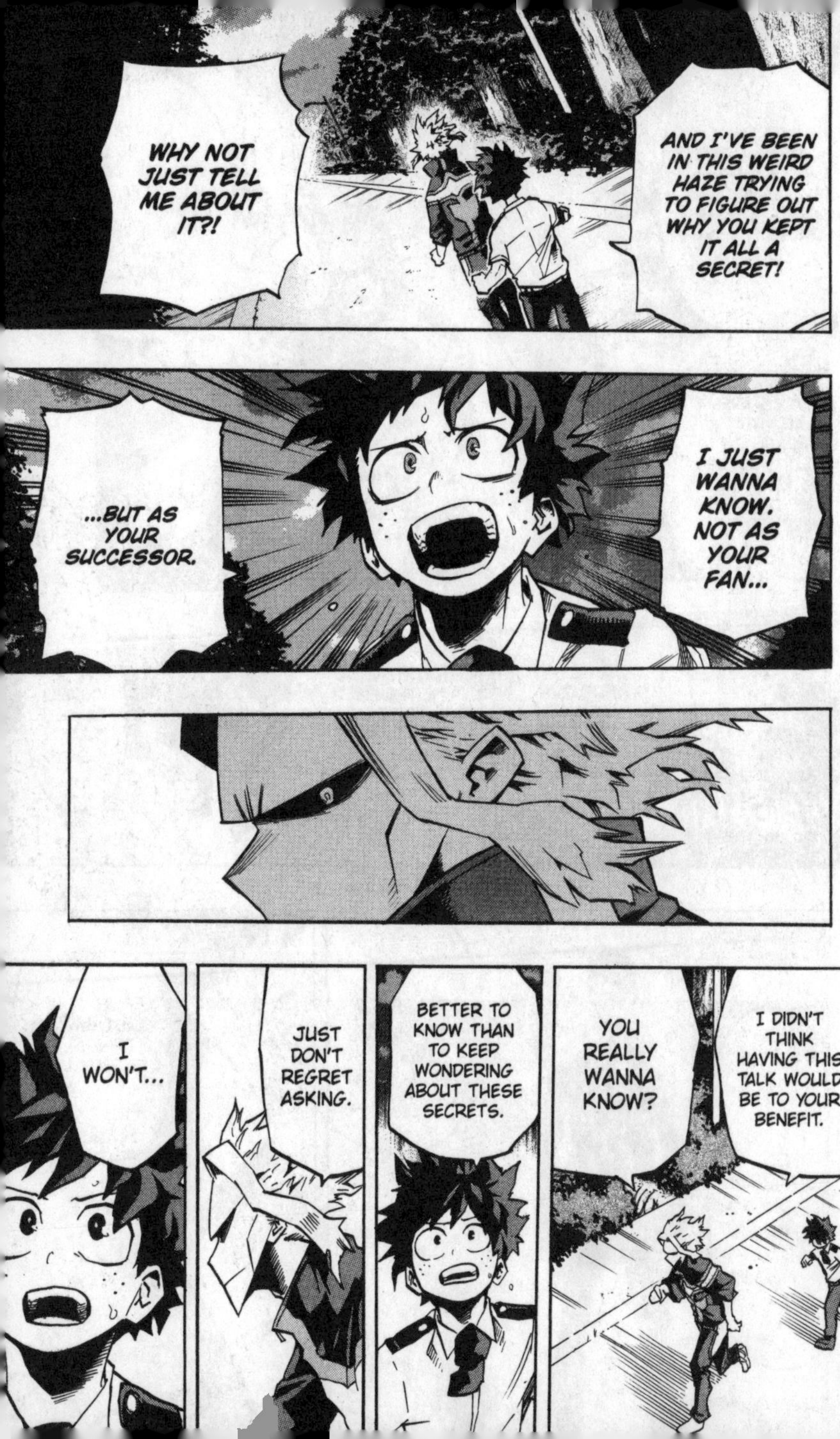
AND I'VE BEEN IN THIS WEIRD HAZE TRYING TO FIGURE OUT WHY YOU KEPT IT ALL A SECRET!
WHY NOT JUST TELL ME ABOUT IT?!
I JUST WANNA KNOW. NOT AS YOUR FAN...
...BUT AS YOUR SUCCESSOR.
I DIDN'T THINK HAVING THIS TALK WOULD BE TO YOUR BENEFIT.
YOU REALLY WANNA KNOW?
BETTER TO KNOW THAN TO KEEP WONDERING ABOUT THESE SECRETS.
JUST DON'T REGRET ASKING.
I WON'T...

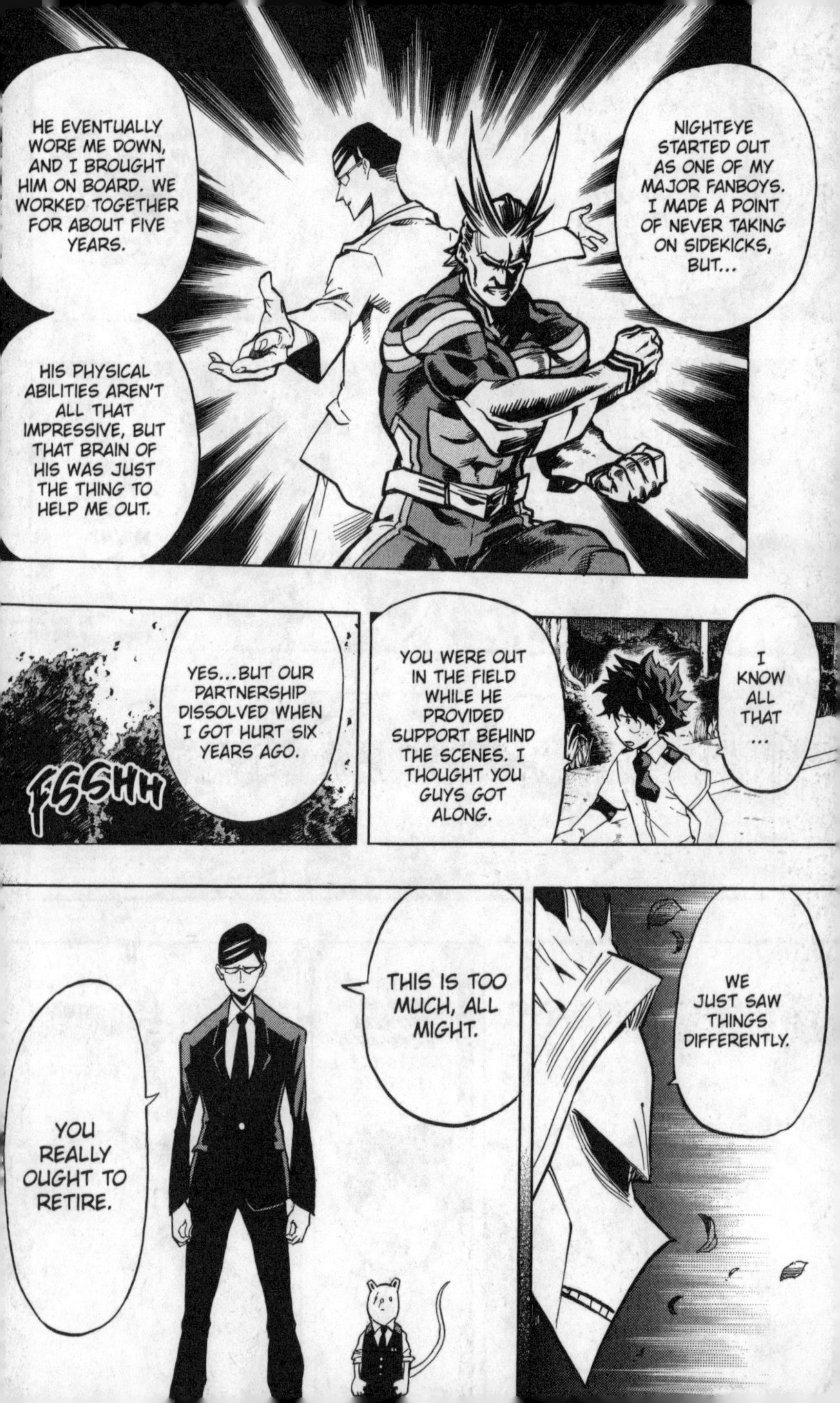
NIGHTEYE STARTED OUT AS ONE OF MY MAJOR FANBOYS. I MADE A POINT OF NEVER TAKING ON SIDEKICKS, BUT...
HE EVENTUALLY WORE ME DOWN, AND I BROUGHT HIM ON BOARD. WE WORKED TOGETHER FOR ABOUT FIVE YEARS.
HIS PHYSICAL ABILITIES AREN'T ALL THAT IMPRESSIVE, BUT THAT BRAIN OF HIS WAS JUST THE THING TO HELP ME OUT.
I KNOW ALL THAT...
YOU WERE OUT IN THE FIELD WHILE HE PROVIDED SUPPORT BEHIND THE SCENES. I THOUGHT YOU GUYS GOT ALONG.
YES...BUT OUR PARTNERSHIP DISSOLVED WHEN I GOT HURT SIX YEARS AGO.
FSSHH
WE JUST SAW THINGS DIFFERENTLY.
THIS IS TOO MUCH, ALL MIGHT.
YOU REALLY OUGHT TO RETIRE.

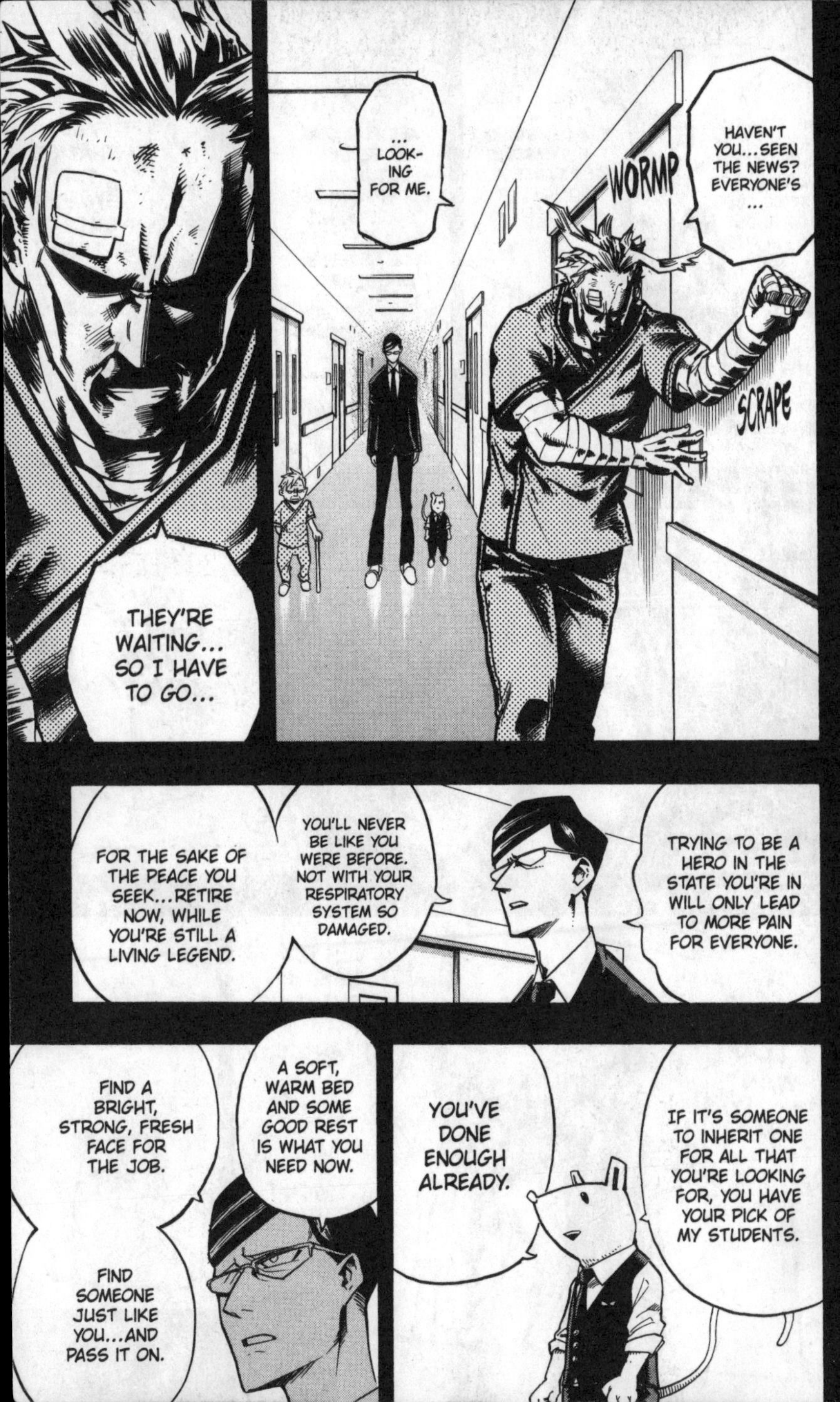
WORMP
HAVEN'T YOU...SEEN THE NEWS? EVERYONE'S ...
SCRAPE
... LOOK-ING FOR ME.
THEY'RE WAITING... SO I HAVE TO GO...
TRYING TO BE A HERO IN THE STATE YOU'RE IN WILL ONLY LEAD TO MORE PAIN FOR EVERYONE.
YOU'LL NEVER BE LIKE YOU WERE BEFORE. NOT WITH YOUR RESPIRATORY SYSTEM SO DAMAGED.
FOR THE SAKE OF THE PEACE YOU SEEK...RETIRE NOW, WHILE YOU'RE STILL A LIVING LEGEND.
IF IT'S SOMEONE TO INHERIT ONE FOR ALL THAT YOU'RE LOOKING FOR, YOU HAVE YOUR PICK OF MY STUDENTS.
YOU'VE DONE ENOUGH ALREADY.
A SOFT, WARM BED AND SOME GOOD REST IS WHAT YOU NEED NOW.
FIND A BRIGHT, STRONG, FRESH FACE FOR THE JOB.
FIND SOMEONE JUST LIKE YOU...AND PASS IT ON.

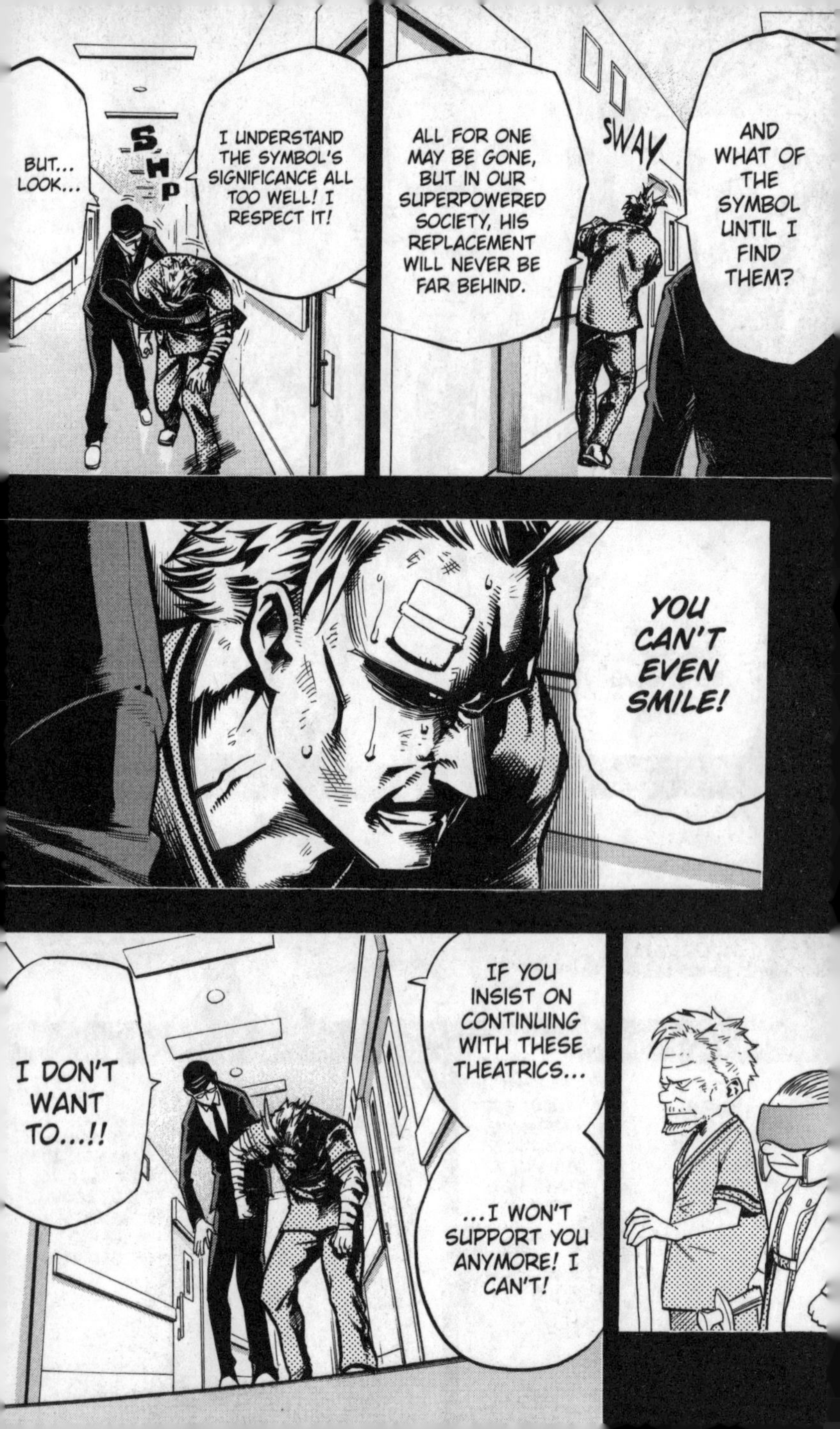
AND WHAT OF THE SYMBOL UNTIL I FIND THEM?
SWAY
ALL FOR ONE MAY BE GONE, BUT IN OUR SUPERPOWERED SOCIETY, HIS REPLACEMENT WILL NEVER BE FAR BEHIND.
I UNDERSTAND THE SYMBOL'S SIGNIFICANCE ALL TOO WELL! I RESPECT IT!
SHP
BUT... LOOK...
YOU CAN'T EVEN SMILE!
IF YOU INSIST ON CONTINUING WITH THESE THEATRICS...
...I WON'T SUPPORT YOU ANYMORE! I CAN'T!
I DON'T WANT TO...!!

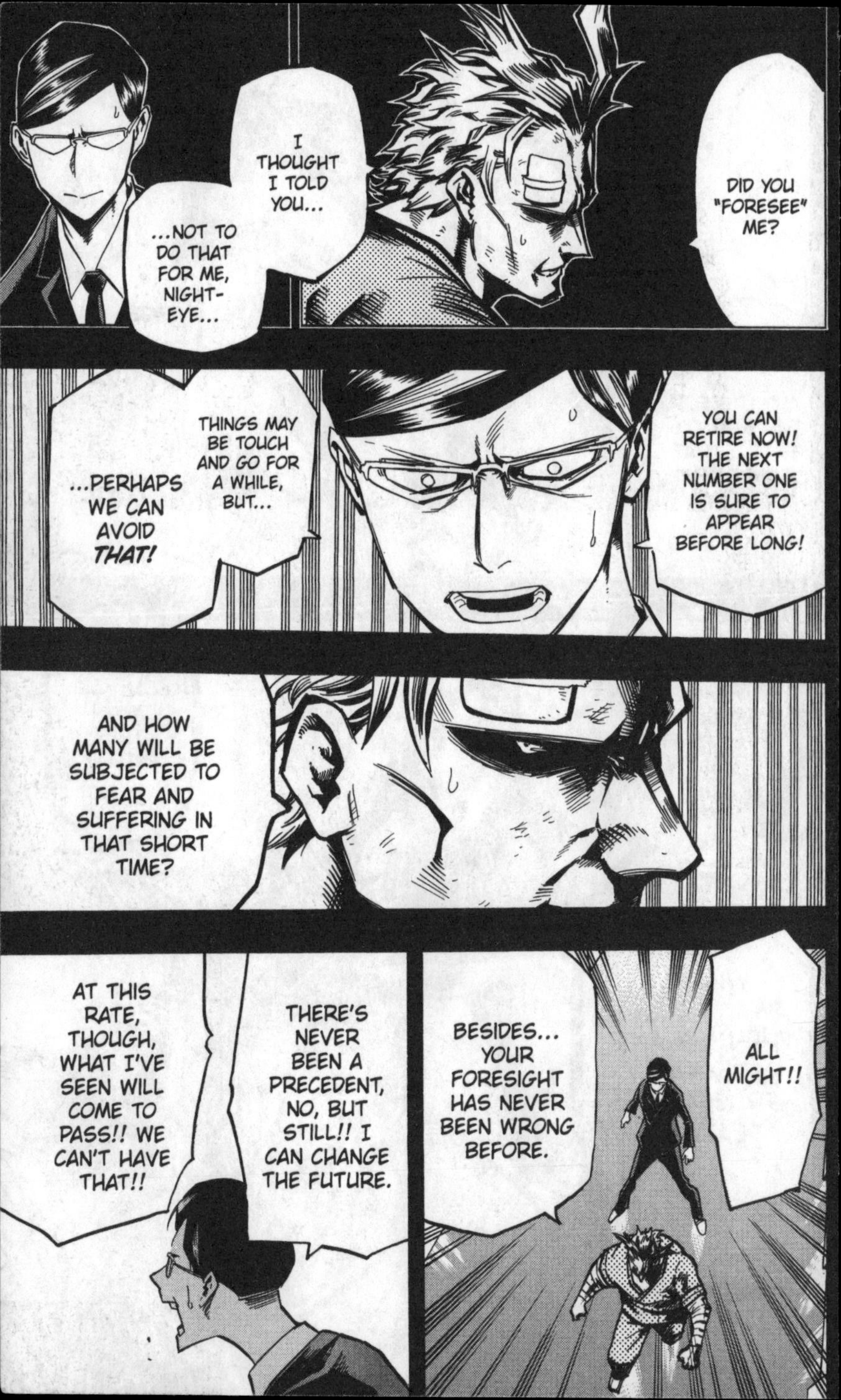
DID YOU "FORESEE" ME?
I THOUGHT I TOLD YOU...
...NOT TO DO THAT FOR ME, NIGHT-EYE...
YOU CAN RETIRE NOW! THE NEXT NUMBER ONE IS SURE TO APPEAR BEFORE LONG!
THINGS MAY BE TOUCH AND GO FOR A WHILE, BUT...
...PERHAPS WE CAN AVOID *THAT!*
AND HOW MANY WILL BE SUBJECTED TO FEAR AND SUFFERING IN THAT SHORT TIME?
ALL MIGHT!!
BESIDES... YOUR FORESIGHT HAS NEVER BEEN WRONG BEFORE.
THERE'S NEVER BEEN A PRECEDENT, NO, BUT STILL!! I CAN CHANGE THE FUTURE.
AT THIS RATE, THOUGH, WHAT I'VE SEEN WILL COME TO PASS!! WE CAN'T HAVE THAT!!

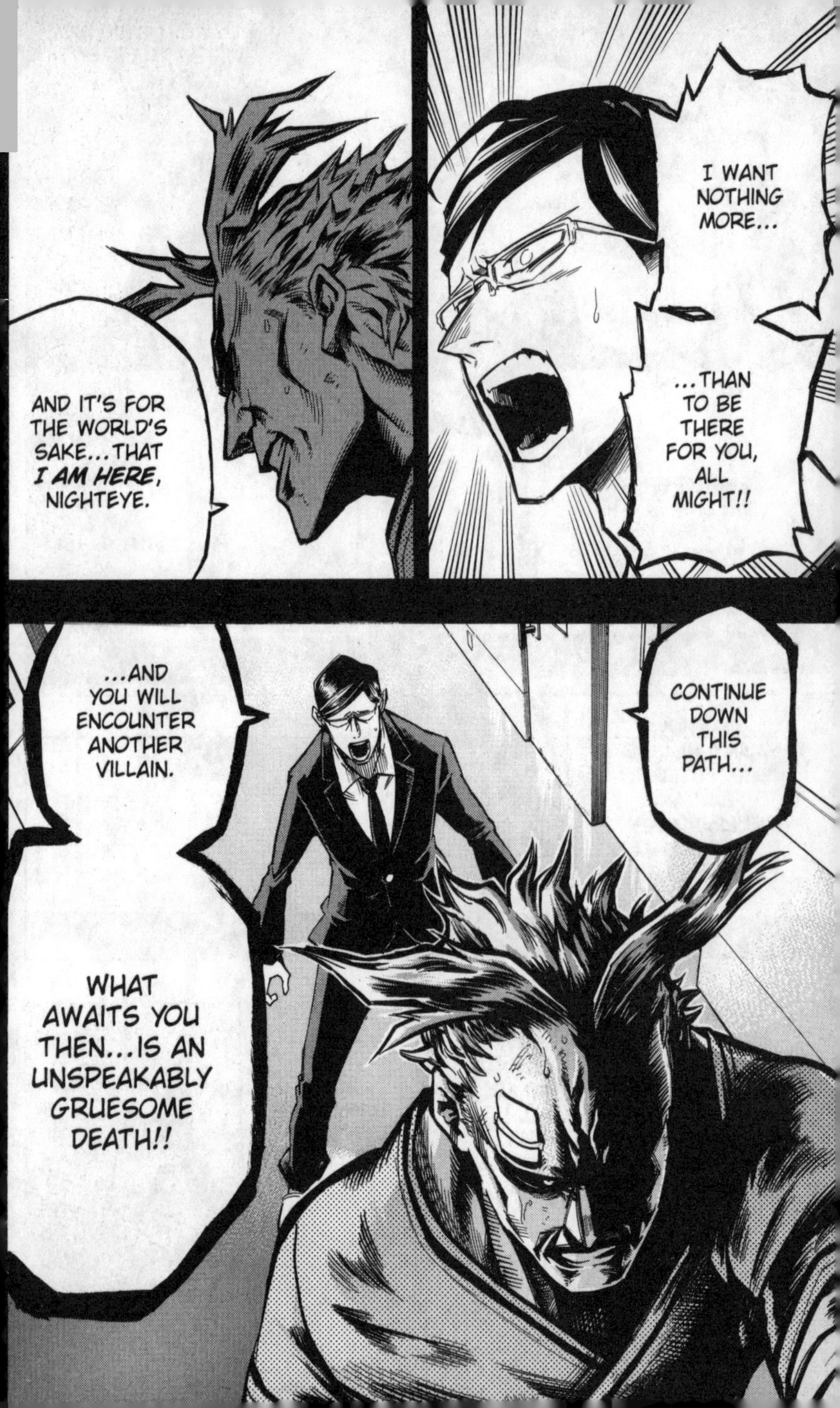
I WANT NOTHING MORE...
...THAN TO BE THERE FOR YOU, ALL MIGHT!!
AND IT'S FOR THE WORLD'S SAKE...THAT *I AM HERE*, NIGHTEYE.
CONTINUE DOWN THIS PATH...
...AND YOU WILL ENCOUNTER ANOTHER VILLAIN.
WHAT AWAITS YOU THEN...IS AN UNSPEAKABLY GRUESOME DEATH!!

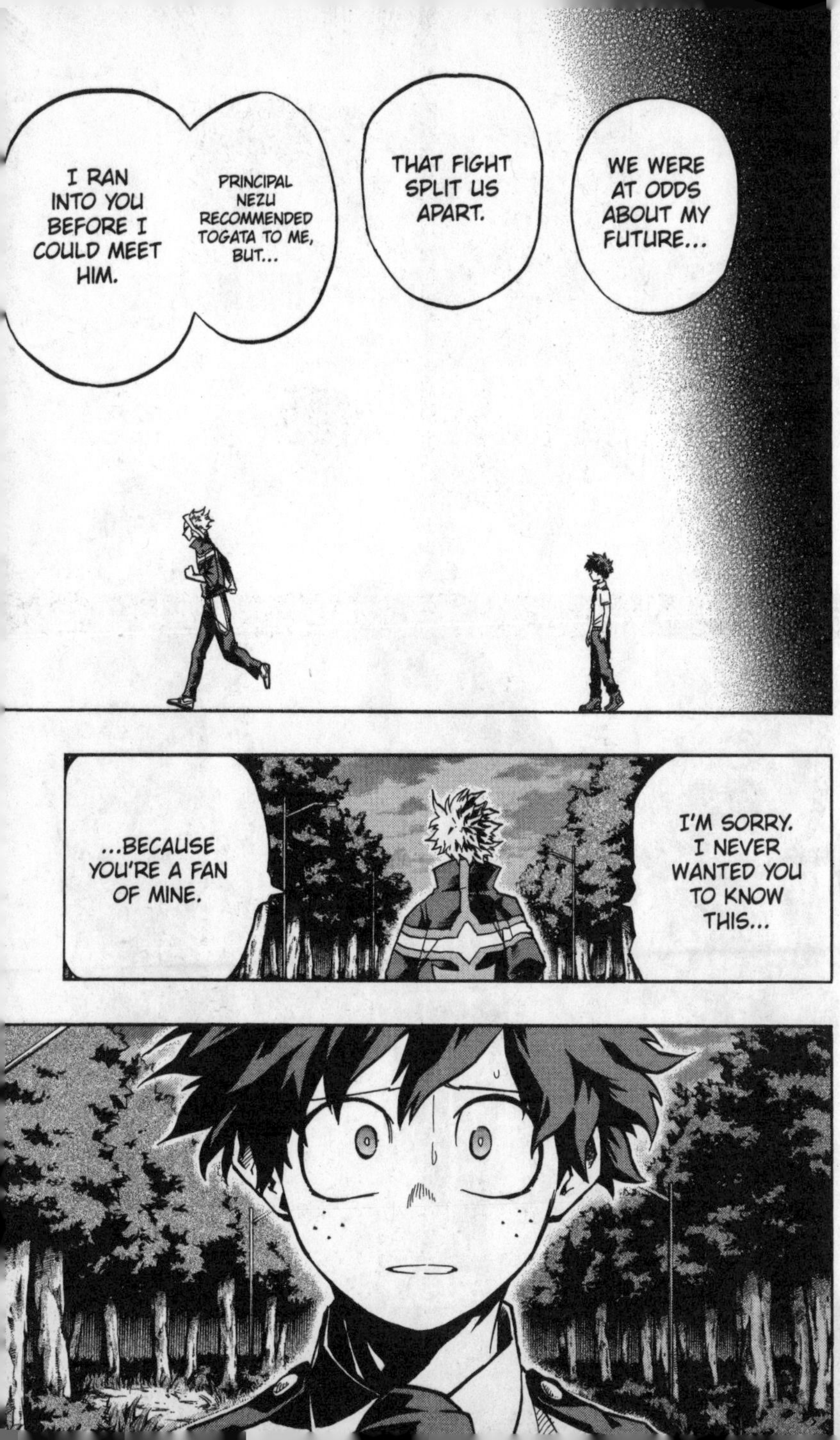
WE WERE AT ODDS ABOUT MY FUTURE...
THAT FIGHT SPLIT US APART.
PRINCIPAL NEZU RECOMMENDED TOGATA TO ME, BUT...
I RAN INTO YOU BEFORE I COULD MEET HIM.
I'M SORRY. I NEVER WANTED YOU TO KNOW THIS...
...BECAUSE YOU'RE A FAN OF MINE.

No. 131 - Fighting Fate

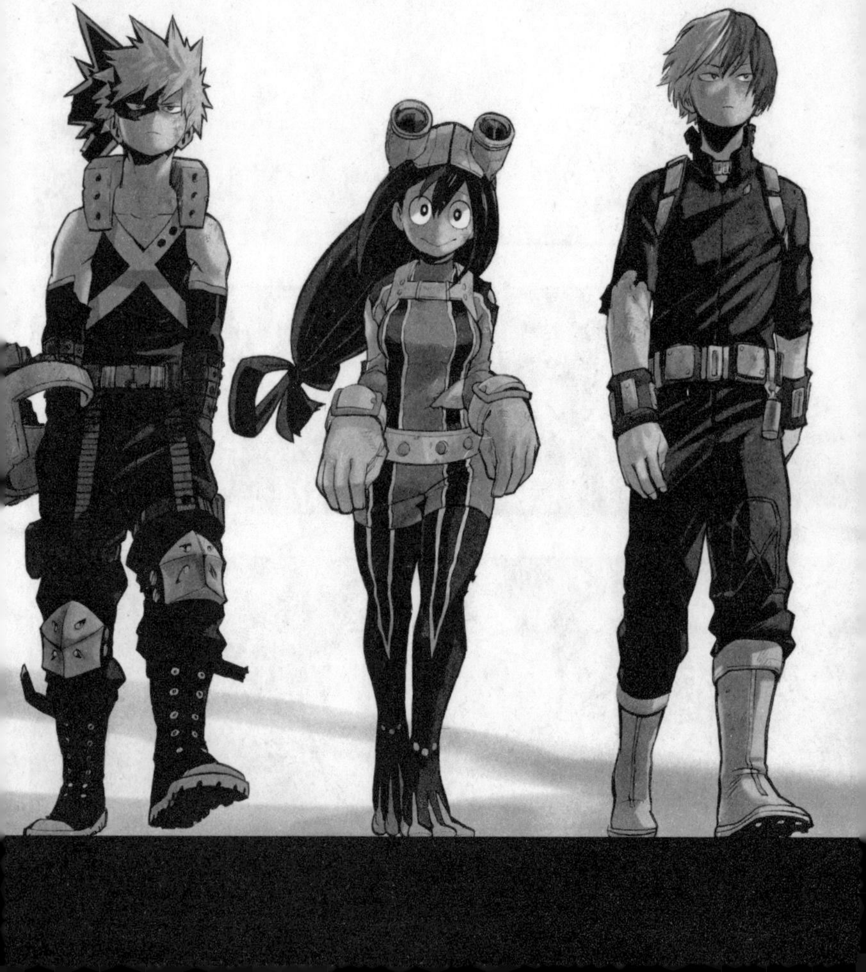

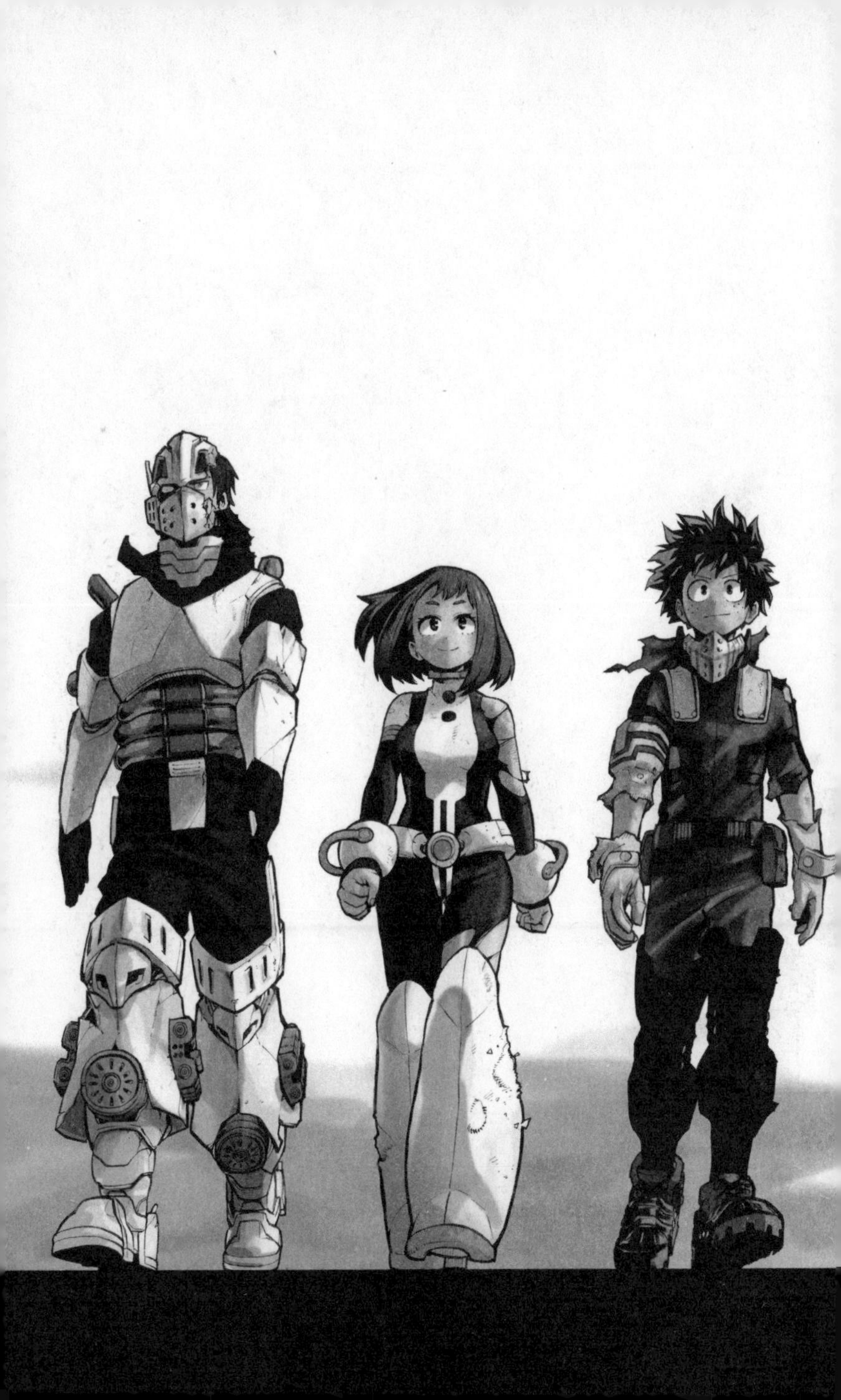

MY HERO ACADEMIA

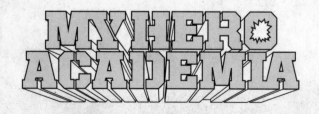

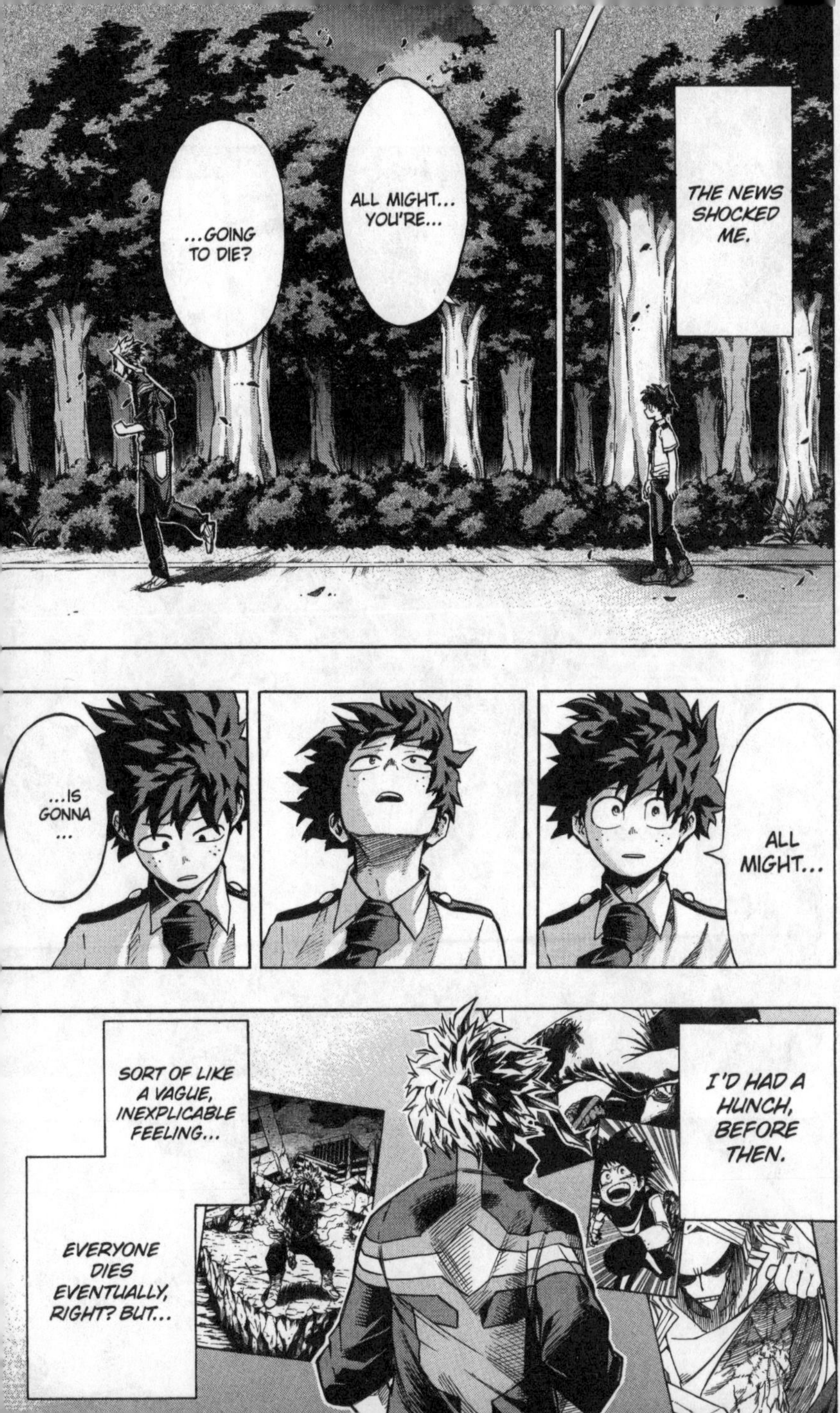
THE NEWS SHOCKED ME.
ALL MIGHT... YOU'RE...
...GOING TO DIE?
ALL MIGHT...
...IS GONNA ...
I'D HAD A HUNCH, BEFORE THEN.
SORT OF LIKE A VAGUE, INEXPLICABLE FEELING...
EVERYONE DIES EVENTUALLY, RIGHT? BUT...

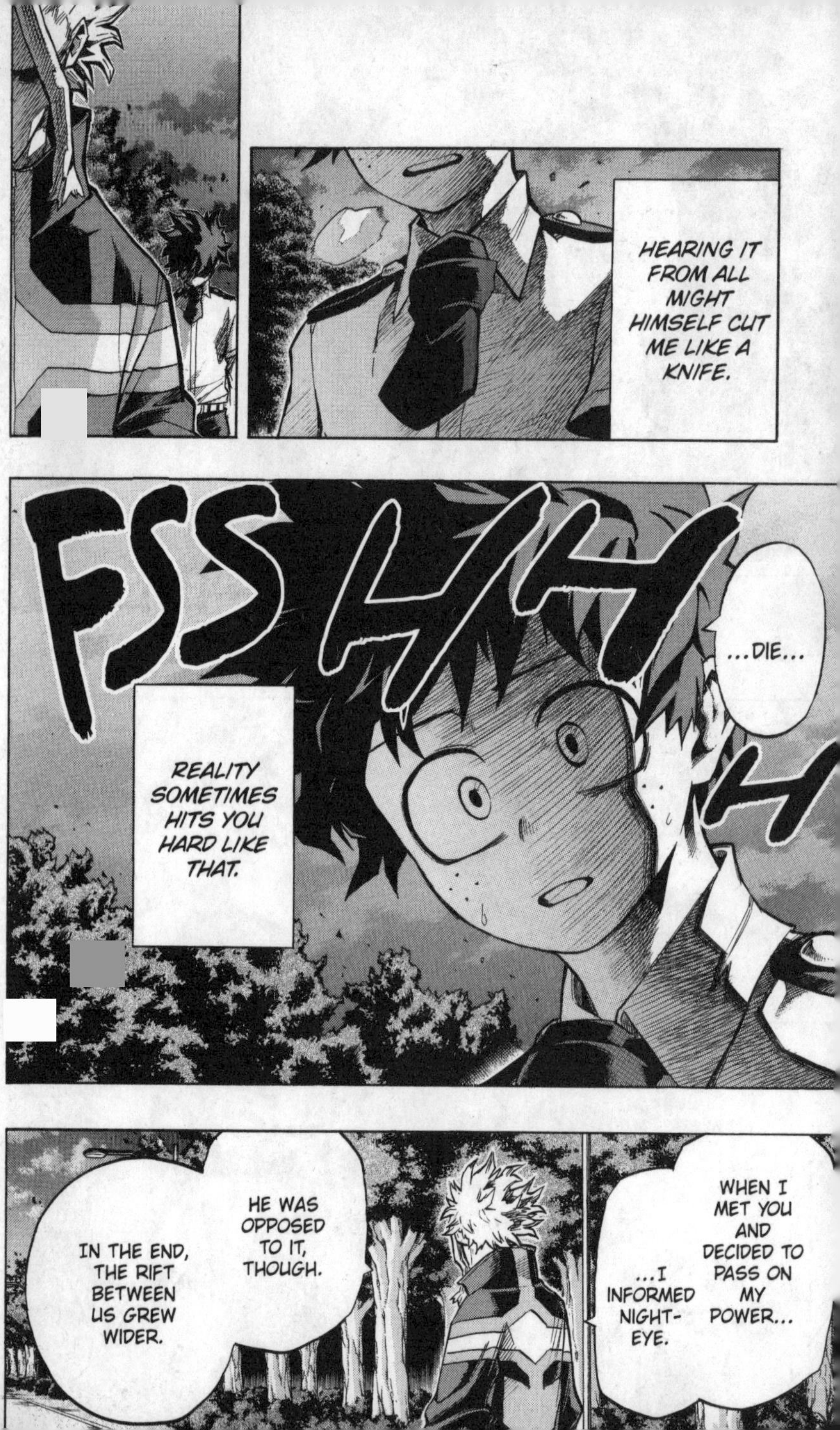
HEARING IT FROM ALL MIGHT HIMSELF CUT ME LIKE A KNIFE.
FSSHHH
...DIE...
REALITY SOMETIMES HITS YOU HARD LIKE THAT.
WHEN I MET YOU AND DECIDED TO PASS ON MY POWER...
...I INFORMED NIGHT-EYE.
HE WAS OPPOSED TO IT, THOUGH.
IN THE END, THE RIFT BETWEEN US GREW WIDER.

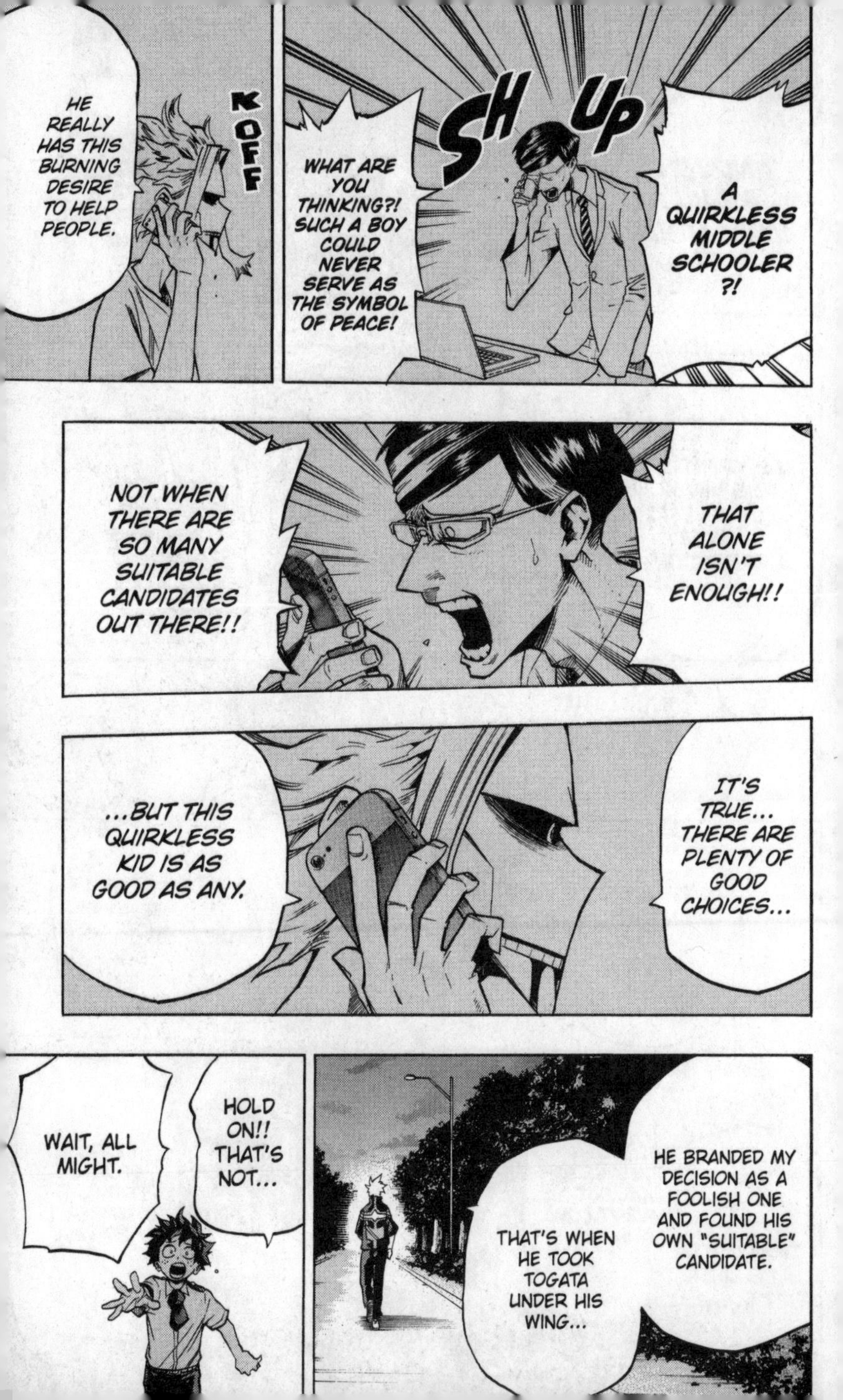
A QUIRKLESS MIDDLE SCHOOLER?!
SHUP
WHAT ARE YOU THINKING?! SUCH A BOY COULD NEVER SERVE AS THE SYMBOL OF PEACE!
KOFF
HE REALLY HAS THIS BURNING DESIRE TO HELP PEOPLE.
THAT ALONE ISN'T ENOUGH!!
NOT WHEN THERE ARE SO MANY SUITABLE CANDIDATES OUT THERE!!
IT'S TRUE... THERE ARE PLENTY OF GOOD CHOICES...
...BUT THIS QUIRKLESS KID IS AS GOOD AS ANY.
HE BRANDED MY DECISION AS A FOOLISH ONE AND FOUND HIS OWN "SUITABLE" CANDIDATE.
THAT'S WHEN HE TOOK TOGATA UNDER HIS WING...
HOLD ON!! THAT'S NOT...
WAIT, ALL MIGHT.

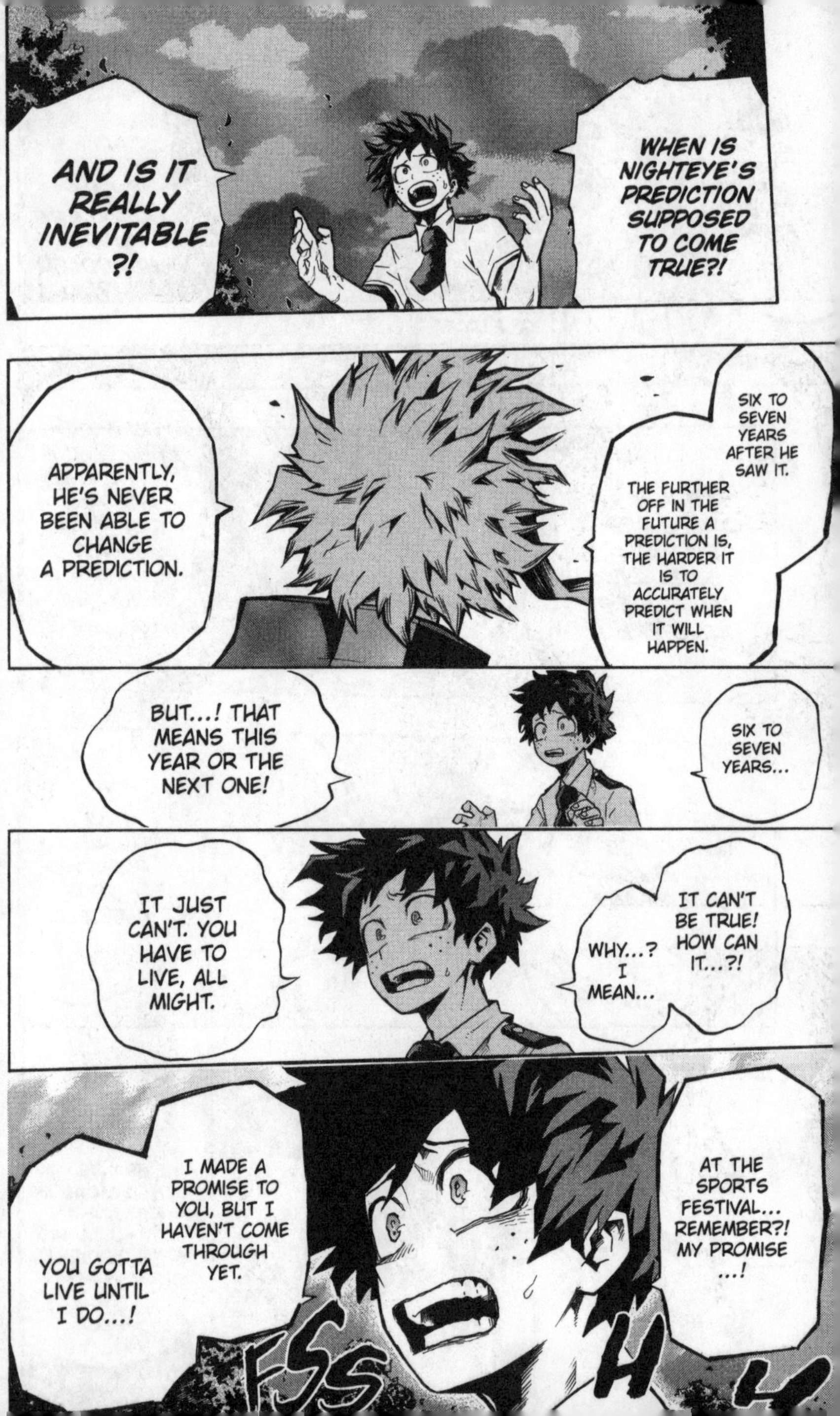
WHEN IS NIGHTEYE'S PREDICTION SUPPOSED TO COME TRUE?!
AND IS IT REALLY INEVITABLE?!
SIX TO SEVEN YEARS AFTER HE SAW IT.
THE FURTHER OFF IN THE FUTURE A PREDICTION IS, THE HARDER IT IS TO ACCURATELY PREDICT WHEN IT WILL HAPPEN.
APPARENTLY, HE'S NEVER BEEN ABLE TO CHANGE A PREDICTION.
SIX TO SEVEN YEARS...
BUT...! THAT MEANS THIS YEAR OR THE NEXT ONE!
IT CAN'T BE TRUE! HOW CAN IT...?!
WHY...? I MEAN...
IT JUST CAN'T. YOU HAVE TO LIVE, ALL MIGHT.
AT THE SPORTS FESTIVAL... REMEMBER?! MY PROMISE...!
I MADE A PROMISE TO YOU, BUT I HAVEN'T COME THROUGH YET.
YOU GOTTA LIVE UNTIL I DO...!

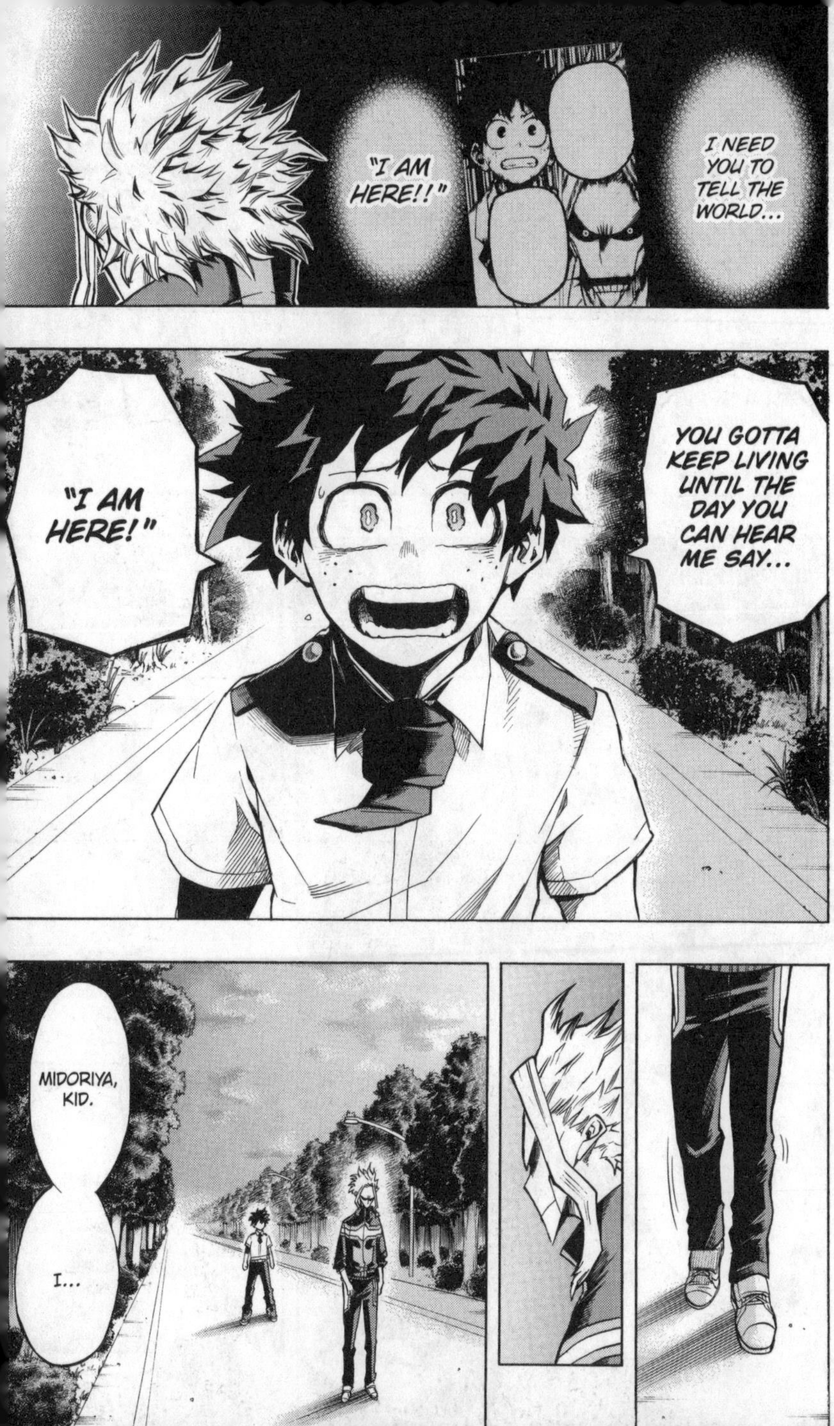
I NEED YOU TO TELL THE WORLD...
"I AM HERE!!"
YOU GOTTA KEEP LIVING UNTIL THE DAY YOU CAN HEAR ME SAY...
"I AM HERE!"
MIDORIYA, KID.
I...

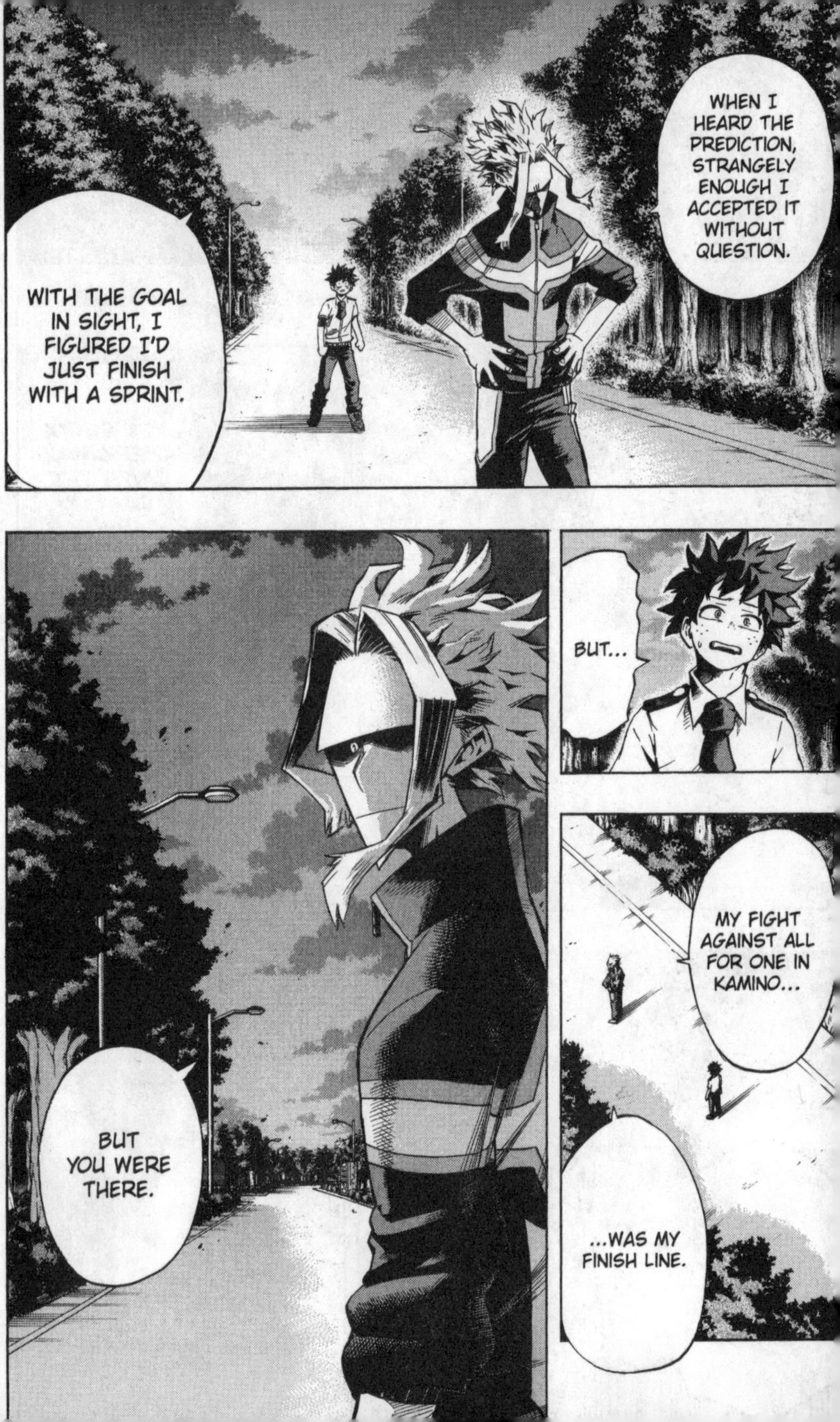
WHEN I HEARD THE PREDICTION, STRANGELY ENOUGH I ACCEPTED IT WITHOUT QUESTION.
WITH THE GOAL IN SIGHT, I FIGURED I'D JUST FINISH WITH A SPRINT.
BUT...
MY FIGHT AGAINST ALL FOR ONE IN KAMINO...
...WAS MY FINISH LINE.
BUT YOU WERE THERE.

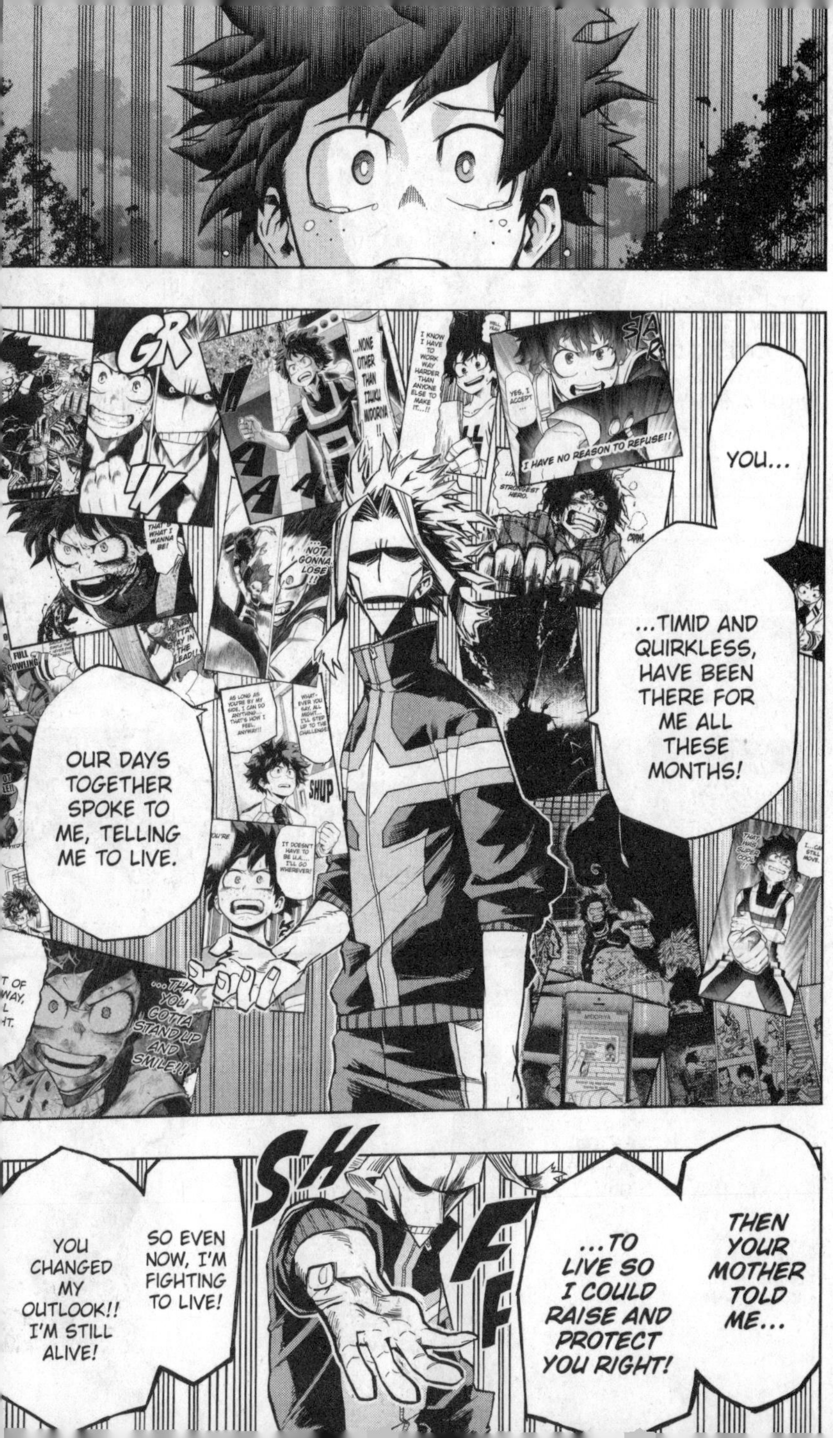
YOU...
...TIMID AND QUIRKLESS, HAVE BEEN THERE FOR ME ALL THESE MONTHS!
I HAVE NO REASON TO REFUSE!!
YES, I ACCEPT...
I KNOW I HAVE TO WORK WAY HARDER THAN ANYONE ELSE TO MAKE IT...!!
...NONE OTHER THAN IZUKU MIDORIYA!!
GR
IN
...NOT GONNA LOSE!!
THAT'S WHAT I WANNA BE!
FULL COWLING
WHAT-EVER YOU SAY, ALL MIGHT... I'LL STEP UP TO THE CHALLENGE!
AS LONG AS YOU'RE BY MY SIDE, I CAN DO ANYTHING!... THAT'S HOW I FEEL, ANYWAY!!
SHUP
IT DOESN'T HAVE TO BE U.A.... I'LL GO WHEREVER!
...THAT YOU GOTTA STAND UP AND SMILE!!
OUR DAYS TOGETHER SPOKE TO ME, TELLING ME TO LIVE.
THEN YOUR MOTHER TOLD ME...
...TO LIVE SO I COULD RAISE AND PROTECT YOU RIGHT!
SH
FF
SO EVEN NOW, I'M FIGHTING TO LIVE!
YOU CHANGED MY OUTLOOK!! I'M STILL ALIVE!

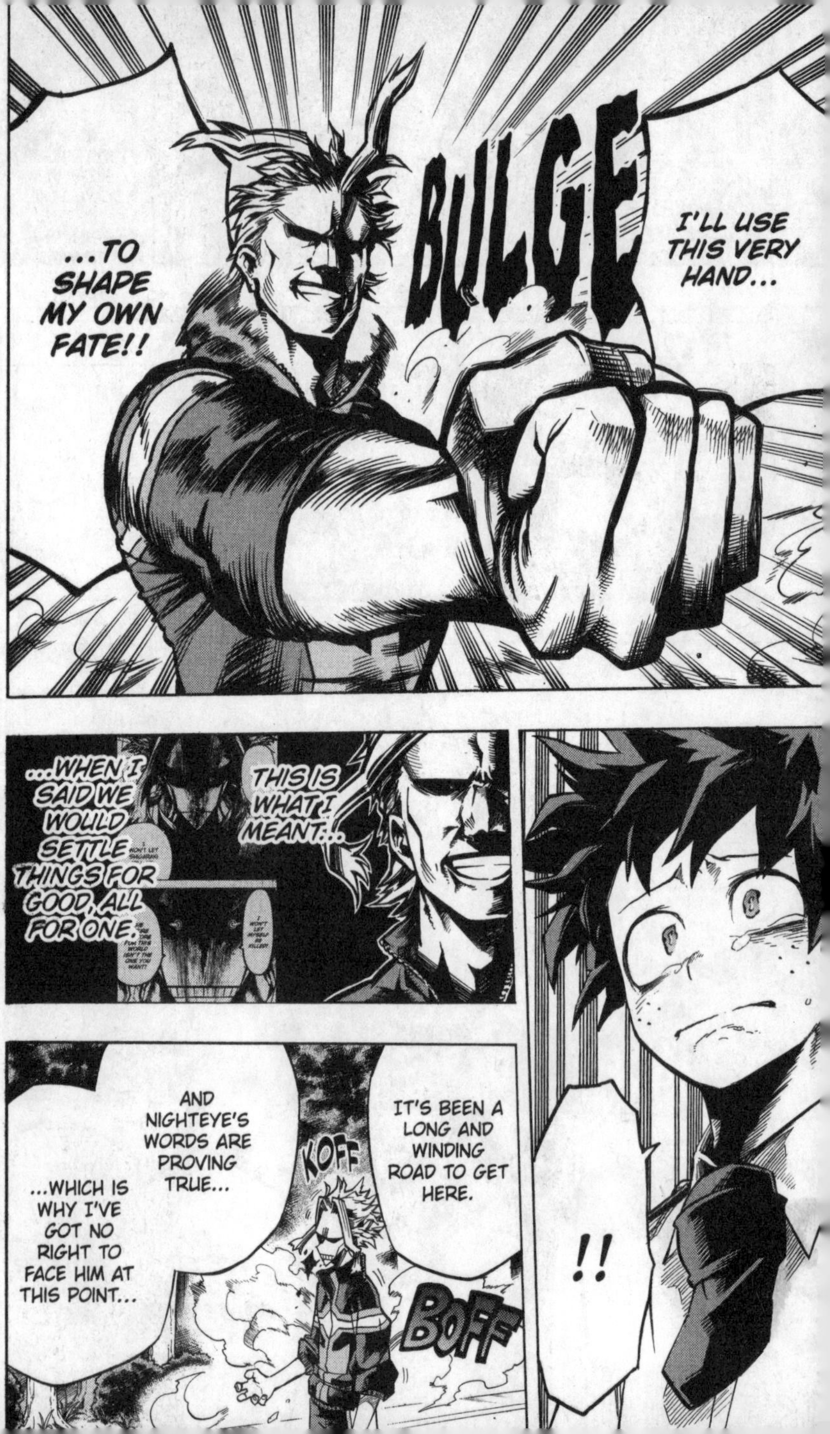
I'LL USE THIS VERY HAND...
BULGE
...TO SHAPE MY OWN FATE!!
!!
THIS IS WHAT I MEANT...
...WHEN I SAID WE WOULD SETTLE THINGS FOR GOOD, ALL FOR ONE.
I WON'T LET MYSELF BE KILLED!
IT'S BEEN A LONG AND WINDING ROAD TO GET HERE.
KOFF
AND NIGHTEYE'S WORDS ARE PROVING TRUE...
BOFF
...WHICH IS WHY I'VE GOT NO RIGHT TO FACE HIM AT THIS POINT...

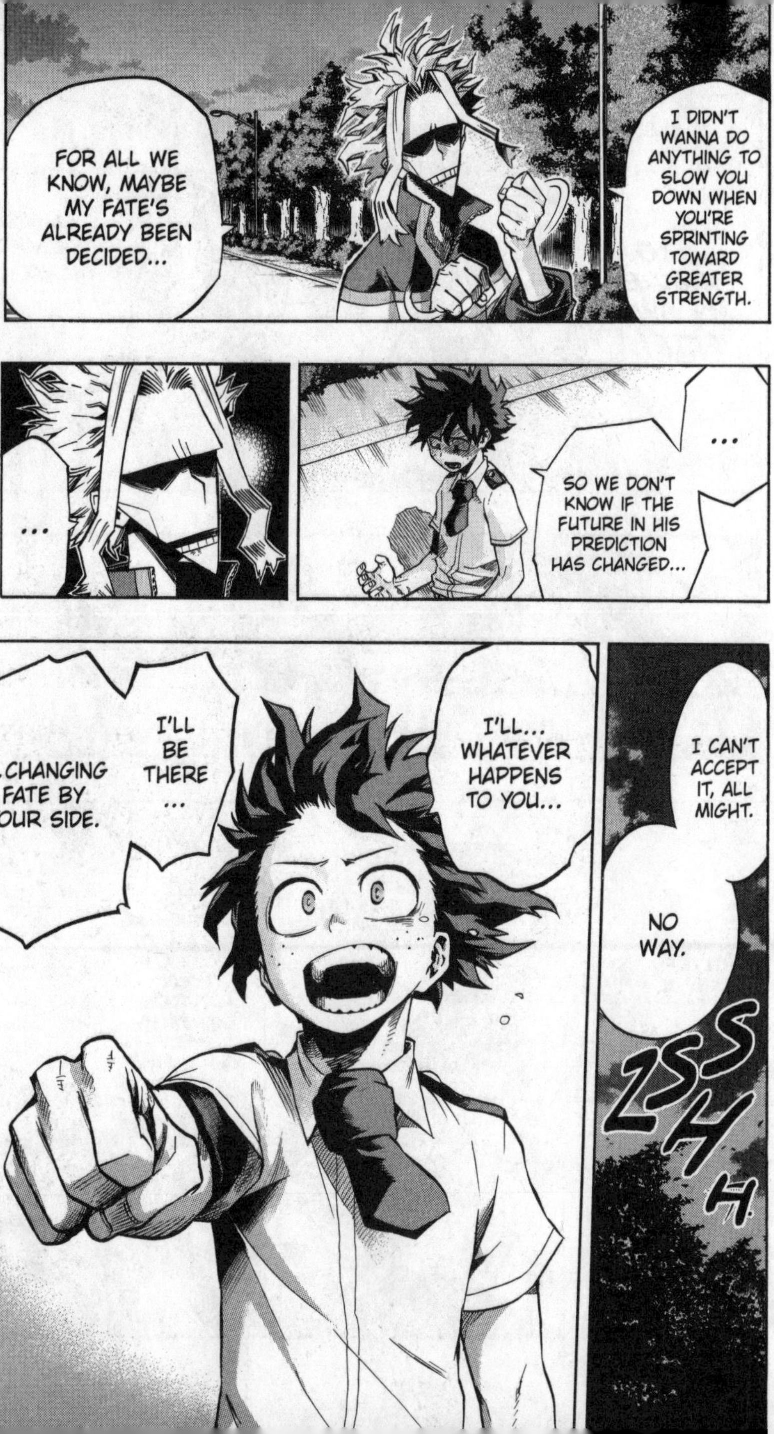
I DIDN'T WANNA DO ANYTHING TO SLOW YOU DOWN WHEN YOU'RE SPRINTING TOWARD GREATER STRENGTH.
FOR ALL WE KNOW, MAYBE MY FATE'S ALREADY BEEN DECIDED...
...
SO WE DON'T KNOW IF THE FUTURE IN HIS PREDICTION HAS CHANGED...
...
I CAN'T ACCEPT IT, ALL MIGHT.
NO WAY.
ZSSHH
I'LL... WHATEVER HAPPENS TO YOU...
I'LL BE THERE ...
...CHANGING FATE BY YOUR SIDE.

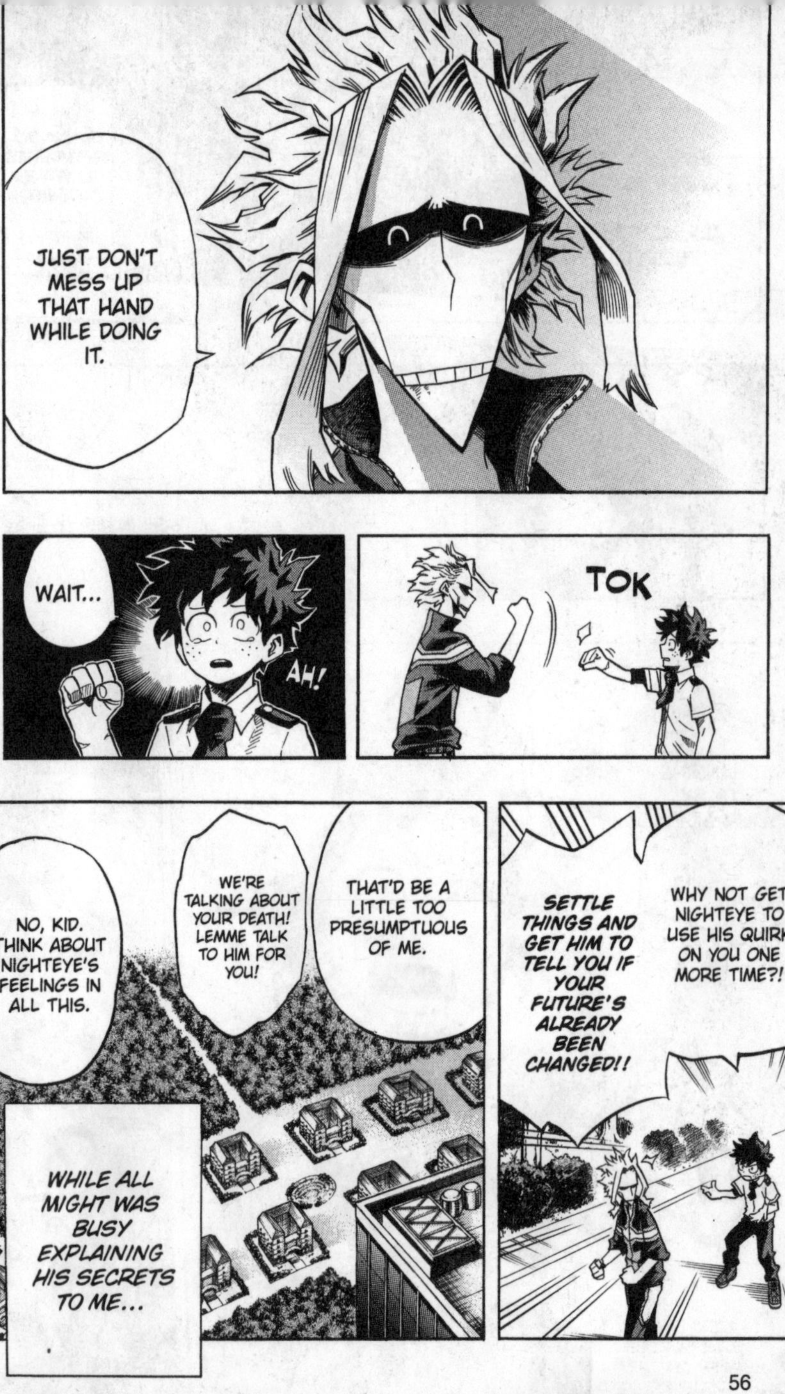
JUST DON'T MESS UP THAT HAND WHILE DOING IT.
TOK
WAIT...
AH!
WHY NOT GET NIGHTEYE TO USE HIS QUIRK ON YOU ONE MORE TIME?!
SETTLE THINGS AND GET HIM TO TELL YOU IF YOUR FUTURE'S ALREADY BEEN CHANGED!!
THAT'D BE A LITTLE TOO PRESUMPTUOUS OF ME.
WE'RE TALKING ABOUT YOUR DEATH! LEMME TALK TO HIM FOR YOU!
NO, KID. THINK ABOUT NIGHTEYE'S FEELINGS IN ALL THIS.
WHILE ALL MIGHT WAS BUSY EXPLAINING HIS SECRETS TO ME...

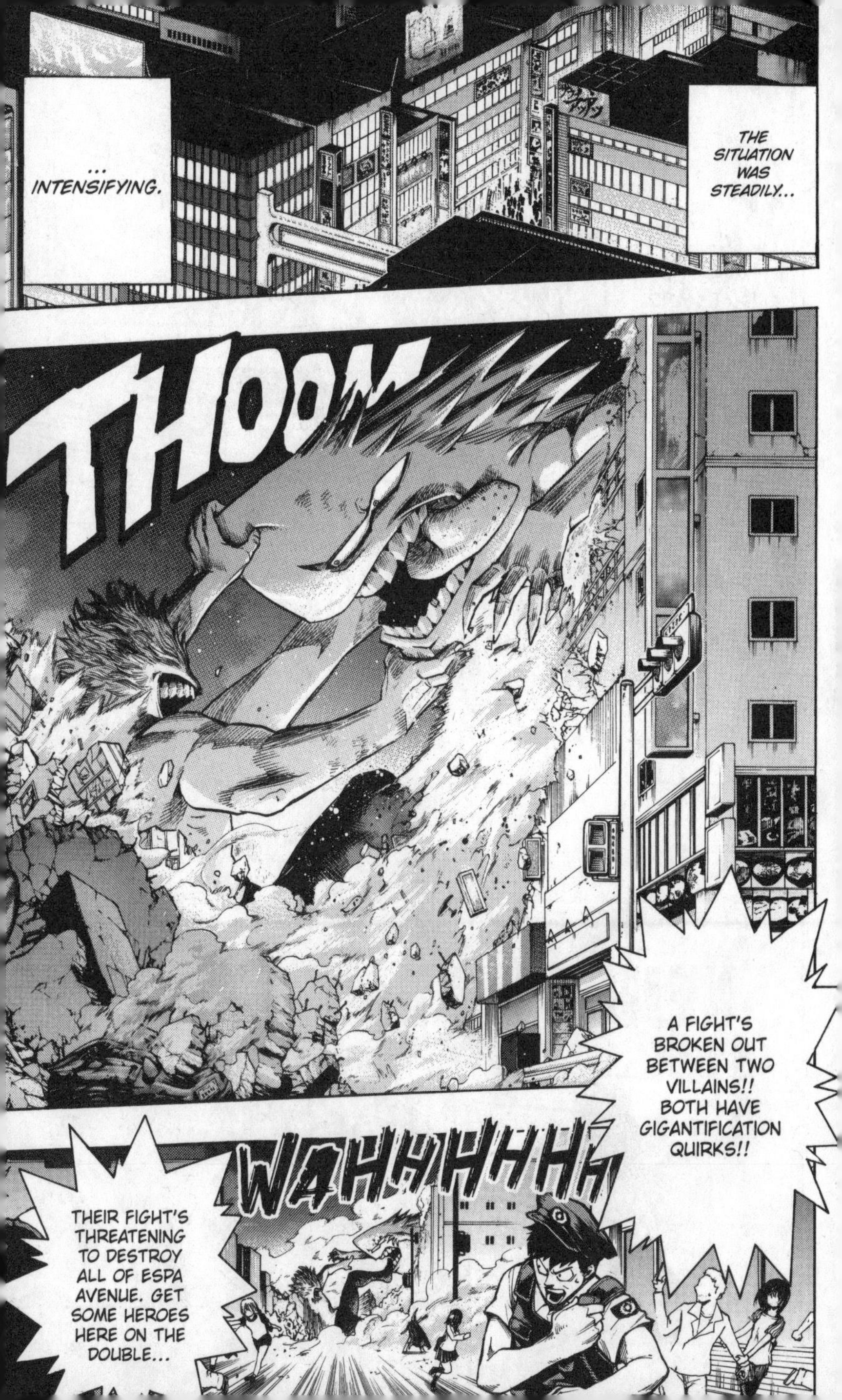

THE SITUATION WAS STEADILY...
... INTENSIFYING.
THOOM
A FIGHT'S BROKEN OUT BETWEEN TWO VILLAINS!! BOTH HAVE GIGANTIFICATION QUIRKS!!
WAHHHHHHH
THEIR FIGHT'S THREATENING TO DESTROY ALL OF ESPA AVENUE. GET SOME HEROES HERE ON THE DOUBLE...

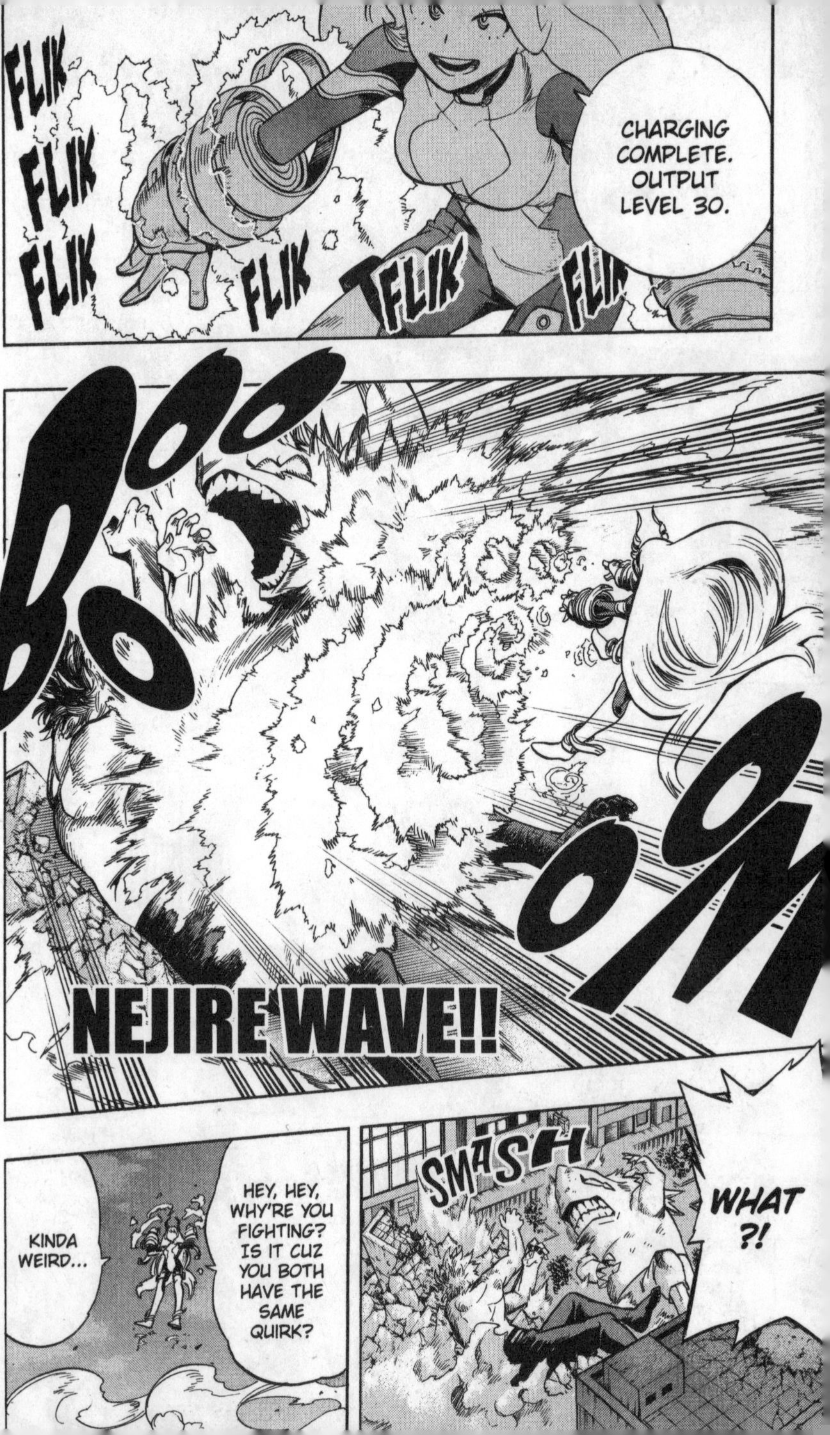
CHARGING COMPLETE. OUTPUT LEVEL 30.
FLIK
FLIK
FLIK
FLIK FLIK FLIK
BOOOOOM
NEJIRE WAVE!!
WHAT ?!
SMASH
HEY, HEY, WHY'RE YOU FIGHTING? IS IT CUZ YOU BOTH HAVE THE SAME QUIRK?
KINDA WEIRD...

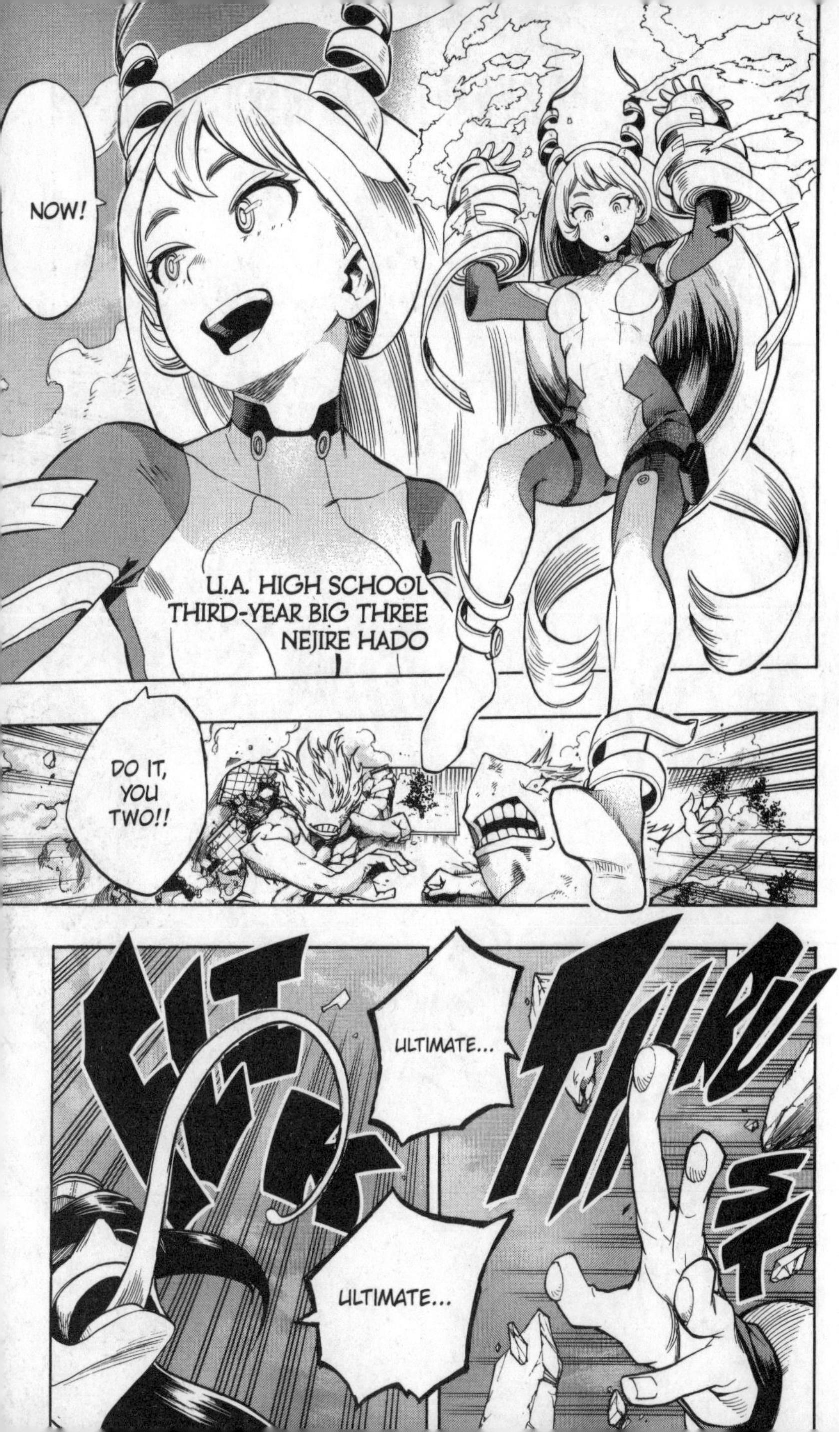
NOW!
U.A. HIGH SCHOOL THIRD-YEAR BIG THREE NEJIRE HADO
DO IT, YOU TWO!!
ULTIMATE...
ULTIMATE...

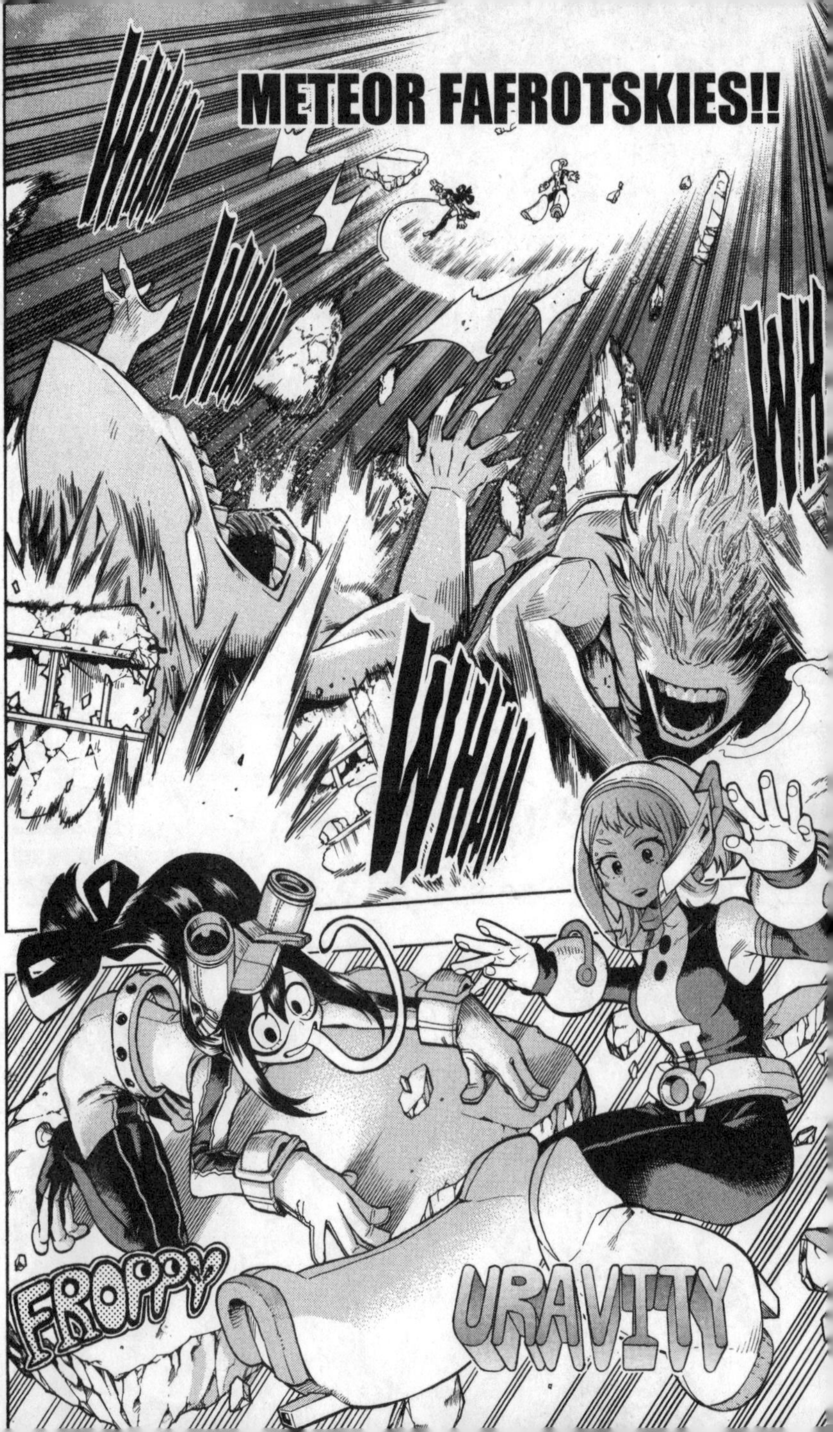
METEOR FAFROTSKIES!!
WHH
WHH
WHH
WHH
URAVITY
FROPPY

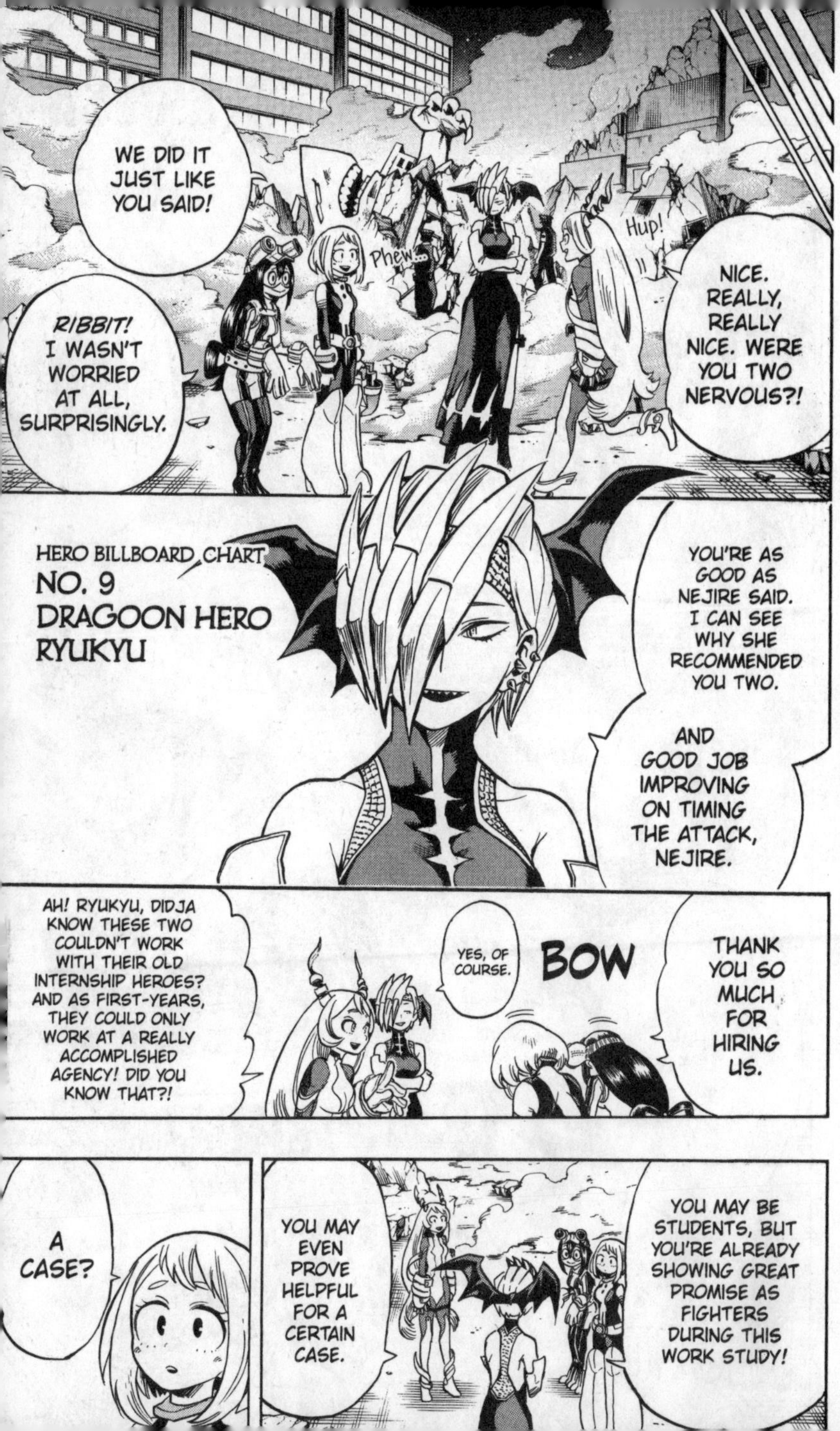
Hup!
NICE. REALLY, REALLY NICE. WERE YOU TWO NERVOUS?!
WE DID IT JUST LIKE YOU SAID!
Phew...
RIBBIT! I WASN'T WORRIED AT ALL, SURPRISINGLY.
YOU'RE AS GOOD AS NEJIRE SAID. I CAN SEE WHY SHE RECOMMENDED YOU TWO.
AND GOOD JOB IMPROVING ON TIMING THE ATTACK, NEJIRE.
HERO BILLBOARD CHART NO. 9 DRAGOON HERO RYUKYU
THANK YOU SO MUCH FOR HIRING US.
BOW
YES, OF COURSE.
AH! RYUKYU, DIDJA KNOW THESE TWO COULDN'T WORK WITH THEIR OLD INTERNSHIP HEROES? AND AS FIRST-YEARS, THEY COULD ONLY WORK AT A REALLY ACCOMPLISHED AGENCY! DID YOU KNOW THAT?!
YOU MAY BE STUDENTS, BUT YOU'RE ALREADY SHOWING GREAT PROMISE AS FIGHTERS DURING THIS WORK STUDY!
YOU MAY EVEN PROVE HELPFUL FOR A CERTAIN CASE.
A CASE?

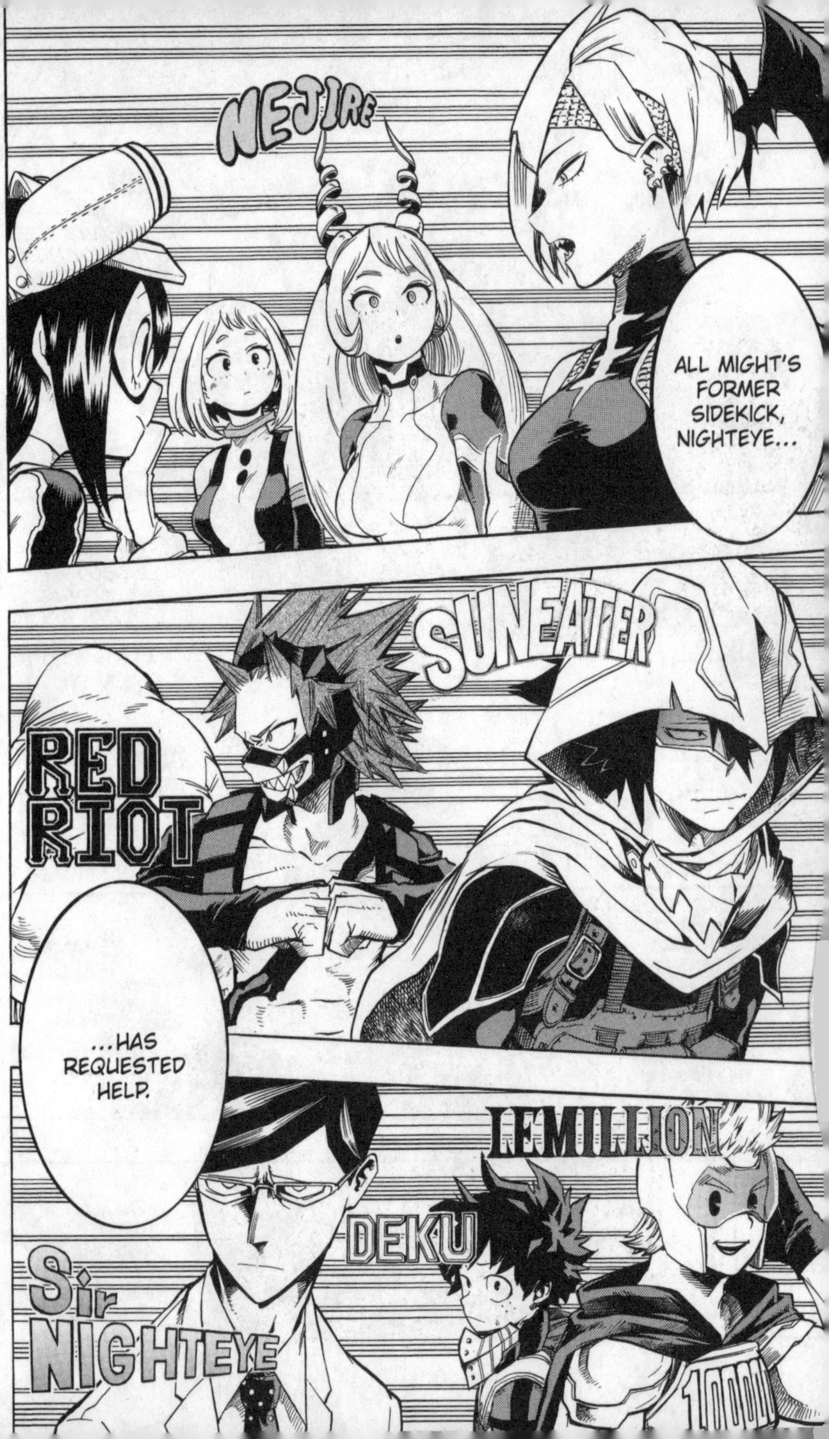
NEJIRE
ALL MIGHT'S FORMER SIDEKICK, NIGHTEYE...
SUNEATER
RED RIOT
...HAS REQUESTED HELP.
LEMILLION
DEKU
Sir NIGHTEYE

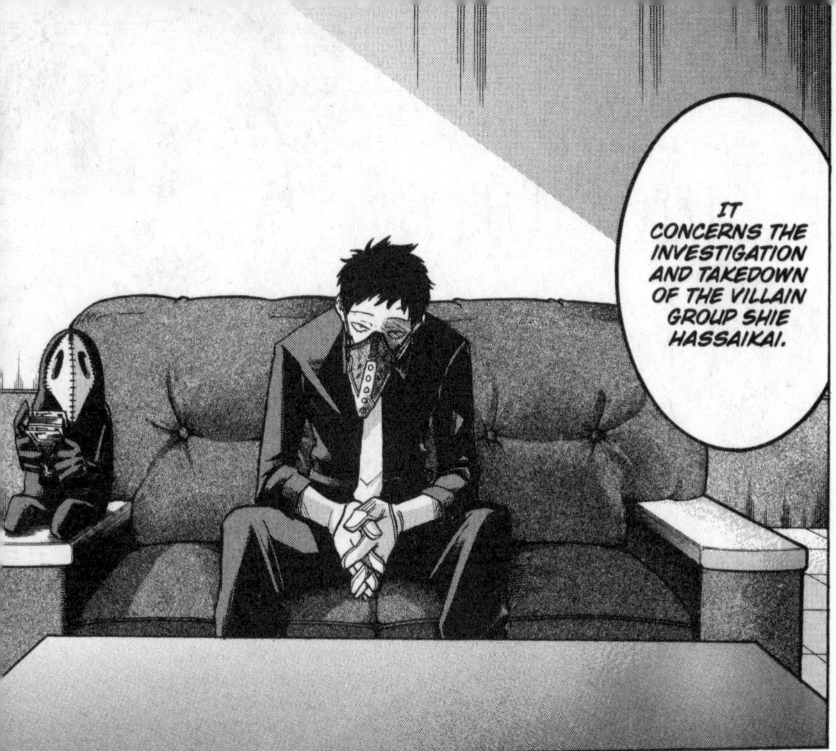
IT CONCERNS THE INVESTIGATION AND TAKEDOWN OF THE VILLAIN GROUP SHIE HASSAIKAI.
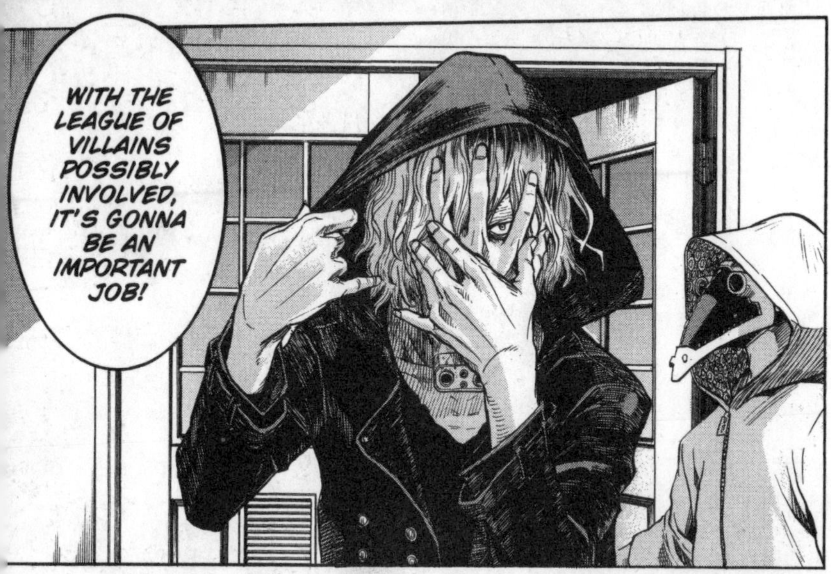
WITH THE LEAGUE OF VILLAINS POSSIBLY INVOLVED, IT'S GONNA BE AN IMPORTANT JOB!

HERO

RYUKYU [26] [RYUKO TATSUMA]

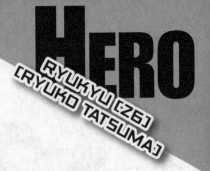

STREET CLOTHES

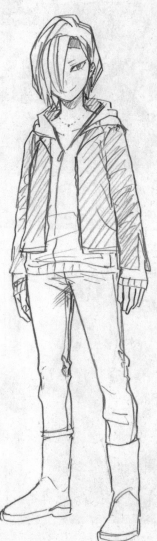

Birthday: 9/22
Height: 166 cm
Favorite Things: Anything sparkly

THE RYUKYU

A cool beauty. Has an impressive amount of support for someone so young, basically because her Quirk is just too freaking cool. Everyone loves her.

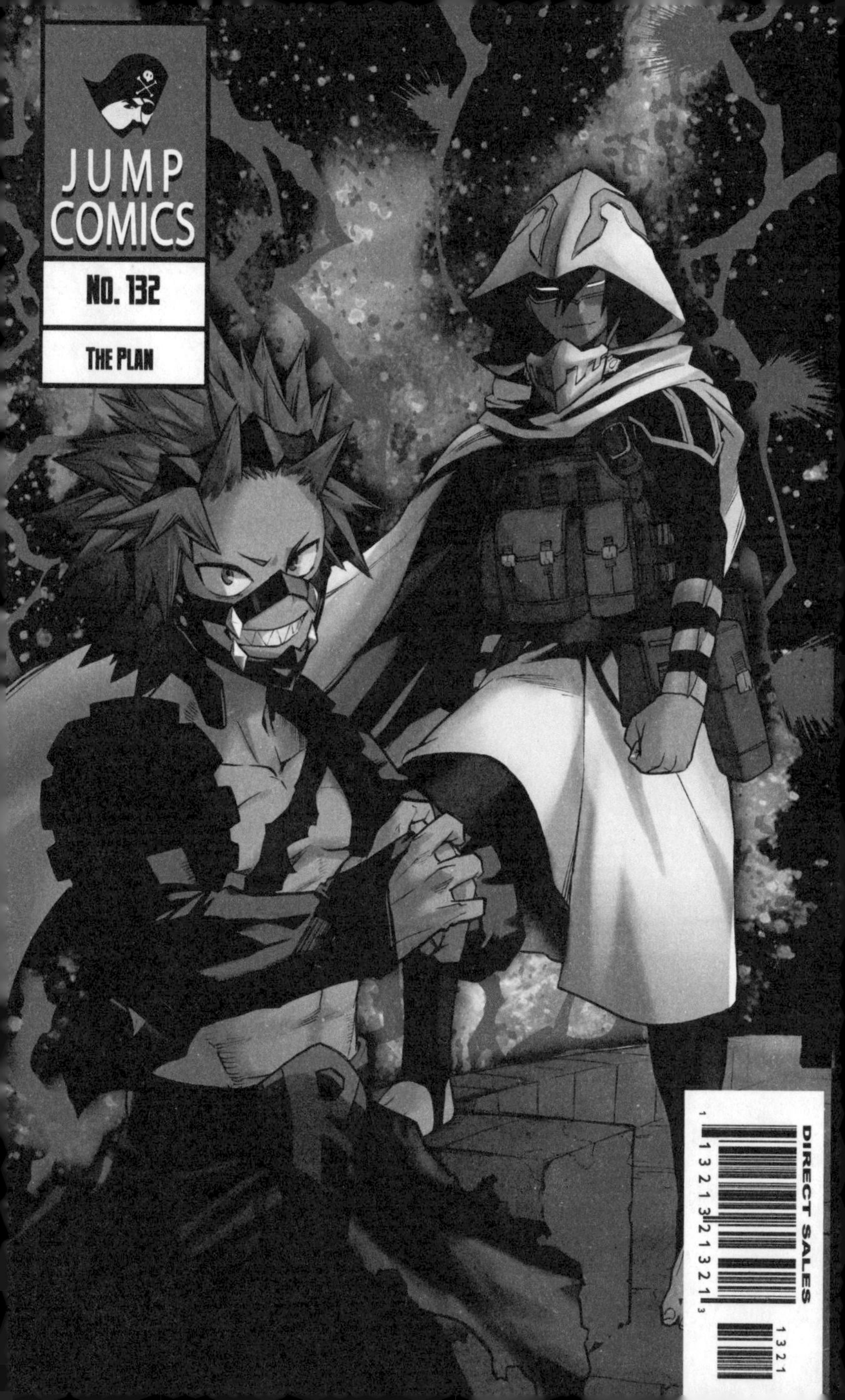
JUMP COMICS
No. 132
The Plan
DIRECT SALES

MY HERO ACADEMIA

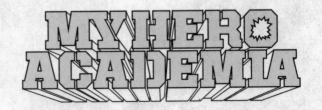

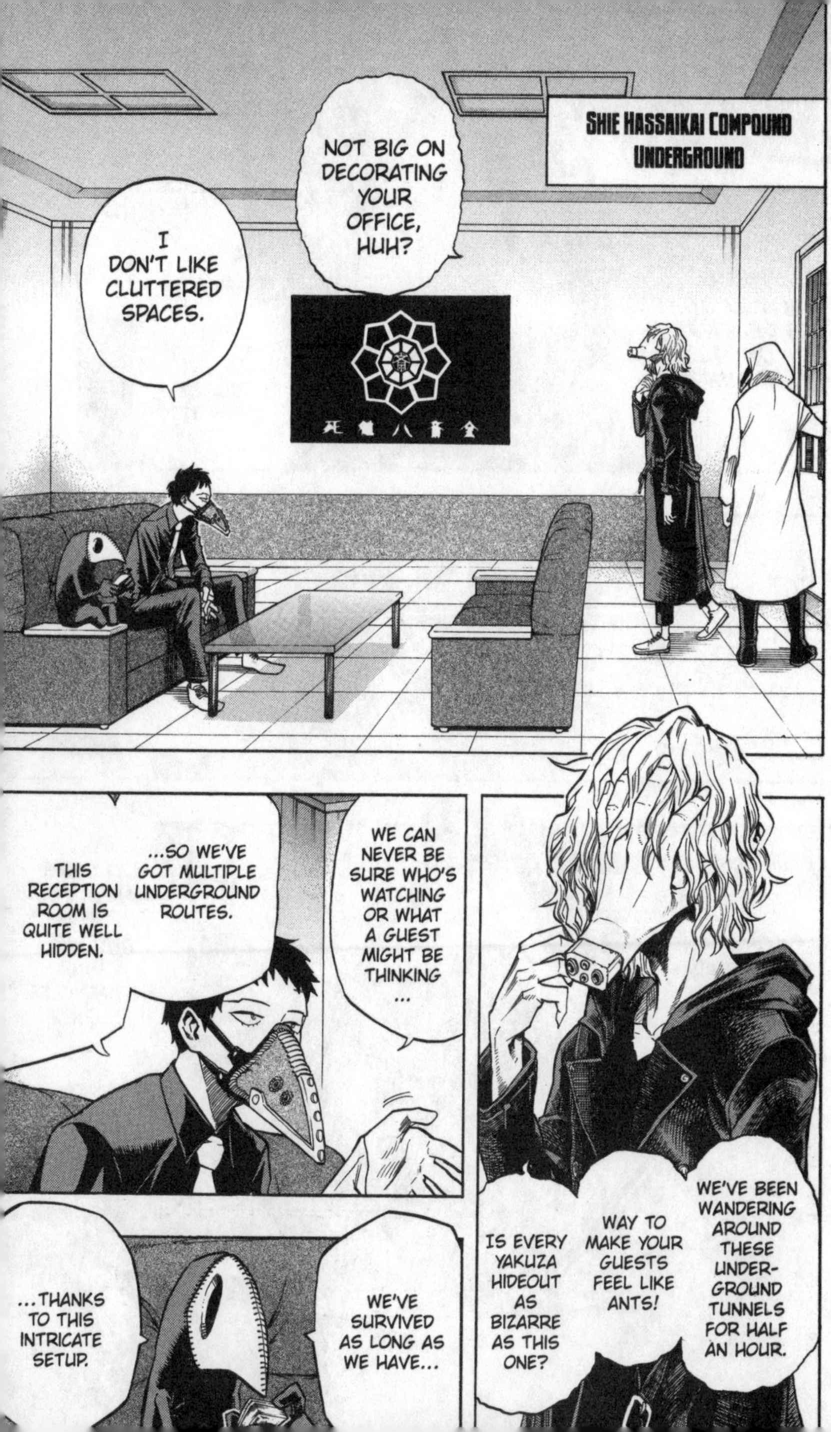
SHIE HASSAIKAI COMPOUND UNDERGROUND
NOT BIG ON DECORATING YOUR OFFICE, HUH?
I DON'T LIKE CLUTTERED SPACES.
WE'VE BEEN WANDERING AROUND THESE UNDER-GROUND TUNNELS FOR HALF AN HOUR.
WAY TO MAKE YOUR GUESTS FEEL LIKE ANTS!
IS EVERY YAKUZA HIDEOUT AS BIZARRE AS THIS ONE?
WE CAN NEVER BE SURE WHO'S WATCHING OR WHAT A GUEST MIGHT BE THINKING...
...SO WE'VE GOT MULTIPLE UNDERGROUND ROUTES.
THIS RECEPTION ROOM IS QUITE WELL HIDDEN.
WE'VE SURVIVED AS LONG AS WE HAVE...
...THANKS TO THIS INTRICATE SETUP.

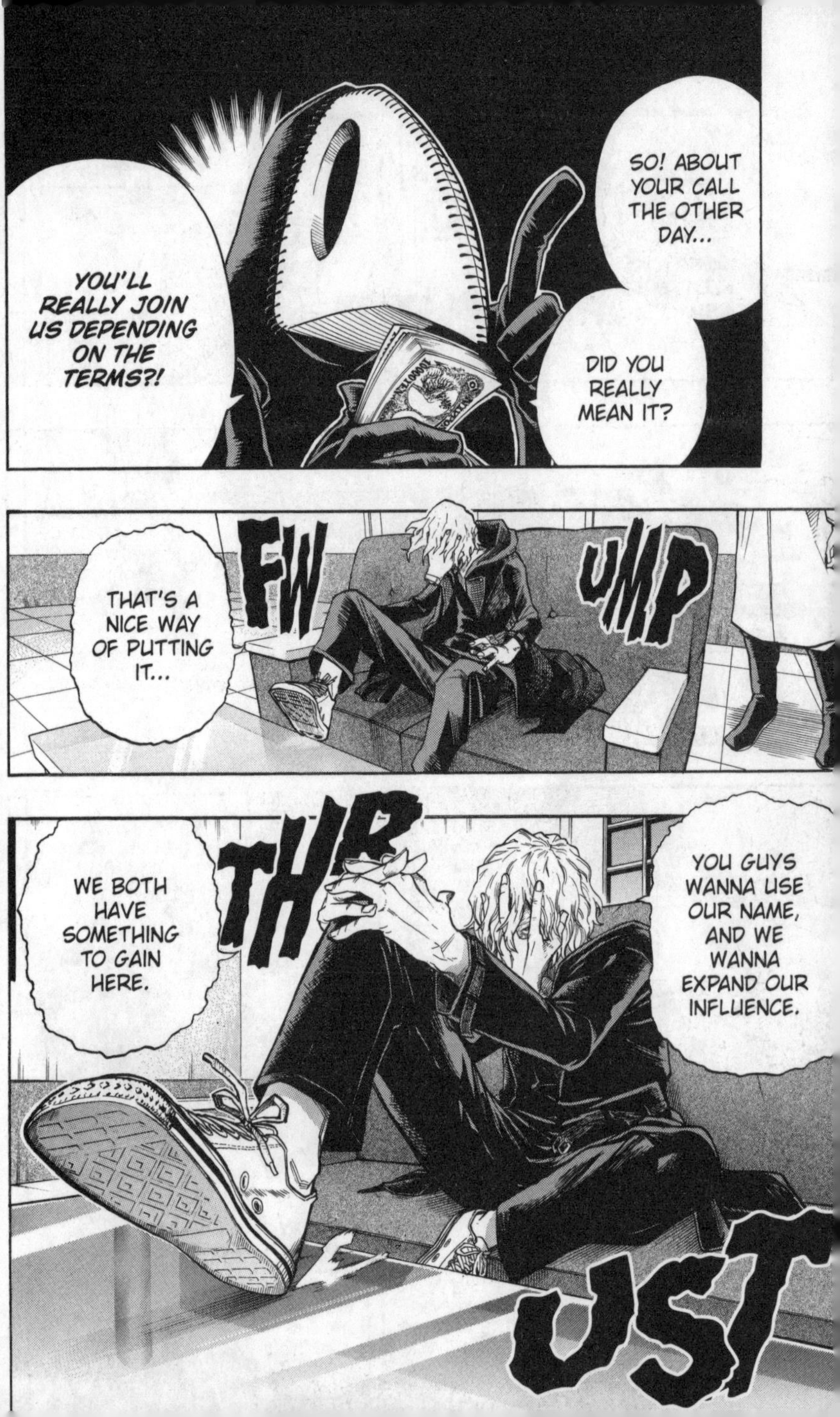

SO! ABOUT YOUR CALL THE OTHER DAY...
DID YOU REALLY MEAN IT?
YOU'LL REALLY JOIN US DEPENDING ON THE TERMS?!
FWUMP
THAT'S A NICE WAY OF PUTTING IT...
YOU GUYS WANNA USE OUR NAME, AND WE WANNA EXPAND OUR INFLUENCE.
WE BOTH HAVE SOMETHING TO GAIN HERE.
THRUST

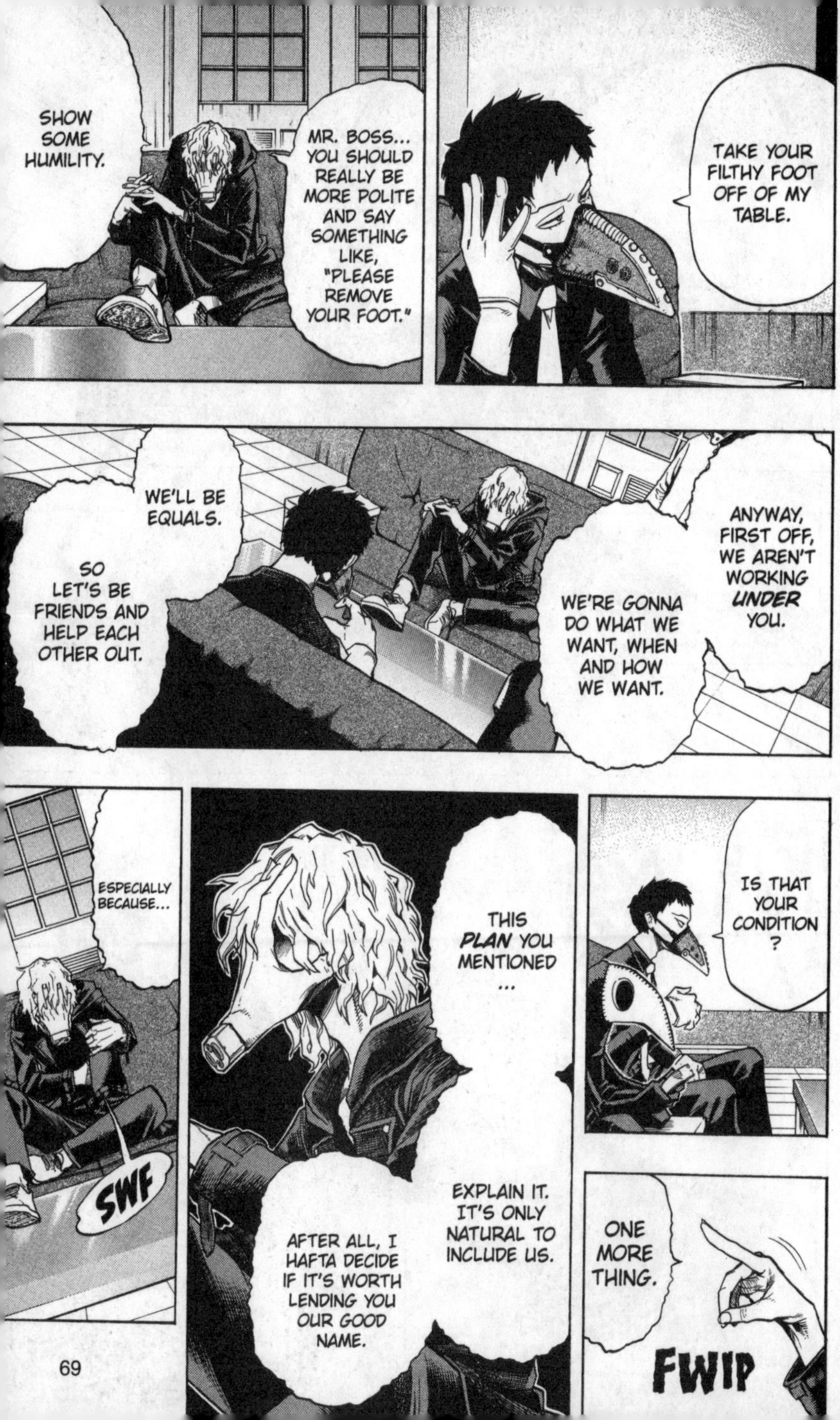
TAKE YOUR FILTHY FOOT OFF OF MY TABLE.
MR. BOSS... YOU SHOULD REALLY BE MORE POLITE AND SAY SOMETHING LIKE, "PLEASE REMOVE YOUR FOOT."
SHOW SOME HUMILITY.
ANYWAY, FIRST OFF, WE AREN'T WORKING *UNDER* YOU.
WE'RE GONNA DO WHAT WE WANT, WHEN AND HOW WE WANT.
WE'LL BE EQUALS.
SO LET'S BE FRIENDS AND HELP EACH OTHER OUT.
IS THAT YOUR CONDITION?
ONE MORE THING.
FWIP
THIS *PLAN* YOU MENTIONED...
EXPLAIN IT. IT'S ONLY NATURAL TO INCLUDE US.
AFTER ALL, I HAFTA DECIDE IF IT'S WORTH LENDING YOU OUR GOOD NAME.
ESPECIALLY BECAUSE...
SWF

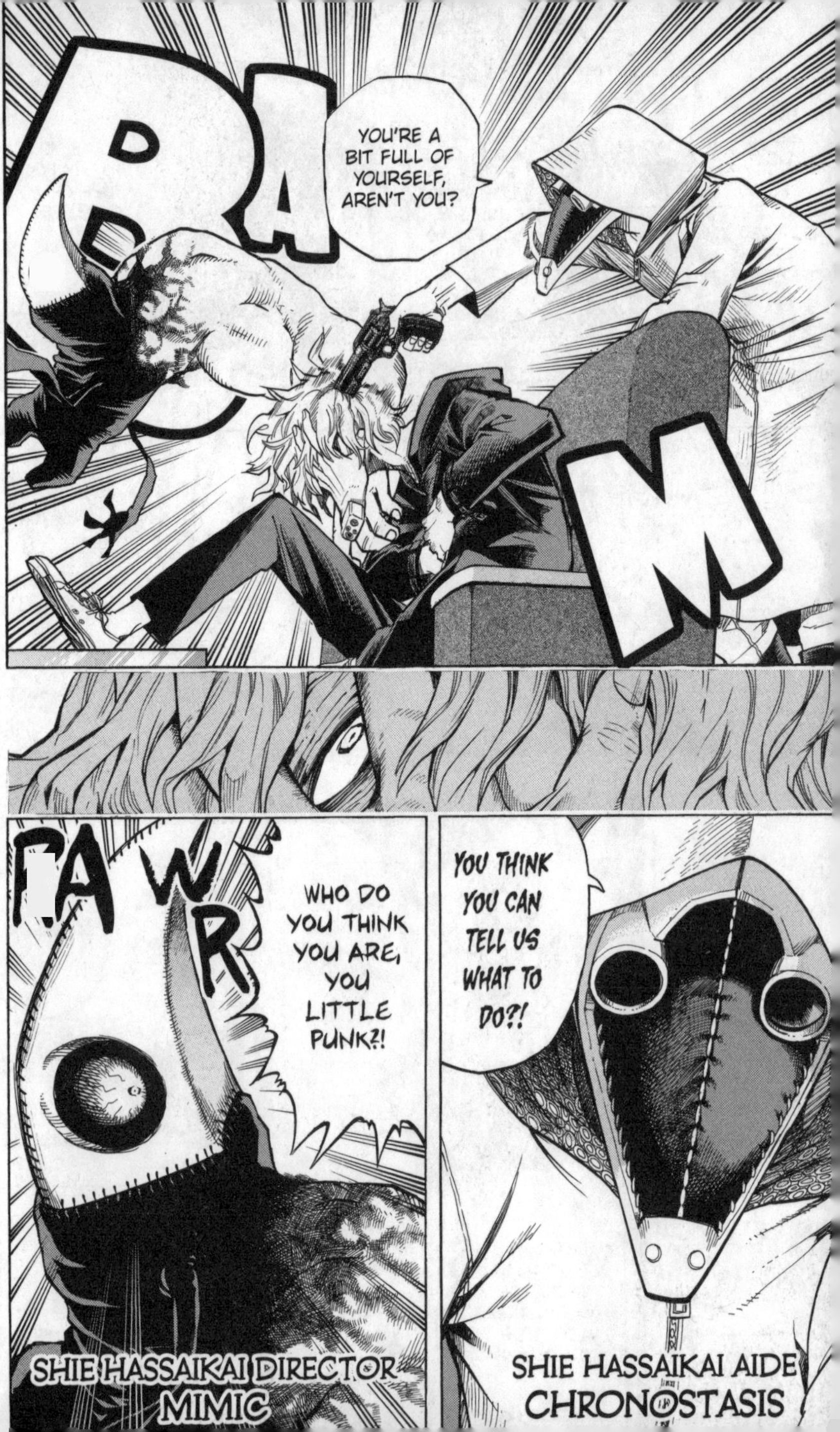
YOU'RE A BIT FULL OF YOURSELF, AREN'T YOU?
BAM
YOU THINK YOU CAN TELL US WHAT TO DO?!
SHIE HASSAIKAI AIDE CHRONOSTASIS
WHO DO YOU THINK YOU ARE, YOU LITTLE PUNK?!
SHIE HASSAIKAI DIRECTOR MIMIC

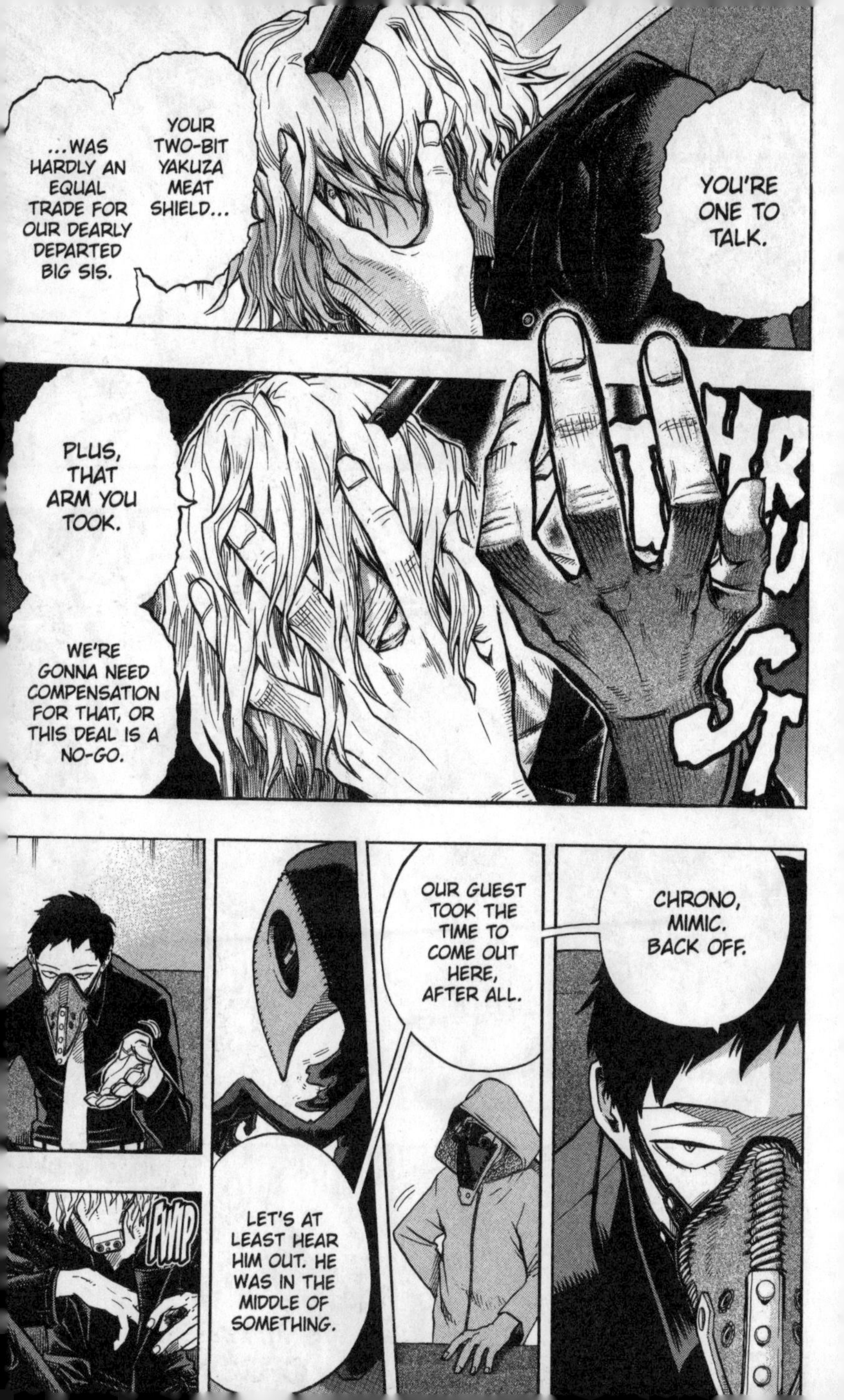
YOU'RE ONE TO TALK.
YOUR TWO-BIT YAKUZA MEAT SHIELD...
...WAS HARDLY AN EQUAL TRADE FOR OUR DEARLY DEPARTED BIG SIS.
THRUST
PLUS, THAT ARM YOU TOOK.
WE'RE GONNA NEED COMPENSATION FOR THAT, OR THIS DEAL IS A NO-GO.
CHRONO, MIMIC. BACK OFF.
OUR GUEST TOOK THE TIME TO COME OUT HERE, AFTER ALL.
LET'S AT LEAST HEAR HIM OUT. HE WAS IN THE MIDDLE OF SOMETHING.
FWIP

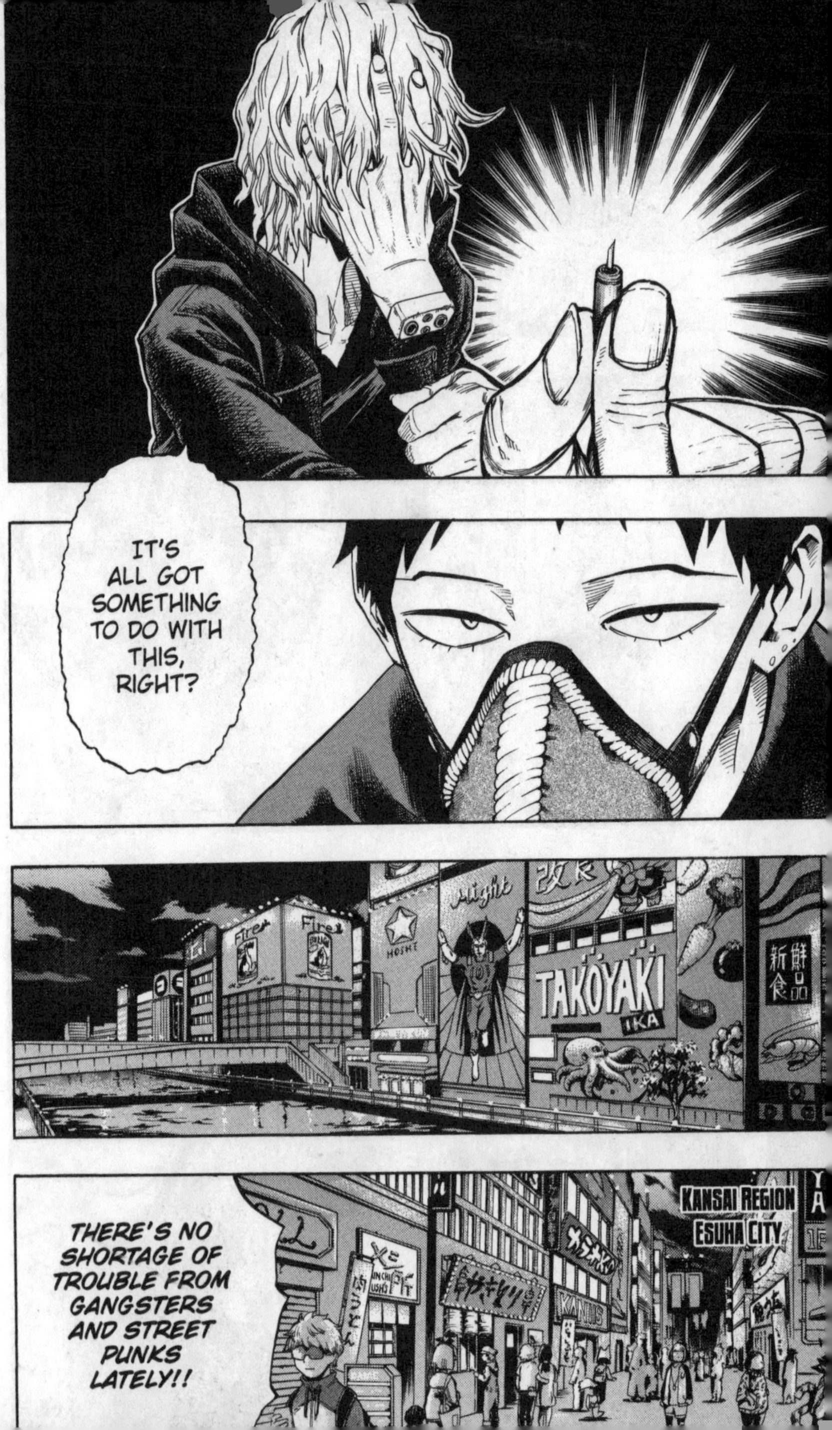
IT'S ALL GOT SOMETHING TO DO WITH THIS, RIGHT?
TAKOYAKI
IKA
KANSAI REGION ESUHA CITY
THERE'S NO SHORTAGE OF TROUBLE FROM GANGSTERS AND STREET PUNKS LATELY!!

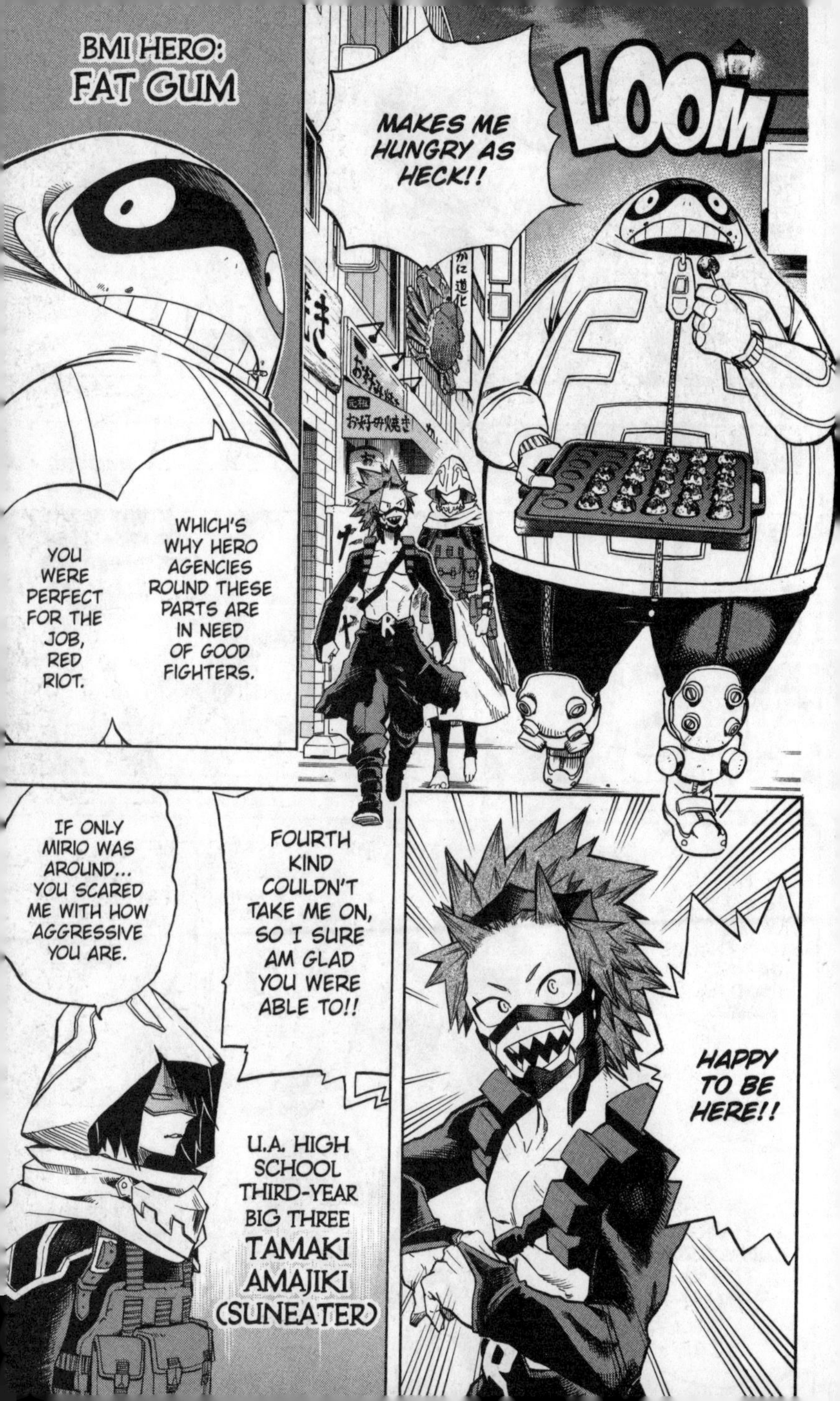
LOOM
MAKES ME HUNGRY AS HECK!!
BMI HERO: FAT GUM
WHICH'S WHY HERO AGENCIES ROUND THESE PARTS ARE IN NEED OF GOOD FIGHTERS.
YOU WERE PERFECT FOR THE JOB, RED RIOT.
FOURTH KIND COULDN'T TAKE ME ON, SO I SURE AM GLAD YOU WERE ABLE TO!!
HAPPY TO BE HERE!!
IF ONLY MIRIO WAS AROUND... YOU SCARED ME WITH HOW AGGRESSIVE YOU ARE.
U.A. HIGH SCHOOL THIRD-YEAR BIG THREE TAMAKI AMAJIKI (SUNEATER)

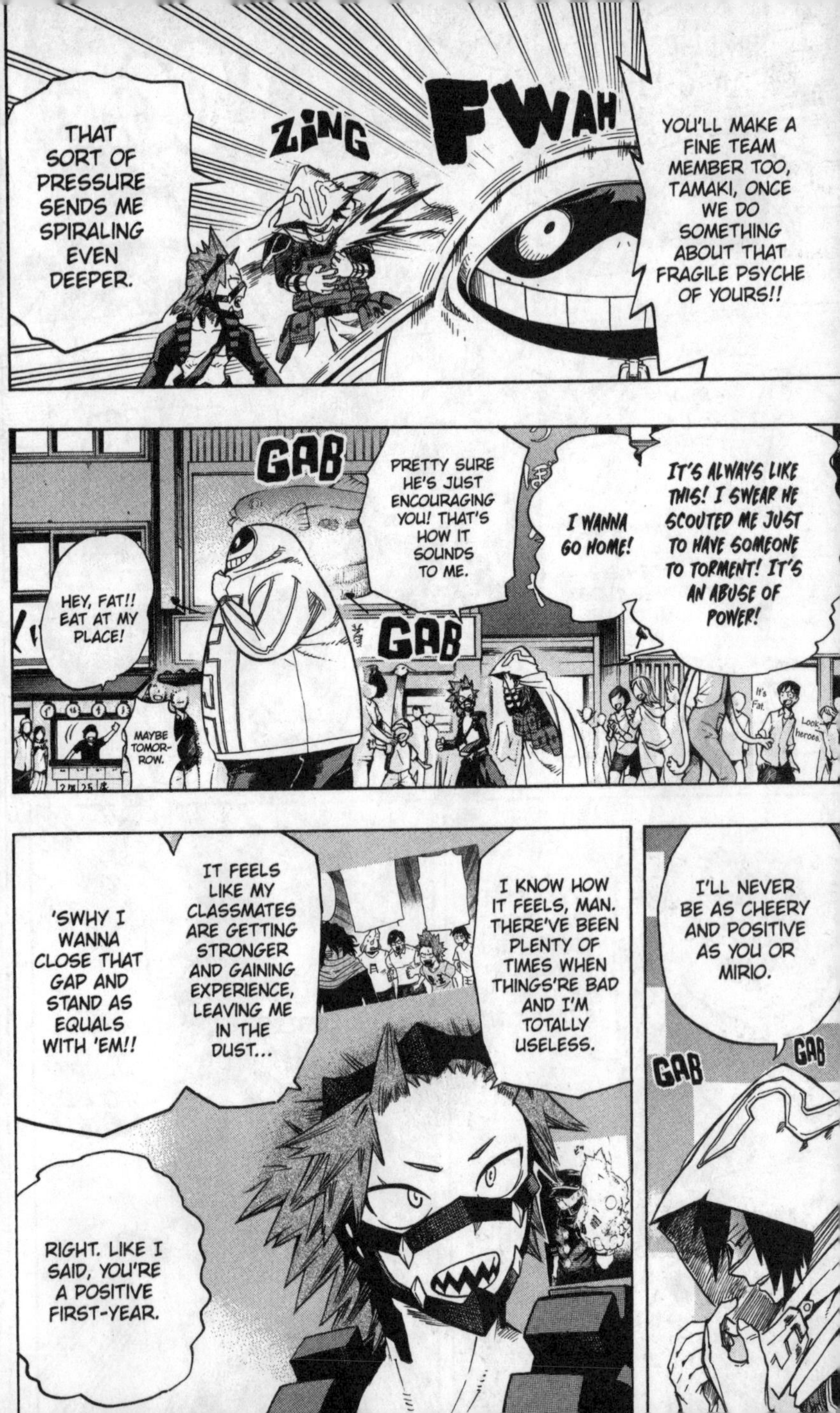
FWAH
YOU'LL MAKE A FINE TEAM MEMBER TOO, TAMAKI, ONCE WE DO SOMETHING ABOUT THAT FRAGILE PSYCHE OF YOURS!!
ZING
THAT SORT OF PRESSURE SENDS ME SPIRALING EVEN DEEPER.
IT'S ALWAYS LIKE THIS! I SWEAR HE SCOUTED ME JUST TO HAVE SOMEONE TO TORMENT! IT'S AN ABUSE OF POWER!
I WANNA GO HOME!
GAB
PRETTY SURE HE'S JUST ENCOURAGING YOU! THAT'S HOW IT SOUNDS TO ME.
GAB
HEY, FAT!! EAT AT MY PLACE!
Look, heroes.
It's Fat.
MAYBE TOMORROW.
I'LL NEVER BE AS CHEERY AND POSITIVE AS YOU OR MIRIO.
GAB
GAB
I KNOW HOW IT FEELS, MAN. THERE'VE BEEN PLENTY OF TIMES WHEN THINGS'RE BAD AND I'M TOTALLY USELESS.
IT FEELS LIKE MY CLASSMATES ARE GETTING STRONGER AND GAINING EXPERIENCE, LEAVING ME IN THE DUST...
'SWHY I WANNA CLOSE THAT GAP AND STAND AS EQUALS WITH 'EM!!
RIGHT. LIKE I SAID, YOU'RE A POSITIVE FIRST-YEAR.

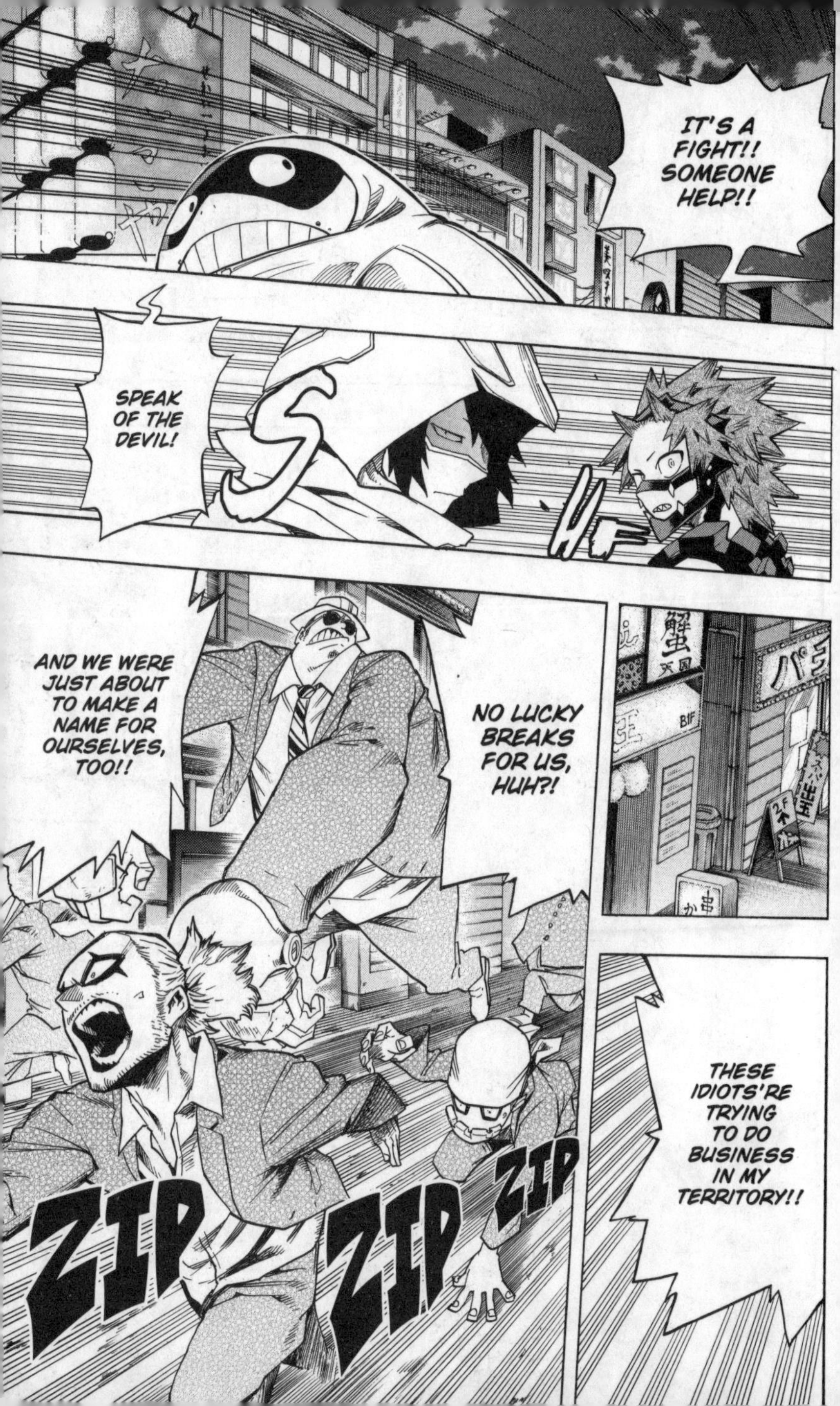
IT'S A FIGHT!! SOMEONE HELP!!
SPEAK OF THE DEVIL!
THESE IDIOTS'RE TRYING TO DO BUSINESS IN MY TERRITORY!!
NO LUCKY BREAKS FOR US, HUH?!
AND WE WERE JUST ABOUT TO MAKE A NAME FOR OURSELVES, TOO!!
ZIP
ZIP
ZIP

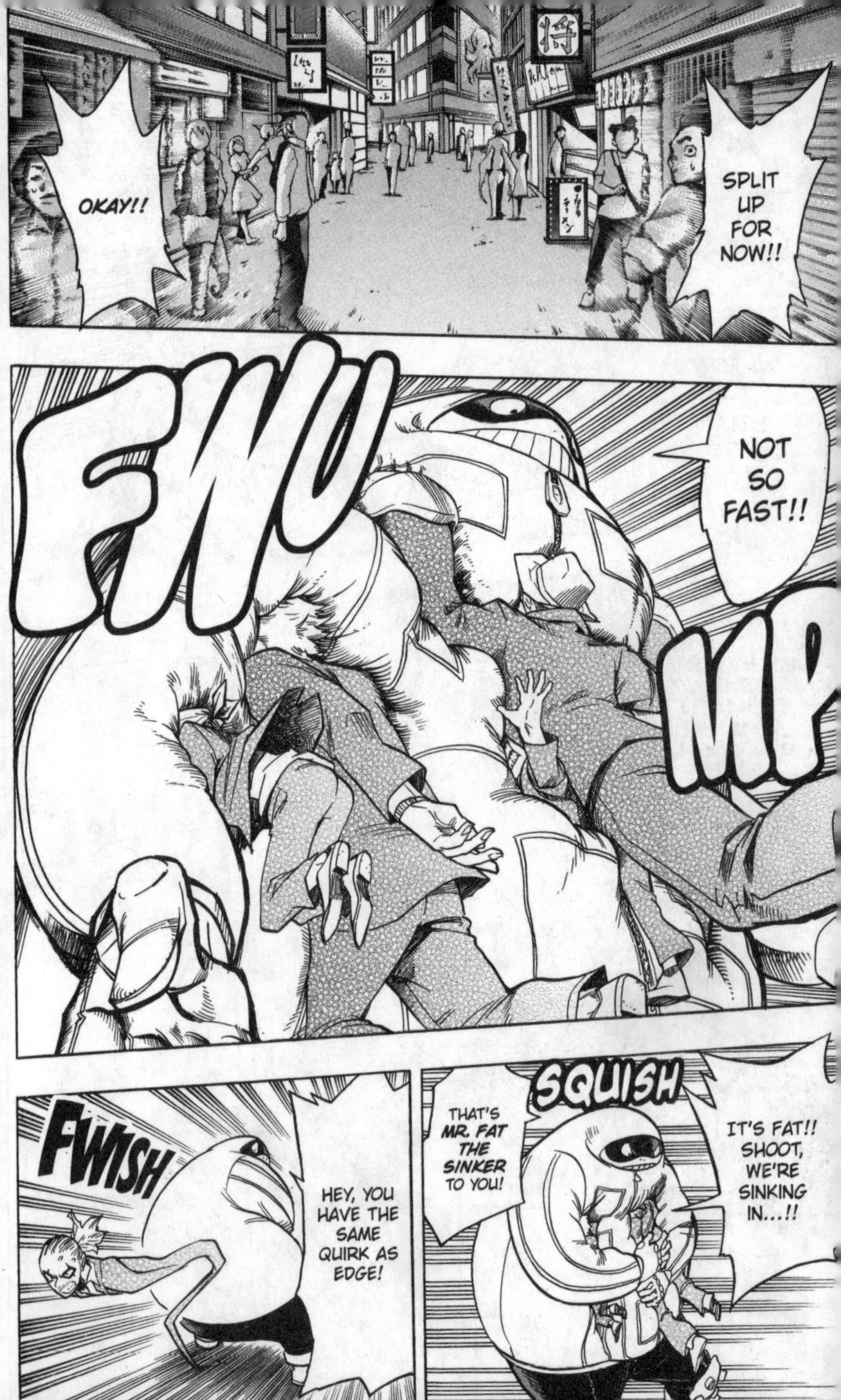
SPLIT UP FOR NOW!!
OKAY!!
NOT SO FAST!!
FWUMP
IT'S FAT!! SHOOT, WE'RE SINKING IN...!!
SQUISH
THAT'S *MR. FAT THE SINKER* TO YOU!
HEY, YOU HAVE THE SAME QUIRK AS EDGE!
FWISH

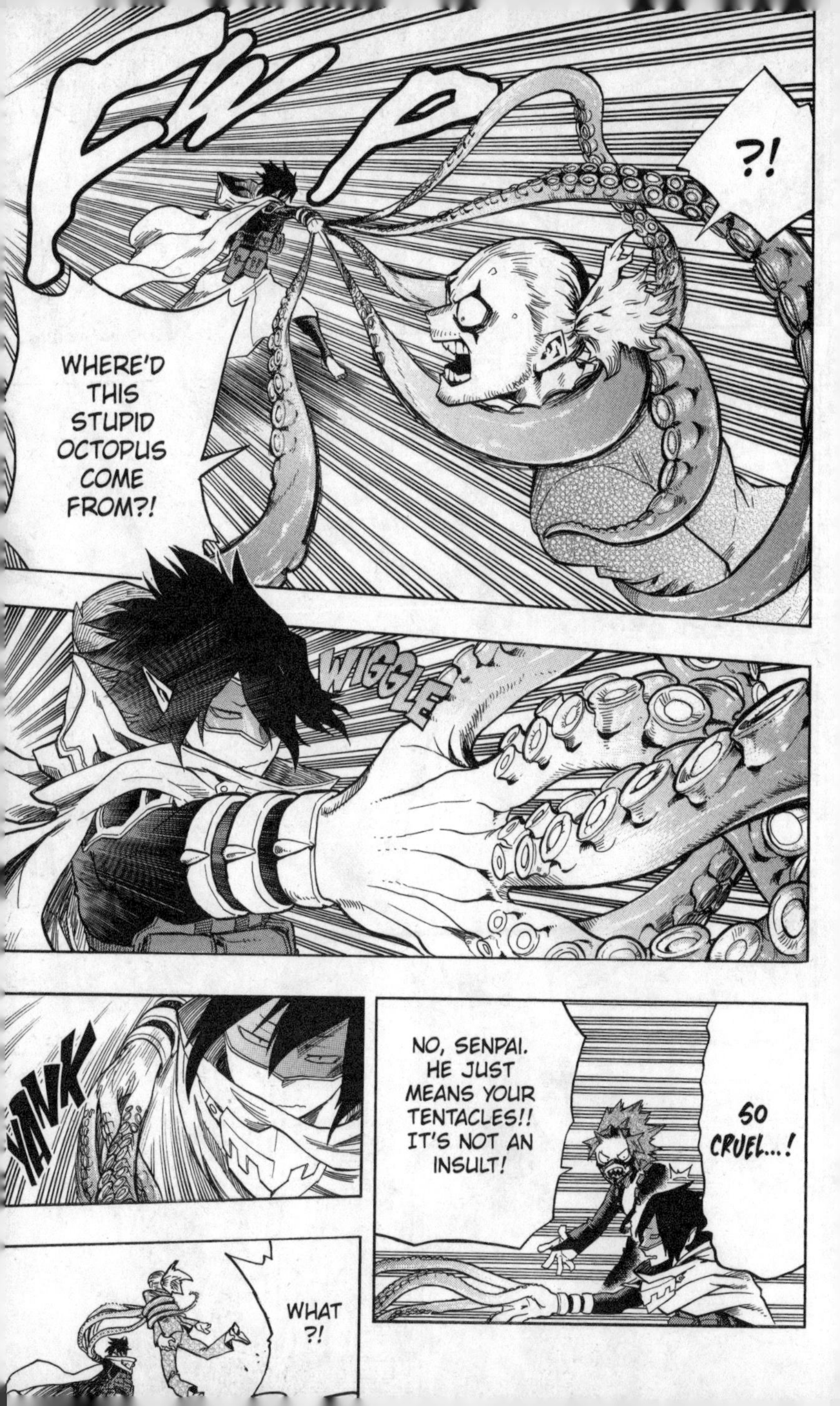
?!
WHERE'D THIS STUPID OCTOPUS COME FROM?!
WIGGLE
SO CRUEL...!
NO, SENPAI. HE JUST MEANS YOUR TENTACLES!! IT'S NOT AN INSULT!
YANK
WHAT?!

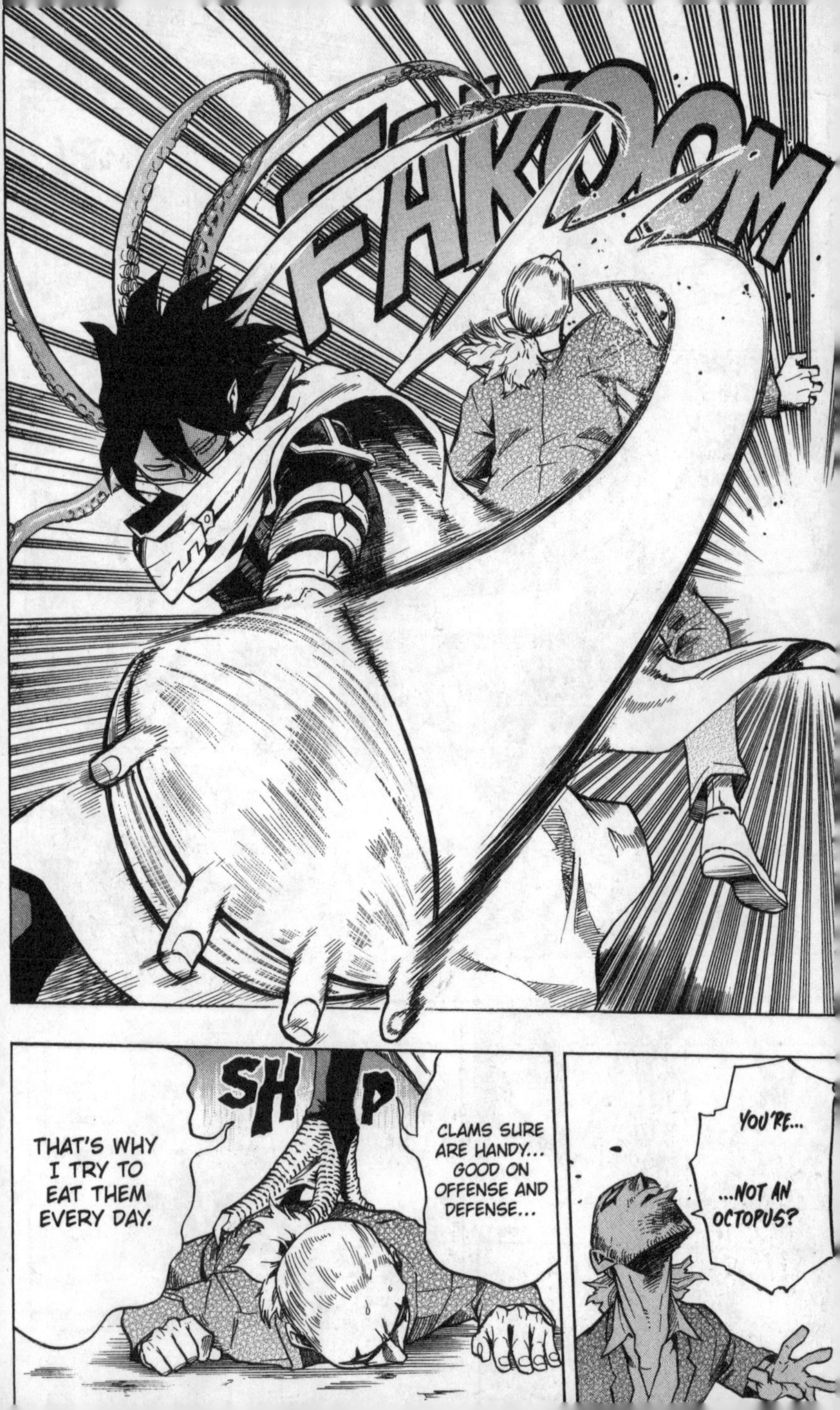
FAKOOM
YOU'RE...
...NOT AN OCTOPUS?
SHP
CLAMS SURE ARE HANDY... GOOD ON OFFENSE AND DEFENSE...
THAT'S WHY I TRY TO EAT THEM EVERY DAY.

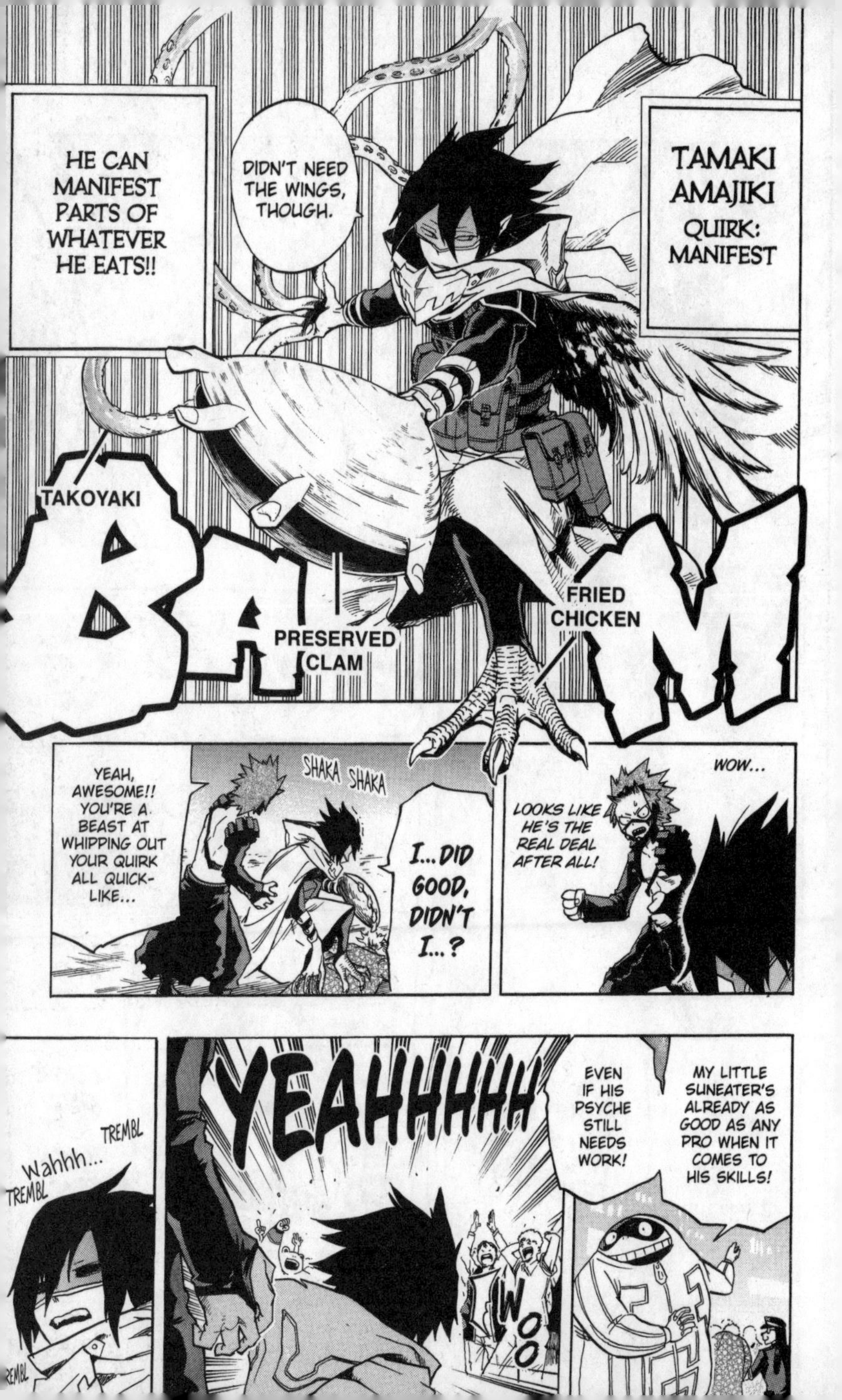

TAMAKI AMAJIKI
QUIRK: MANIFEST
DIDN'T NEED THE WINGS, THOUGH.
HE CAN MANIFEST PARTS OF WHATEVER HE EATS!!
TAKOYAKI
FRIED CHICKEN
PRESERVED CLAM
BAM
WOW...
LOOKS LIKE HE'S THE REAL DEAL AFTER ALL!
I...DID GOOD, DIDN'T I...?
SHAKA SHAKA
YEAH, AWESOME!! YOU'RE A BEAST AT WHIPPING OUT YOUR QUIRK ALL QUICK-LIKE...
MY LITTLE SUNEATER'S ALREADY AS GOOD AS ANY PRO WHEN IT COMES TO HIS SKILLS!
EVEN IF HIS PSYCHE STILL NEEDS WORK!
YEAHHHHH
WOO
TREMBL
Wahhh...
TREMBL
TREMBL

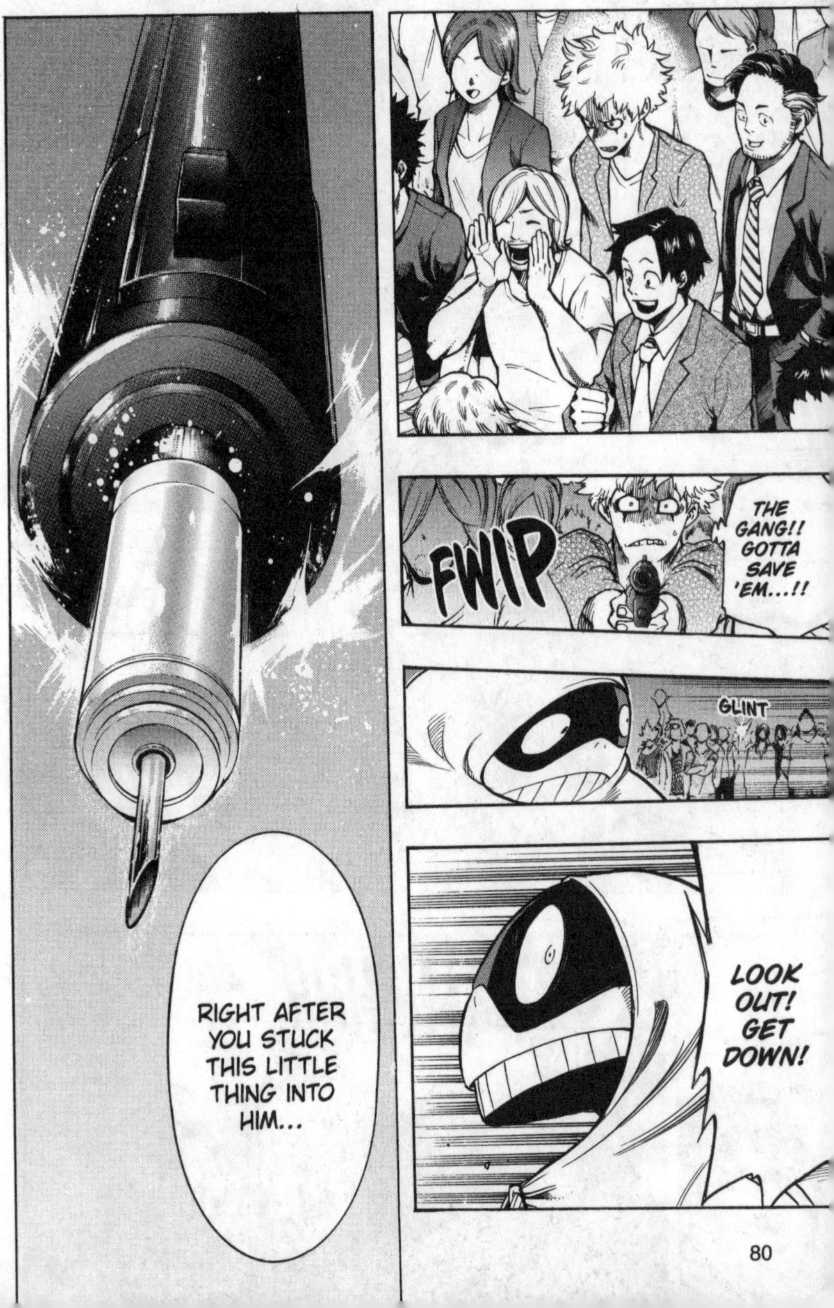
THE GANG!! GOTTA SAVE 'EM...!!
FWIP
GLINT
LOOK OUT! GET DOWN!
RIGHT AFTER YOU STUCK THIS LITTLE THING INTO HIM...

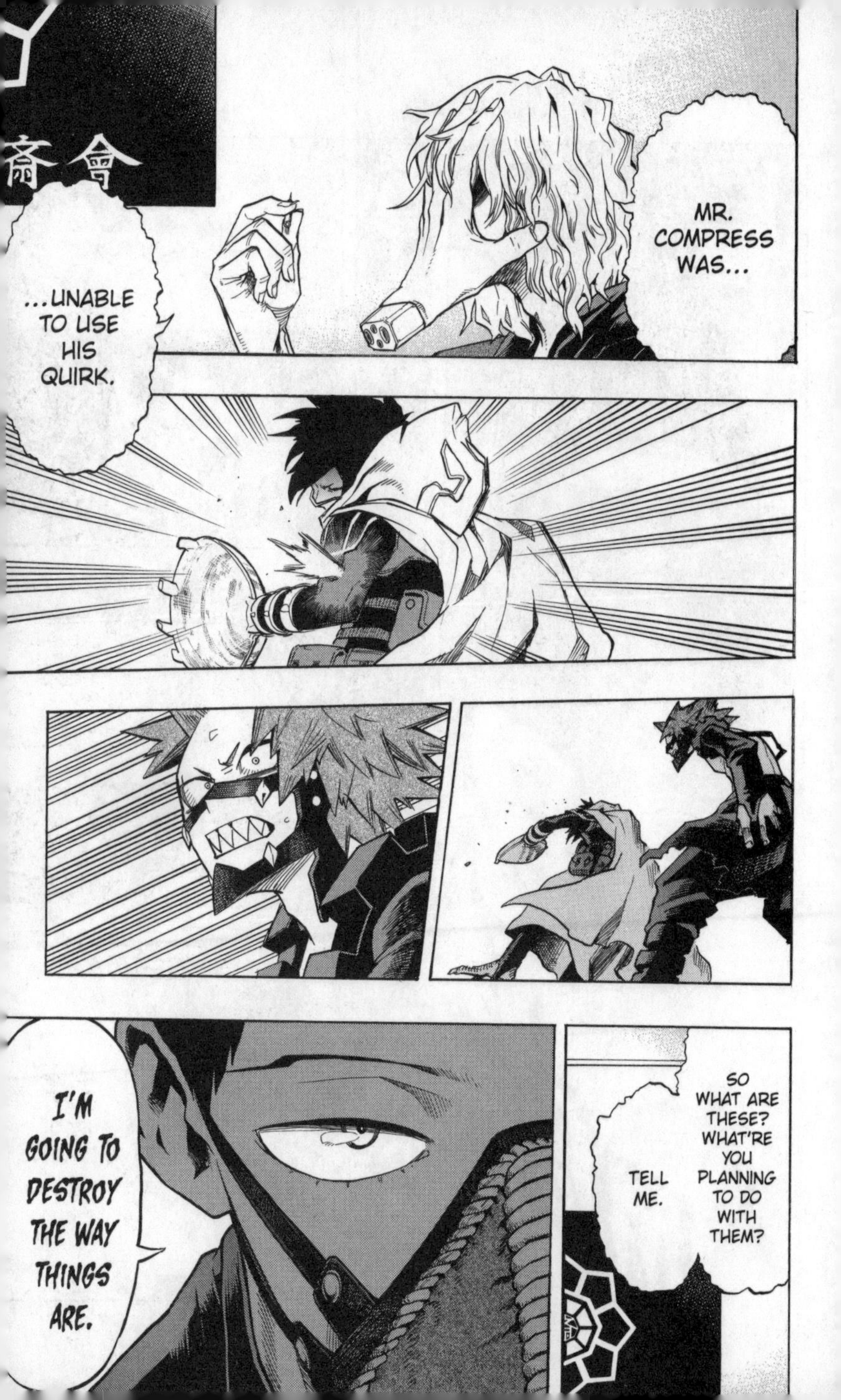
MR. COMPRESS WAS...
斎會
...UNABLE TO USE HIS QUIRK.
SO WHAT ARE THESE? WHAT'RE YOU PLANNING TO DO WITH THEM?
TELL ME.
I'M GOING TO DESTROY THE WAY THINGS ARE.

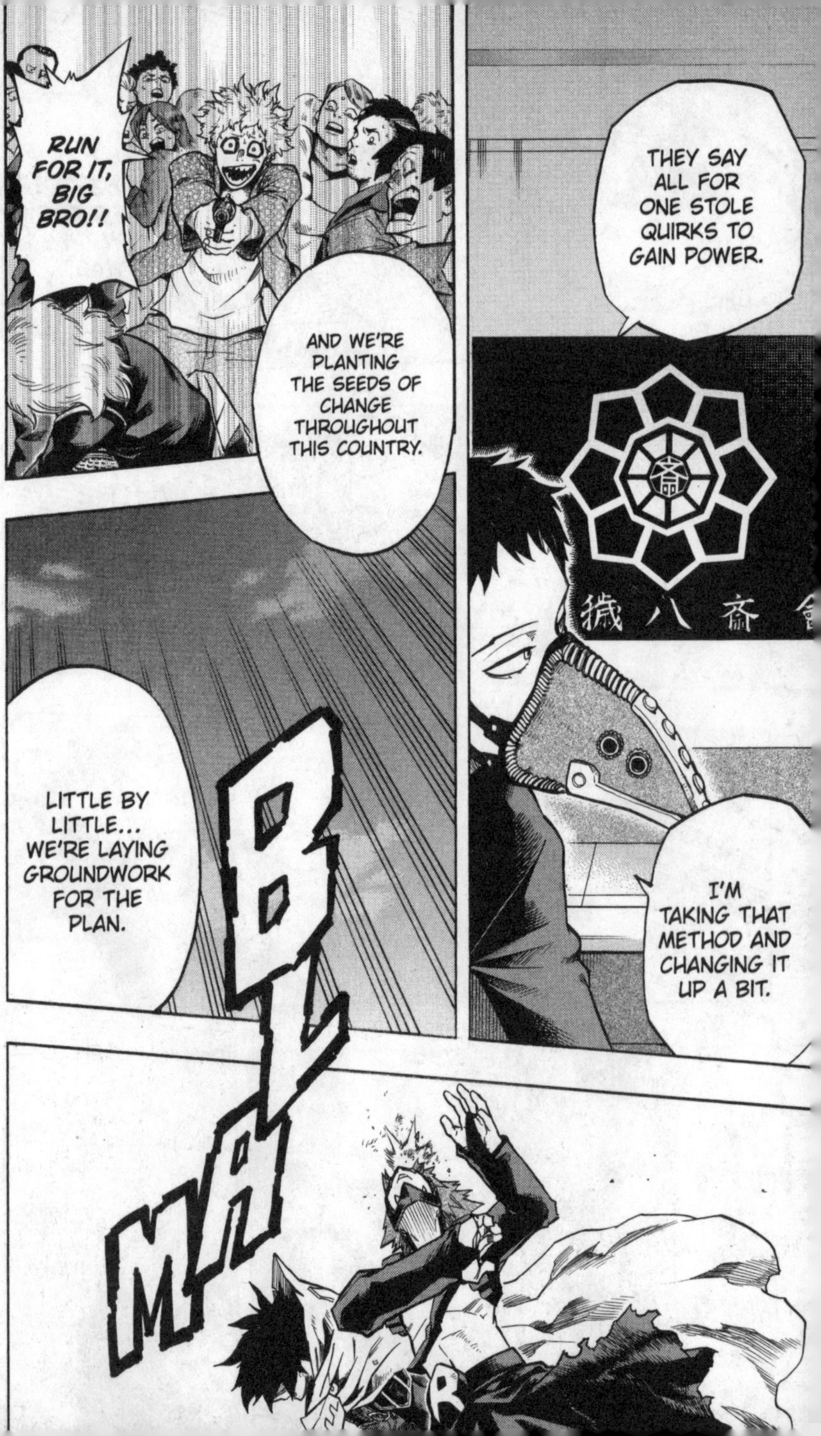
THEY SAY ALL FOR ONE STOLE QUIRKS TO GAIN POWER.
RUN FOR IT, BIG BRO!!
AND WE'RE PLANTING THE SEEDS OF CHANGE THROUGHOUT THIS COUNTRY.
織八斎
I'M TAKING THAT METHOD AND CHANGING IT UP A BIT.
LITTLE BY LITTLE... WE'RE LAYING GROUNDWORK FOR THE PLAN.
BLAM

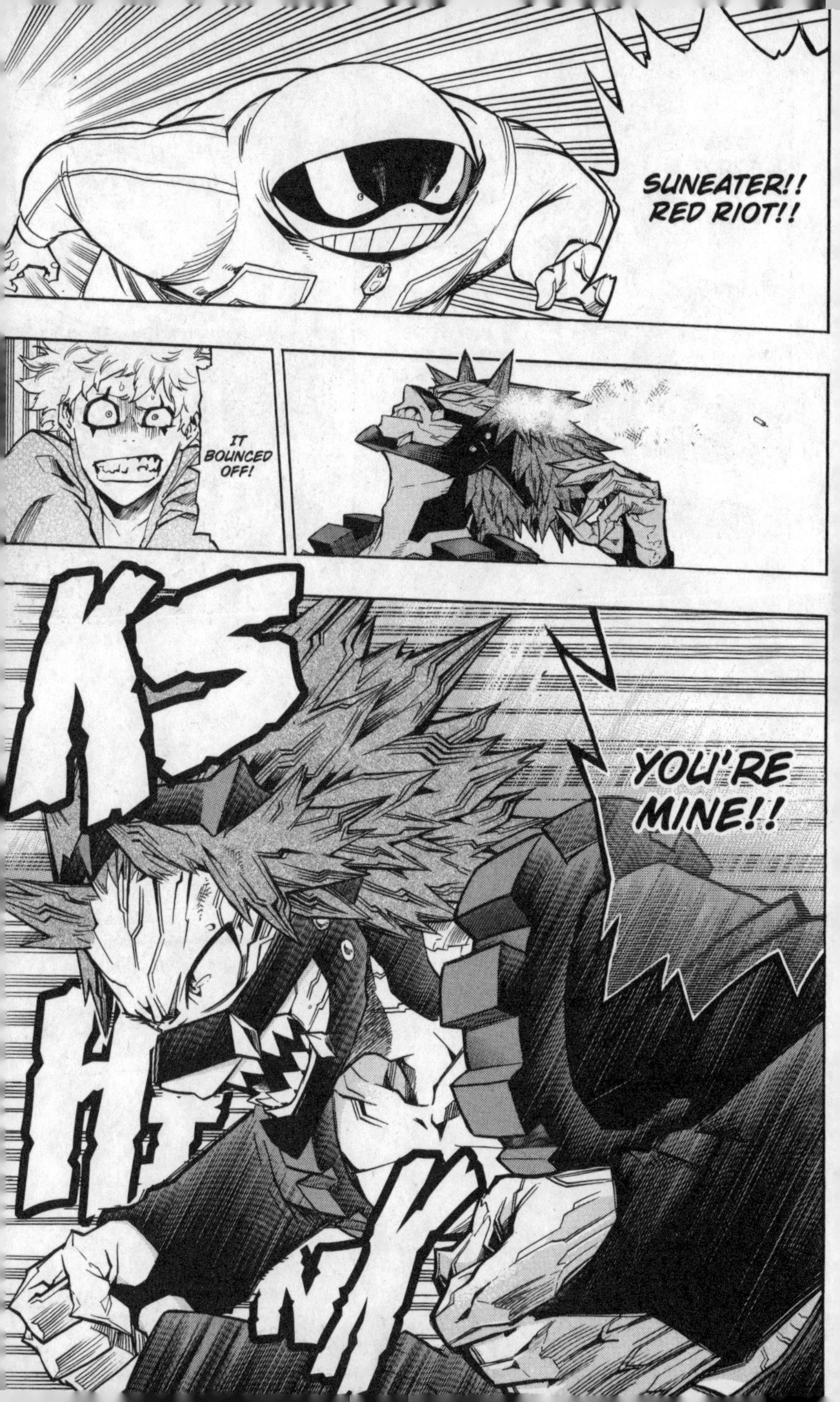

SUNEATER!! RED RIOT!!
IT BOUNCED OFF!
YOU'RE MINE!!

No. 133 - Catch Up, Kirishima

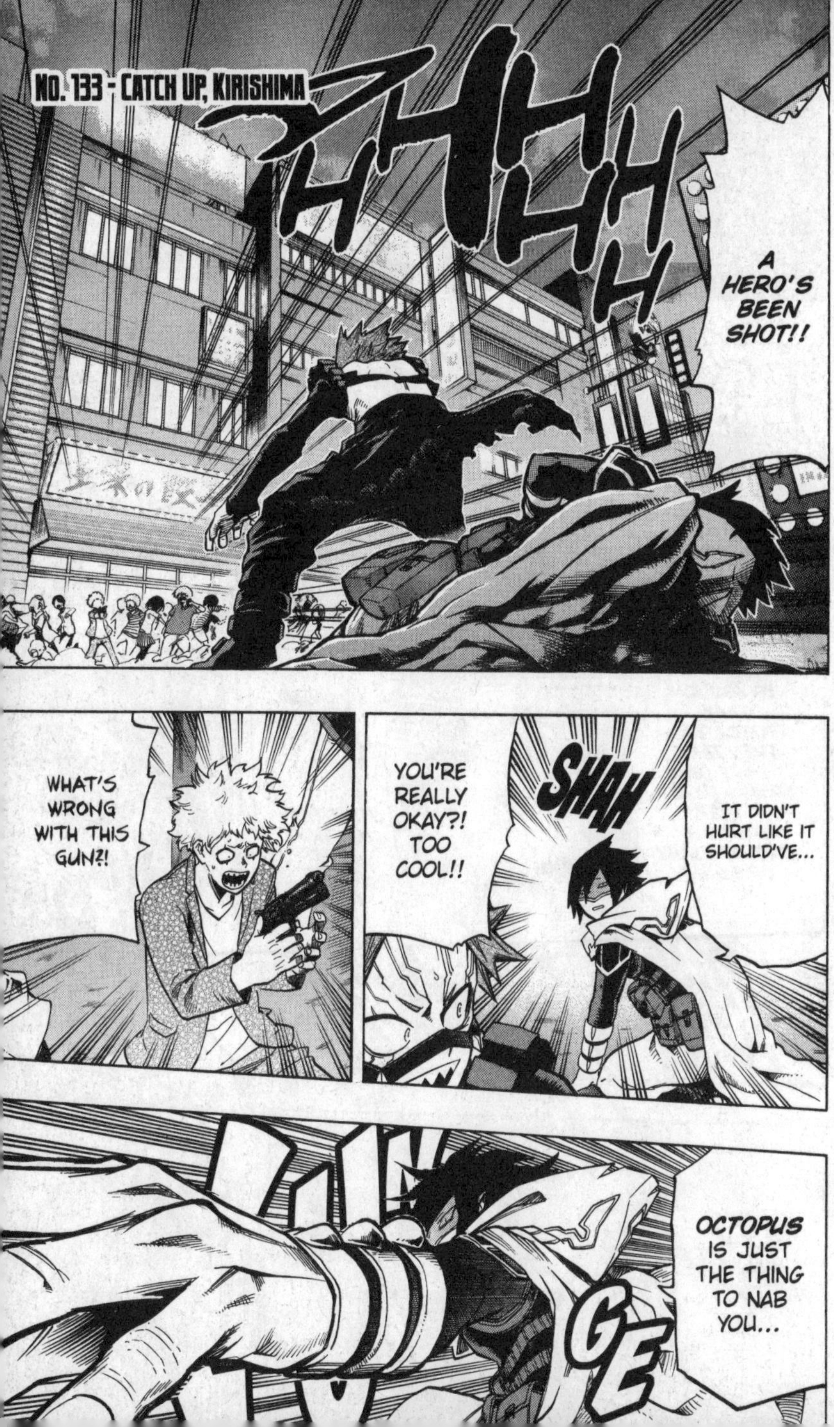
A HERO'S BEEN SHOT!!
SHAH
IT DIDN'T HURT LIKE IT SHOULD'VE...
YOU'RE REALLY OKAY?! TOO COOL!!
WHAT'S WRONG WITH THIS GUN?!
OCTOPUS IS JUST THE THING TO NAB YOU...
GE

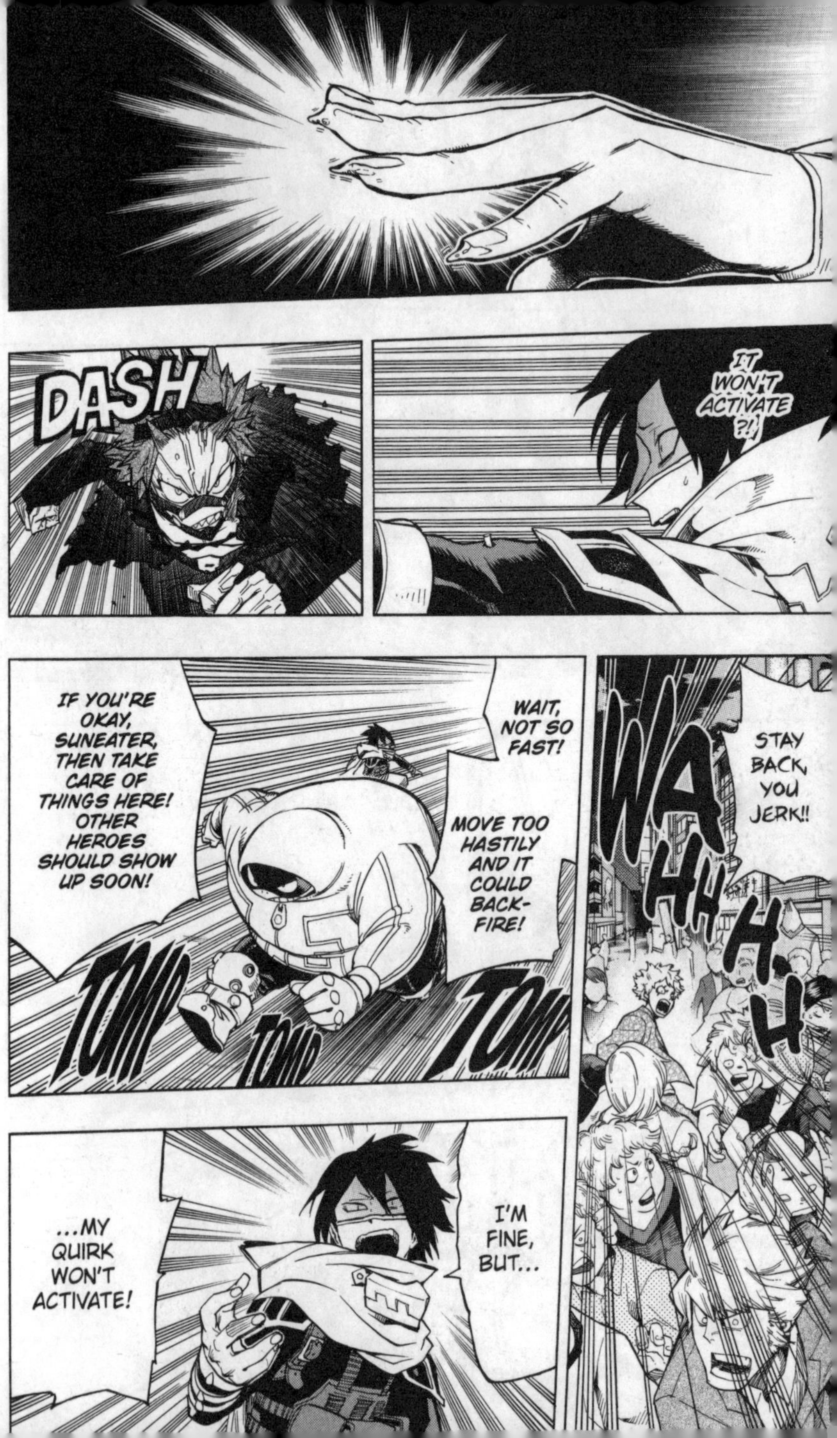
IT WON'T ACTIVATE ?!
DASH
WAHHHH
STAY BACK, YOU JERK!!
WAIT, NOT SO FAST!
MOVE TOO HASTILY AND IT COULD BACKFIRE!
IF YOU'RE OKAY, SUNEATER, THEN TAKE CARE OF THINGS HERE! OTHER HEROES SHOULD SHOW UP SOON!
TOMP
TOMP
TOMP
I'M FINE, BUT...
...MY QUIRK WON'T ACTIVATE!

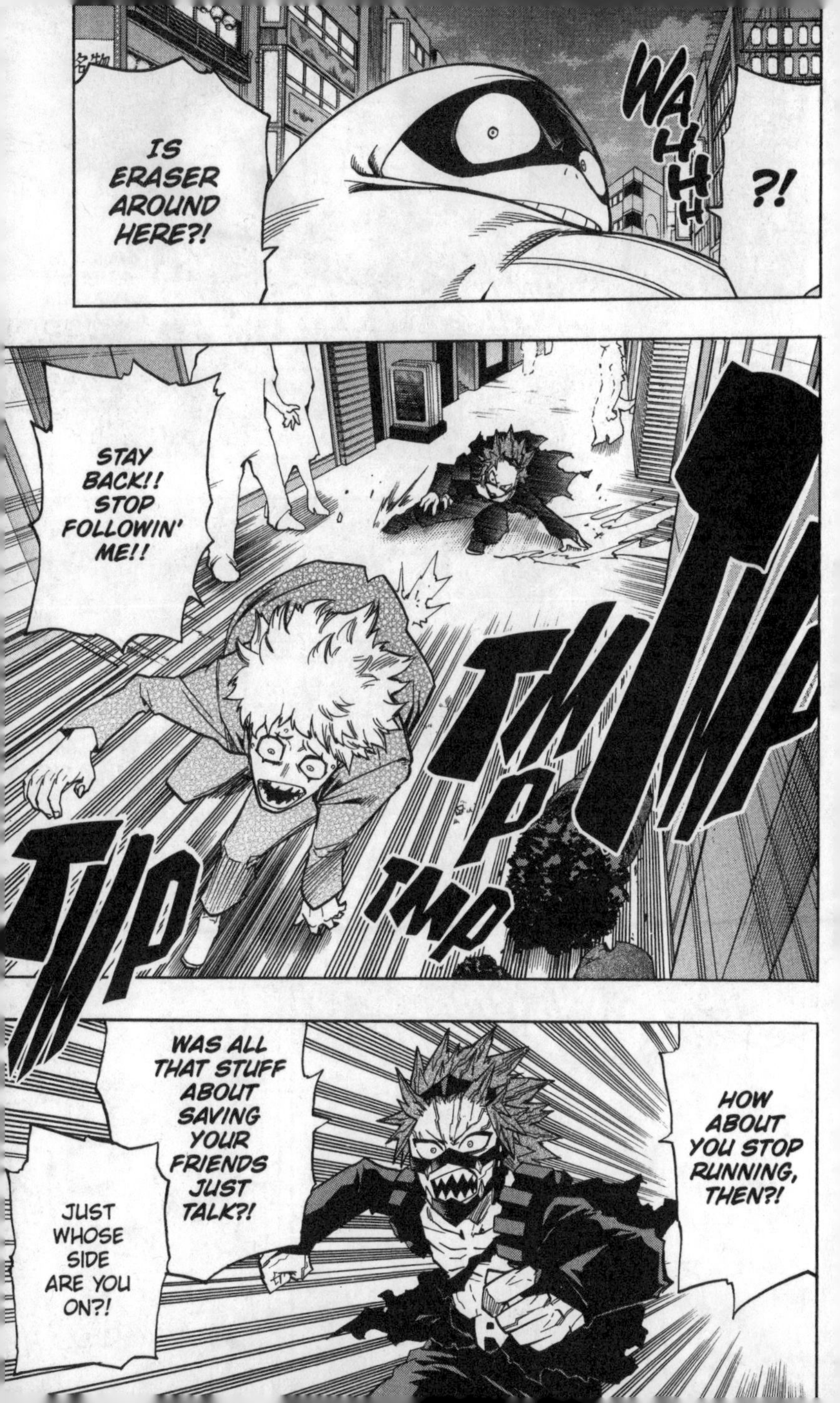
WAHHHH?!
IS ERASER AROUND HERE?!
TMP
TMP
TMP
STAY BACK!! STOP FOLLOWIN' ME!!
TMP
HOW ABOUT YOU STOP RUNNING, THEN?!
WAS ALL THAT STUFF ABOUT SAVING YOUR FRIENDS JUST TALK?!
JUST WHOSE SIDE ARE YOU ON?!

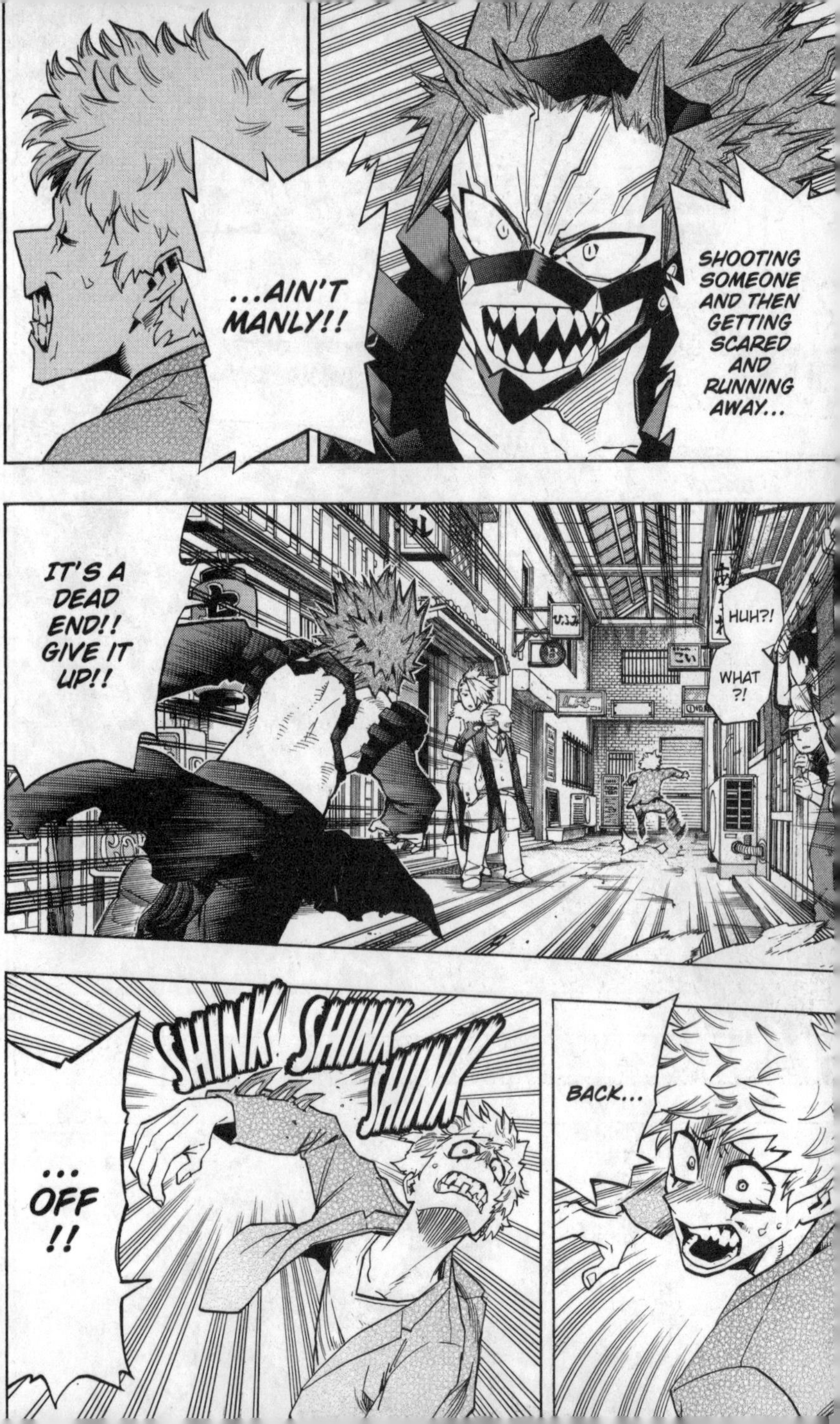
SHOOTING SOMEONE AND THEN GETTING SCARED AND RUNNING AWAY...
...AIN'T MANLY!!
HUH?!
WHAT ?!
IT'S A DEAD END!! GIVE IT UP!!
BACK...
SHINK SHINK SHINK
...OFF !!

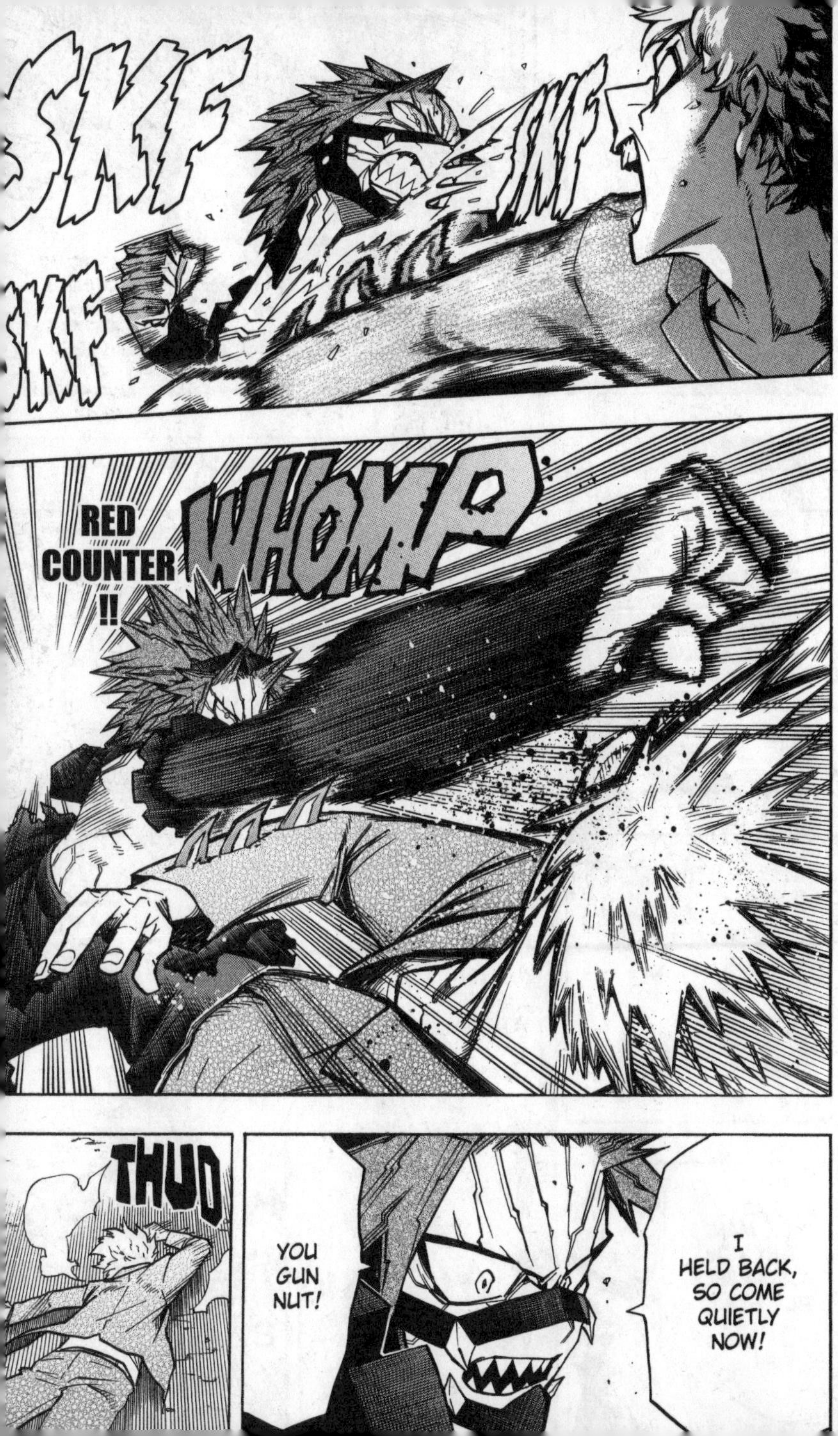

SKF
SKF
WHOMP
RED COUNTER!!
I HELD BACK, SO COME QUIETLY NOW!
YOU GUN NUT!
THUD

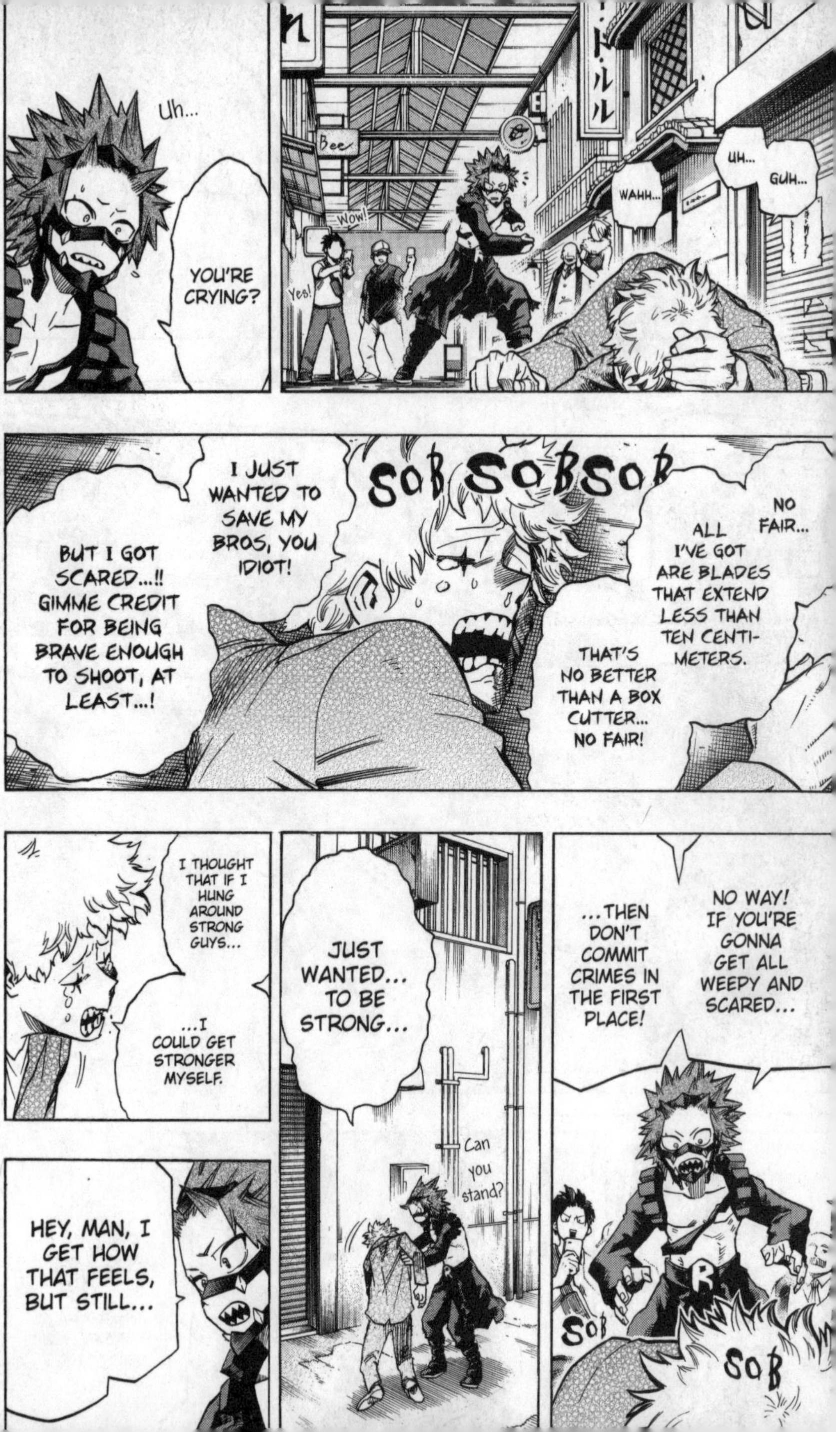
UH... GUH...
WAHH...
Wow!
Yes!
Uh...
YOU'RE CRYING?
NO FAIR...
ALL I'VE GOT ARE BLADES THAT EXTEND LESS THAN TEN CENTIMETERS.
THAT'S NO BETTER THAN A BOX CUTTER... NO FAIR!
SOB SOB SOB
I JUST WANTED TO SAVE MY BROS, YOU IDIOT!
BUT I GOT SCARED...!! GIMME CREDIT FOR BEING BRAVE ENOUGH TO SHOOT, AT LEAST...!
NO WAY! IF YOU'RE GONNA GET ALL WEEPY AND SCARED...
...THEN DON'T COMMIT CRIMES IN THE FIRST PLACE!
SOB
SOB
JUST WANTED... TO BE STRONG...
Can you stand?
I THOUGHT THAT IF I HUNG AROUND STRONG GUYS...
...I COULD GET STRONGER MYSELF.
HEY, MAN, I GET HOW THAT FEELS, BUT STILL...

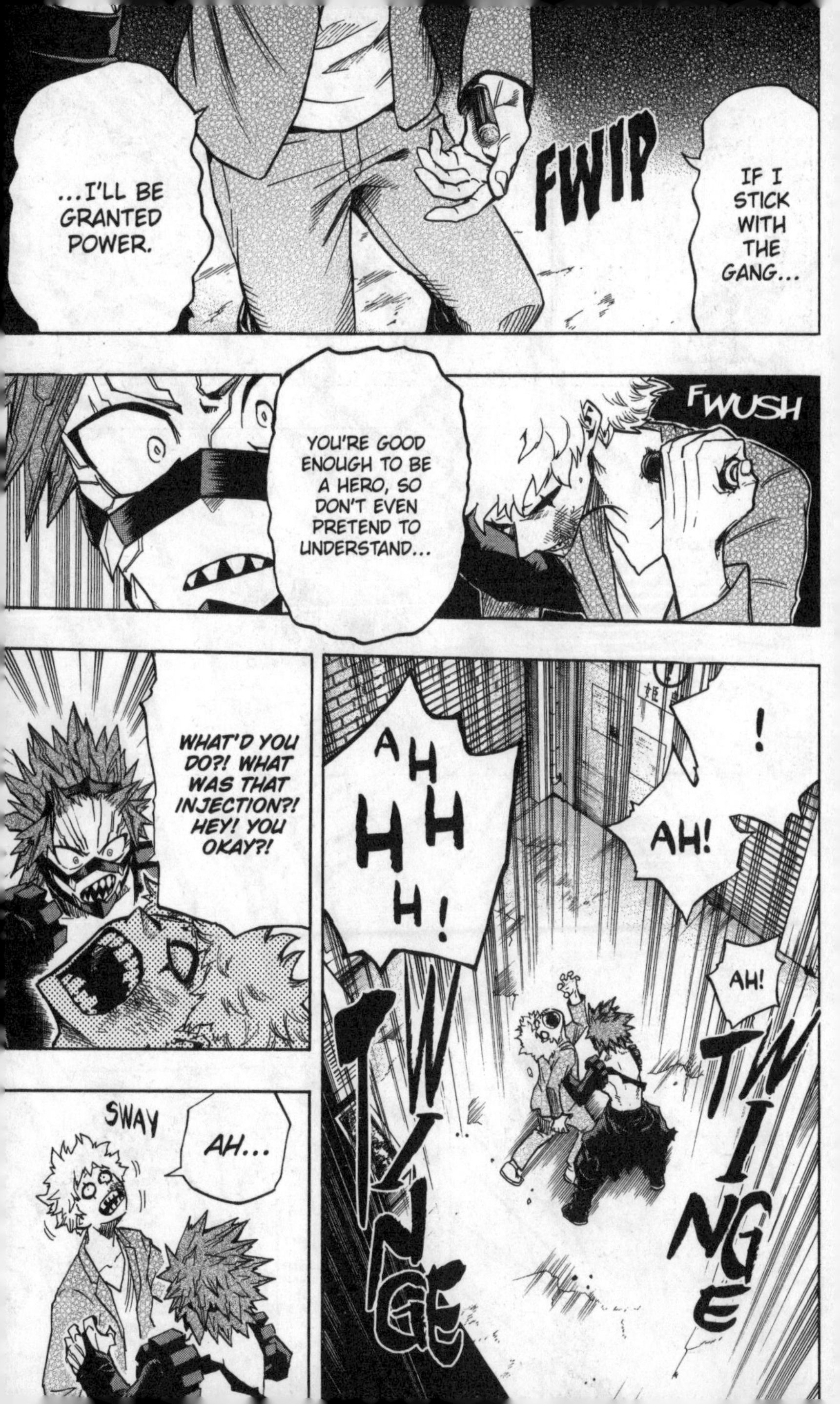
IF I STICK WITH THE GANG...
FWIP
...I'LL BE GRANTED POWER.
FWUSH
YOU'RE GOOD ENOUGH TO BE A HERO, SO DON'T EVEN PRETEND TO UNDERSTAND...
!
AH!
AHHHH!
AH!
TWINGE
TWINGE
WHAT'D YOU DO?! WHAT WAS THAT INJECTION?! HEY! YOU OKAY?!
SWAY
AH...

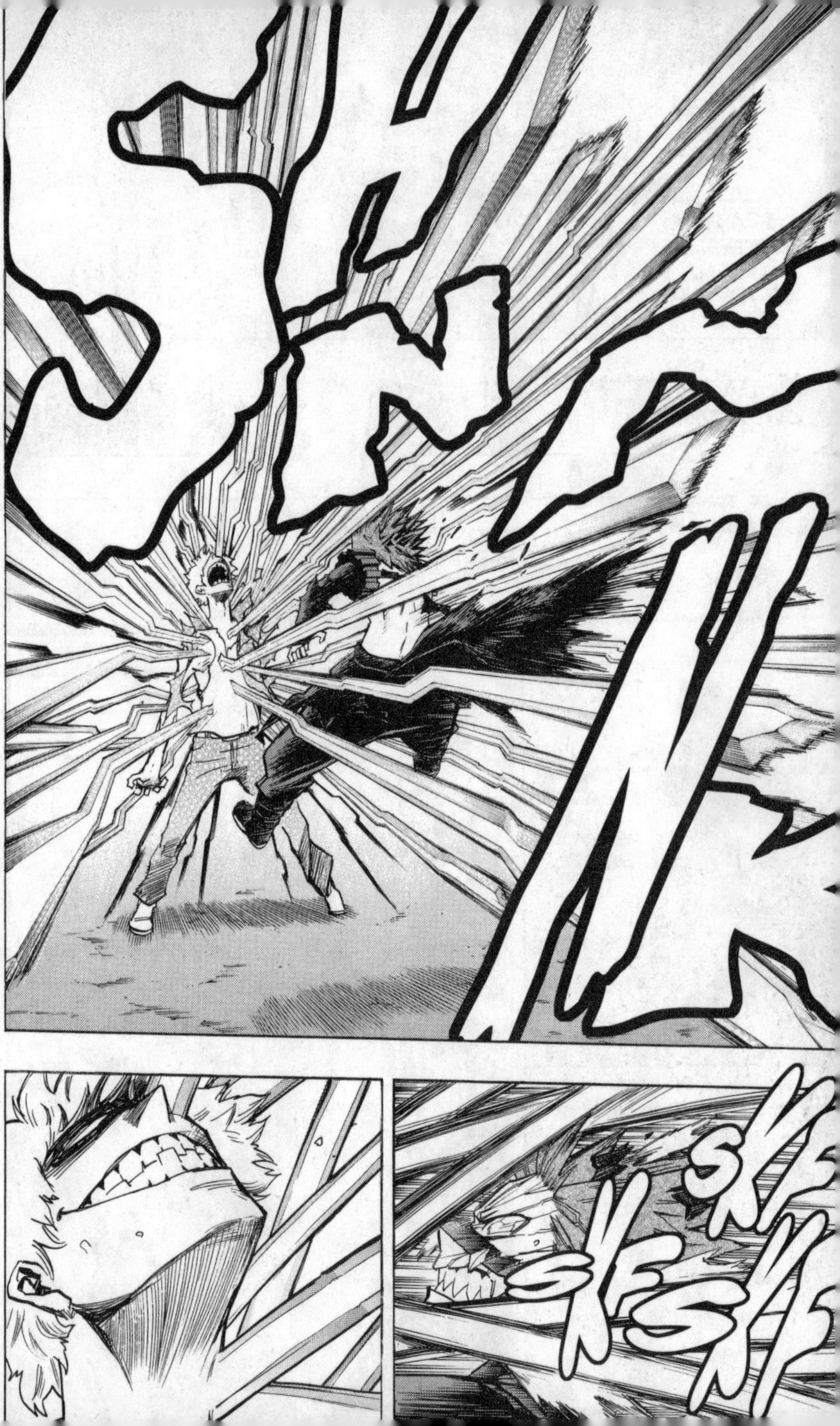

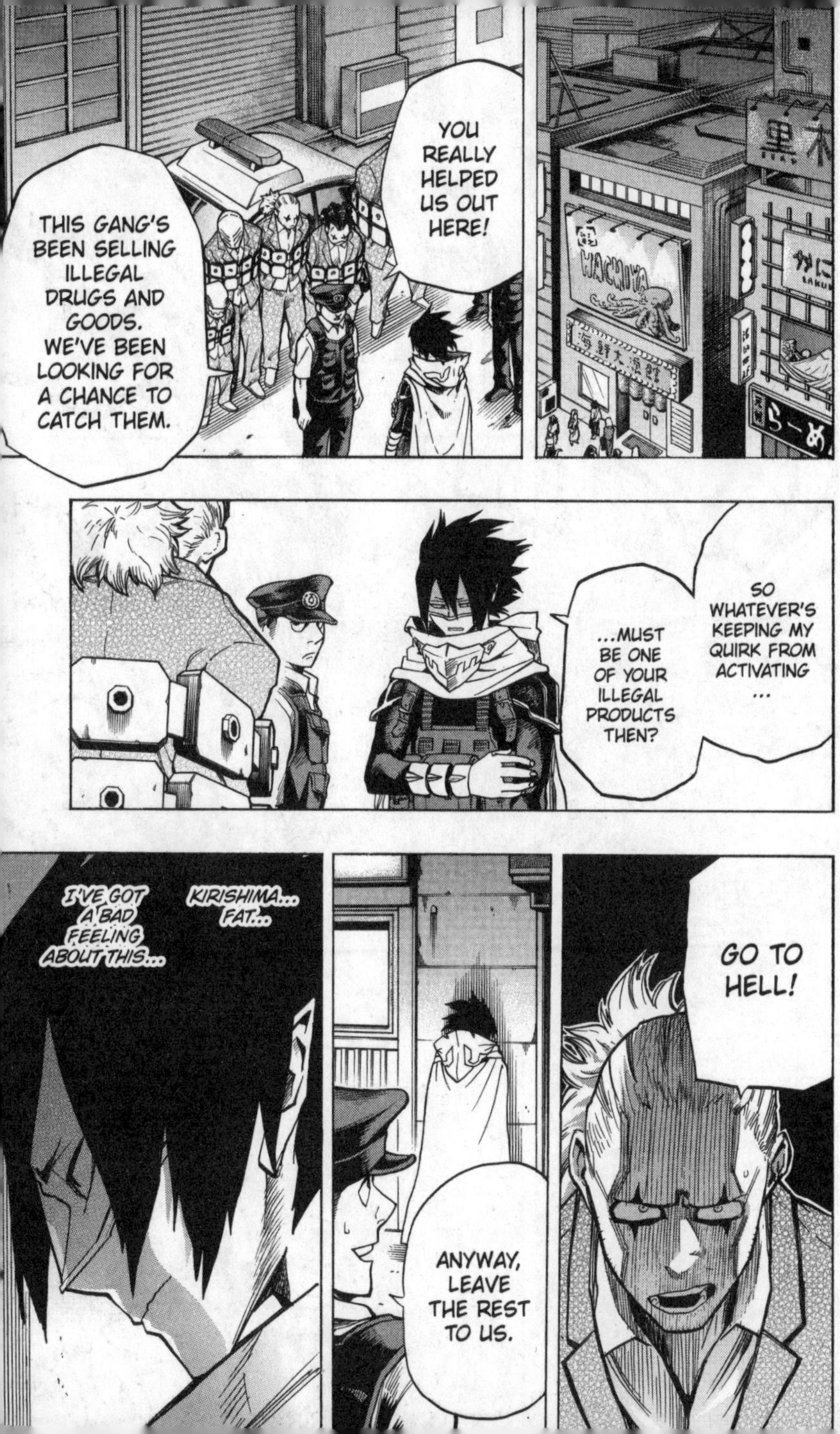
WACHIYA
YOU REALLY HELPED US OUT HERE!
THIS GANG'S BEEN SELLING ILLEGAL DRUGS AND GOODS. WE'VE BEEN LOOKING FOR A CHANCE TO CATCH THEM.
SO WHATEVER'S KEEPING MY QUIRK FROM ACTIVATING...
...MUST BE ONE OF YOUR ILLEGAL PRODUCTS THEN?
GO TO HELL!
ANYWAY, LEAVE THE REST TO US.
KIRISHIMA... FAT...
I'VE GOT A BAD FEELING ABOUT THIS...

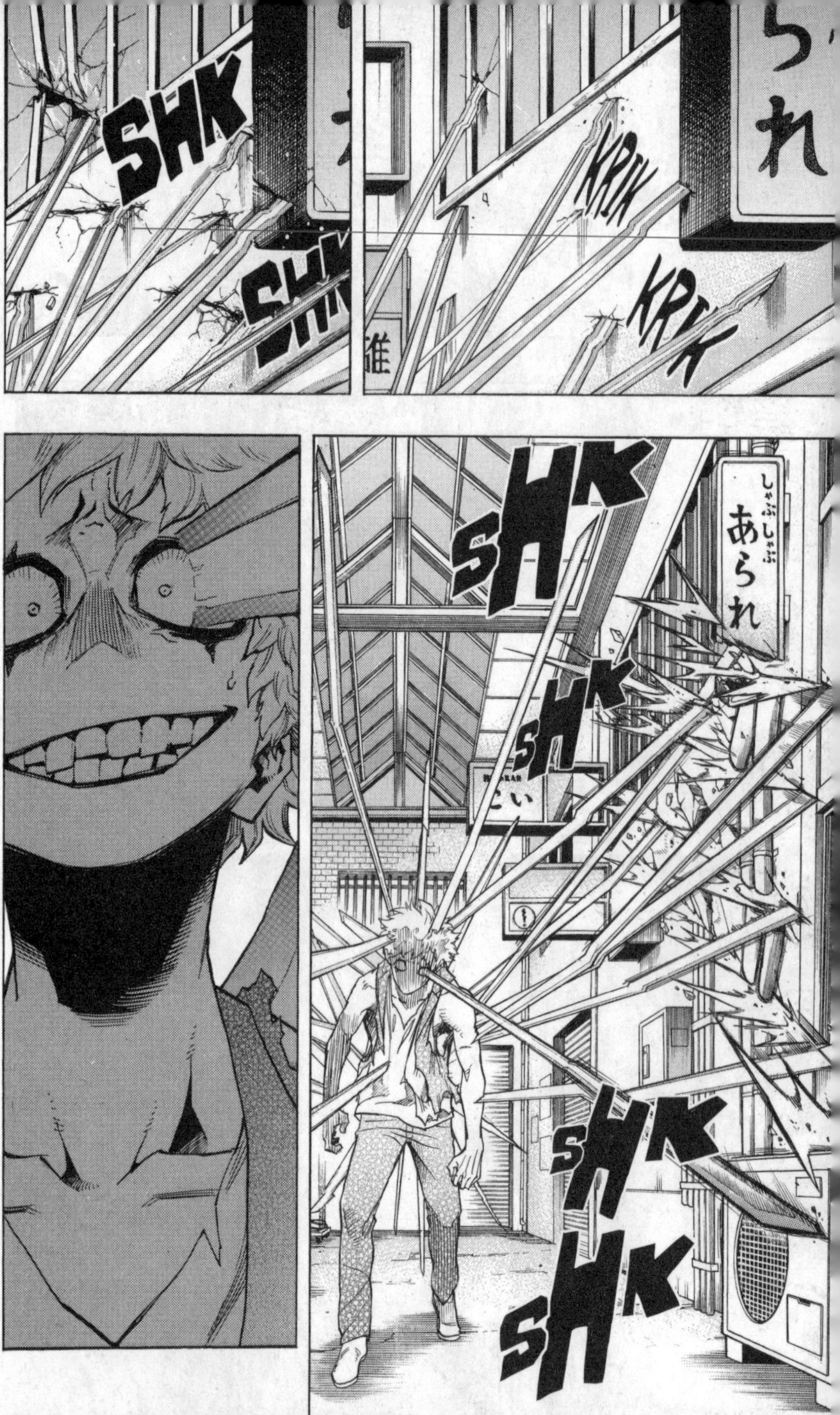

られ
KRIK
KRIK
SHK
SHK
SHK
しゃぶしゃぶ
あられ
SHK
こい
SHK
SHK

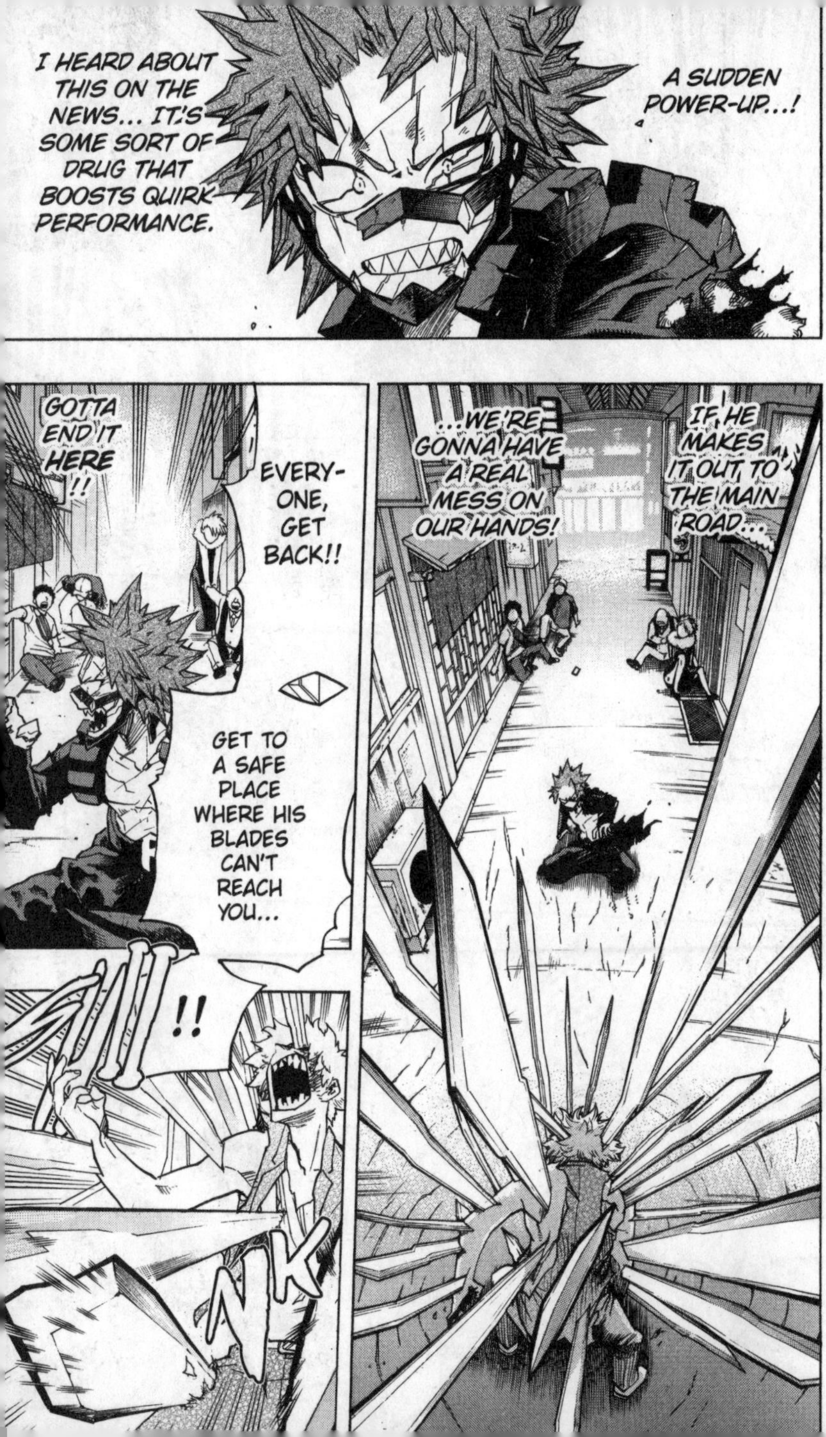

A SUDDEN POWER-UP...!
I HEARD ABOUT THIS ON THE NEWS... IT'S SOME SORT OF DRUG THAT BOOSTS QUIRK PERFORMANCE.
IF HE MAKES IT OUT TO THE MAIN ROAD...
...WE'RE GONNA HAVE A REAL MESS ON OUR HANDS!
EVERY-ONE, GET BACK!!
GOTTA END IT HERE!!
GET TO A SAFE PLACE WHERE HIS BLADES CAN'T REACH YOU...
!!
NK

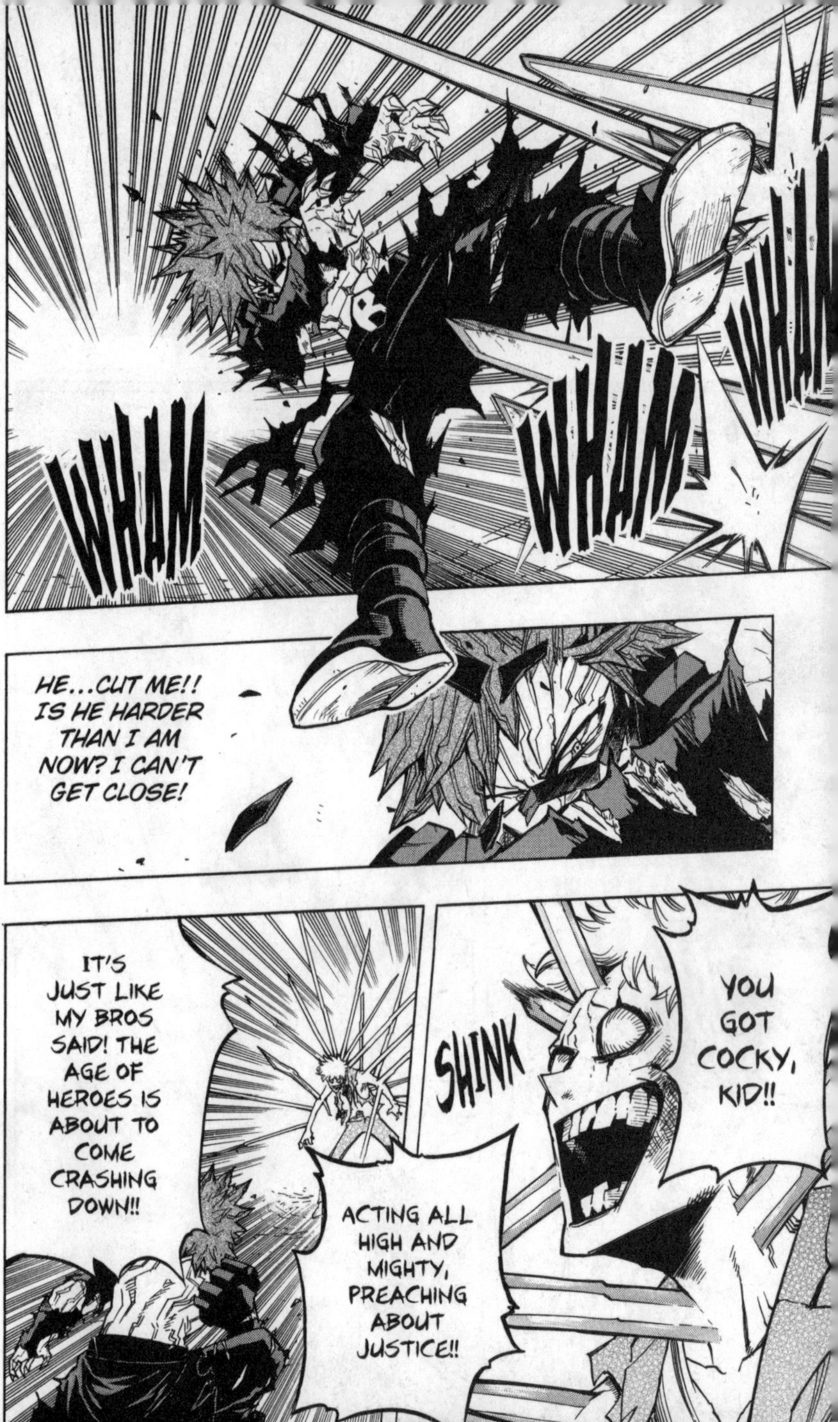
WHAM
WHAM
WHAM
WHAM
HE...CUT ME!! IS HE HARDER THAN I AM NOW? I CAN'T GET CLOSE!
YOU GOT COCKY, KID!!
SHINK
ACTING ALL HIGH AND MIGHTY, PREACHING ABOUT JUSTICE!!
IT'S JUST LIKE MY BROS SAID! THE AGE OF HEROES IS ABOUT TO COME CRASHING DOWN!!

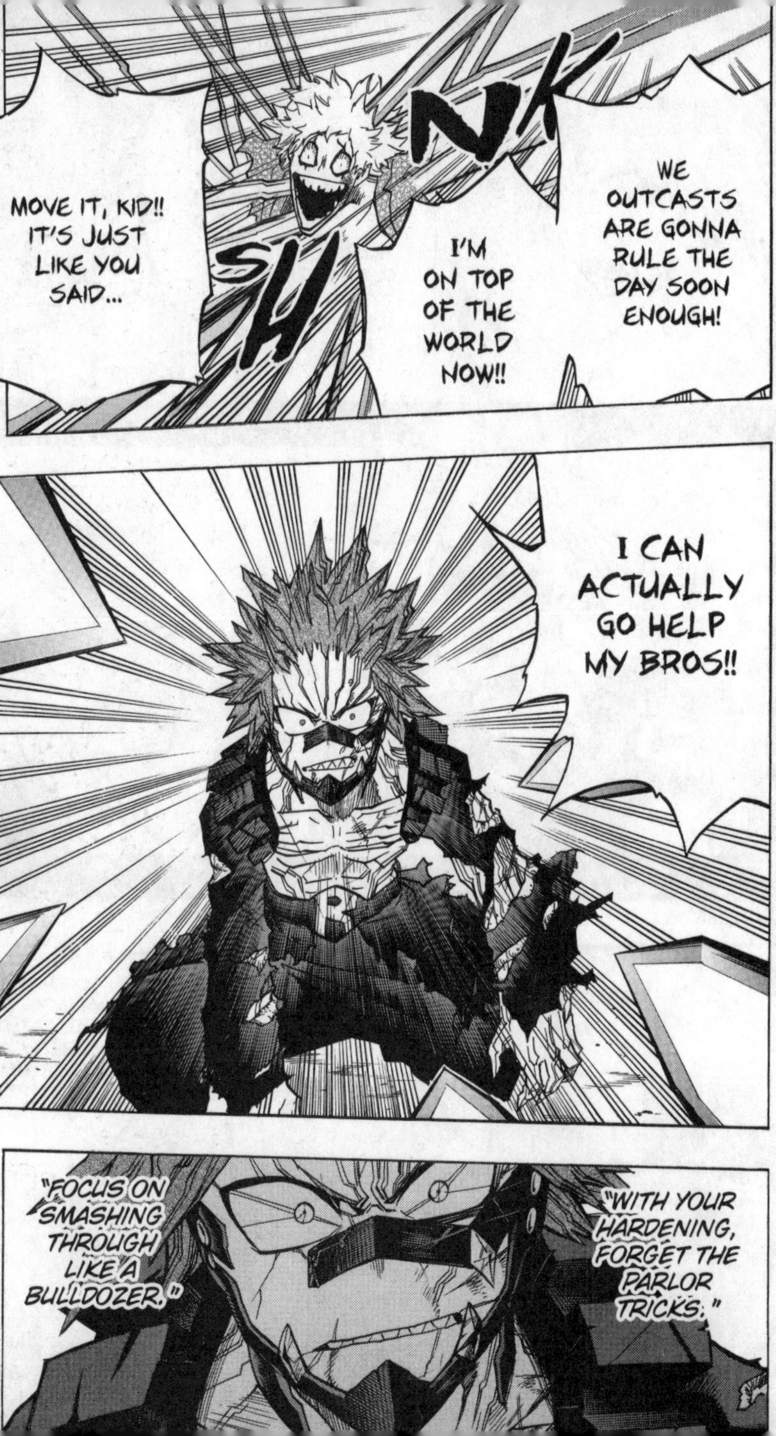
WE OUTCASTS ARE GONNA RULE THE DAY SOON ENOUGH!
I'M ON TOP OF THE WORLD NOW!!
SHNK
MOVE IT, KID!! IT'S JUST LIKE YOU SAID...
I CAN ACTUALLY GO HELP MY BROS!!
"WITH YOUR HARDENING, FORGET THE PARLOR TRICKS."
"FOCUS ON SMASHING THROUGH LIKE A BULLDOZER."

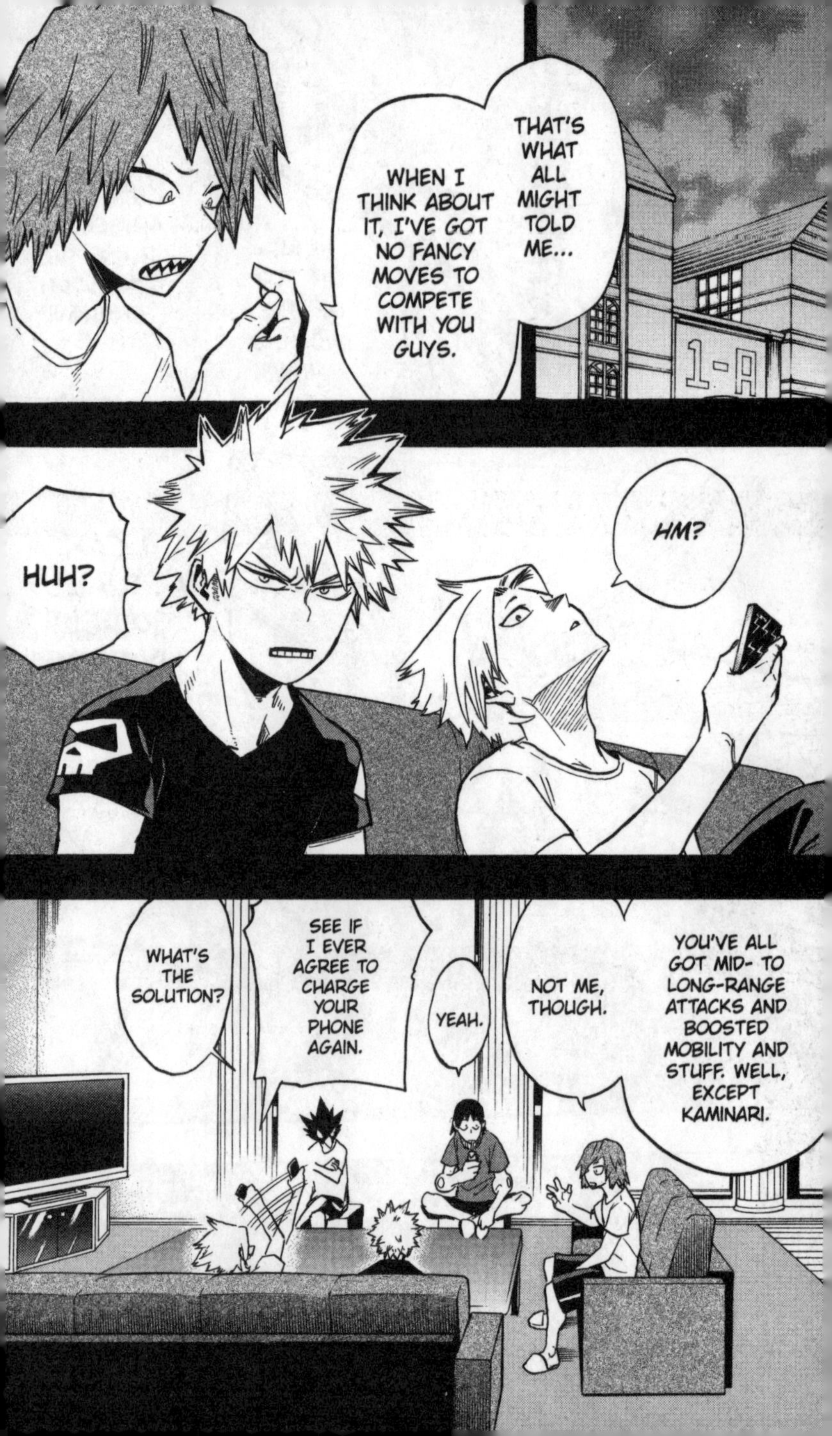
THAT'S WHAT ALL MIGHT TOLD ME...
WHEN I THINK ABOUT IT, I'VE GOT NO FANCY MOVES TO COMPETE WITH YOU GUYS.
1-A
HM?
HUH?
YOU'VE ALL GOT MID- TO LONG-RANGE ATTACKS AND BOOSTED MOBILITY AND STUFF. WELL, EXCEPT KAMINARI.
NOT ME, THOUGH.
YEAH.
SEE IF I EVER AGREE TO CHARGE YOUR PHONE AGAIN.
WHAT'S THE SOLUTION?

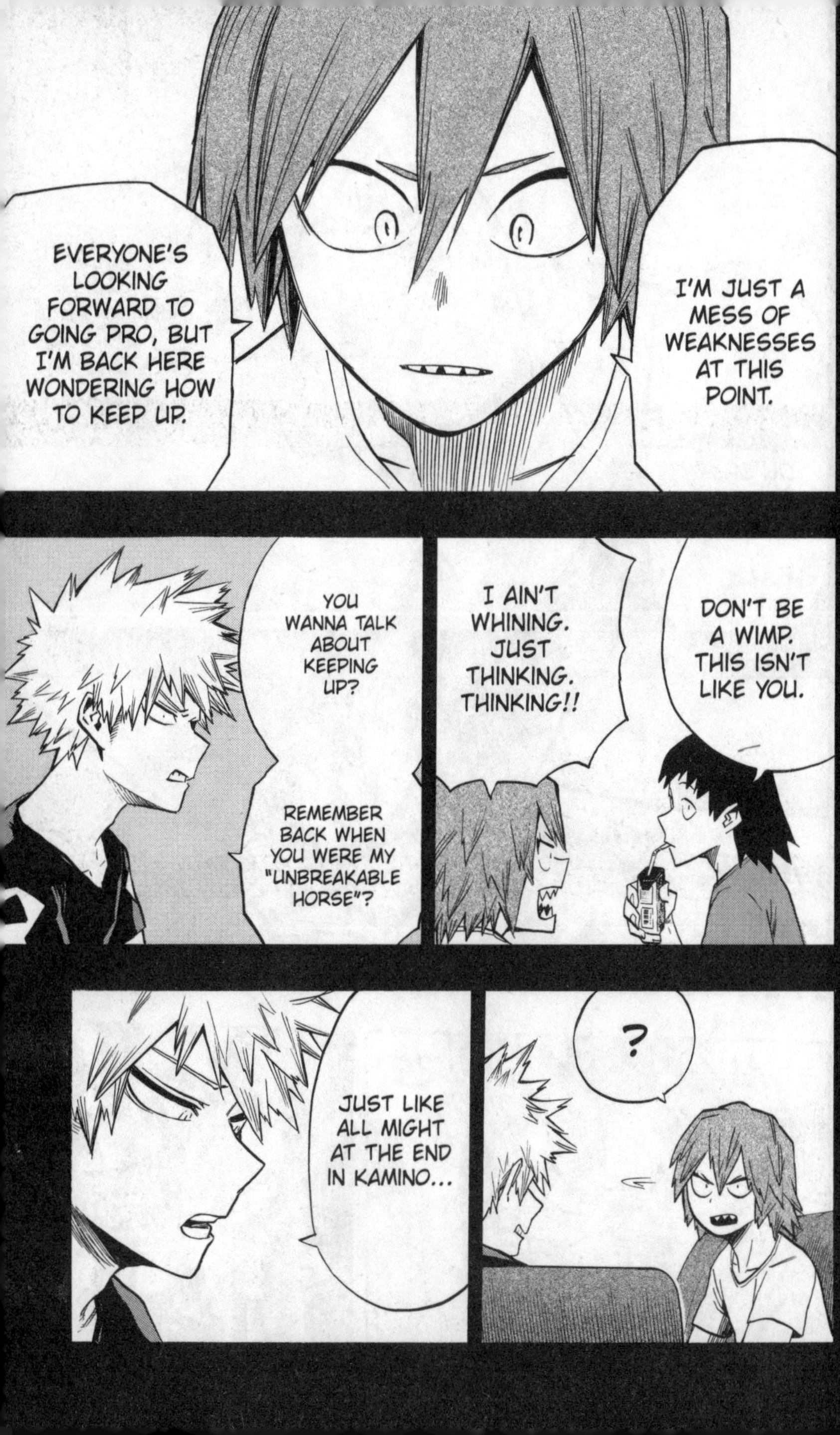
I'M JUST A MESS OF WEAKNESSES AT THIS POINT.
EVERYONE'S LOOKING FORWARD TO GOING PRO, BUT I'M BACK HERE WONDERING HOW TO KEEP UP.
DON'T BE A WIMP. THIS ISN'T LIKE YOU.
I AIN'T WHINING. JUST THINKING. THINKING!!
YOU WANNA TALK ABOUT KEEPING UP?
REMEMBER BACK WHEN YOU WERE MY "UNBREAKABLE HORSE"?
?
JUST LIKE ALL MIGHT AT THE END IN KAMINO...

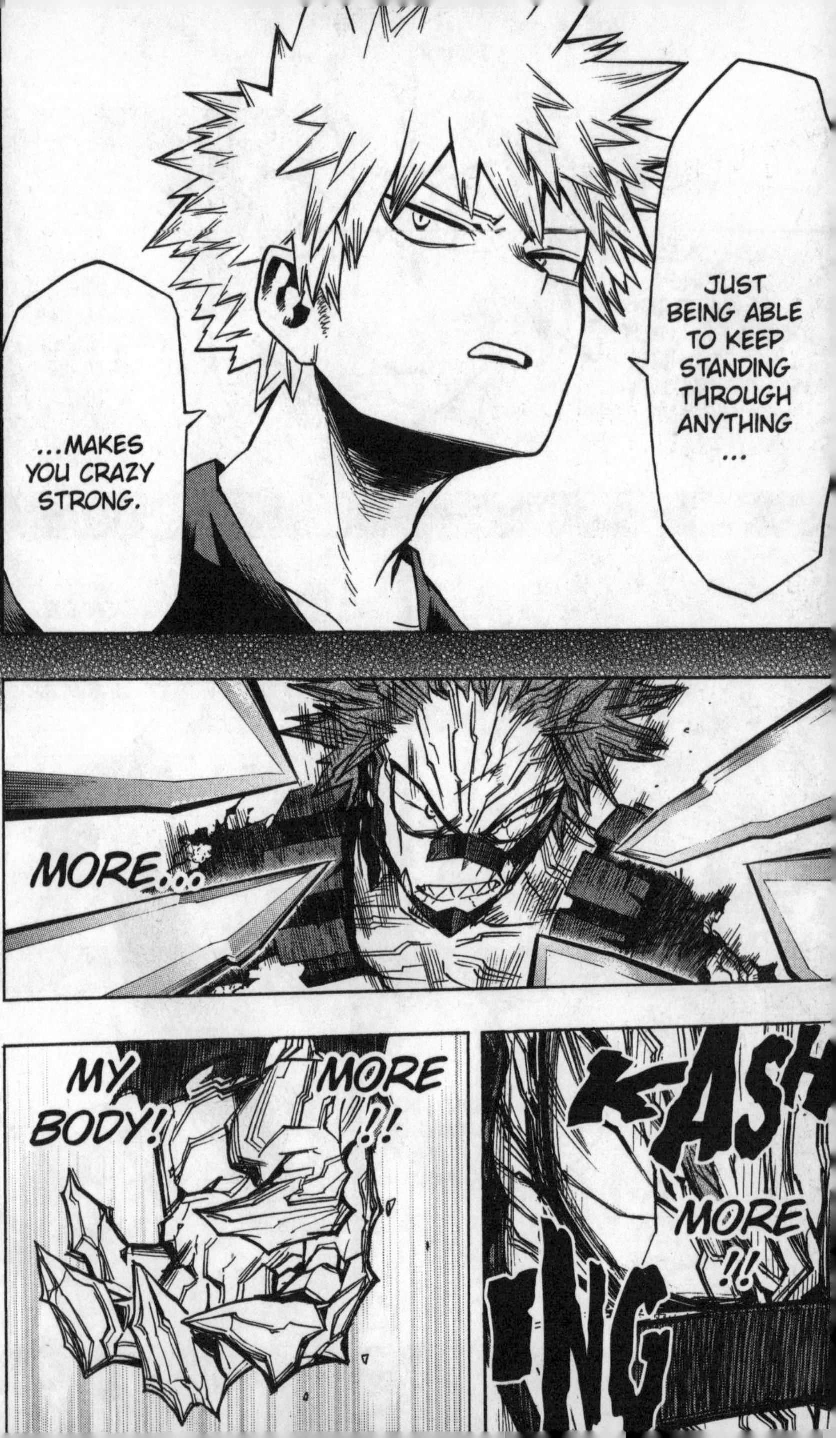
JUST BEING ABLE TO KEEP STANDING THROUGH ANYTHING ...
...MAKES YOU CRAZY STRONG.
MORE...
KASH
MORE !!
ING
MORE !!
MY BODY!!

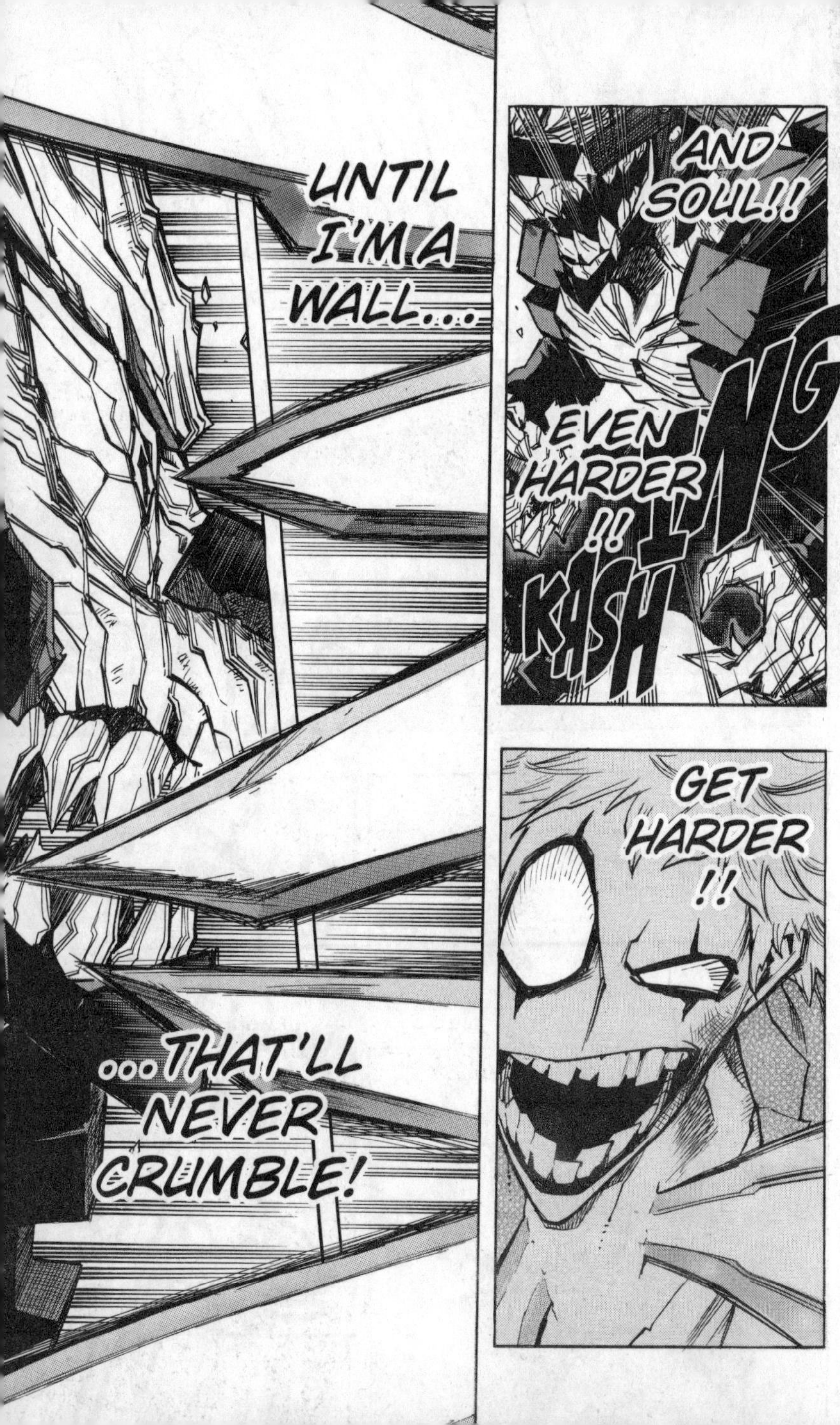
AND SOUL!!
EVEN HARDER!!
KASHING
GET HARDER!!
UNTIL I'M A WALL...
...THAT'LL NEVER CRUMBLE!

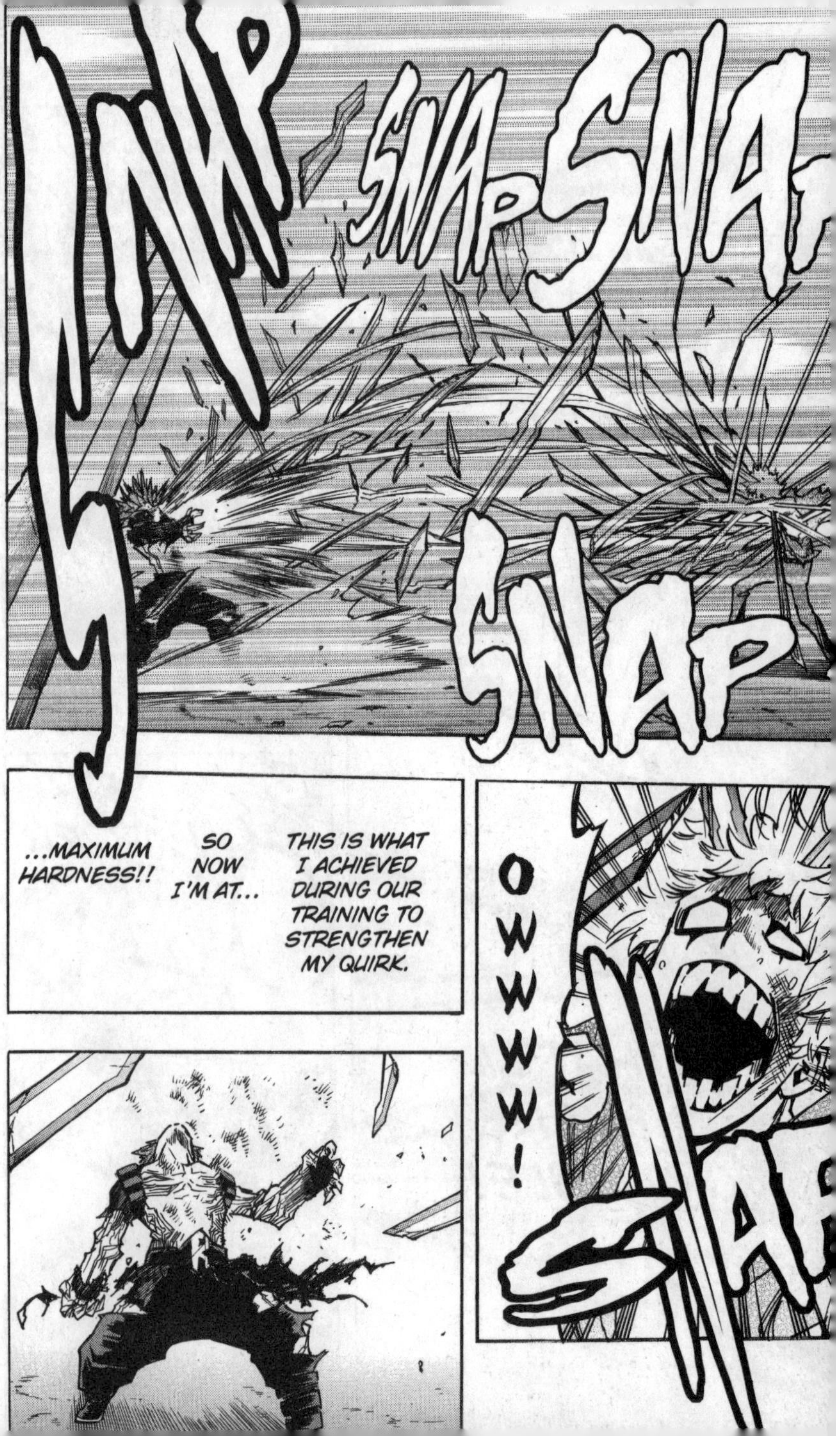
SNA
SNAP
SNAP
SNAP
OWWWWW!
SNA
THIS IS WHAT I ACHIEVED DURING OUR TRAINING TO STRENGTHEN MY QUIRK.
SO NOW I'M AT...
...MAXIMUM HARDNESS!!

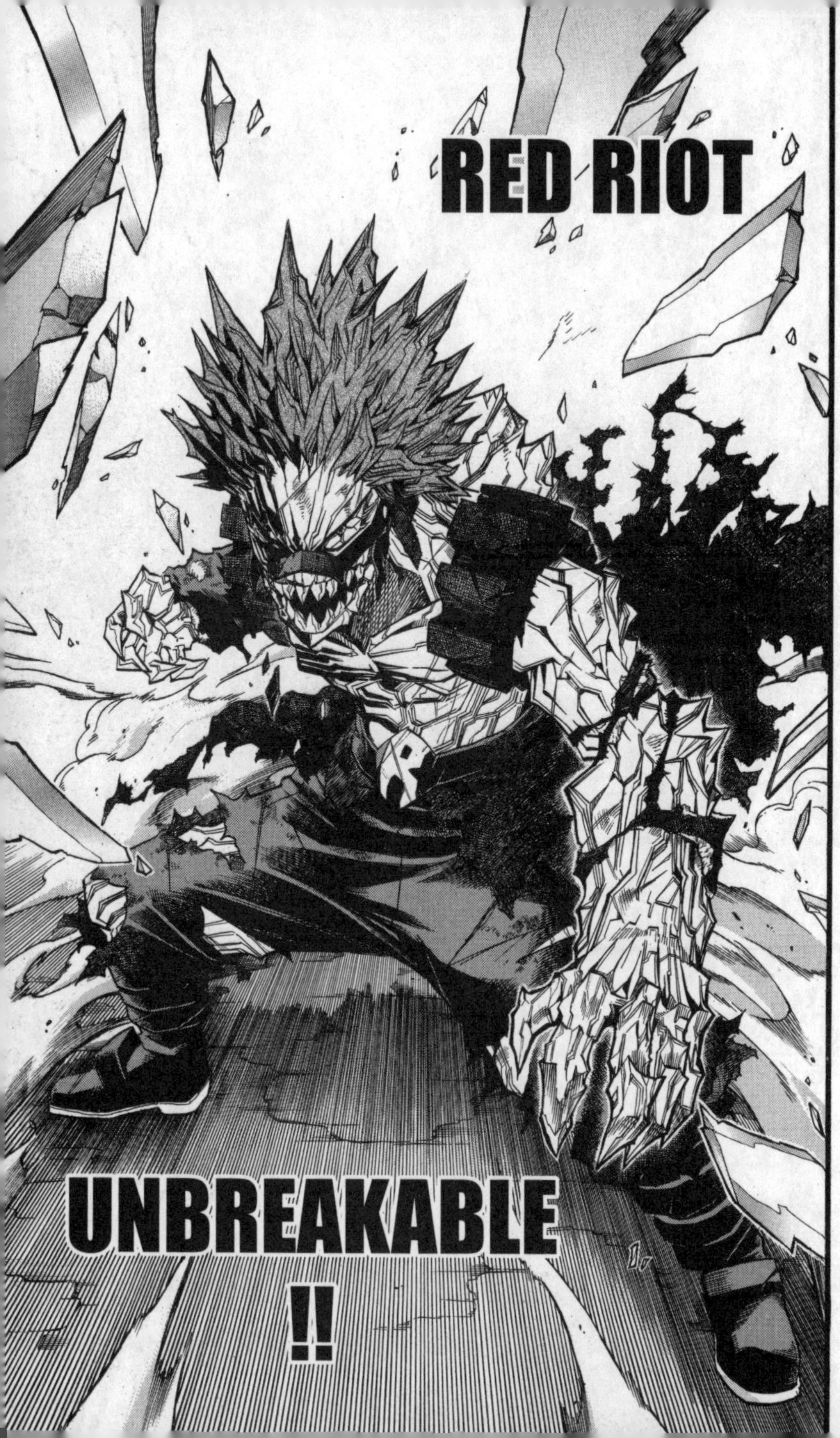
RED RIOT
UNBREAKABLE
!!

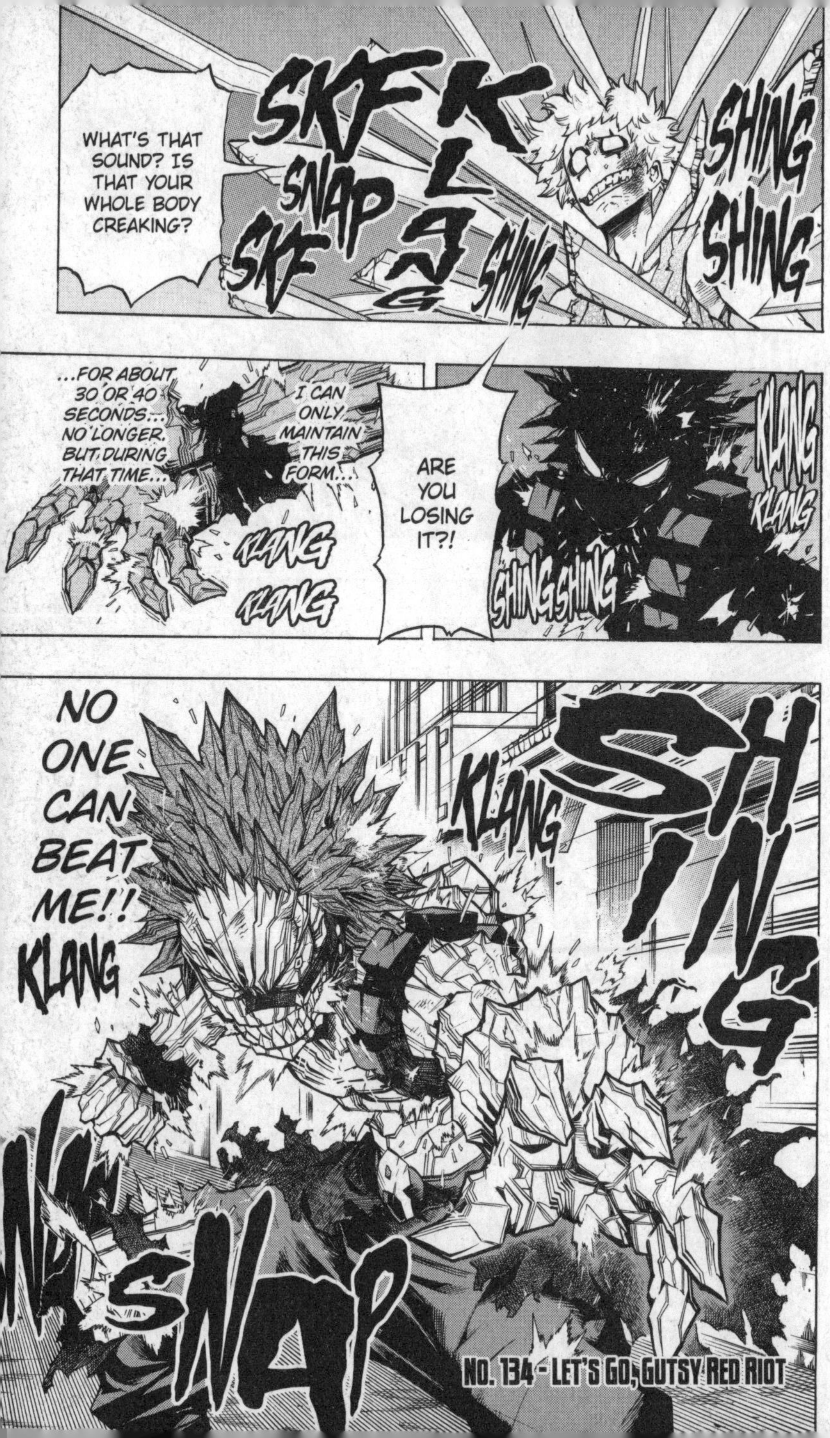
SHING
SHING
KLANG
SKF
SNAP
SKF
SHING
WHAT'S THAT SOUND? IS THAT YOUR WHOLE BODY CREAKING?
KLANG
KLANG
SHING SHING
ARE YOU LOSING IT?!
I CAN ONLY MAINTAIN THIS FORM...
...FOR ABOUT 30 OR 40 SECONDS... NO LONGER. BUT DURING THAT TIME...
KLANG
KLANG
SHING
KLANG
NO ONE CAN BEAT ME!!
KLANG
SNAP
NO. 134 - LET'S GO, GUTSY RED RIOT

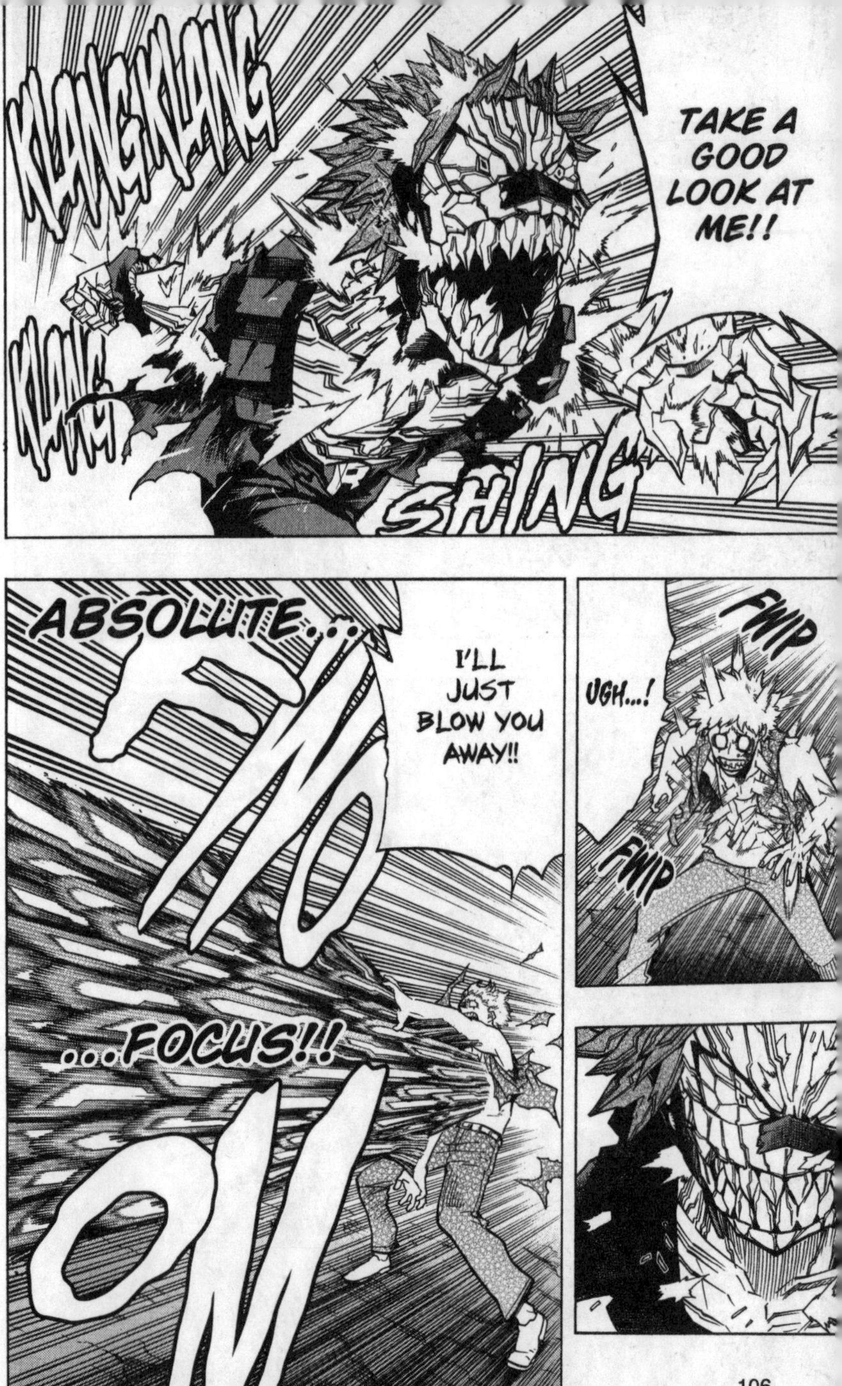
TAKE A GOOD LOOK AT ME!!
KLANGKLANG
SHING
KLANG
FWIP
UGH...!
FWIP
ABSOLUTE...
I'LL JUST BLOW YOU AWAY!!
...FOCUS!!

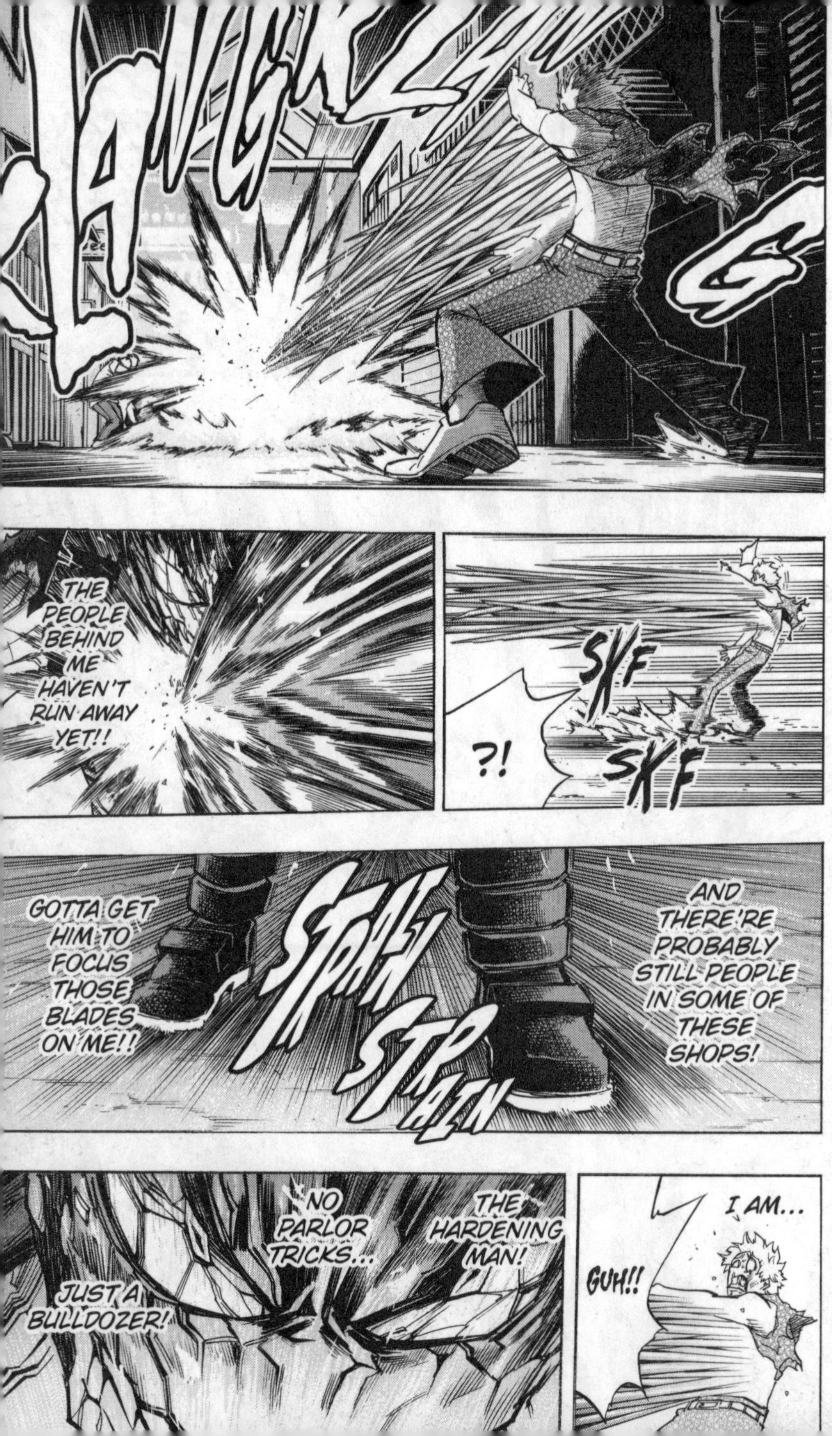
SKF
SKF
?!
THE PEOPLE BEHIND ME HAVEN'T RUN AWAY YET!!
AND THERE'RE PROBABLY STILL PEOPLE IN SOME OF THESE SHOPS!
GOTTA GET HIM TO FOCUS THOSE BLADES ON ME!!
I AM...
GUH!!
THE HARDENING MAN!
NO PARLOR TRICKS...
JUST A BULLDOZER!

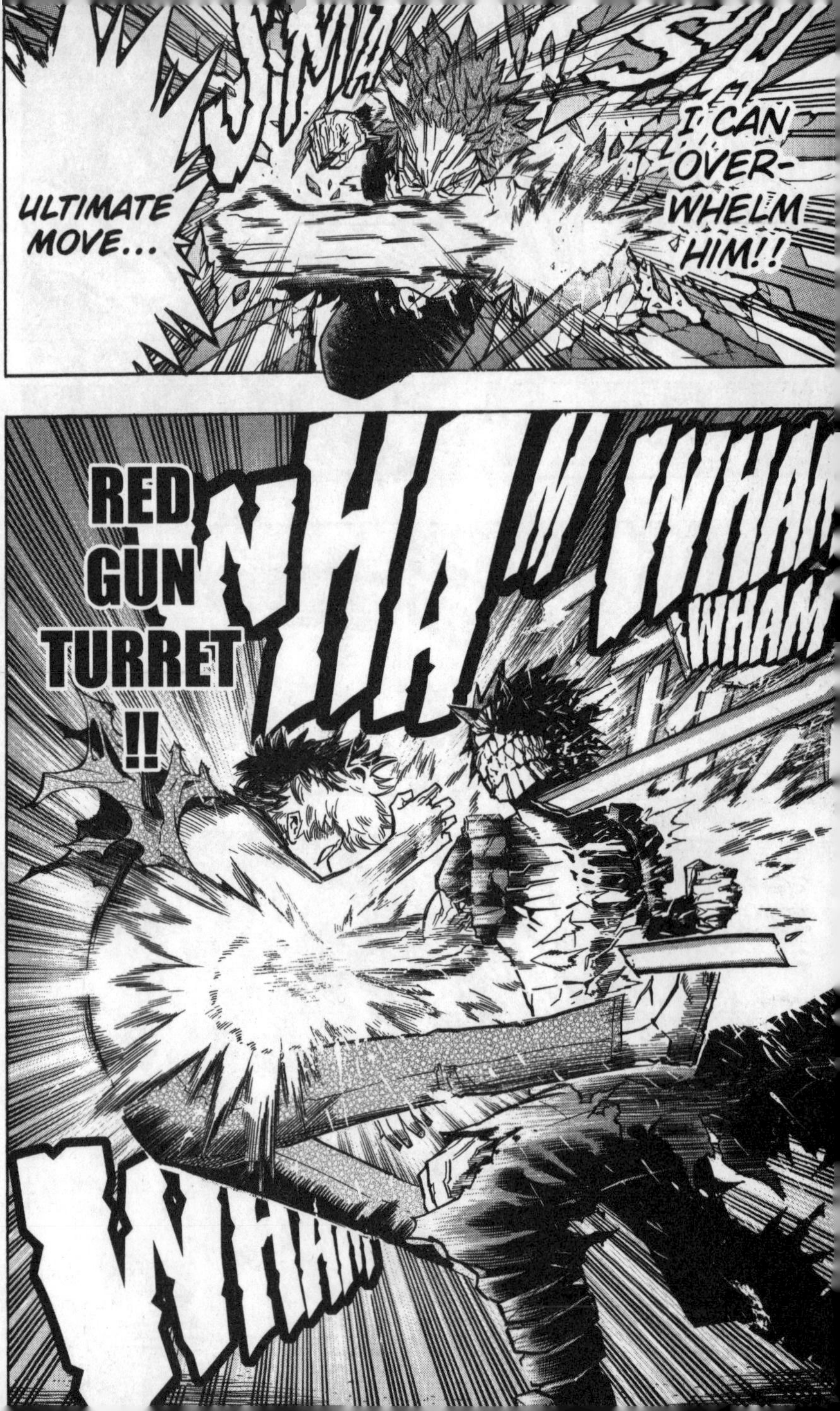
I CAN OVER-WHELM HIM!!
ULTIMATE MOVE...
WHAM
RED GUN TURRET!!

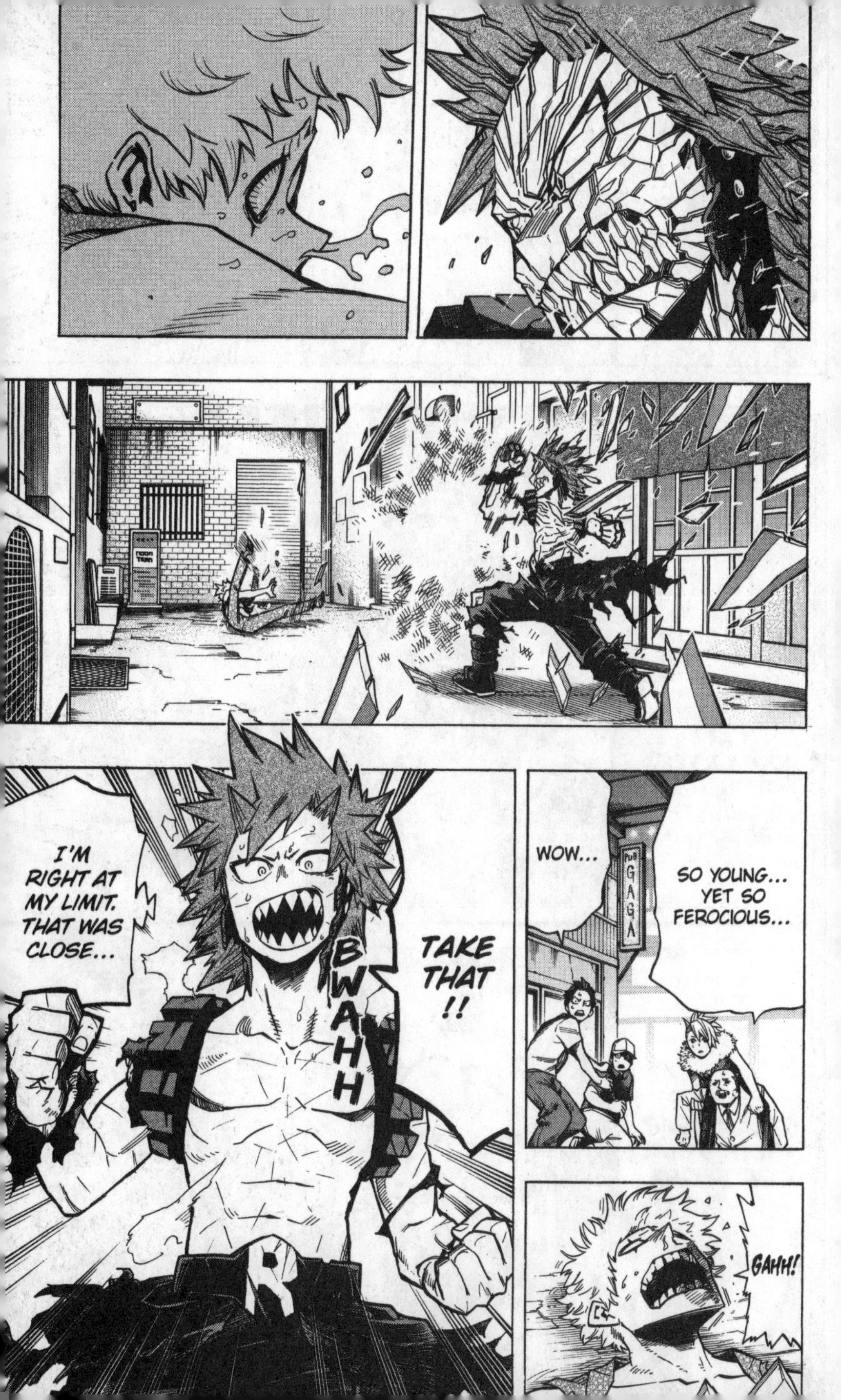
SO YOUNG... YET SO FEROCIOUS...
WOW...
PUB GAGA
GAHH!
TAKE THAT!!
BWAHH
I'M RIGHT AT MY LIMIT. THAT WAS CLOSE...

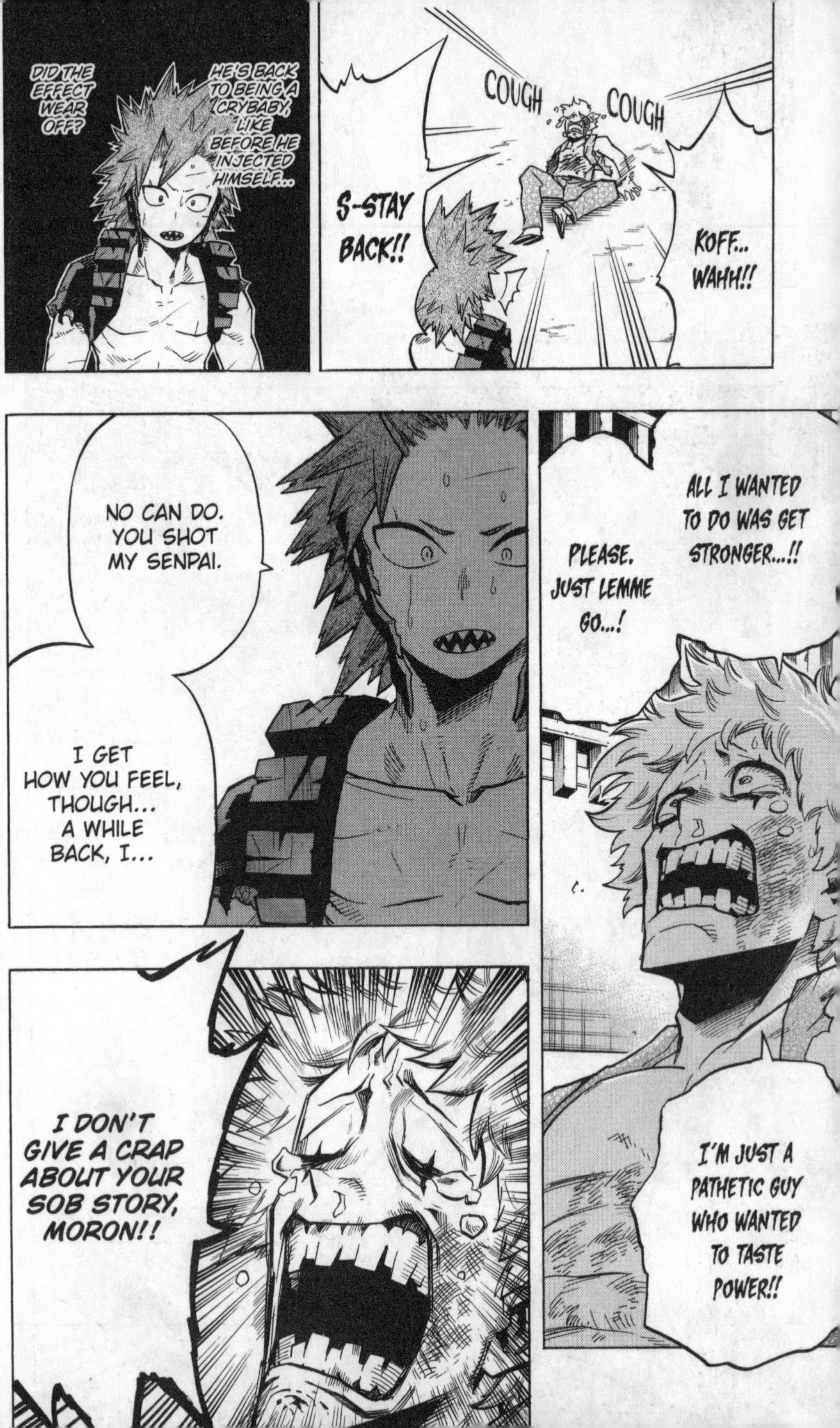
COUGH
COUGH
KOFF... WAHH!!
S-STAY BACK!!
HE'S BACK TO BEING A CRYBABY, LIKE BEFORE HE INJECTED HIMSELF...
DID THE EFFECT WEAR OFF?
ALL I WANTED TO DO WAS GET STRONGER...!!
PLEASE. JUST LEMME GO...!
I'M JUST A PATHETIC GUY WHO WANTED TO TASTE POWER!!
NO CAN DO. YOU SHOT MY SENPAI.
I GET HOW YOU FEEL, THOUGH... A WHILE BACK, I...
I DON'T GIVE A CRAP ABOUT YOUR SOB STORY, MORON!!

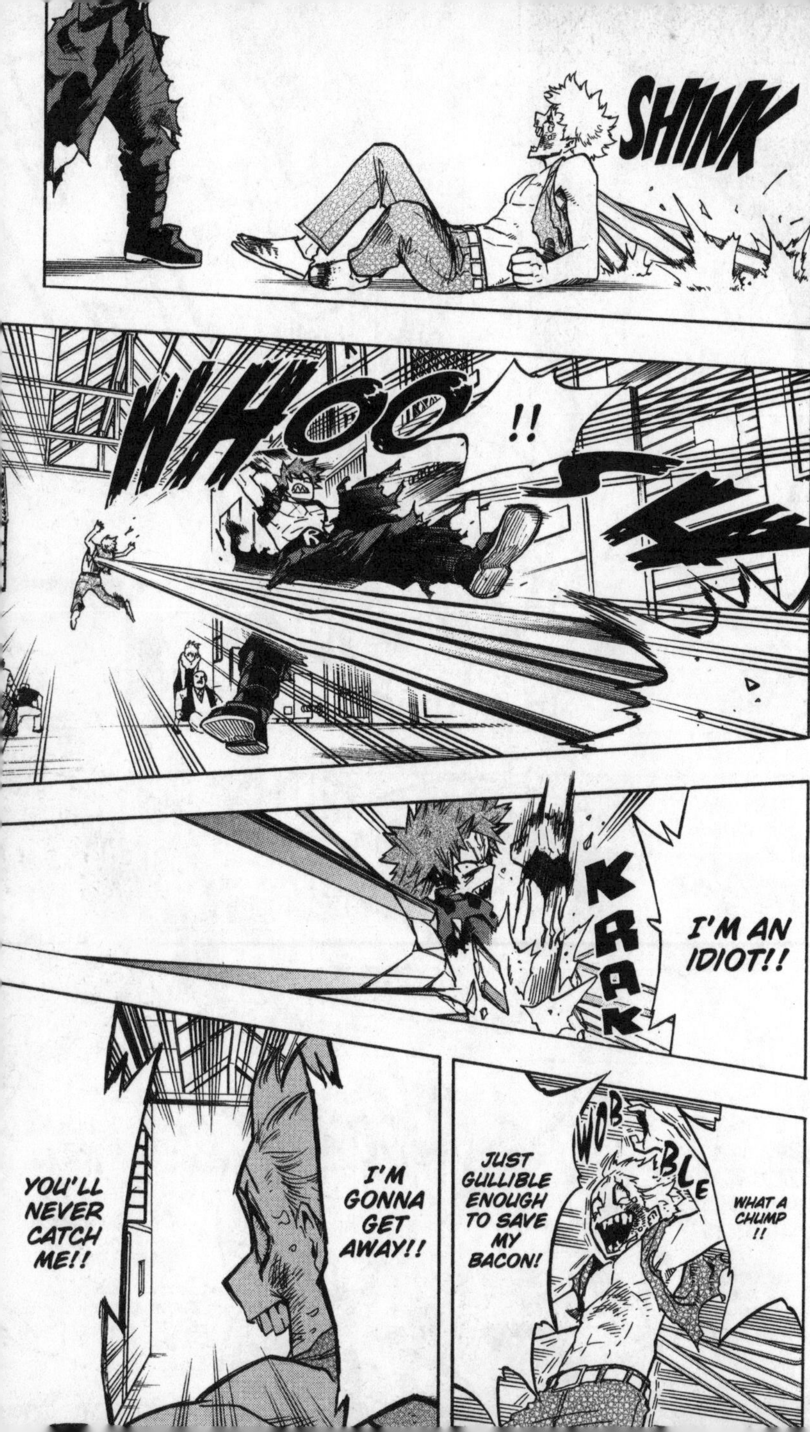
SHINK
WHOOSH
!!
KRAK
I'M AN IDIOT!!
WOBBLE
WHAT A CHUMP!!
JUST GULLIBLE ENOUGH TO SAVE MY BACON!
I'M GONNA GET AWAY!!
YOU'LL NEVER CATCH ME!!

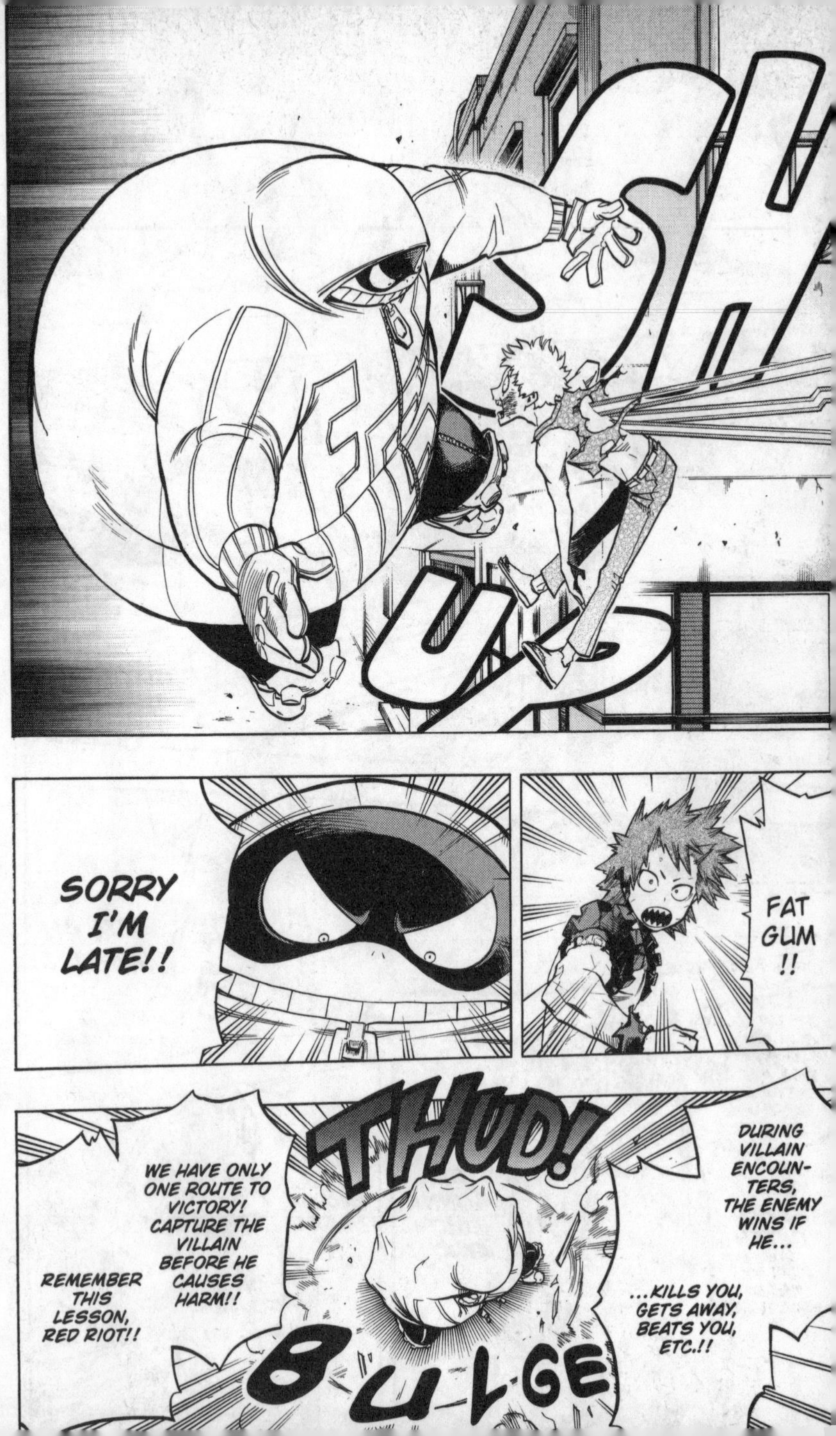
FAT GUM !!
SORRY I'M LATE!!
THUD!
DURING VILLAIN ENCOUN-TERS, THE ENEMY WINS IF HE...
WE HAVE ONLY ONE ROUTE TO VICTORY! CAPTURE THE VILLAIN BEFORE HE CAUSES HARM!!
...KILLS YOU, GETS AWAY, BEATS YOU, ETC.!!
REMEMBER THIS LESSON, RED RIOT!!
BULGE

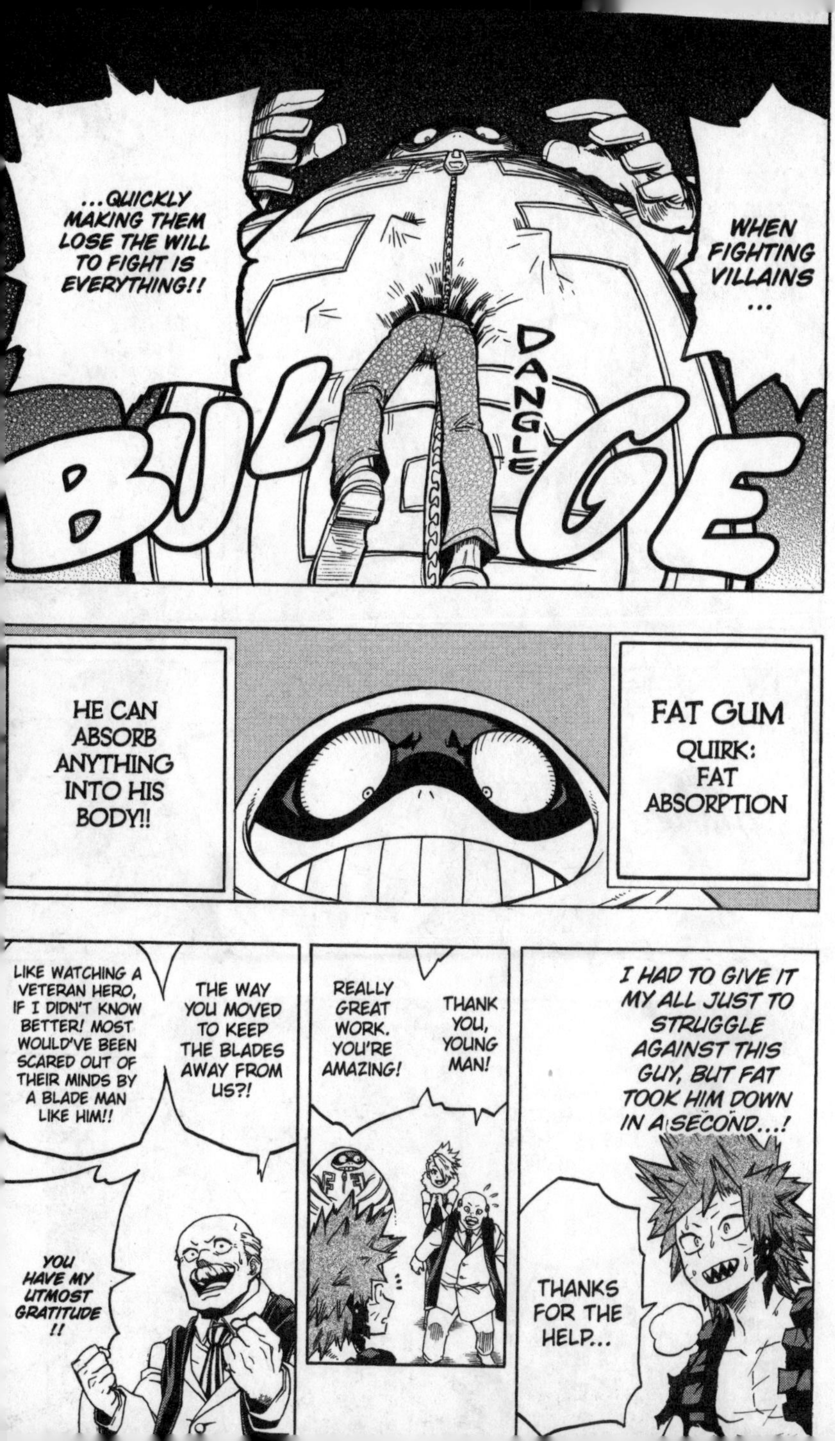
WHEN FIGHTING VILLAINS ...
...QUICKLY MAKING THEM LOSE THE WILL TO FIGHT IS EVERYTHING!!
DANGLE
BULGE
FAT GUM
QUIRK: FAT ABSORPTION
HE CAN ABSORB ANYTHING INTO HIS BODY!!
I HAD TO GIVE IT MY ALL JUST TO STRUGGLE AGAINST THIS GUY, BUT FAT TOOK HIM DOWN IN A SECOND...!
THANKS FOR THE HELP...
THANK YOU, YOUNG MAN!
REALLY GREAT WORK. YOU'RE AMAZING!
THE WAY YOU MOVED TO KEEP THE BLADES AWAY FROM US?!
LIKE WATCHING A VETERAN HERO, IF I DIDN'T KNOW BETTER! MOST WOULD'VE BEEN SCARED OUT OF THEIR MINDS BY A BLADE MAN LIKE HIM!!
YOU HAVE MY UTMOST GRATITUDE!!

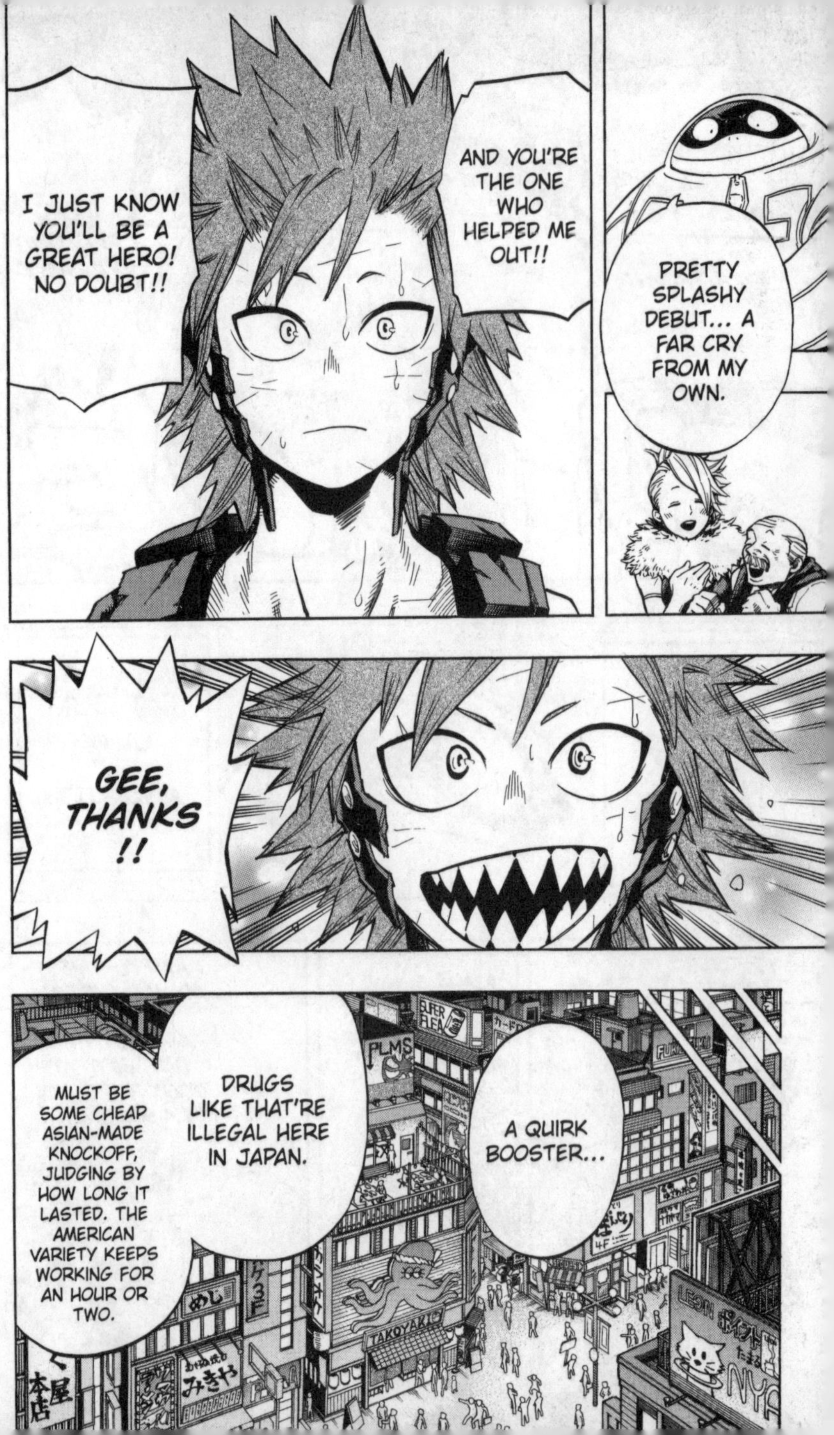
PRETTY SPLASHY DEBUT... A FAR CRY FROM MY OWN.
AND YOU'RE THE ONE WHO HELPED ME OUT!!
I JUST KNOW YOU'LL BE A GREAT HERO! NO DOUBT!!
GEE, THANKS !!
A QUIRK BOOSTER...
DRUGS LIKE THAT'RE ILLEGAL HERE IN JAPAN.
MUST BE SOME CHEAP ASIAN-MADE KNOCKOFF, JUDGING BY HOW LONG IT LASTED. THE AMERICAN VARIETY KEEPS WORKING FOR AN HOUR OR TWO.

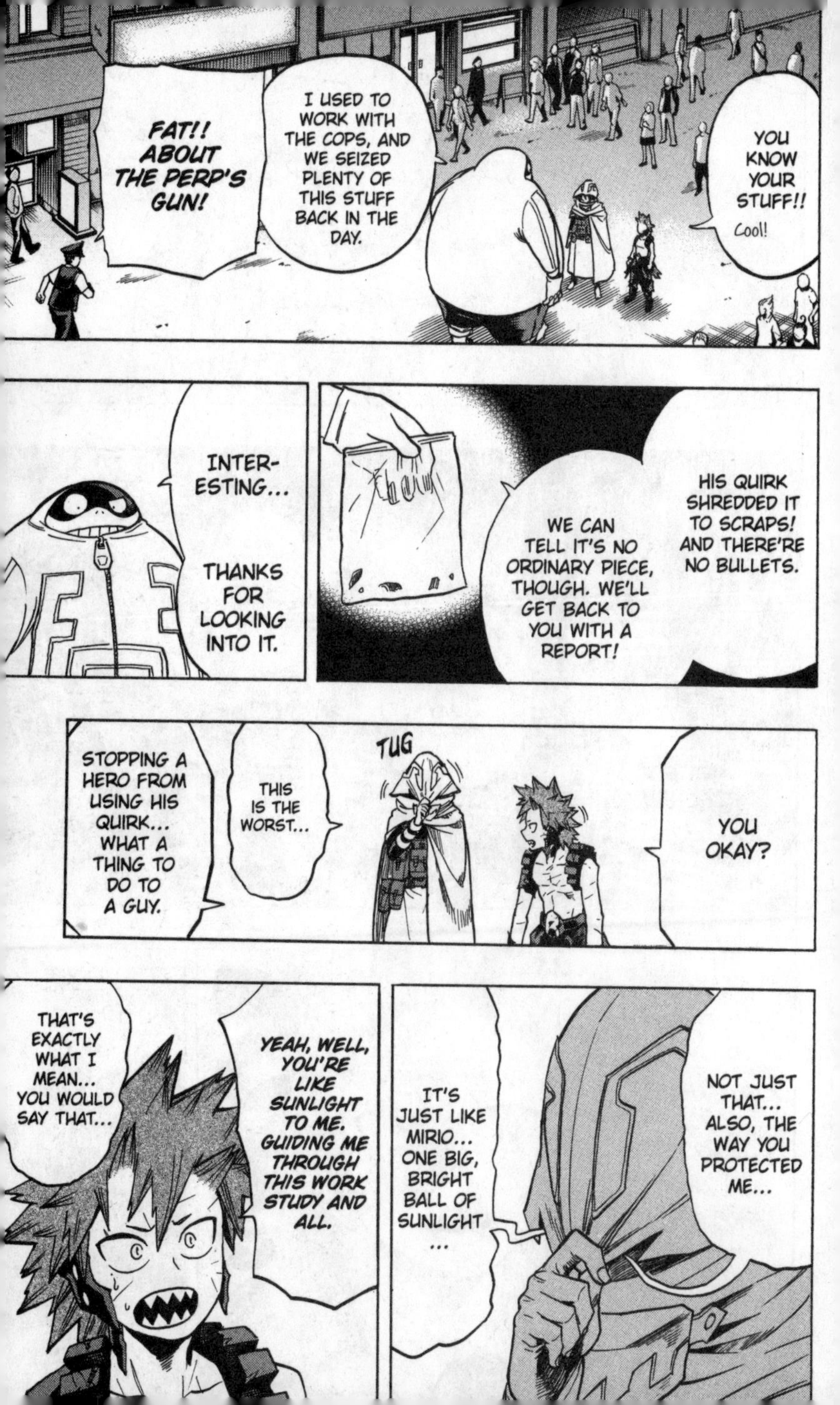
YOU KNOW YOUR STUFF!!
Cool!
I USED TO WORK WITH THE COPS, AND WE SEIZED PLENTY OF THIS STUFF BACK IN THE DAY.
FAT!! ABOUT THE PERP'S GUN!
HIS QUIRK SHREDDED IT TO SCRAPS! AND THERE'RE NO BULLETS.
WE CAN TELL IT'S NO ORDINARY PIECE, THOUGH. WE'LL GET BACK TO YOU WITH A REPORT!
INTER-ESTING...
THANKS FOR LOOKING INTO IT.
YOU OKAY?
TUG
THIS IS THE WORST...
STOPPING A HERO FROM USING HIS QUIRK... WHAT A THING TO DO TO A GUY.
NOT JUST THAT... ALSO, THE WAY YOU PROTECTED ME...
IT'S JUST LIKE MIRIO... ONE BIG, BRIGHT BALL OF SUNLIGHT ...
YEAH, WELL, YOU'RE LIKE SUNLIGHT TO ME. GUIDING ME THROUGH THIS WORK STUDY AND ALL.
THAT'S EXACTLY WHAT I MEAN... YOU WOULD SAY THAT...

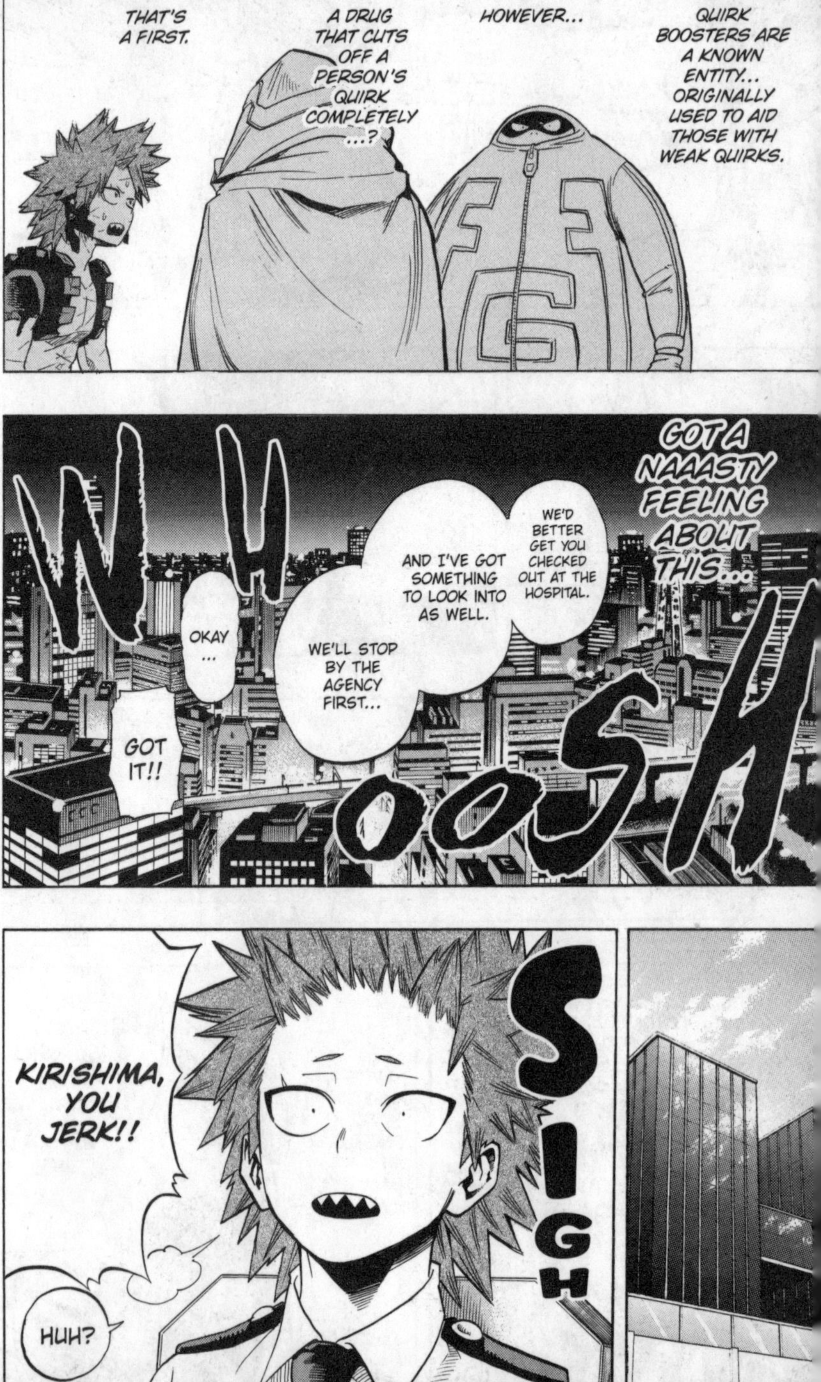
QUIRK BOOSTERS ARE A KNOWN ENTITY... ORIGINALLY USED TO AID THOSE WITH WEAK QUIRKS.
HOWEVER...
A DRUG THAT CUTS OFF A PERSON'S QUIRK COMPLETELY ...?
THAT'S A FIRST.
GOT A NAAASTY FEELING ABOUT THIS...
WHOOSH
WE'D BETTER GET YOU CHECKED OUT AT THE HOSPITAL.
AND I'VE GOT SOMETHING TO LOOK INTO AS WELL.
WE'LL STOP BY THE AGENCY FIRST...
OKAY ...
GOT IT!!
SIGH
KIRISHIMA, YOU JERK!!
HUH?

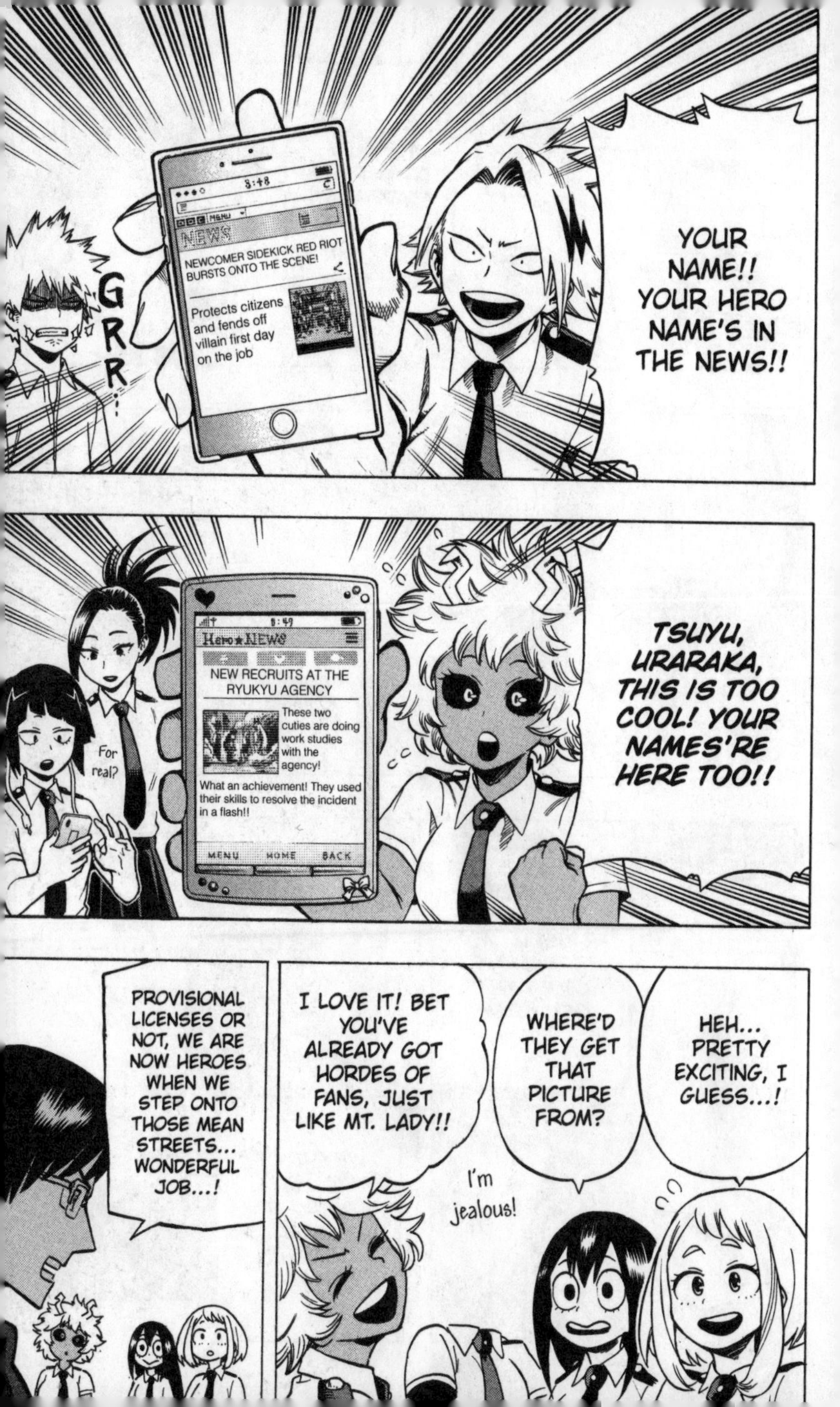

YOUR NAME!! YOUR HERO NAME'S IN THE NEWS!!
NEWS
NEWCOMER SIDEKICK RED RIOT BURSTS ONTO THE SCENE!
Protects citizens and fends off villain first day on the job
GRR
TSUYU, URARAKA, THIS IS TOO COOL! YOUR NAMES'RE HERE TOO!!
Hero★NEWS
NEW RECRUITS AT THE RYUKYU AGENCY
These two cuties are doing work studies with the agency!
What an achievement! They used their skills to resolve the incident in a flash!!
MENU
HOME
BACK
For real?
HEH... PRETTY EXCITING, I GUESS...!
WHERE'D THEY GET THAT PICTURE FROM?
I LOVE IT! BET YOU'VE ALREADY GOT HORDES OF FANS, JUST LIKE MT. LADY!!
I'm jealous!
PROVISIONAL LICENSES OR NOT, WE ARE NOW HEROES WHEN WE STEP ONTO THOSE MEAN STREETS... WONDERFUL JOB...!

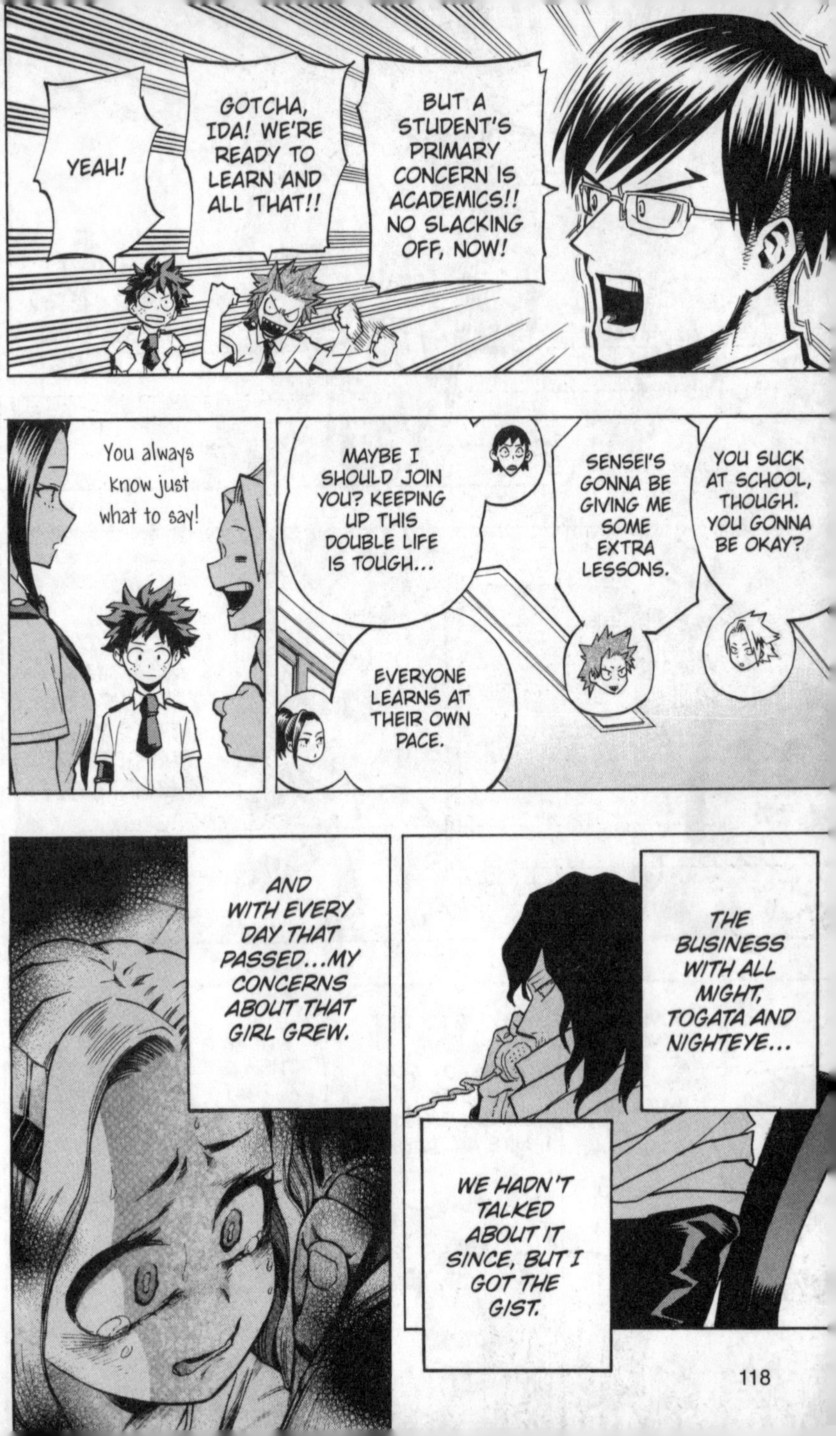
BUT A STUDENT'S PRIMARY CONCERN IS ACADEMICS!! NO SLACKING OFF, NOW!
GOTCHA, IDA! WE'RE READY TO LEARN AND ALL THAT!!
YEAH!
YOU SUCK AT SCHOOL, THOUGH. YOU GONNA BE OKAY?
SENSEI'S GONNA BE GIVING ME SOME EXTRA LESSONS.
MAYBE I SHOULD JOIN YOU? KEEPING UP THIS DOUBLE LIFE IS TOUGH...
EVERYONE LEARNS AT THEIR OWN PACE.
You always know just what to say!
THE BUSINESS WITH ALL MIGHT, TOGATA AND NIGHTEYE...
WE HADN'T TALKED ABOUT IT SINCE, BUT I GOT THE GIST.
AND WITH EVERY DAY THAT PASSED...MY CONCERNS ABOUT THAT GIRL GREW.

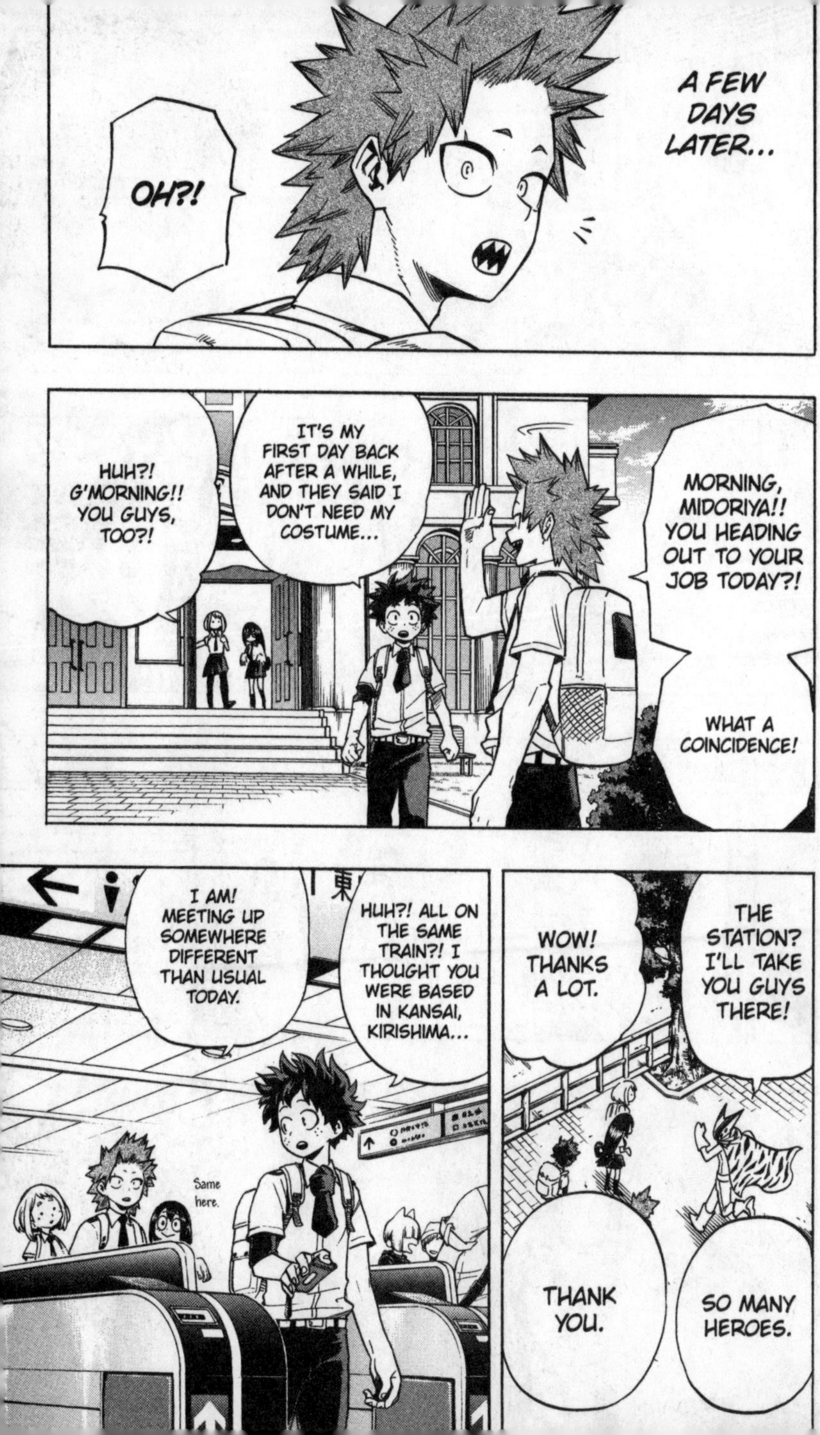
A FEW DAYS LATER...
OH?!
MORNING, MIDORIYA!! YOU HEADING OUT TO YOUR JOB TODAY?!
WHAT A COINCIDENCE!
IT'S MY FIRST DAY BACK AFTER A WHILE, AND THEY SAID I DON'T NEED MY COSTUME...
HUH?! G'MORNING!! YOU GUYS, TOO?!
THE STATION? I'LL TAKE YOU GUYS THERE!
WOW! THANKS A LOT.
SO MANY HEROES.
THANK YOU.
HUH?! ALL ON THE SAME TRAIN?! I THOUGHT YOU WERE BASED IN KANSAI, KIRISHIMA...
I AM! MEETING UP SOMEWHERE DIFFERENT THAN USUAL TODAY.
Same here.

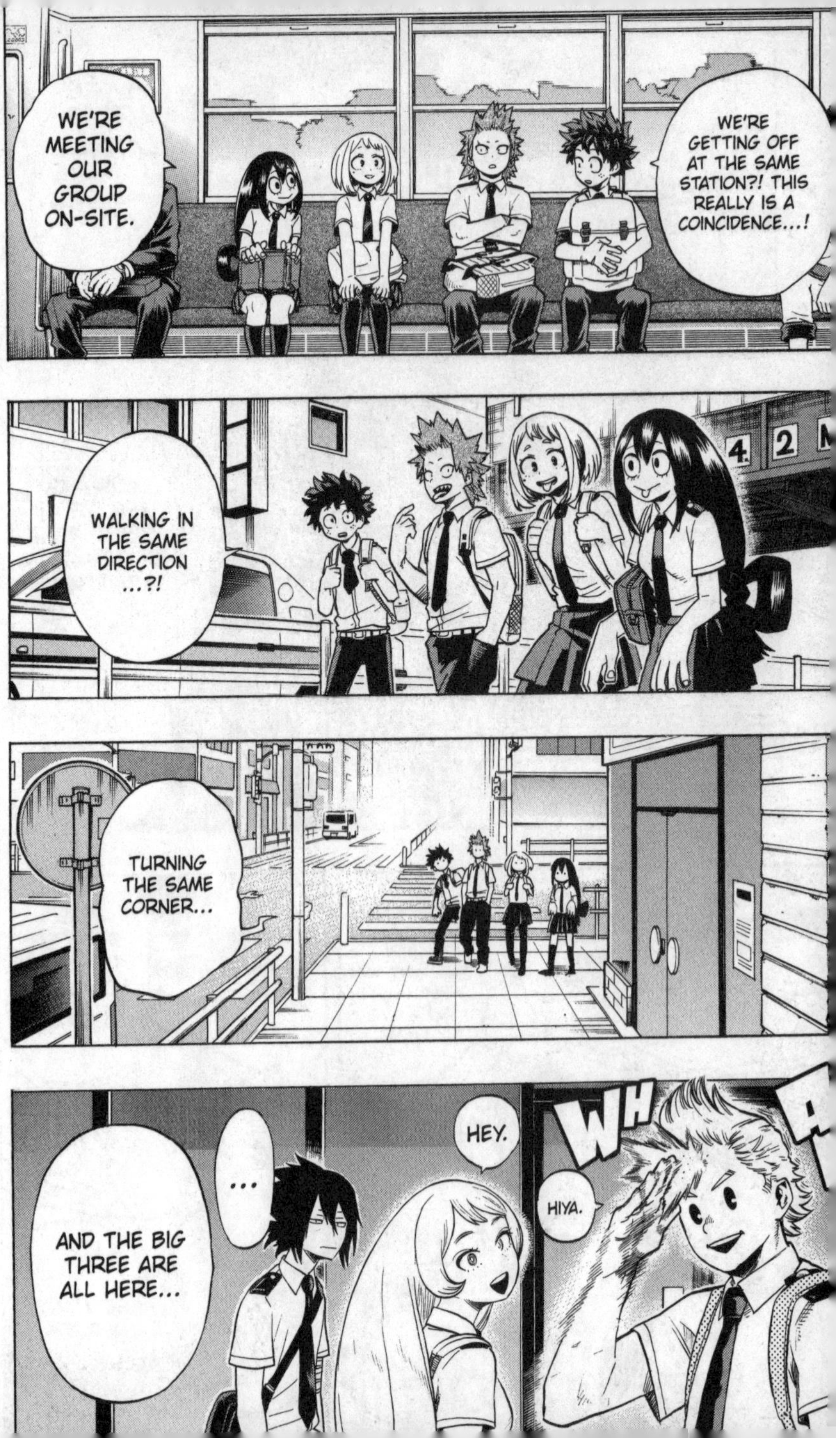
WE'RE GETTING OFF AT THE SAME STATION?! THIS REALLY IS A COINCIDENCE...!
WE'RE MEETING OUR GROUP ON-SITE.
WALKING IN THE SAME DIRECTION ...?!
TURNING THE SAME CORNER...
WH A
HIYA.
HEY.
...
AND THE BIG THREE ARE ALL HERE...

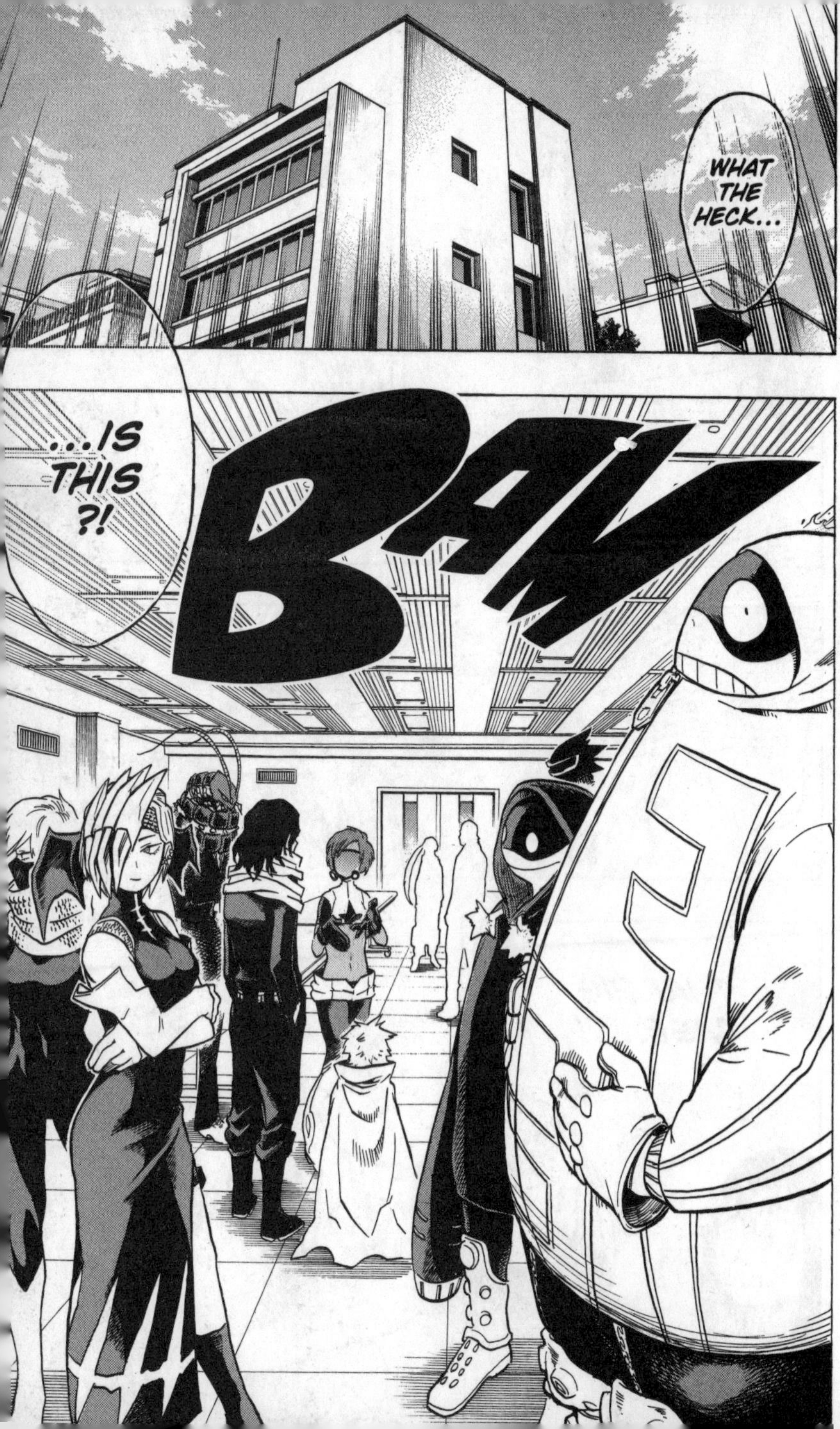
WHAT THE HECK...
...IS THIS ?!
BAM

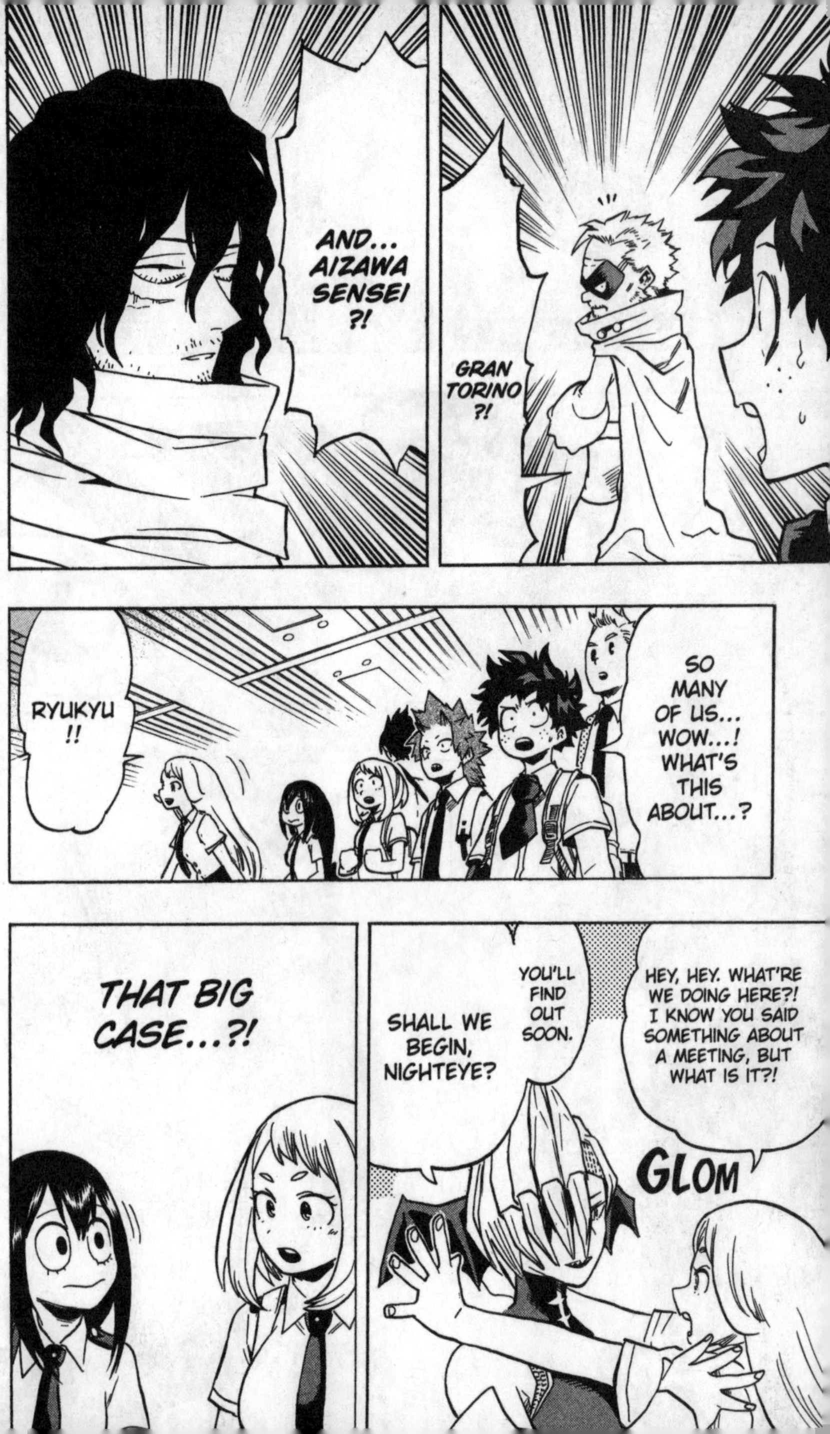
GRAN TORINO ?!
AND... AIZAWA SENSEI ?!
SO MANY OF US... WOW...! WHAT'S THIS ABOUT...?
RYUKYU !!
HEY, HEY. WHAT'RE WE DOING HERE?! I KNOW YOU SAID SOMETHING ABOUT A MEETING, BUT WHAT IS IT?!
GLOM
YOU'LL FIND OUT SOON.
SHALL WE BEGIN, NIGHTEYE?
THAT BIG CASE...?!

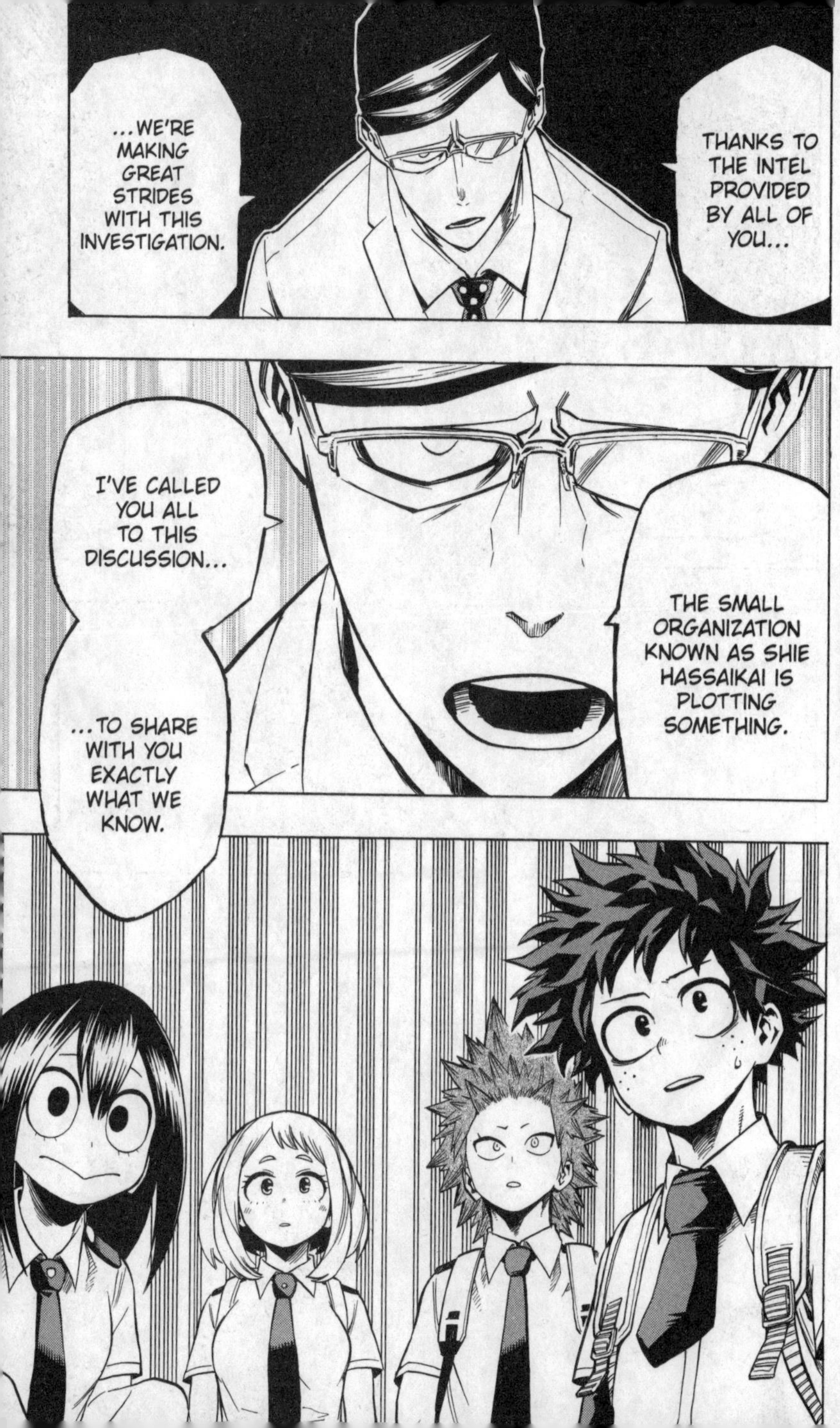
THANKS TO THE INTEL PROVIDED BY ALL OF YOU...
...WE'RE MAKING GREAT STRIDES WITH THIS INVESTIGATION.
THE SMALL ORGANIZATION KNOWN AS SHIE HASSAIKAI IS PLOTTING SOMETHING.
I'VE CALLED YOU ALL TO THIS DISCUSSION...
...TO SHARE WITH YOU EXACTLY WHAT WE KNOW.

MY HERO ACADEMIA

NO. 135 - AN UNPLEASANT TALK

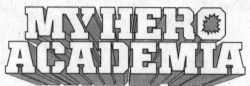

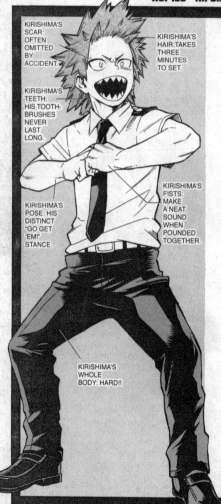

KIRISHIMA'S SCAR: OFTEN OMITTED BY ACCIDENT.
KIRISHIMA'S HAIR: TAKES THREE MINUTES TO SET.
KIRISHIMA'S TEETH: HIS TOOTH-BRUSHES NEVER LAST LONG.
KIRISHIMA'S FISTS: MAKE A NEAT SOUND WHEN POUNDED TOGETHER.
KIRISHIMA'S POSE: HIS DISTINCT "GO GET 'EM!" STANCE.
KIRISHIMA'S WHOLE BODY: HARD!!

U.A. FILE.12

CLASS No.08

EIJIRO KIRISHIMA

QUIRK

HARDENING

He makes his body hard by tensing up!! But it's hard to keep moving around while keeping up the hardness! He can maintain that ordinary hard state for about ten minutes, but the "unbreakable" form we saw recently is only available for 30 to 40 seconds at a time! He needs to breathe for a second or two after releasing the hardness, so if you want to beat him, that's your chance! Aim for his chin!!

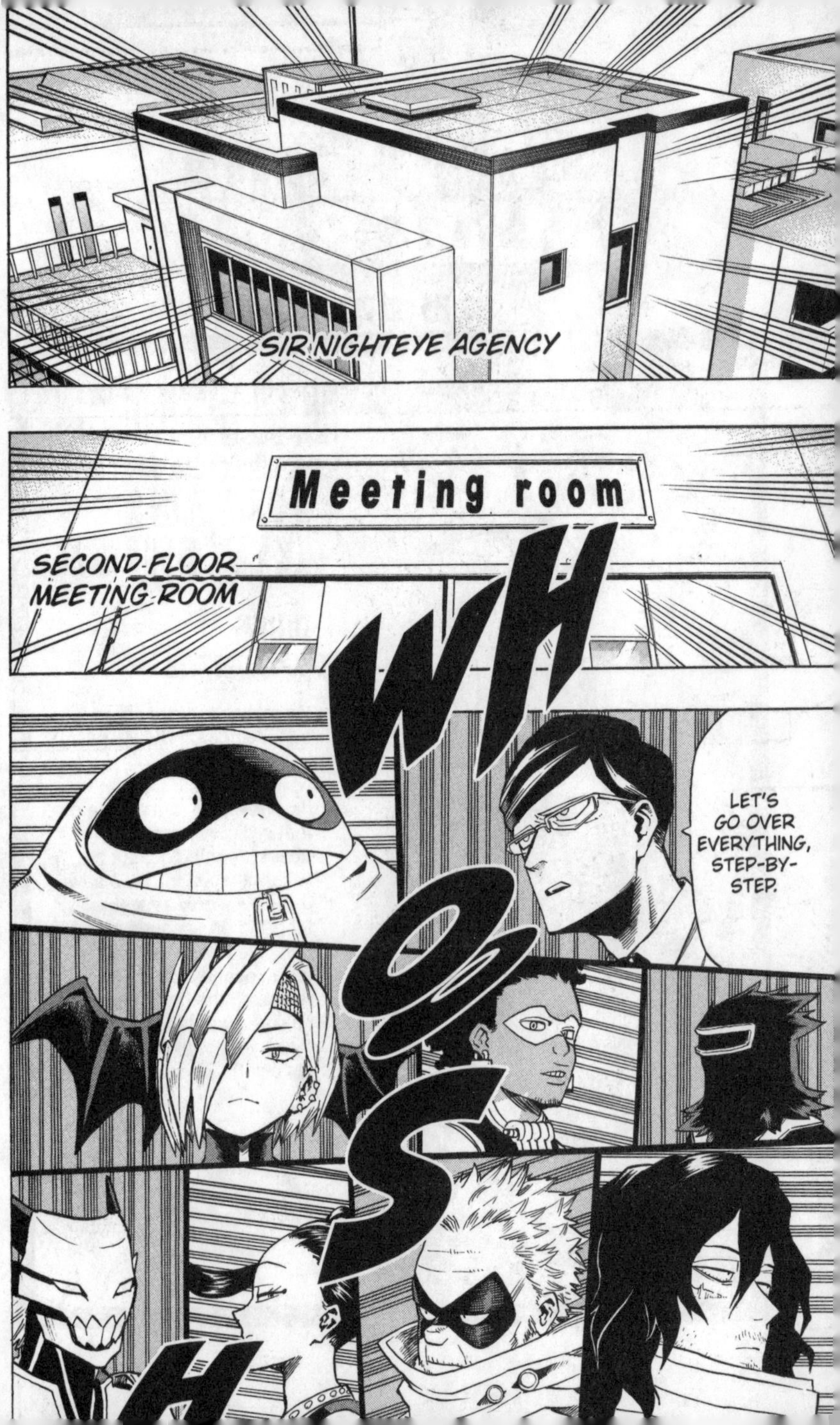
SIR NIGHTEYE AGENCY
Meeting room
SECOND-FLOOR MEETING-ROOM
WHOOSH
LET'S GO OVER EVERYTHING, STEP-BY-STEP.

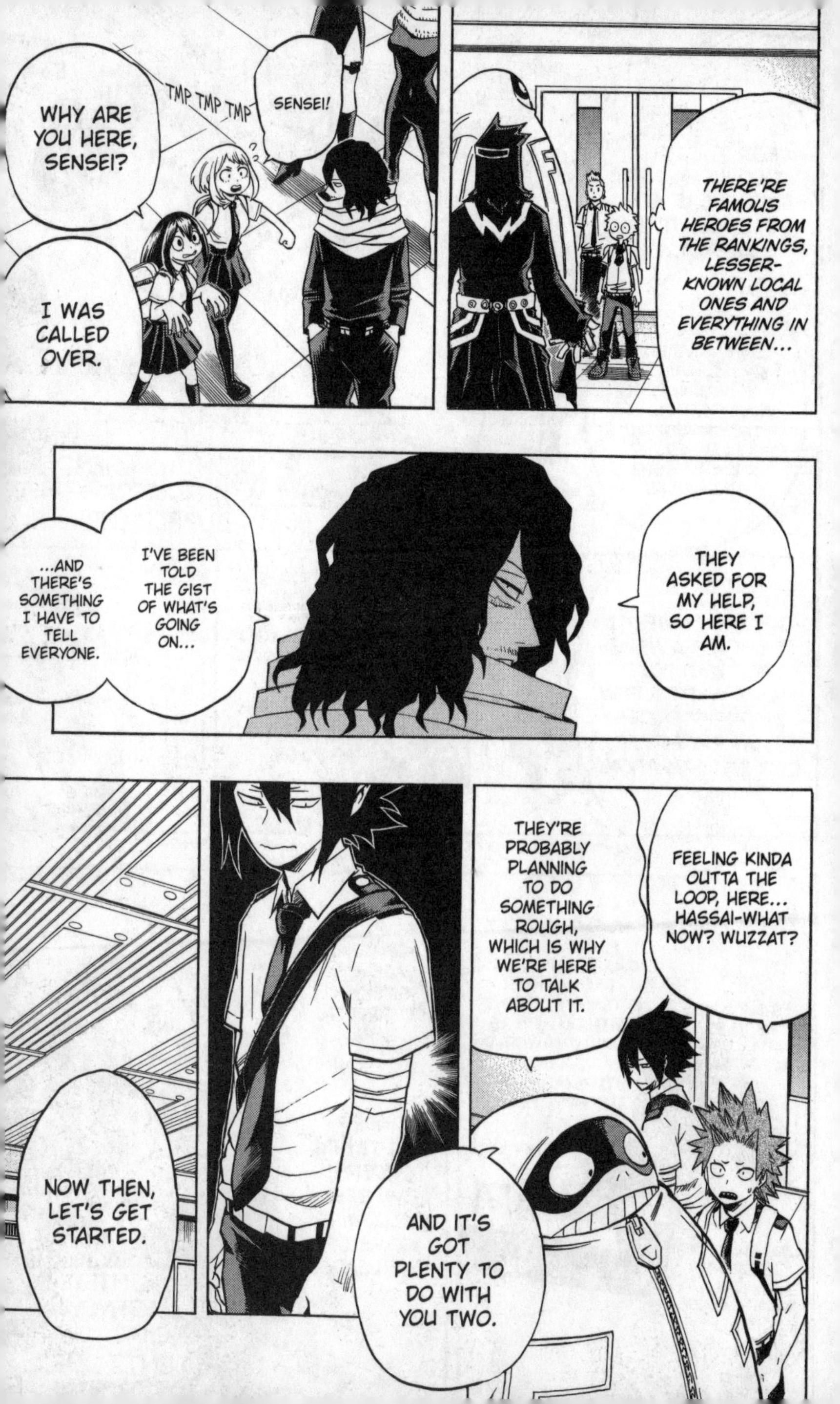
THERE'RE FAMOUS HEROES FROM THE RANKINGS, LESSER-KNOWN LOCAL ONES AND EVERYTHING IN BETWEEN...
SENSEI!
TMP TMP TMP
WHY ARE YOU HERE, SENSEI?
I WAS CALLED OVER.
THEY ASKED FOR MY HELP, SO HERE I AM.
I'VE BEEN TOLD THE GIST OF WHAT'S GOING ON...
...AND THERE'S SOMETHING I HAVE TO TELL EVERYONE.
FEELING KINDA OUTTA THE LOOP, HERE... HASSAI-WHAT NOW? WUZZAT?
THEY'RE PROBABLY PLANNING TO DO SOMETHING ROUGH, WHICH IS WHY WE'RE HERE TO TALK ABOUT IT.
AND IT'S GOT PLENTY TO DO WITH YOU TWO.
NOW THEN, LET'S GET STARTED.

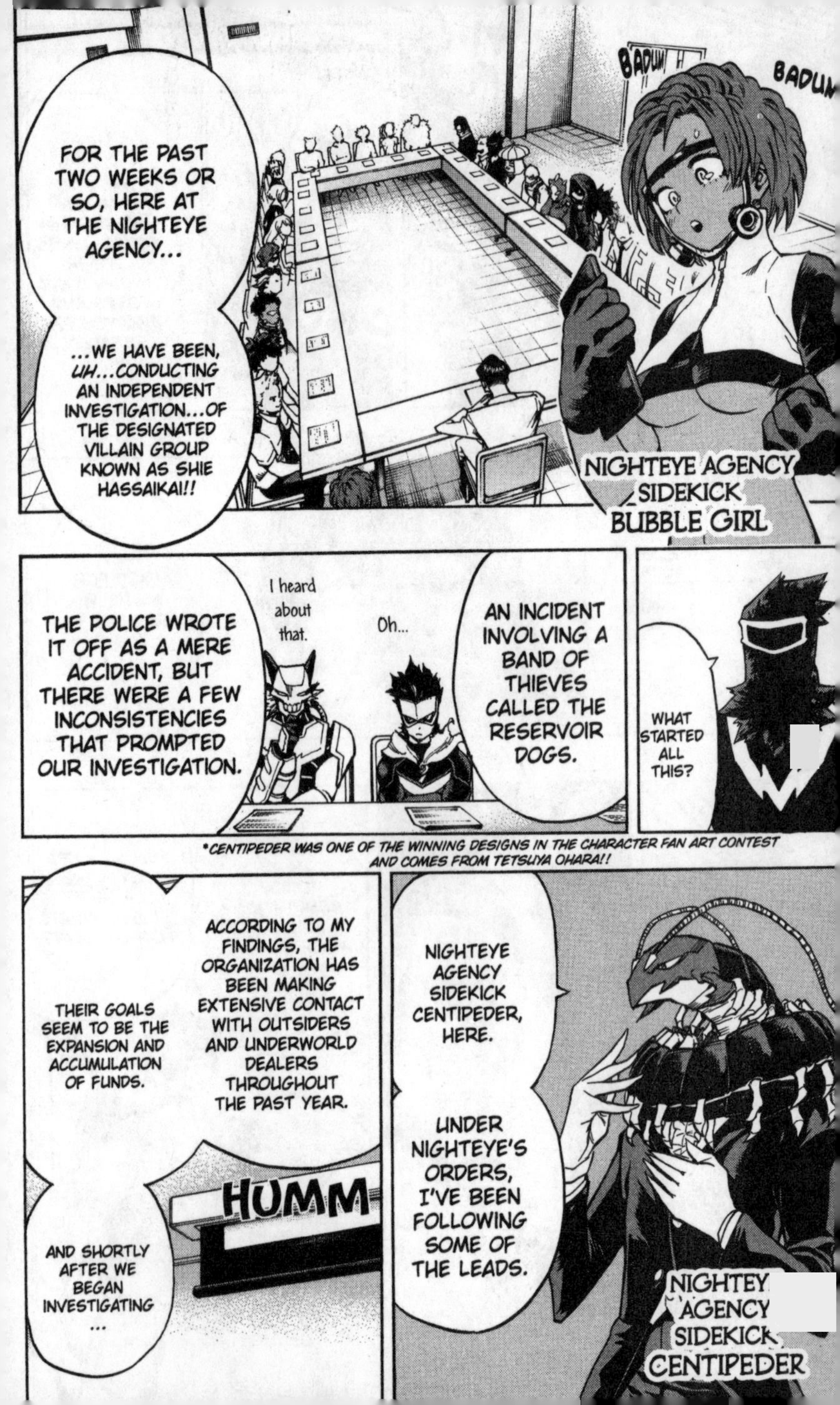
BADUM
BADUM
FOR THE PAST TWO WEEKS OR SO, HERE AT THE NIGHTEYE AGENCY...
...WE HAVE BEEN, UH...CONDUCTING AN INDEPENDENT INVESTIGATION...OF THE DESIGNATED VILLAIN GROUP KNOWN AS SHIE HASSAIKAI!!
NIGHTEYE AGENCY SIDEKICK BUBBLE GIRL
WHAT STARTED ALL THIS?
AN INCIDENT INVOLVING A BAND OF THIEVES CALLED THE RESERVOIR DOGS.
Oh...
I heard about that.
THE POLICE WROTE IT OFF AS A MERE ACCIDENT, BUT THERE WERE A FEW INCONSISTENCIES THAT PROMPTED OUR INVESTIGATION.
NIGHTEYE AGENCY SIDEKICK CENTIPEDER, HERE.
UNDER NIGHTEYE'S ORDERS, I'VE BEEN FOLLOWING SOME OF THE LEADS.
NIGHTEY
AGENCY
SIDEKICK
CENTIPEDER
ACCORDING TO MY FINDINGS, THE ORGANIZATION HAS BEEN MAKING EXTENSIVE CONTACT WITH OUTSIDERS AND UNDERWORLD DEALERS THROUGHOUT THE PAST YEAR.
THEIR GOALS SEEM TO BE THE EXPANSION AND ACCUMULATION OF FUNDS.
HUMM
AND SHORTLY AFTER WE BEGAN INVESTIGATING...

*CENTIPEDER WAS ONE OF THE WINNING DESIGNS IN THE CHARACTER FAN ART CONTEST AND COMES FROM TETSUYA OHARA!!

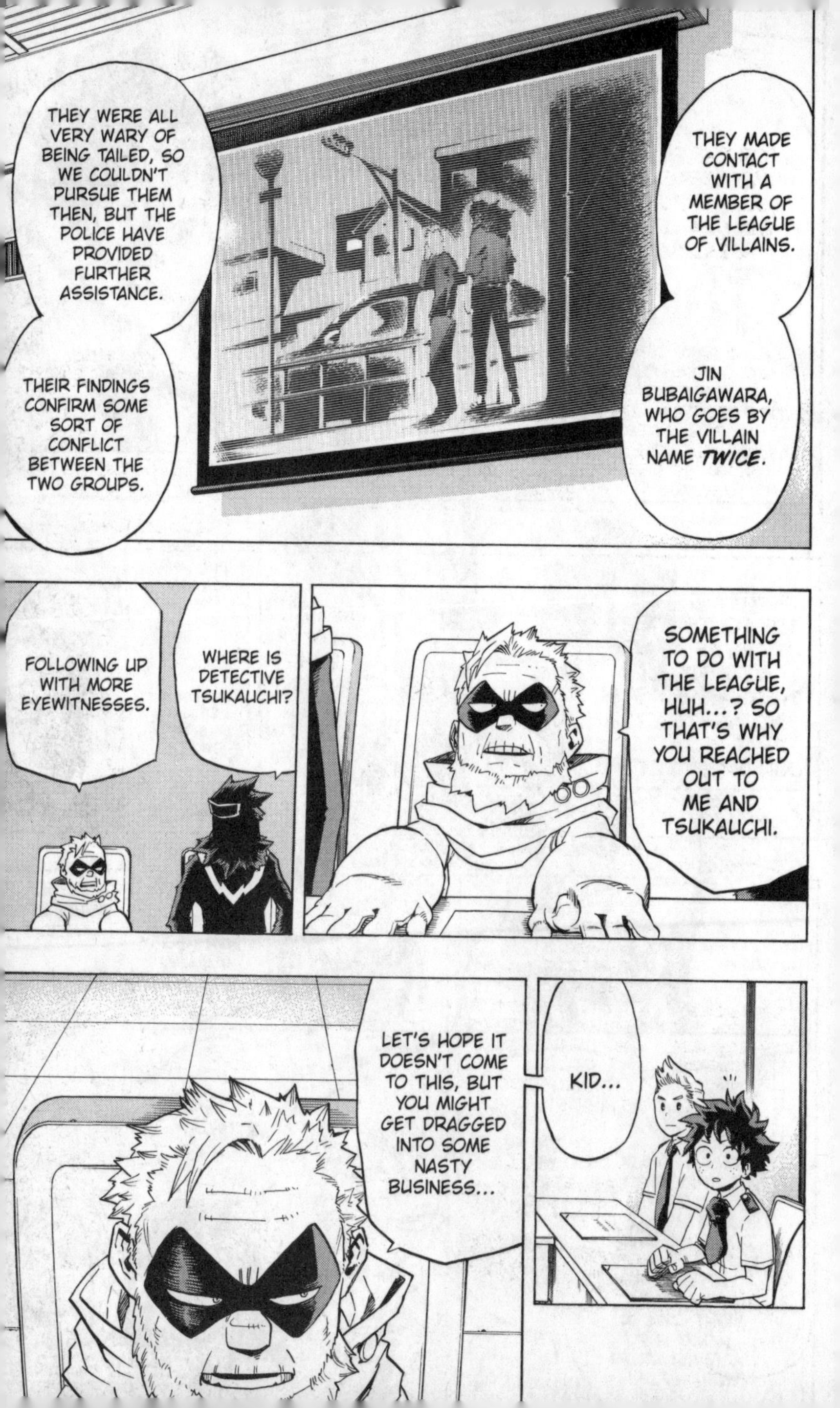
THEY MADE CONTACT WITH A MEMBER OF THE LEAGUE OF VILLAINS.
JIN BUBAIGAWARA, WHO GOES BY THE VILLAIN NAME *TWICE*.
THEY WERE ALL VERY WARY OF BEING TAILED, SO WE COULDN'T PURSUE THEM THEN, BUT THE POLICE HAVE PROVIDED FURTHER ASSISTANCE.
THEIR FINDINGS CONFIRM SOME SORT OF CONFLICT BETWEEN THE TWO GROUPS.
SOMETHING TO DO WITH THE LEAGUE, HUH...? SO THAT'S WHY YOU REACHED OUT TO ME AND TSUKAUCHI.
WHERE IS DETECTIVE TSUKAUCHI?
FOLLOWING UP WITH MORE EYEWITNESSES.
KID...
LET'S HOPE IT DOESN'T COME TO THIS, BUT YOU MIGHT GET DRAGGED INTO SOME NASTY BUSINESS...

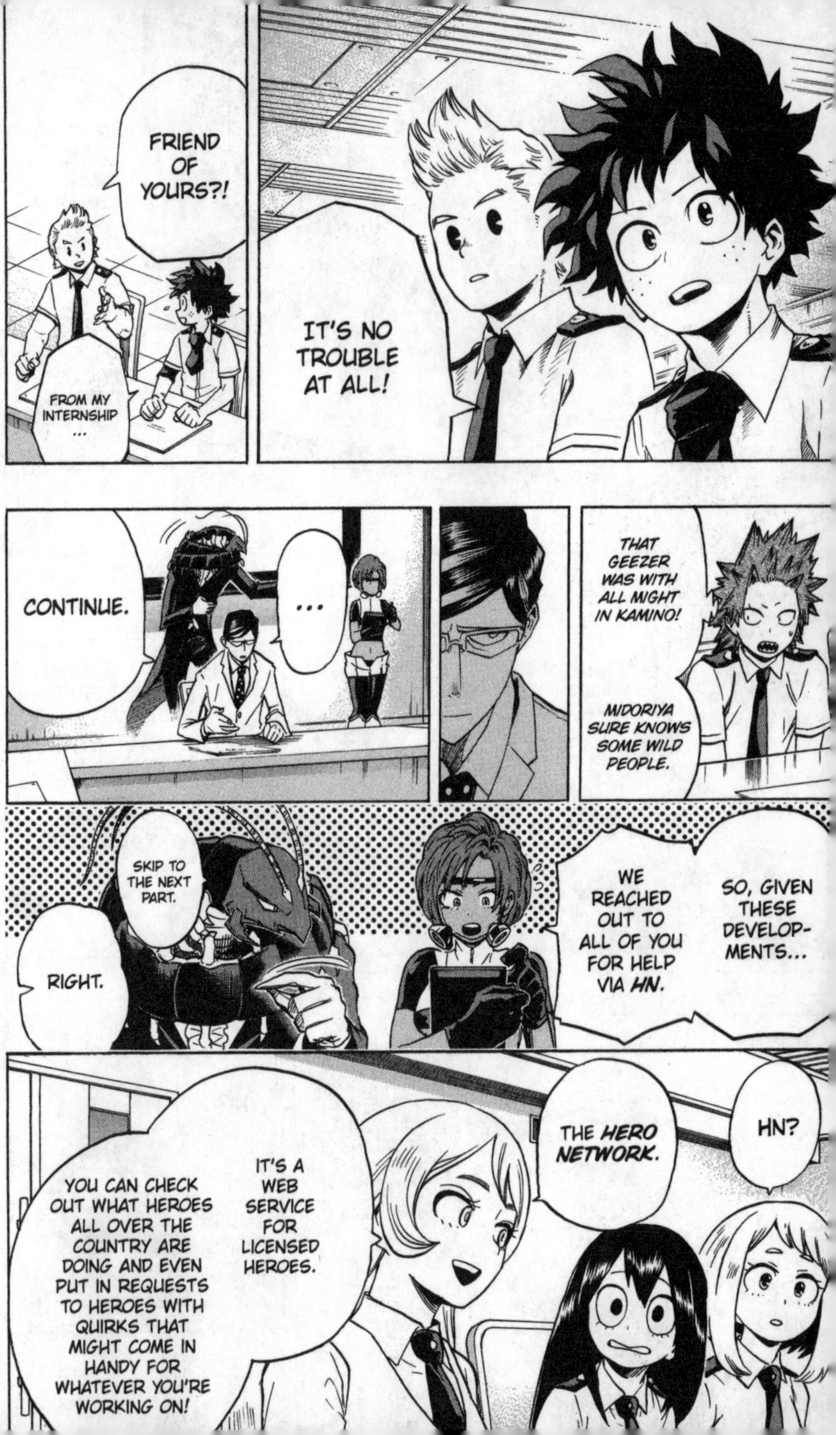
IT'S NO TROUBLE AT ALL!
FRIEND OF YOURS?!
FROM MY INTERNSHIP ...
THAT GEEZER WAS WITH ALL MIGHT IN KAMINO!
MIDORIYA SURE KNOWS SOME WILD PEOPLE.
...
CONTINUE.
SO, GIVEN THESE DEVELOPMENTS...
WE REACHED OUT TO ALL OF YOU FOR HELP VIA *HN*.
SKIP TO THE NEXT PART.
RIGHT.
HN?
THE *HERO NETWORK*.
IT'S A WEB SERVICE FOR LICENSED HEROES.
YOU CAN CHECK OUT WHAT HEROES ALL OVER THE COUNTRY ARE DOING AND EVEN PUT IN REQUESTS TO HEROES WITH QUIRKS THAT MIGHT COME IN HANDY FOR WHATEVER YOU'RE WORKING ON!

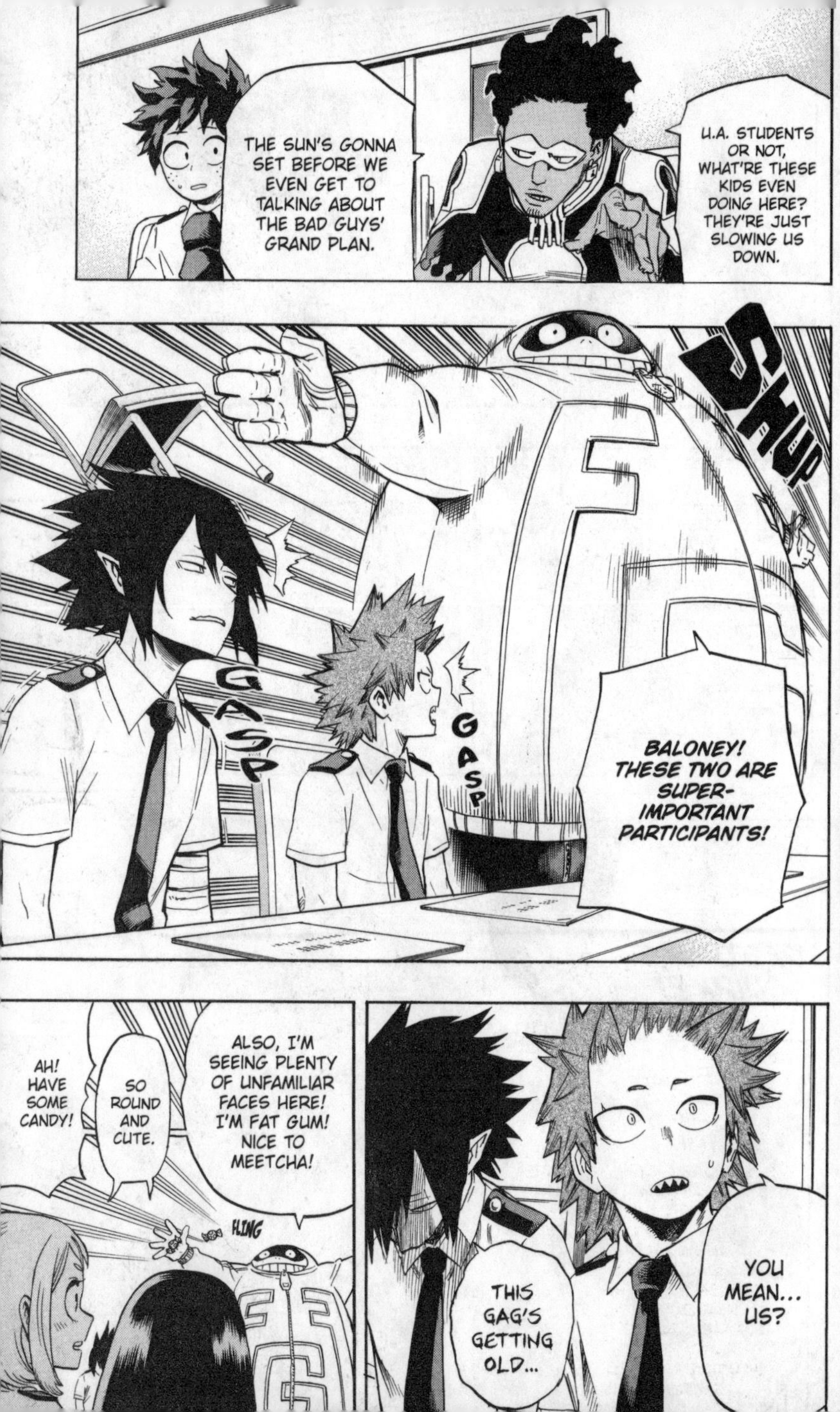
U.A. STUDENTS OR NOT, WHAT'RE THESE KIDS EVEN DOING HERE? THEY'RE JUST SLOWING US DOWN.
THE SUN'S GONNA SET BEFORE WE EVEN GET TO TALKING ABOUT THE BAD GUYS' GRAND PLAN.
SHUP
BALONEY! THESE TWO ARE SUPER-IMPORTANT PARTICIPANTS!
GASP
GASP
YOU MEAN... US?
THIS GAG'S GETTING OLD...
ALSO, I'M SEEING PLENTY OF UNFAMILIAR FACES HERE! I'M FAT GUM! NICE TO MEETCHA!
SO ROUND AND CUTE.
AH! HAVE SOME CANDY!
FLING

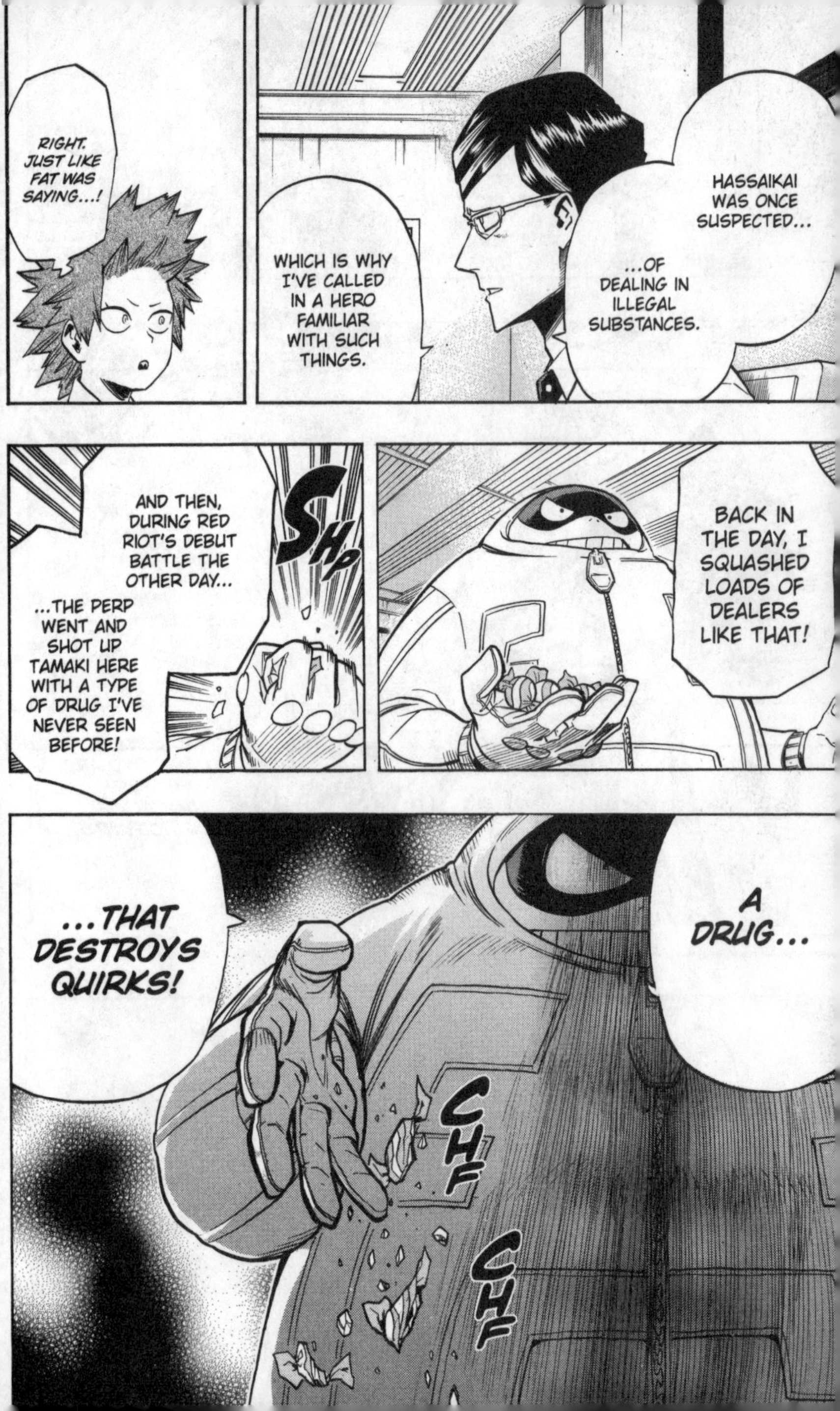
HASSAIKAI WAS ONCE SUSPECTED...
...OF DEALING IN ILLEGAL SUBSTANCES.
WHICH IS WHY I'VE CALLED IN A HERO FAMILIAR WITH SUCH THINGS.
RIGHT. JUST LIKE FAT WAS SAYING...!
BACK IN THE DAY, I SQUASHED LOADS OF DEALERS LIKE THAT!
SHP
AND THEN, DURING RED RIOT'S DEBUT BATTLE THE OTHER DAY...
...THE PERP WENT AND SHOT UP TAMAKI HERE WITH A TYPE OF DRUG I'VE NEVER SEEN BEFORE!
A DRUG...
...THAT DESTROYS QUIRKS!
CHF
CHF

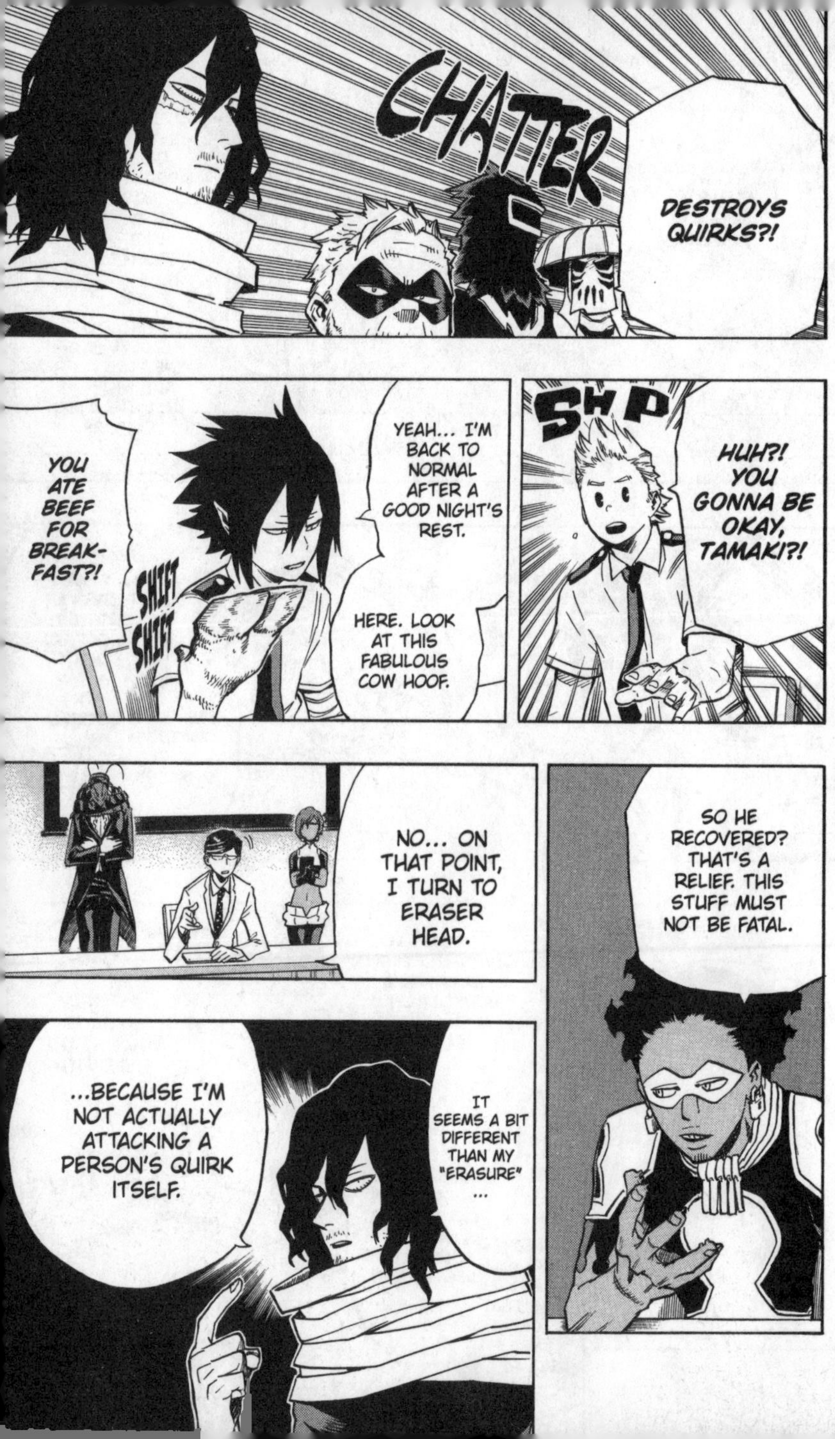
CHATTER
DESTROYS QUIRKS?!
SHP
HUH?! YOU GONNA BE OKAY, TAMAKI?!
YEAH... I'M BACK TO NORMAL AFTER A GOOD NIGHT'S REST.
HERE. LOOK AT THIS FABULOUS COW HOOF.
SHIFT SHIFT
YOU ATE BEEF FOR BREAK-FAST?!
SO HE RECOVERED? THAT'S A RELIEF. THIS STUFF MUST NOT BE FATAL.
NO... ON THAT POINT, I TURN TO ERASER HEAD.
IT SEEMS A BIT DIFFERENT THAN MY "ERASURE" ...
...BECAUSE I'M NOT ACTUALLY ATTACKING A PERSON'S QUIRK ITSELF.

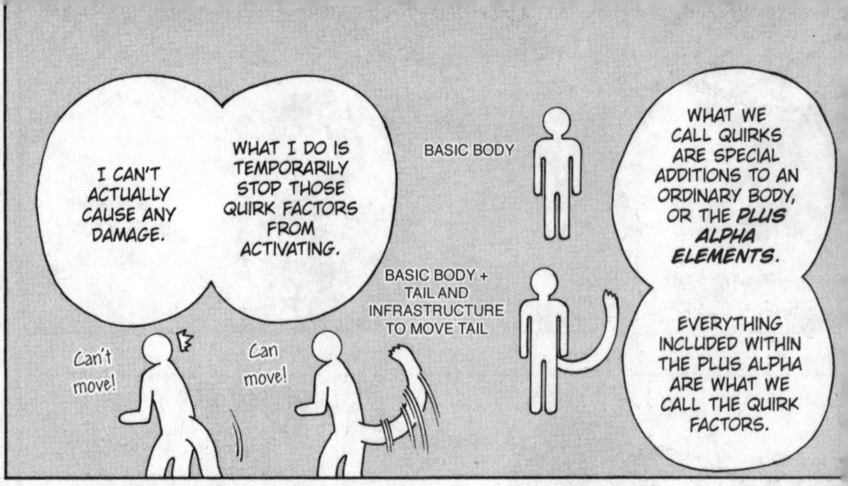
WHAT WE CALL QUIRKS ARE SPECIAL ADDITIONS TO AN ORDINARY BODY, OR THE PLUS ALPHA ELEMENTS.
EVERYTHING INCLUDED WITHIN THE PLUS ALPHA ARE WHAT WE CALL THE QUIRK FACTORS.
BASIC BODY
BASIC BODY + TAIL AND INFRASTRUCTURE TO MOVE TAIL
WHAT I DO IS TEMPORARILY STOP THOSE QUIRK FACTORS FROM ACTIVATING.
I CAN'T ACTUALLY CAUSE ANY DAMAGE.
Can move!
Can't move!
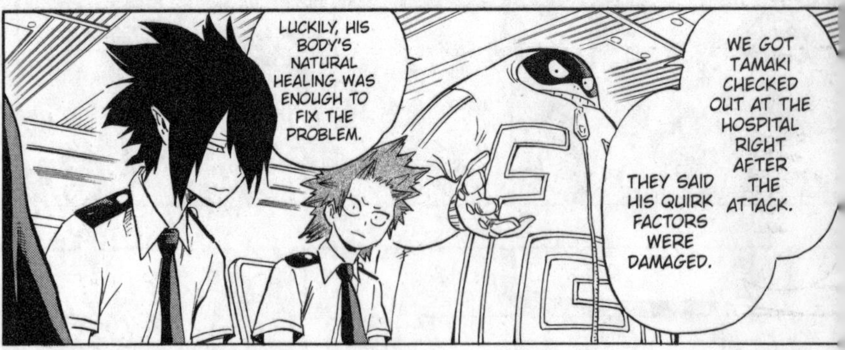
WE GOT TAMAKI CHECKED OUT AT THE HOSPITAL RIGHT AFTER THE ATTACK.
THEY SAID HIS QUIRK FACTORS WERE DAMAGED.
LUCKILY, HIS BODY'S NATURAL HEALING WAS ENOUGH TO FIX THE PROBLEM.
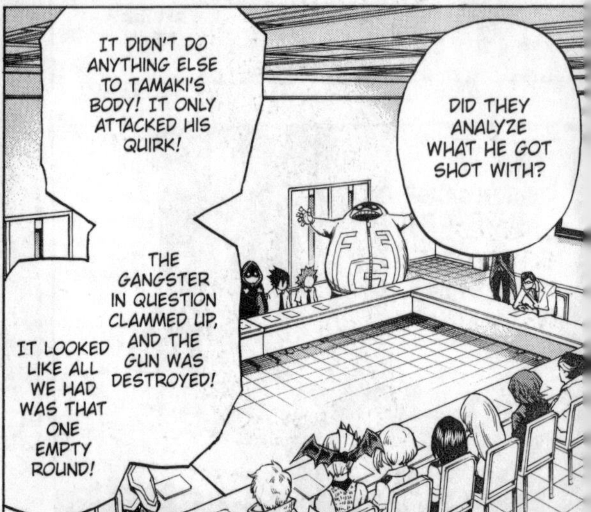
DID THEY ANALYZE WHAT HE GOT SHOT WITH?
IT DIDN'T DO ANYTHING ELSE TO TAMAKI'S BODY! IT ONLY ATTACKED HIS QUIRK!
THE GANGSTER IN QUESTION CLAMMED UP, AND THE GUN WAS DESTROYED!
IT LOOKED LIKE ALL WE HAD WAS THAT ONE EMPTY ROUND!
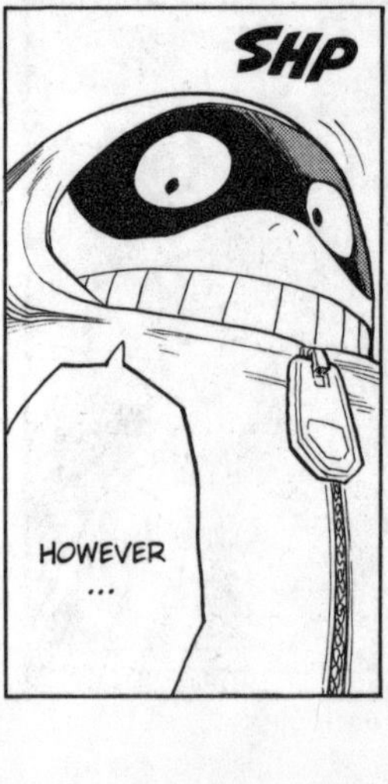
SHP
HOWEVER ...

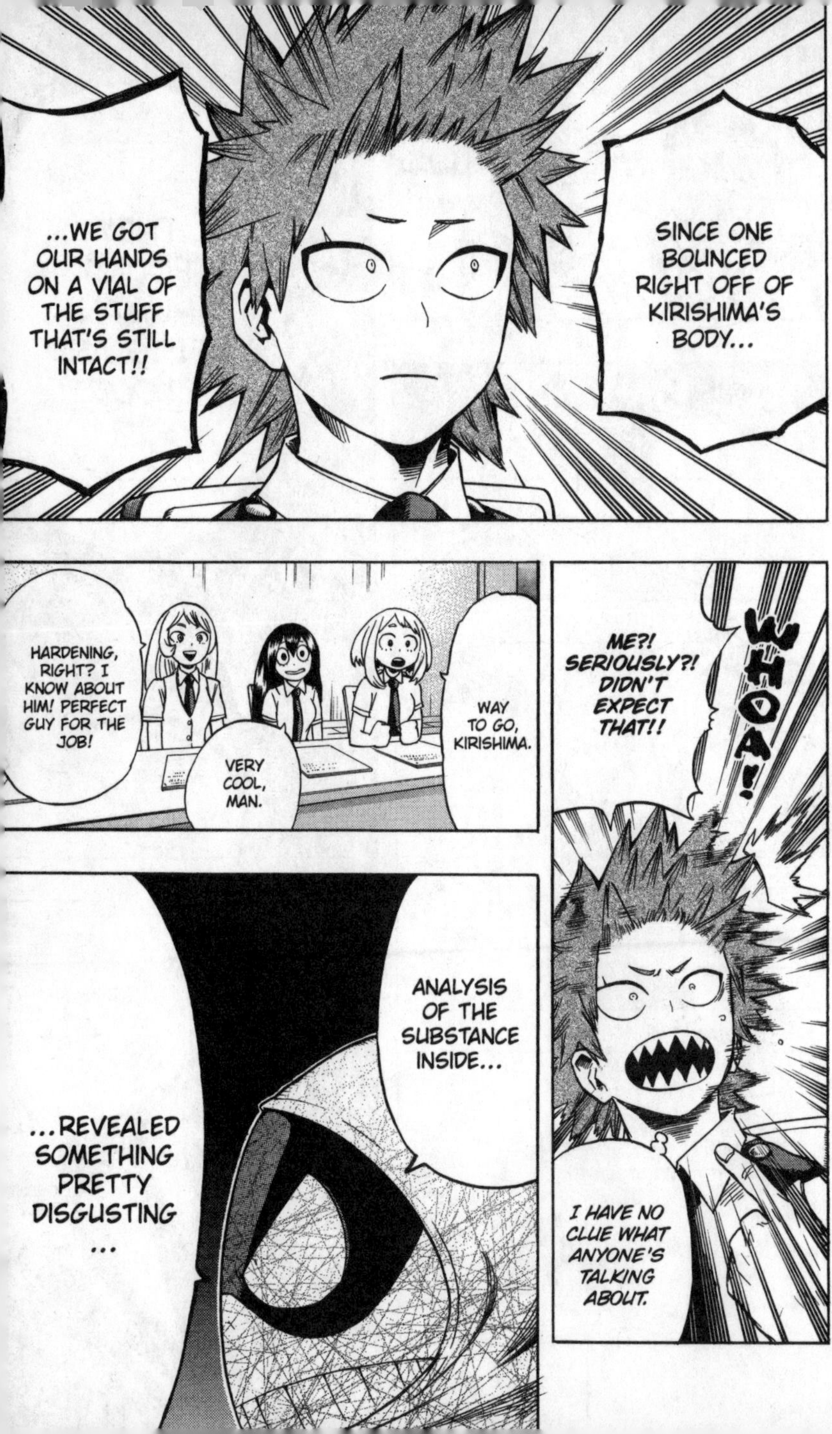
SINCE ONE BOUNCED RIGHT OFF OF KIRISHIMA'S BODY...
...WE GOT OUR HANDS ON A VIAL OF THE STUFF THAT'S STILL INTACT!!
WHOA!
ME?! SERIOUSLY?! DIDN'T EXPECT THAT!!
I HAVE NO CLUE WHAT ANYONE'S TALKING ABOUT.
WAY TO GO, KIRISHIMA.
VERY COOL, MAN.
HARDENING, RIGHT? I KNOW ABOUT HIM! PERFECT GUY FOR THE JOB!
ANALYSIS OF THE SUBSTANCE INSIDE...
...REVEALED SOMETHING PRETTY DISGUSTING ...

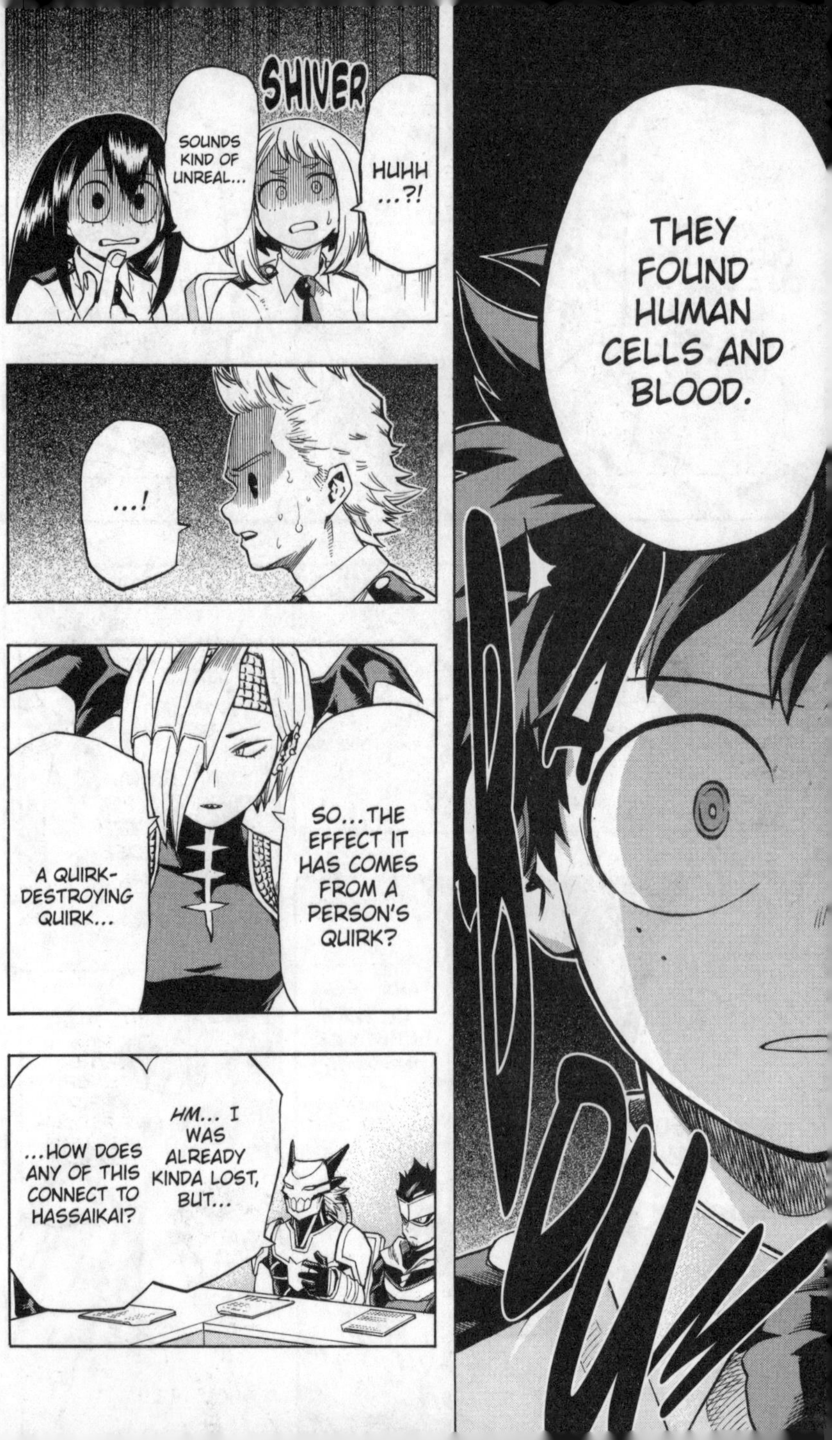
THEY FOUND HUMAN CELLS AND BLOOD.
SHIVER
HUHH ...?!
SOUNDS KIND OF UNREAL...
...!
SO...THE EFFECT IT HAS COMES FROM A PERSON'S QUIRK?
A QUIRK-DESTROYING QUIRK...
HM... I WAS ALREADY KINDA LOST, BUT...
...HOW DOES ANY OF THIS CONNECT TO HASSAIKAI?

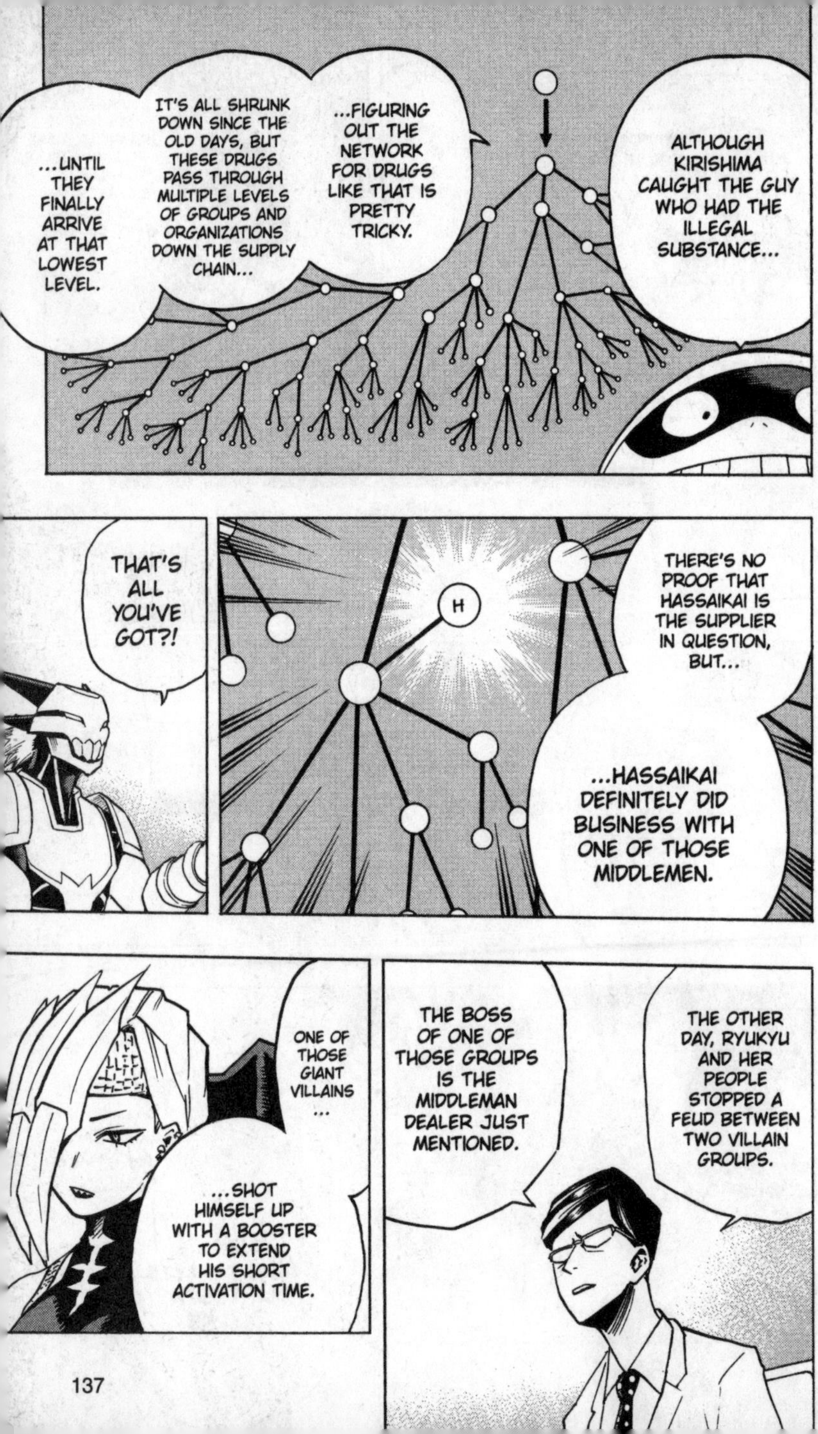
ALTHOUGH KIRISHIMA CAUGHT THE GUY WHO HAD THE ILLEGAL SUBSTANCE...
...FIGURING OUT THE NETWORK FOR DRUGS LIKE THAT IS PRETTY TRICKY.
IT'S ALL SHRUNK DOWN SINCE THE OLD DAYS, BUT THESE DRUGS PASS THROUGH MULTIPLE LEVELS OF GROUPS AND ORGANIZATIONS DOWN THE SUPPLY CHAIN...
...UNTIL THEY FINALLY ARRIVE AT THAT LOWEST LEVEL.
H
THERE'S NO PROOF THAT HASSAIKAI IS THE SUPPLIER IN QUESTION, BUT...
...HASSAIKAI DEFINITELY DID BUSINESS WITH ONE OF THOSE MIDDLEMEN.
THAT'S ALL YOU'VE GOT?!
THE OTHER DAY, RYUKYU AND HER PEOPLE STOPPED A FEUD BETWEEN TWO VILLAIN GROUPS.
THE BOSS OF ONE OF THOSE GROUPS IS THE MIDDLEMAN DEALER JUST MENTIONED.
ONE OF THOSE GIANT VILLAINS...
...SHOT HIMSELF UP WITH A BOOSTER TO EXTEND HIS SHORT ACTIVATION TIME.

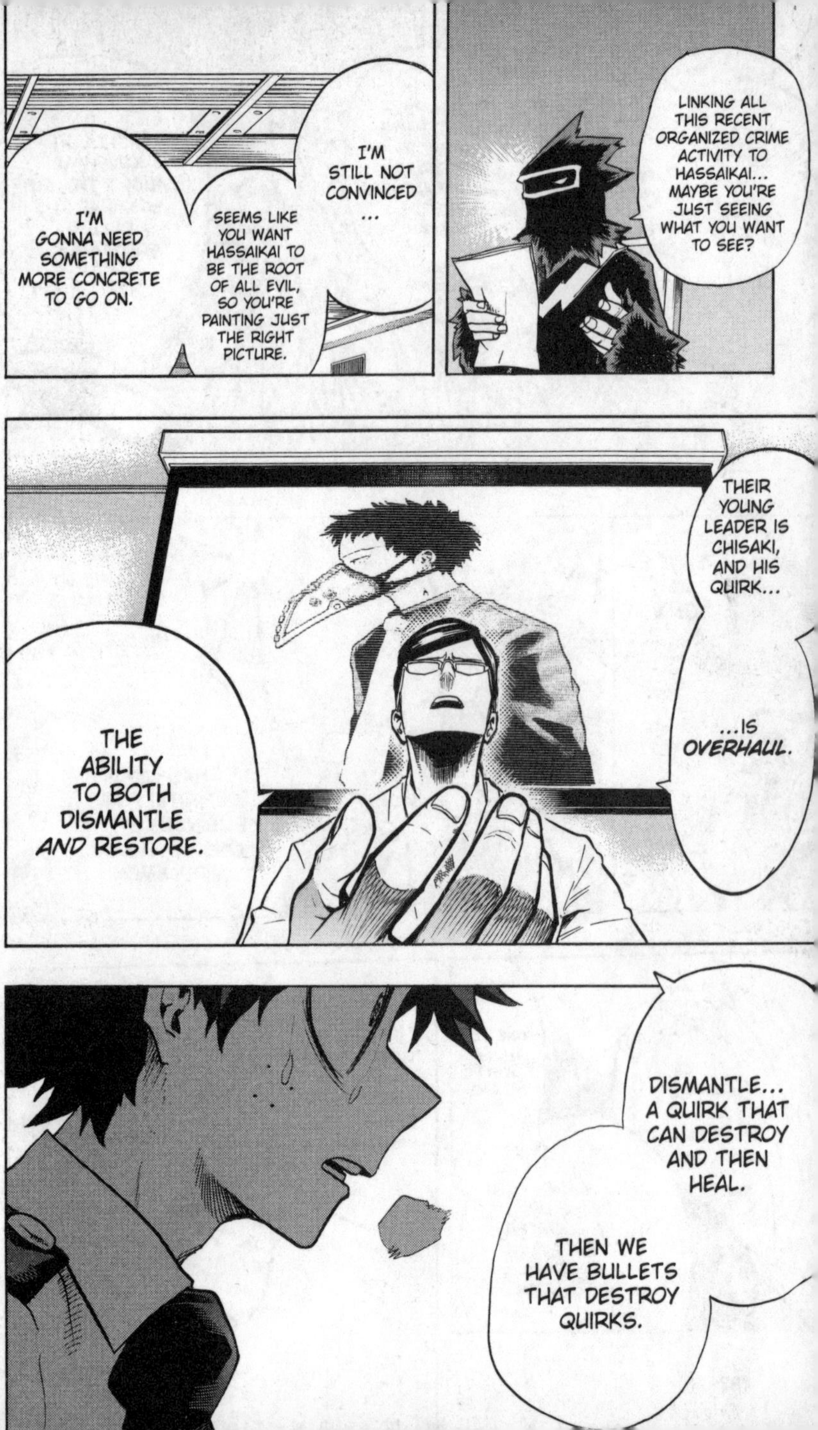
LINKING ALL THIS RECENT ORGANIZED CRIME ACTIVITY TO HASSAIKAI... MAYBE YOU'RE JUST SEEING WHAT YOU WANT TO SEE?
I'M STILL NOT CONVINCED...
SEEMS LIKE YOU WANT HASSAIKAI TO BE THE ROOT OF ALL EVIL, SO YOU'RE PAINTING JUST THE RIGHT PICTURE.
I'M GONNA NEED SOMETHING MORE CONCRETE TO GO ON.
THEIR YOUNG LEADER IS CHISAKI, AND HIS QUIRK...
...IS *OVERHAUL.*
THE ABILITY TO BOTH DISMANTLE *AND* RESTORE.
DISMANTLE... A QUIRK THAT CAN DESTROY AND THEN HEAL.
THEN WE HAVE BULLETS THAT DESTROY QUIRKS.

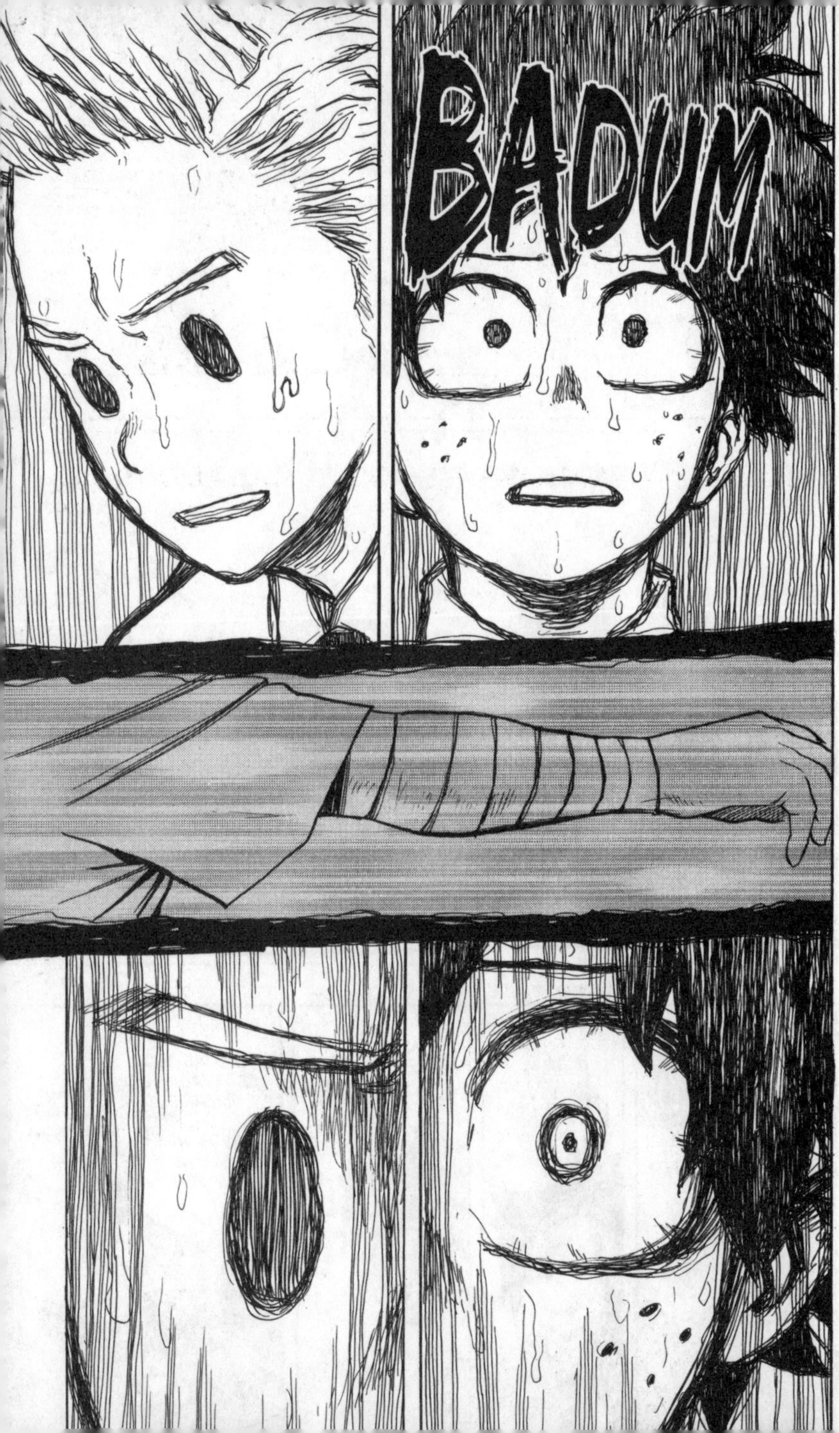
BADUM

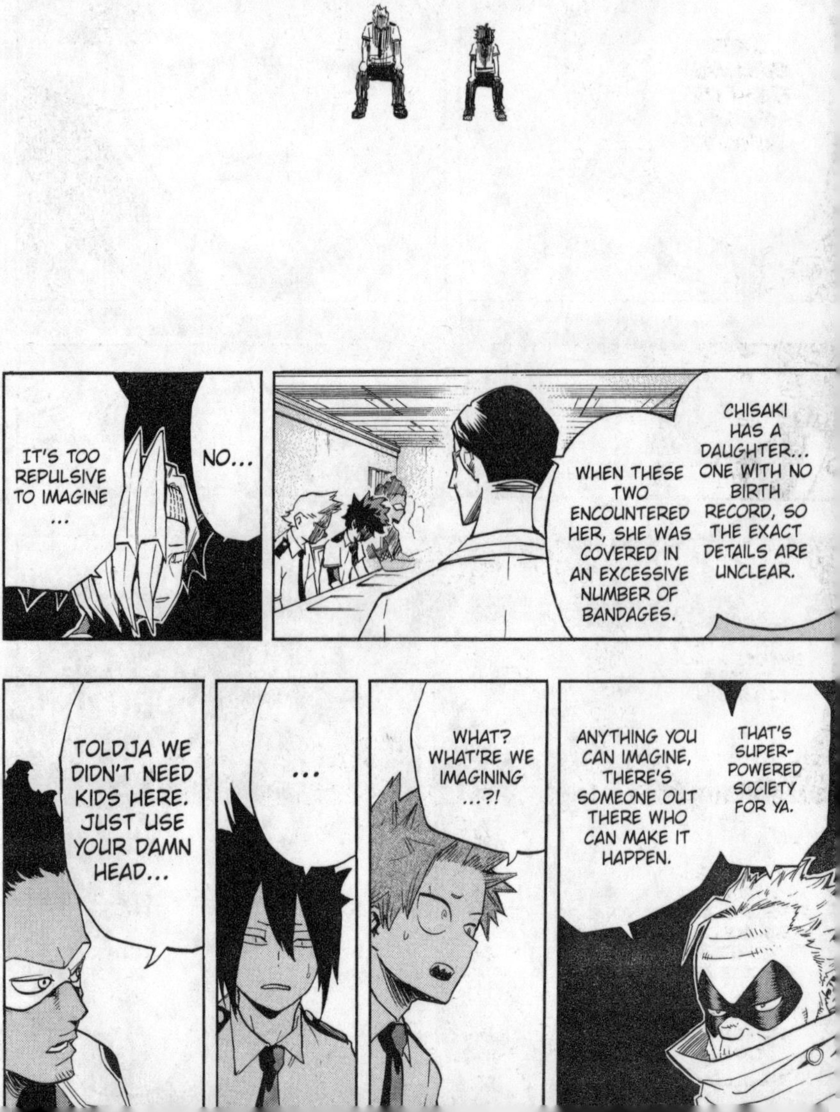
CHISAKI HAS A DAUGHTER... ONE WITH NO BIRTH RECORD, SO THE EXACT DETAILS ARE UNCLEAR.
WHEN THESE TWO ENCOUNTERED HER, SHE WAS COVERED IN AN EXCESSIVE NUMBER OF BANDAGES.
NO...
IT'S TOO REPULSIVE TO IMAGINE ...
THAT'S SUPER-POWERED SOCIETY FOR YA.
ANYTHING YOU CAN IMAGINE, THERE'S SOMEONE OUT THERE WHO CAN MAKE IT HAPPEN.
WHAT? WHAT'RE WE IMAGINING ...?!
...
TOLDJA WE DIDN'T NEED KIDS HERE. JUST USE YOUR DAMN HEAD...

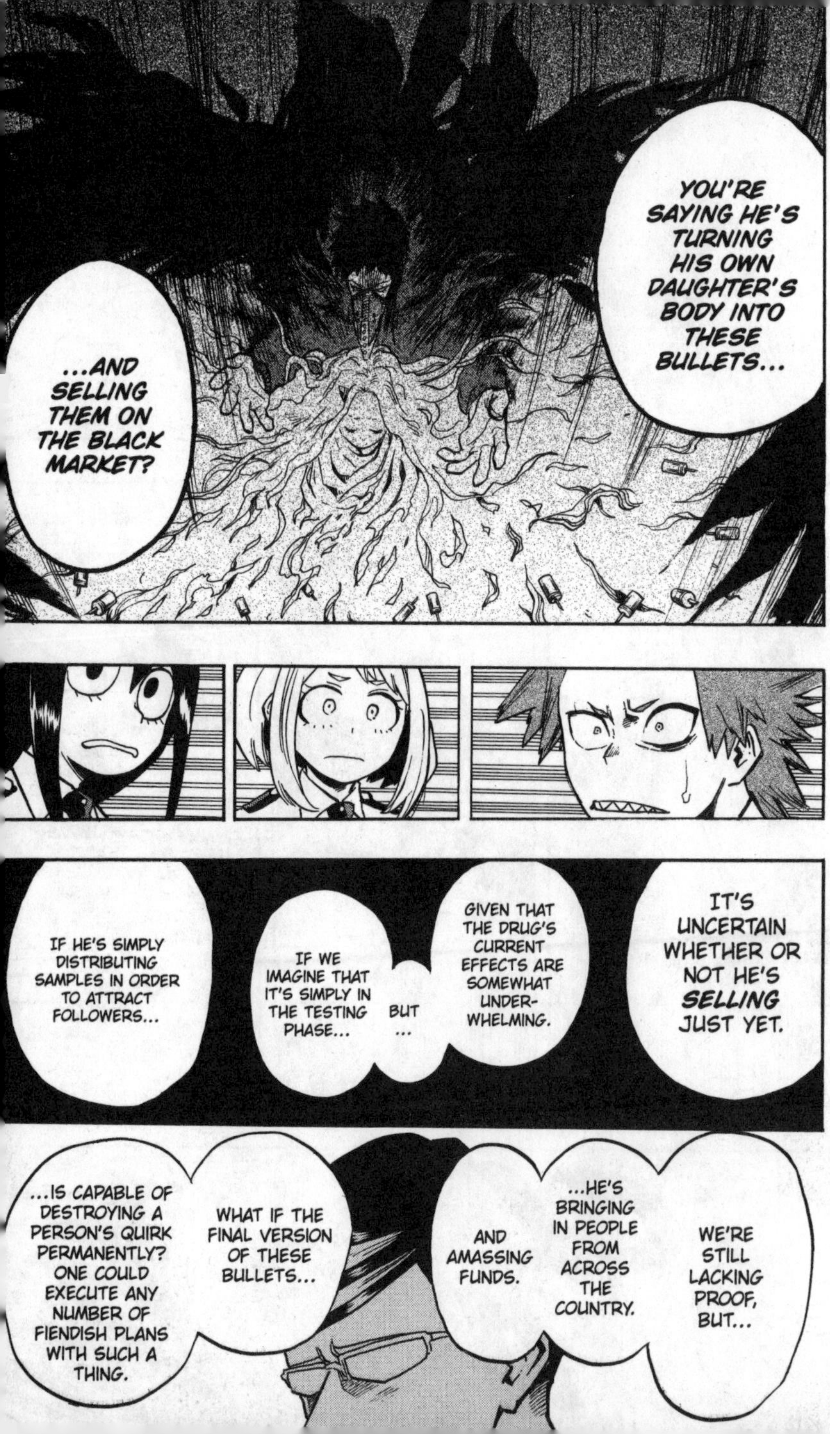
YOU'RE SAYING HE'S TURNING HIS OWN DAUGHTER'S BODY INTO THESE BULLETS...
...AND SELLING THEM ON THE BLACK MARKET?
IT'S UNCERTAIN WHETHER OR NOT HE'S *SELLING* JUST YET.
GIVEN THAT THE DRUG'S CURRENT EFFECTS ARE SOMEWHAT UNDER-WHELMING.
BUT...
IF WE IMAGINE THAT IT'S SIMPLY IN THE TESTING PHASE...
IF HE'S SIMPLY DISTRIBUTING SAMPLES IN ORDER TO ATTRACT FOLLOWERS...
WE'RE STILL LACKING PROOF, BUT...
...HE'S BRINGING IN PEOPLE FROM ACROSS THE COUNTRY.
AND AMASSING FUNDS.
WHAT IF THE FINAL VERSION OF THESE BULLETS...
...IS CAPABLE OF DESTROYING A PERSON'S QUIRK PERMANENTLY? ONE COULD EXECUTE ANY NUMBER OF FIENDISH PLANS WITH SUCH A THING.

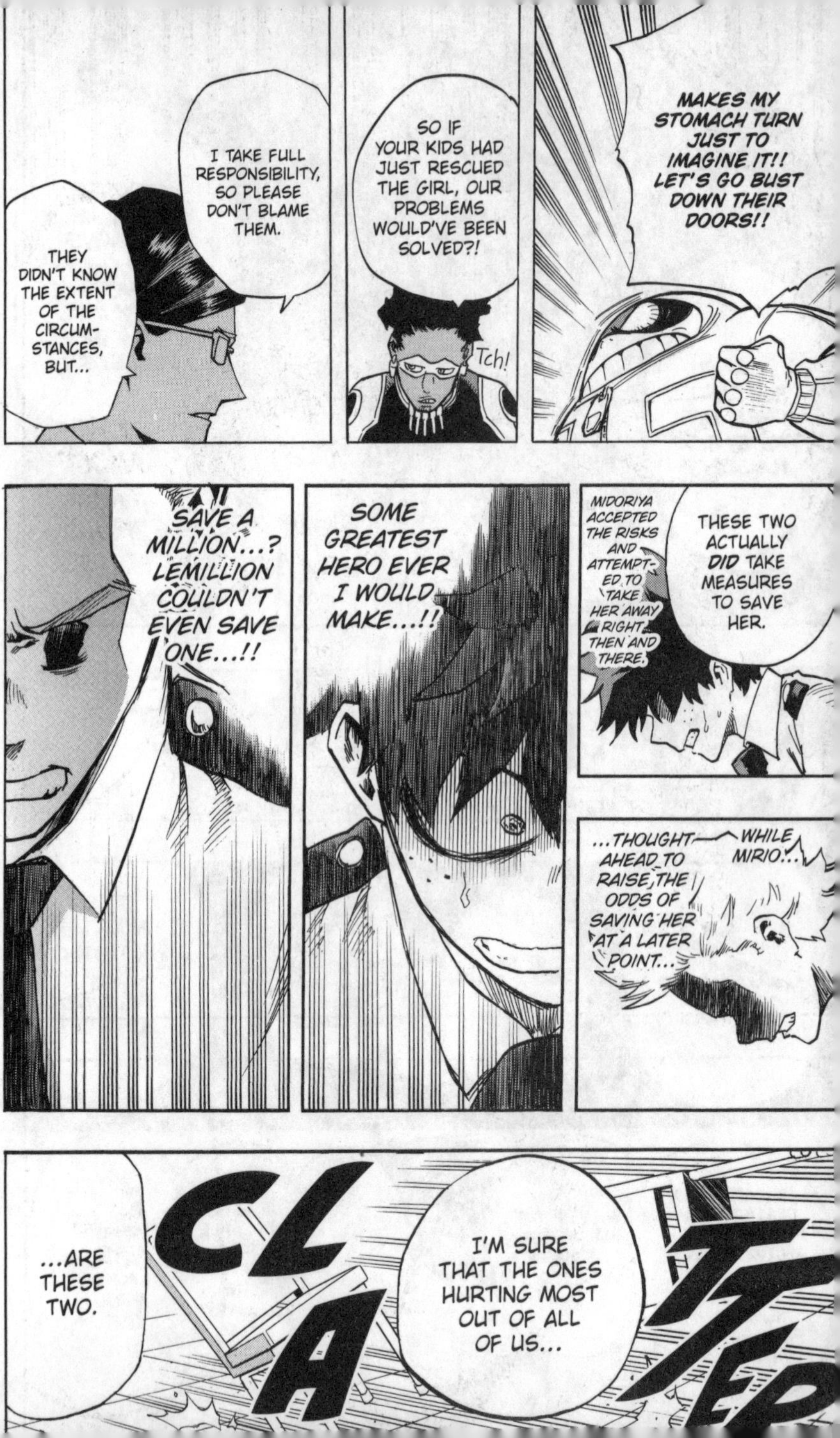
MAKES MY STOMACH TURN JUST TO IMAGINE IT!! LET'S GO BUST DOWN THEIR DOORS!!
SO IF YOUR KIDS HAD JUST RESCUED THE GIRL, OUR PROBLEMS WOULD'VE BEEN SOLVED?!
Tch!
I TAKE FULL RESPONSIBILITY, SO PLEASE DON'T BLAME THEM.
THEY DIDN'T KNOW THE EXTENT OF THE CIRCUM-STANCES, BUT...
THESE TWO ACTUALLY DID TAKE MEASURES TO SAVE HER.
MIDORIYA ACCEPTED THE RISKS AND ATTEMPT-ED TO TAKE HER AWAY RIGHT THEN AND THERE.
WHILE MIRIO...
...THOUGHT AHEAD TO RAISE THE ODDS OF SAVING HER AT A LATER POINT...
SOME GREATEST HERO EVER I WOULD MAKE...!!
SAVE A MILLION...? LEMILLION COULDN'T EVEN SAVE ONE...!!
CLATTER
I'M SURE THAT THE ONES HURTING MOST OUT OF ALL OF US...
...ARE THESE TWO.

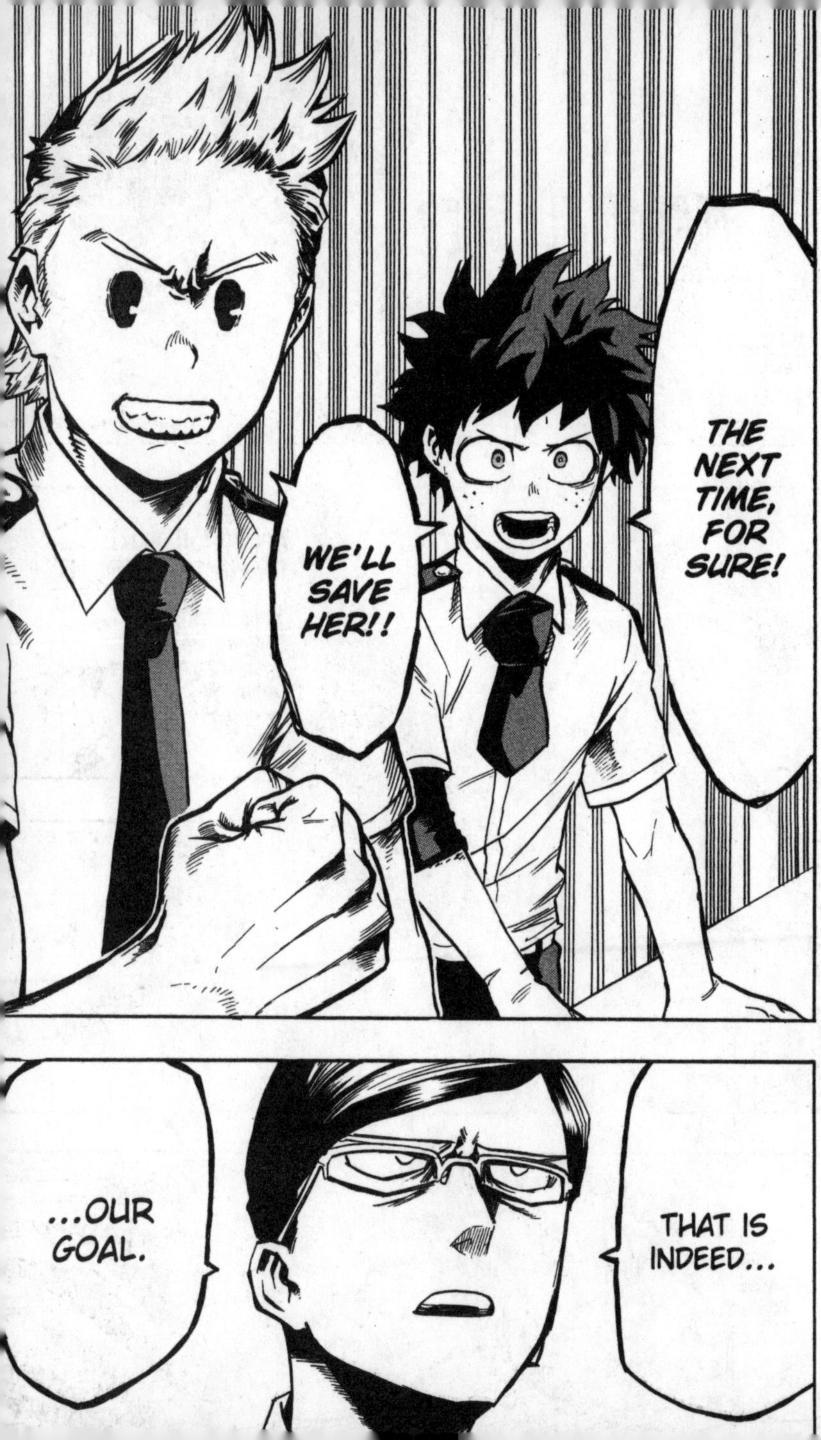

THE NEXT TIME, FOR SURE!
WE'LL SAVE HER!!
THAT IS INDEED...
...OUR GOAL.

HERO

FAT GUM [29]
[TAISHIRO TOYOMITSU]

STREET CLOTHES

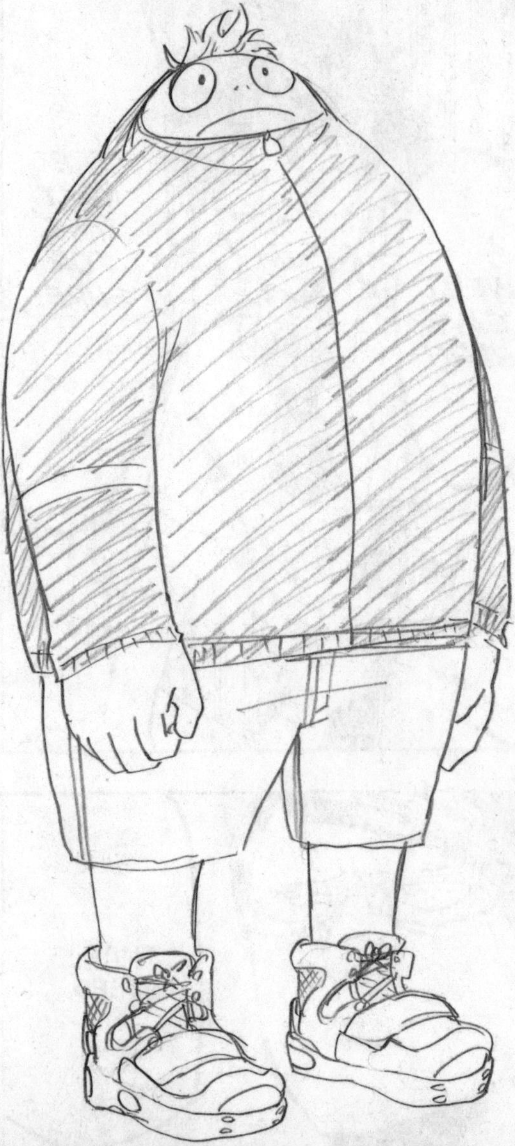

Birthday: 8/8
Height: 250 cm [?]
Favorite Thing: Takoyaki

THE TOYOMITSU

Drawing him is so fun. Definitely a good guy. I wanna climb on him and ride around.

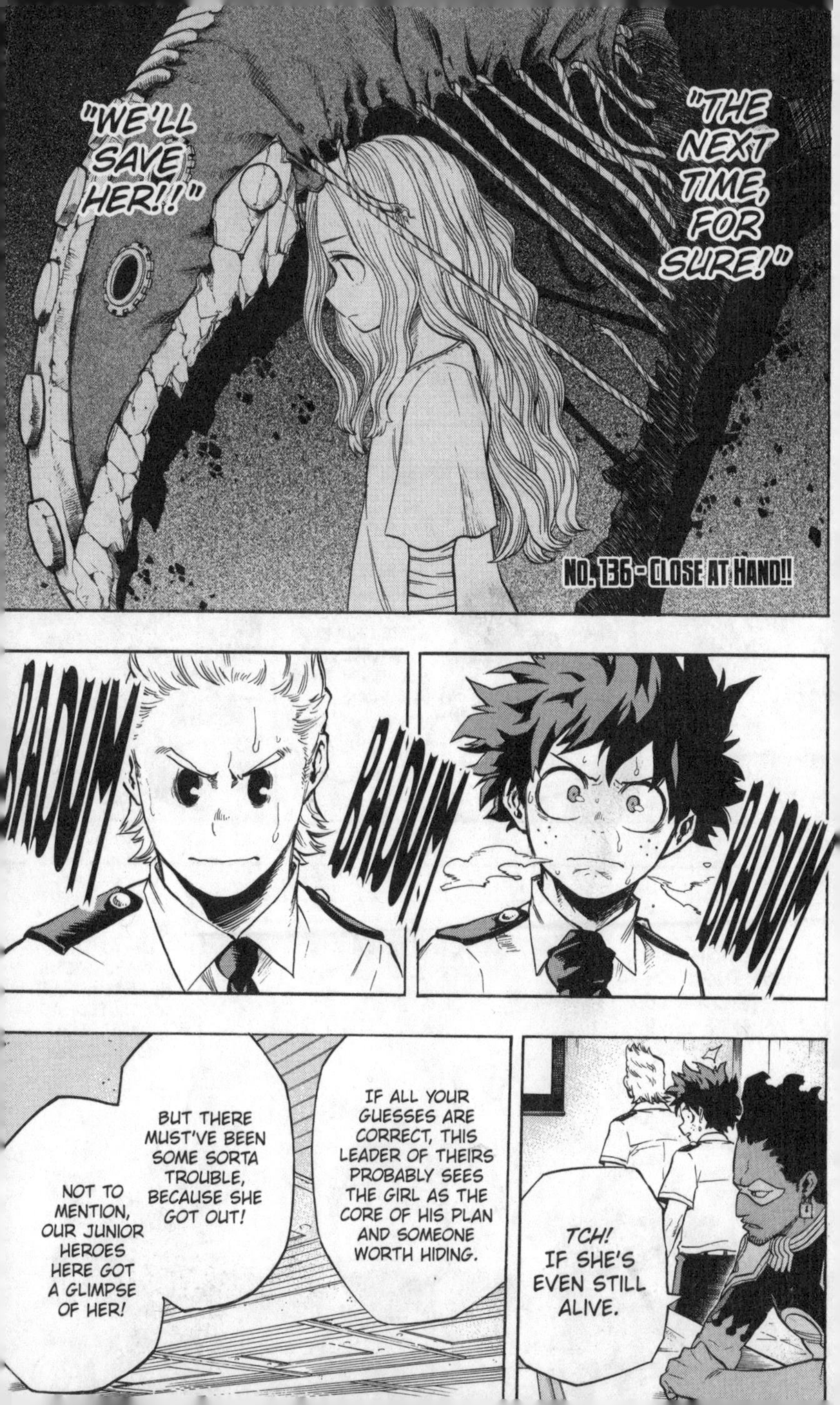
"THE NEXT TIME, FOR SURE!"
"WE'LL SAVE HER!!"
No. 136 - Close at Hand!!
BADUM
BADUM
BADUM
TCH! IF SHE'S EVEN STILL ALIVE.
IF ALL YOUR GUESSES ARE CORRECT, THIS LEADER OF THEIRS PROBABLY SEES THE GIRL AS THE CORE OF HIS PLAN AND SOMEONE WORTH HIDING.
BUT THERE MUST'VE BEEN SOME SORTA TROUBLE, BECAUSE SHE GOT OUT!
NOT TO MENTION, OUR JUNIOR HEROES HERE GOT A GLIMPSE OF HER!

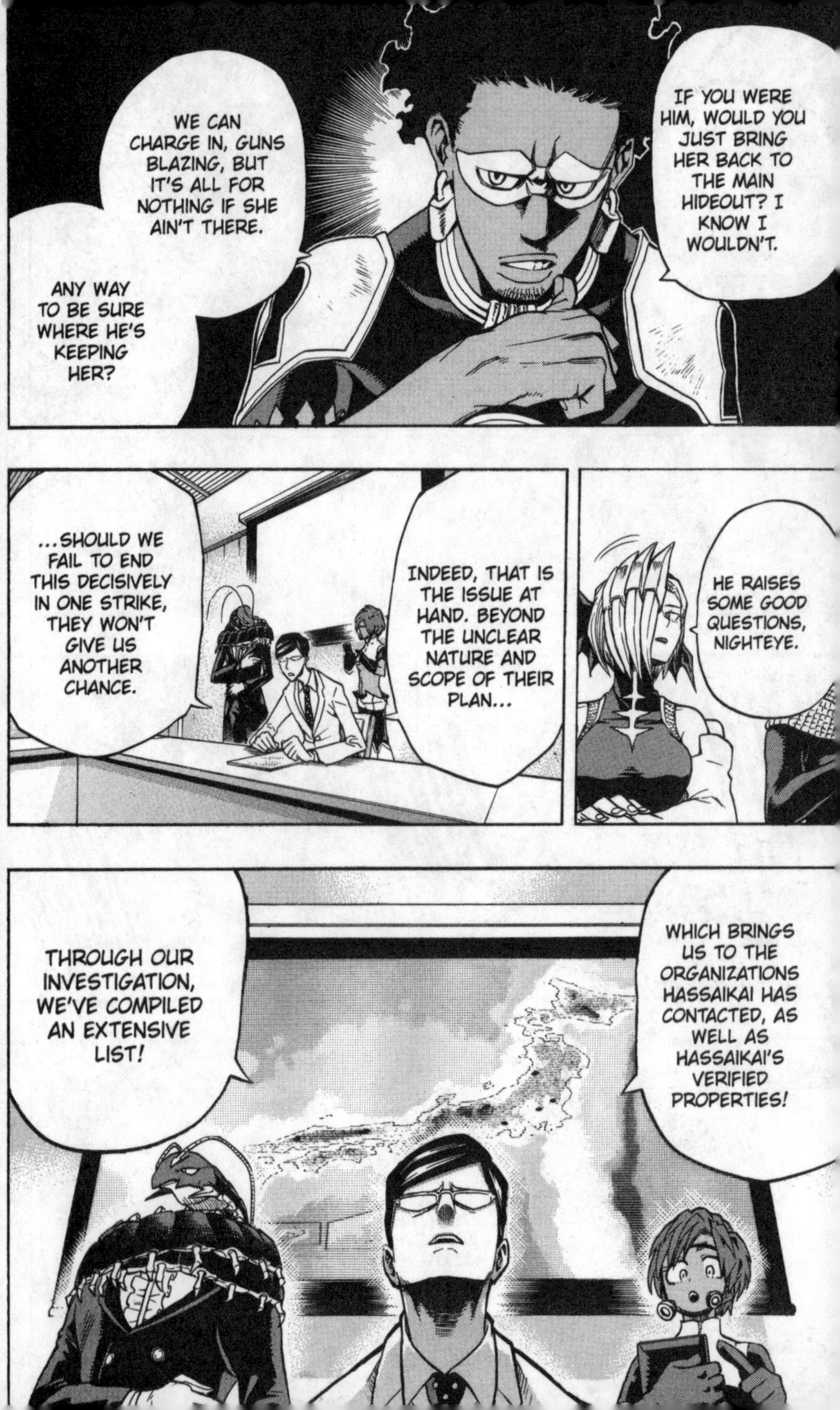
IF YOU WERE HIM, WOULD YOU JUST BRING HER BACK TO THE MAIN HIDEOUT? I KNOW I WOULDN'T.
WE CAN CHARGE IN, GUNS BLAZING, BUT IT'S ALL FOR NOTHING IF SHE AIN'T THERE.
ANY WAY TO BE SURE WHERE HE'S KEEPING HER?
HE RAISES SOME GOOD QUESTIONS, NIGHTEYE.
INDEED, THAT IS THE ISSUE AT HAND. BEYOND THE UNCLEAR NATURE AND SCOPE OF THEIR PLAN...
...SHOULD WE FAIL TO END THIS DECISIVELY IN ONE STRIKE, THEY WON'T GIVE US ANOTHER CHANCE.
WHICH BRINGS US TO THE ORGANIZATIONS HASSAIKAI HAS CONTACTED, AS WELL AS HASSAIKAI'S VERIFIED PROPERTIES!
THROUGH OUR INVESTIGATION, WE'VE COMPILED AN EXTENSIVE LIST!

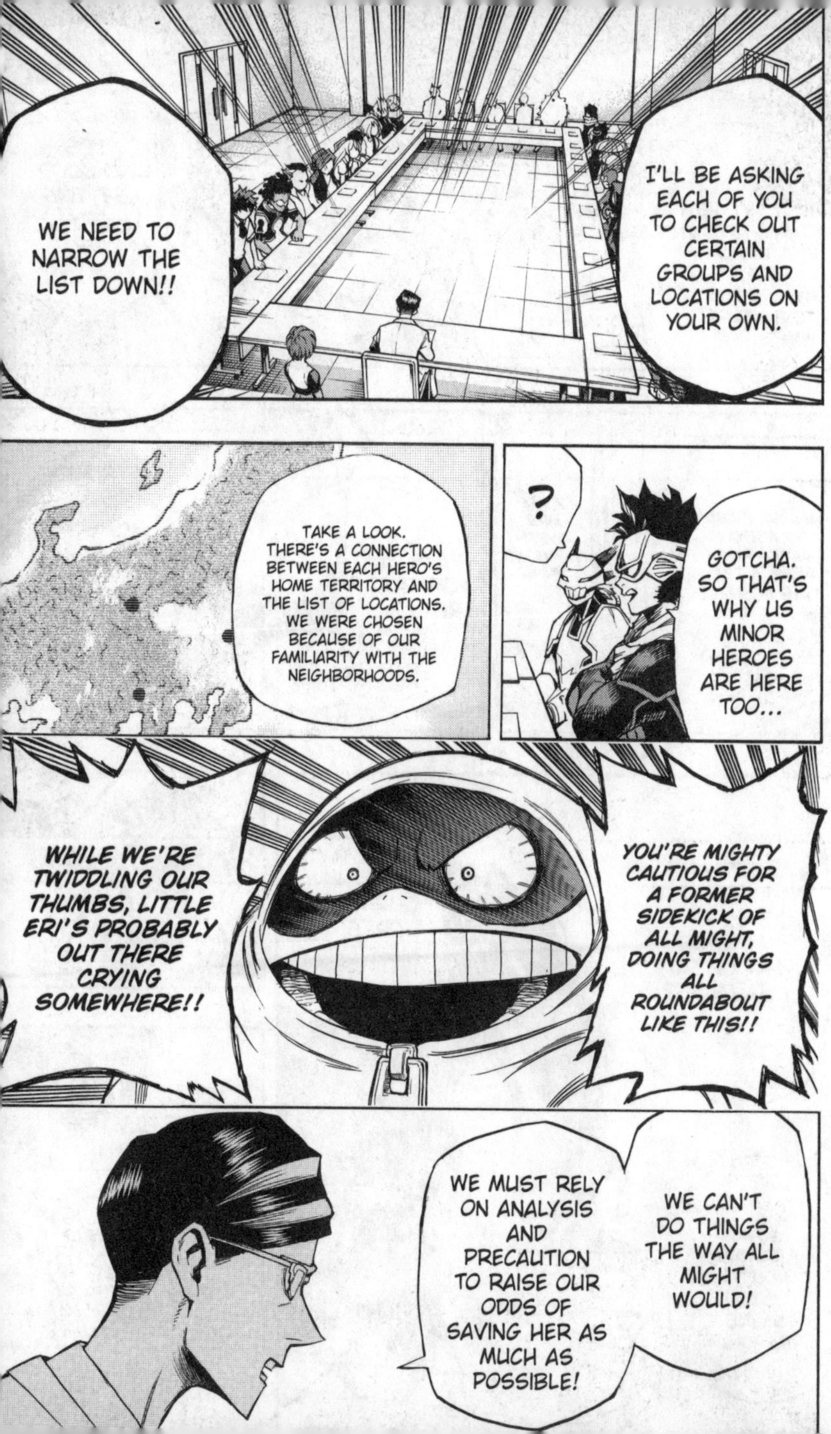
I'LL BE ASKING EACH OF YOU TO CHECK OUT CERTAIN GROUPS AND LOCATIONS ON YOUR OWN.
WE NEED TO NARROW THE LIST DOWN!!
?
GOTCHA. SO THAT'S WHY US MINOR HEROES ARE HERE TOO...
TAKE A LOOK. THERE'S A CONNECTION BETWEEN EACH HERO'S HOME TERRITORY AND THE LIST OF LOCATIONS. WE WERE CHOSEN BECAUSE OF OUR FAMILIARITY WITH THE NEIGHBORHOODS.
YOU'RE MIGHTY CAUTIOUS FOR A FORMER SIDEKICK OF ALL MIGHT, DOING THINGS ALL ROUNDABOUT LIKE THIS!!
WHILE WE'RE TWIDDLING OUR THUMBS, LITTLE ERI'S PROBABLY OUT THERE CRYING SOMEWHERE!!
WE CAN'T DO THINGS THE WAY ALL MIGHT WOULD!
WE MUST RELY ON ANALYSIS AND PRECAUTION TO RAISE OUR ODDS OF SAVING HER AS MUCH AS POSSIBLE!

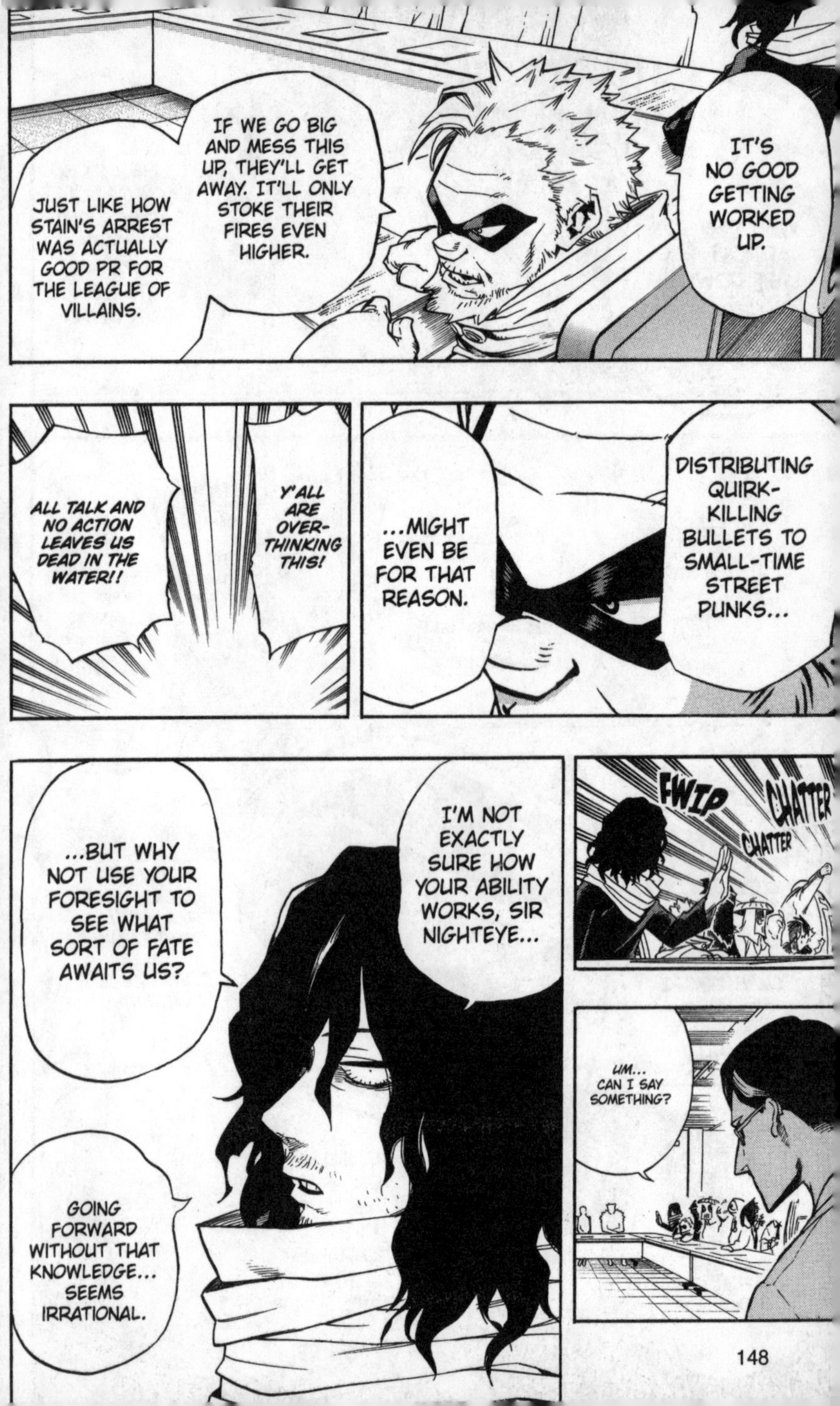
IT'S NO GOOD GETTING WORKED UP.
IF WE GO BIG AND MESS THIS UP, THEY'LL GET AWAY. IT'LL ONLY STOKE THEIR FIRES EVEN HIGHER.
JUST LIKE HOW STAIN'S ARREST WAS ACTUALLY GOOD PR FOR THE LEAGUE OF VILLAINS.
DISTRIBUTING QUIRK-KILLING BULLETS TO SMALL-TIME STREET PUNKS...
...MIGHT EVEN BE FOR THAT REASON.
Y'ALL ARE OVER-THINKING THIS!
ALL TALK AND NO ACTION LEAVES US DEAD IN THE WATER!!
CHATTER
FWIP
CHATTER
UM... CAN I SAY SOMETHING?
I'M NOT EXACTLY SURE HOW YOUR ABILITY WORKS, SIR NIGHTEYE...
...BUT WHY NOT USE YOUR FORESIGHT TO SEE WHAT SORT OF FATE AWAITS US?
GOING FORWARD WITHOUT THAT KNOWLEDGE... SEEMS IRRATIONAL.

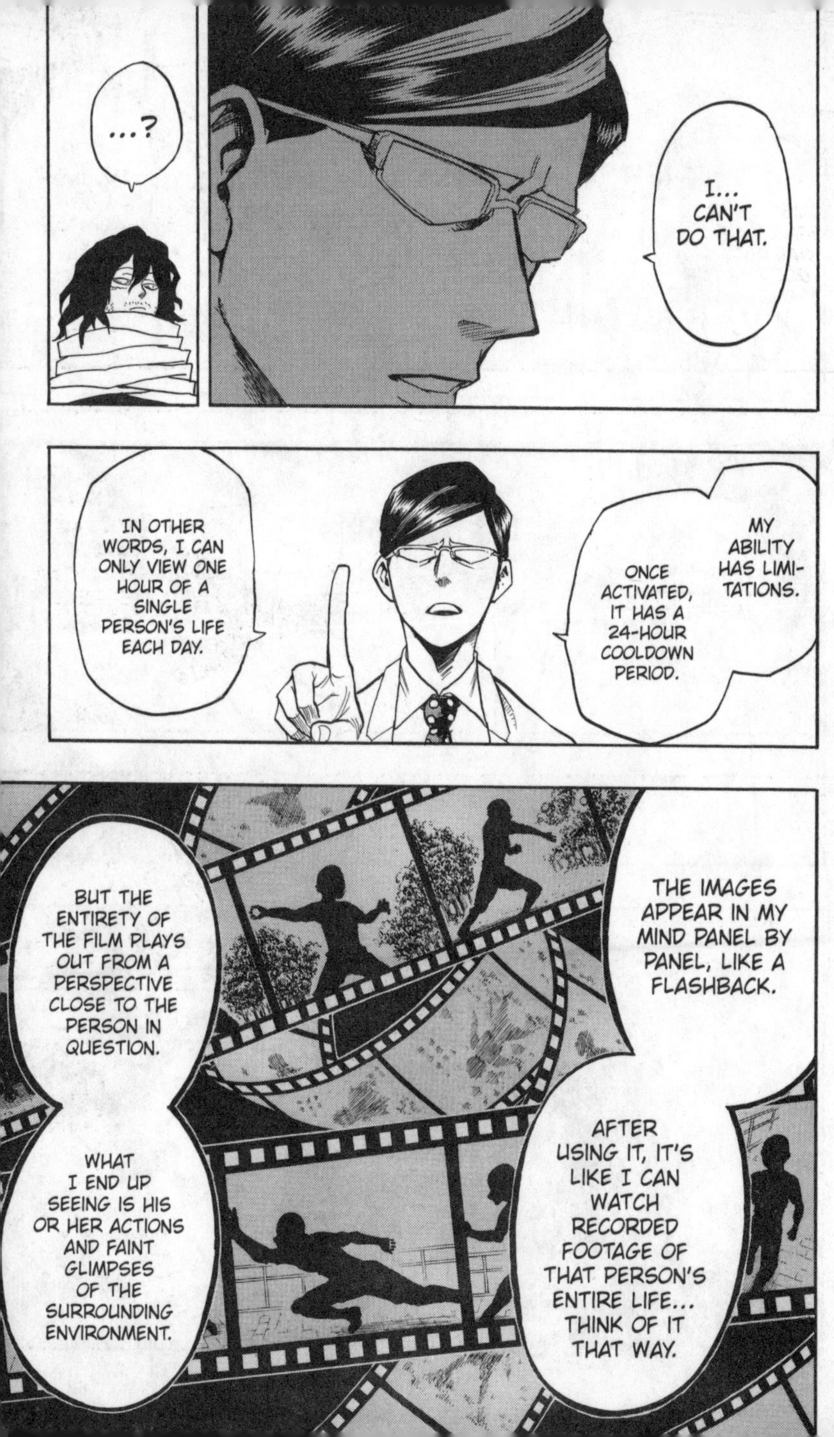
I... CAN'T DO THAT.
...?
MY ABILITY HAS LIMITATIONS.
ONCE ACTIVATED, IT HAS A 24-HOUR COOLDOWN PERIOD.
IN OTHER WORDS, I CAN ONLY VIEW ONE HOUR OF A SINGLE PERSON'S LIFE EACH DAY.
THE IMAGES APPEAR IN MY MIND PANEL BY PANEL, LIKE A FLASHBACK.
AFTER USING IT, IT'S LIKE I CAN WATCH RECORDED FOOTAGE OF THAT PERSON'S ENTIRE LIFE... THINK OF IT THAT WAY.
BUT THE ENTIRETY OF THE FILM PLAYS OUT FROM A PERSPECTIVE CLOSE TO THE PERSON IN QUESTION.
WHAT I END UP SEEING IS HIS OR HER ACTIONS AND FAINT GLIMPSES OF THE SURROUNDING ENVIRONMENT.

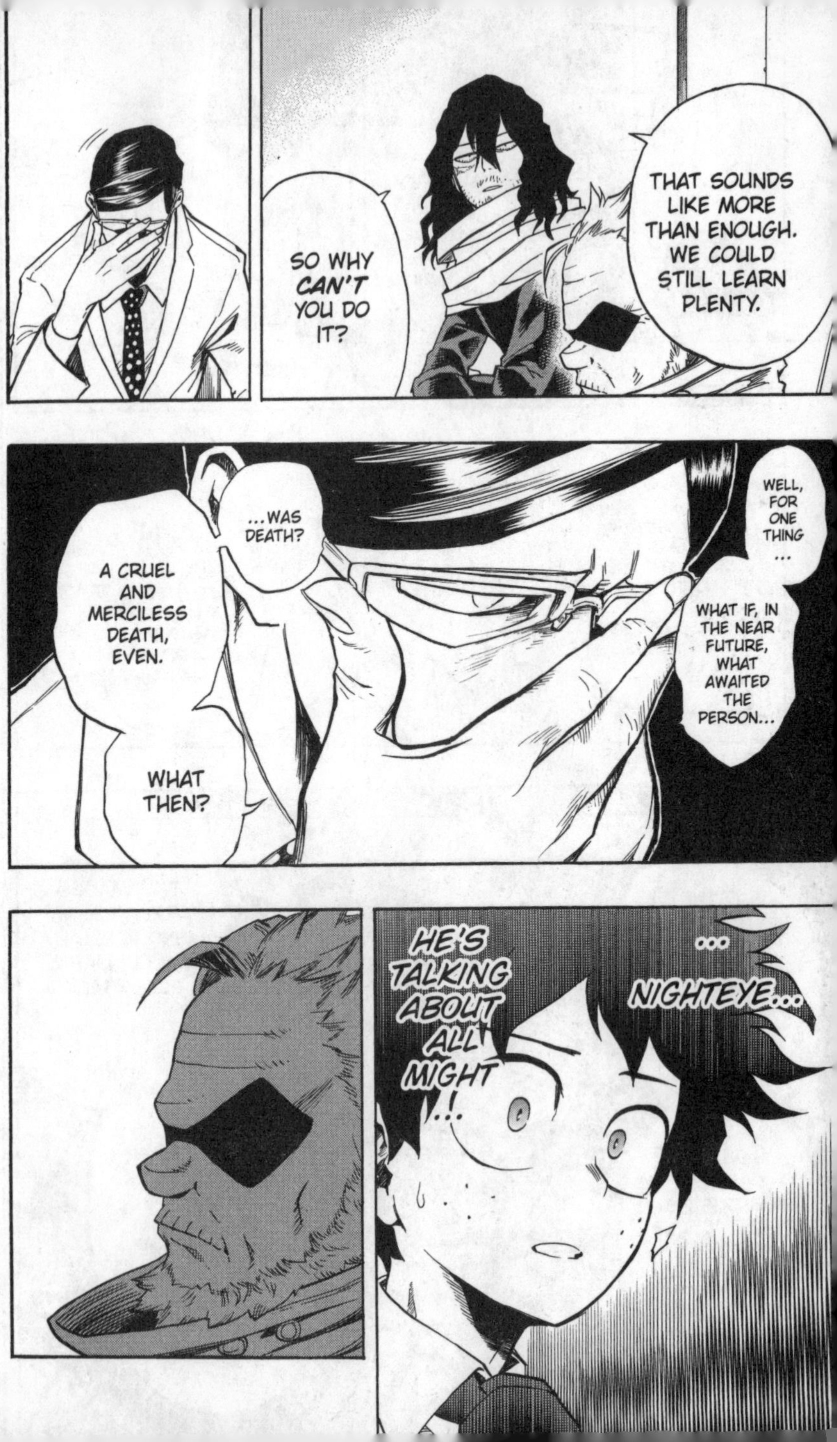
THAT SOUNDS LIKE MORE THAN ENOUGH. WE COULD STILL LEARN PLENTY.
SO WHY *CAN'T* YOU DO IT?
WELL, FOR ONE THING...
WHAT IF, IN THE NEAR FUTURE, WHAT AWAITED THE PERSON...
...WAS DEATH?
A CRUEL AND MERCILESS DEATH, EVEN.
WHAT THEN?
...NIGHTEYE...
HE'S TALKING ABOUT ALL MIGHT...!

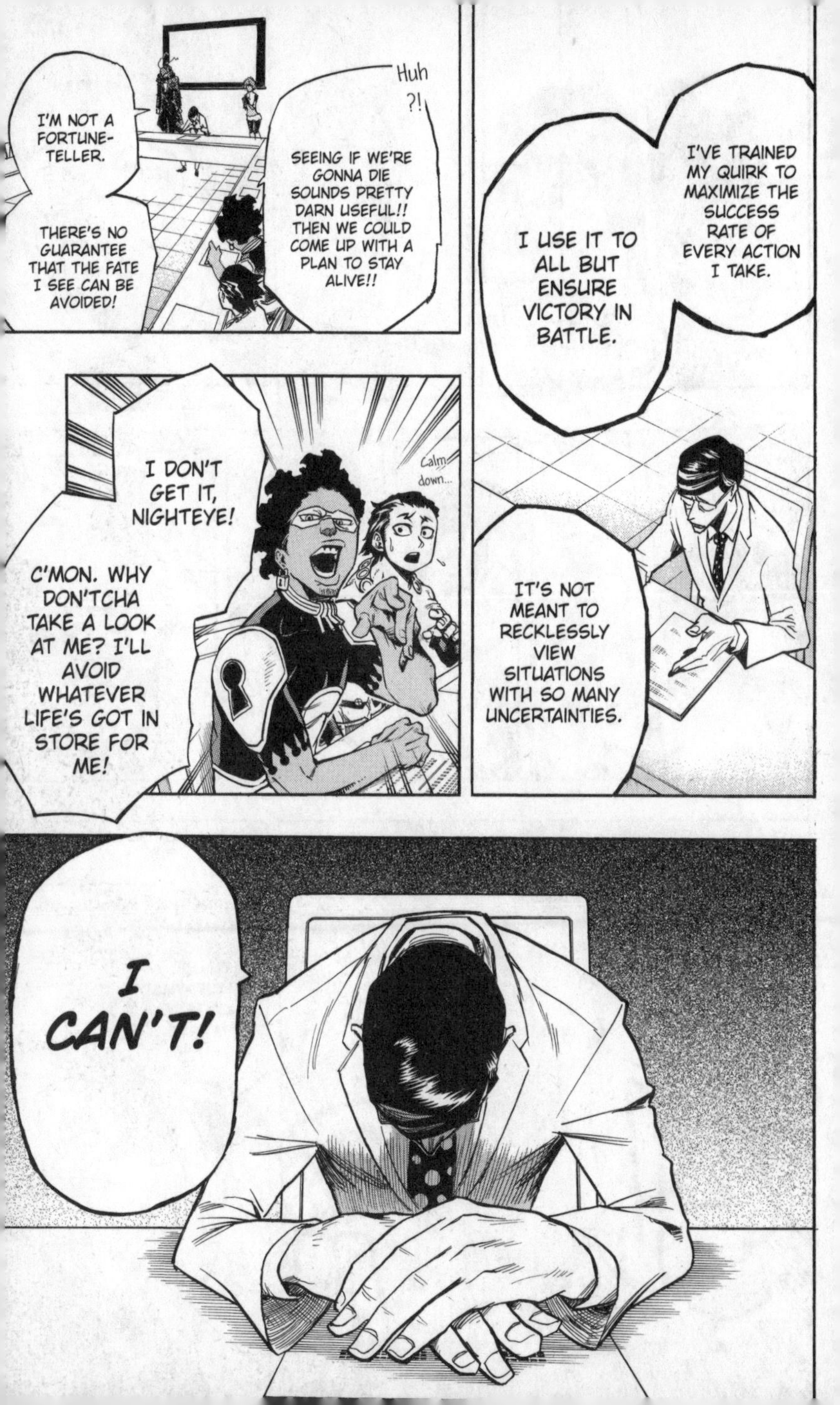
I'VE TRAINED MY QUIRK TO MAXIMIZE THE SUCCESS RATE OF EVERY ACTION I TAKE.
I USE IT TO ALL BUT ENSURE VICTORY IN BATTLE.
IT'S NOT MEANT TO RECKLESSLY VIEW SITUATIONS WITH SO MANY UNCERTAINTIES.
I'M NOT A FORTUNE-TELLER.
THERE'S NO GUARANTEE THAT THE FATE I SEE CAN BE AVOIDED!
Huh ?!
SEEING IF WE'RE GONNA DIE SOUNDS PRETTY DARN USEFUL!! THEN WE COULD COME UP WITH A PLAN TO STAY ALIVE!!
Calm down...
I DON'T GET IT, NIGHTEYE!
C'MON. WHY DON'TCHA TAKE A LOOK AT ME? I'LL AVOID WHATEVER LIFE'S GOT IN STORE FOR ME!
I CAN'T!

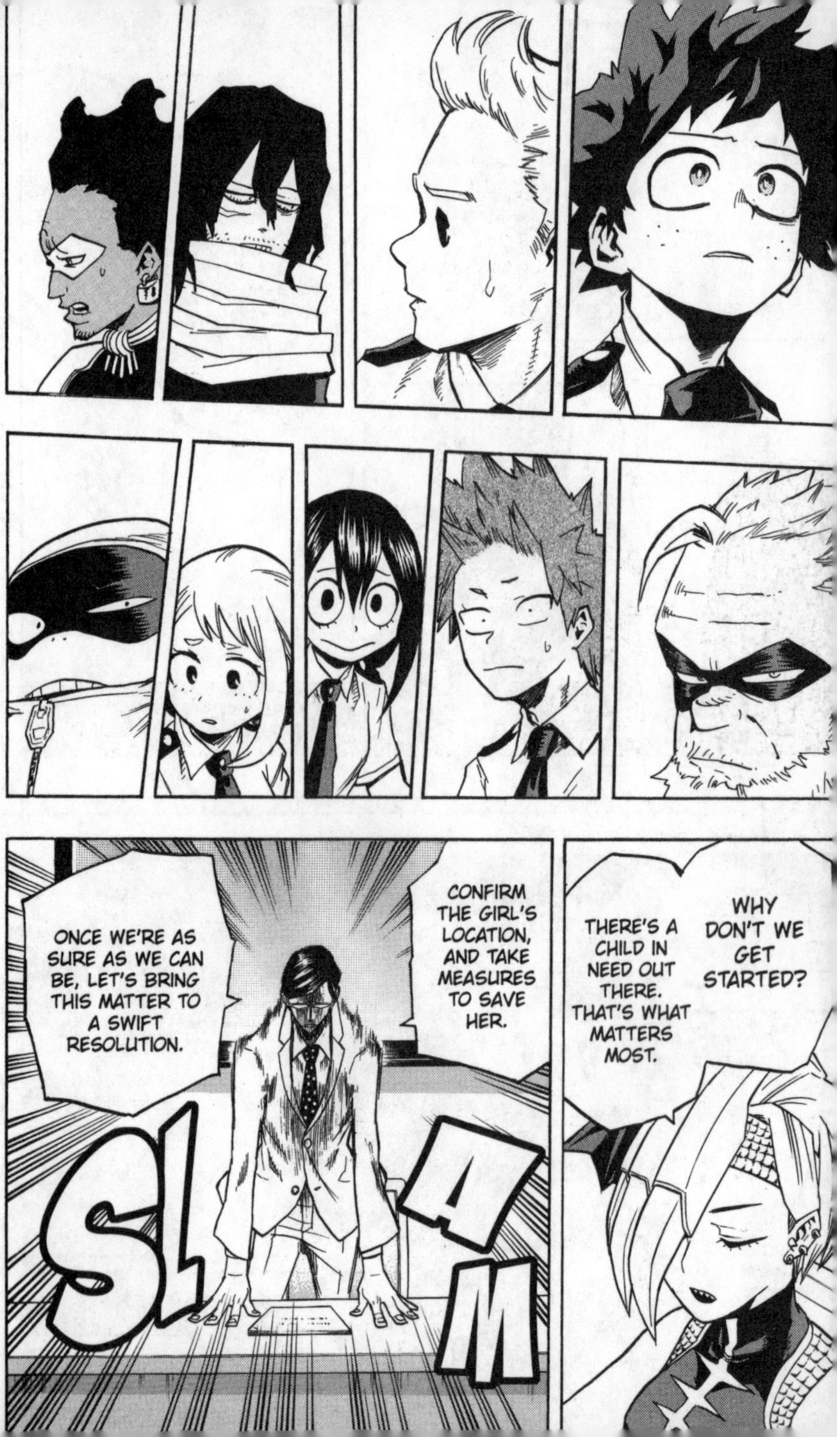
WHY DON'T WE GET STARTED?
THERE'S A CHILD IN NEED OUT THERE. THAT'S WHAT MATTERS MOST.
CONFIRM THE GIRL'S LOCATION, AND TAKE MEASURES TO SAVE HER.
ONCE WE'RE AS SURE AS WE CAN BE, LET'S BRING THIS MATTER TO A SWIFT RESOLUTION.
SLAM

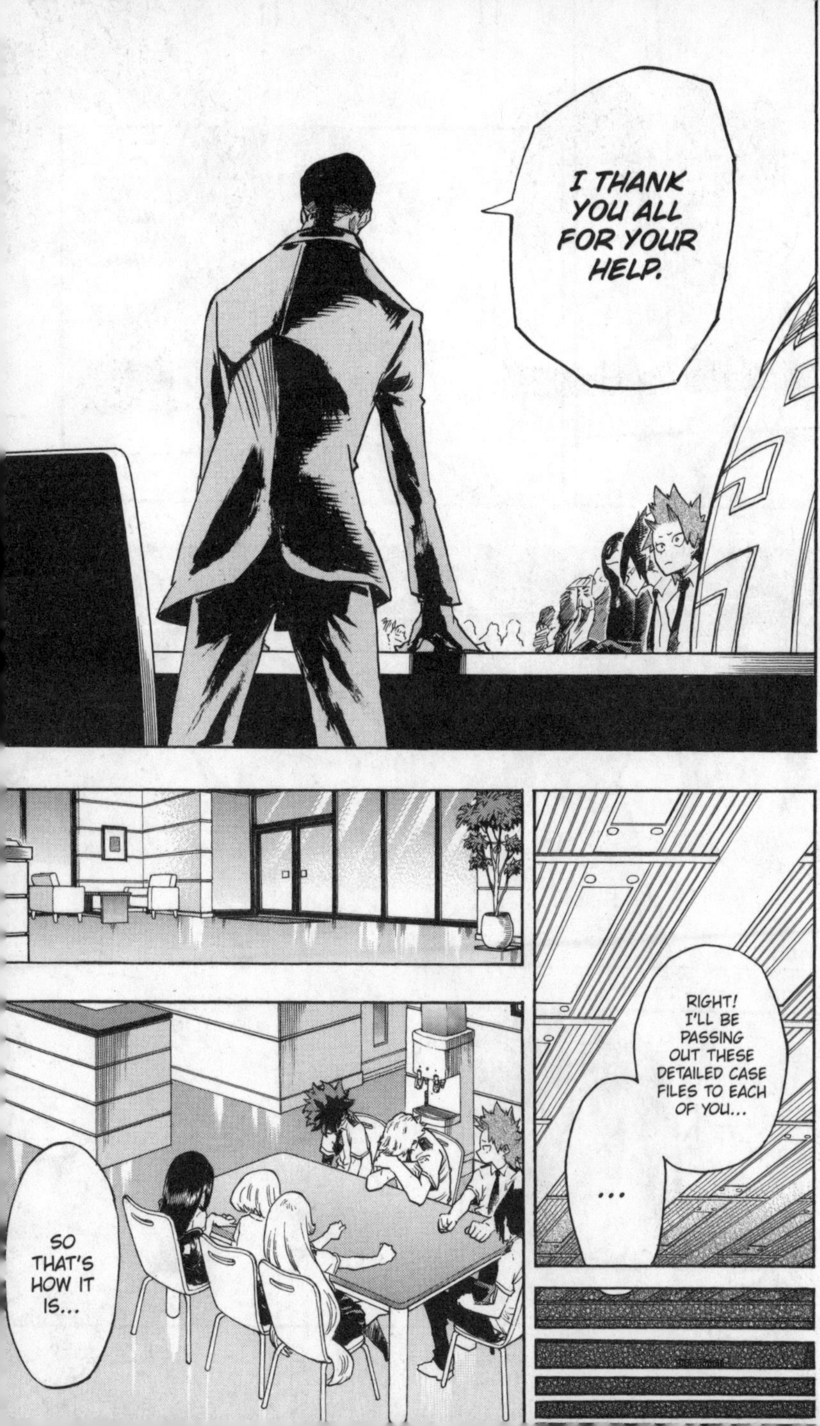
I THANK YOU ALL FOR YOUR HELP.
RIGHT! I'LL BE PASSING OUT THESE DETAILED CASE FILES TO EACH OF YOU...
...
SO THAT'S HOW IT IS...

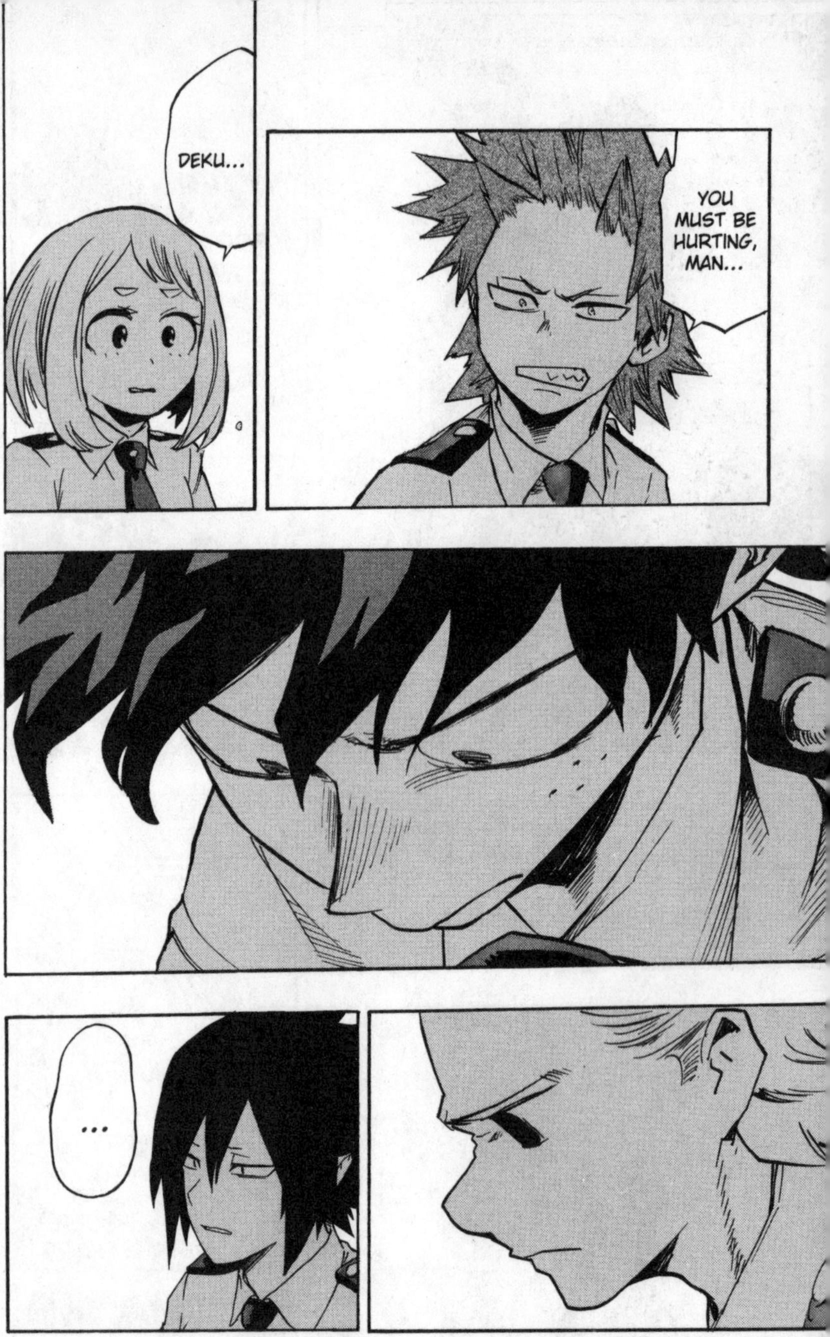
YOU MUST BE HURTING, MAN...
DEKU...
...

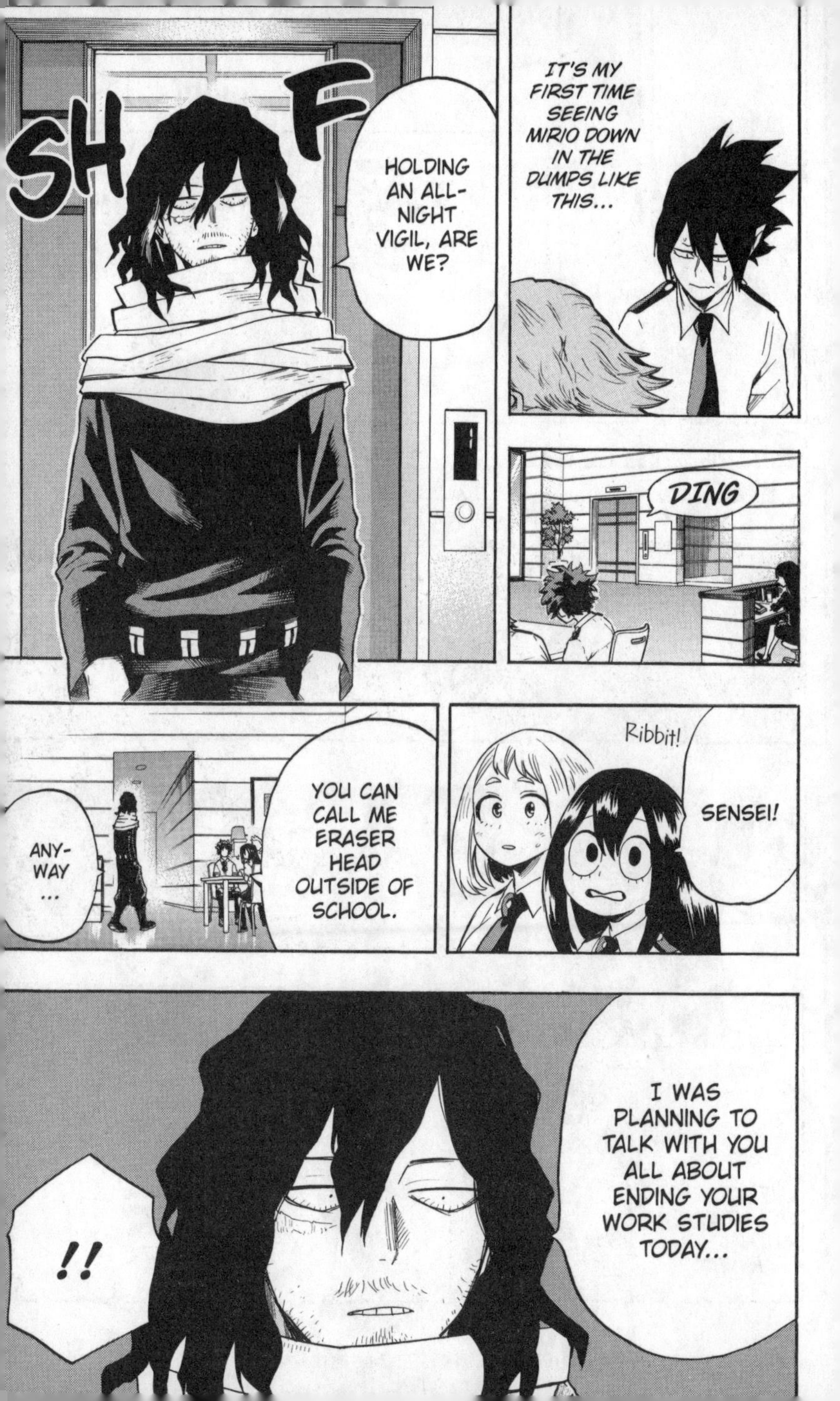
IT'S MY FIRST TIME SEEING MIRIO DOWN IN THE DUMPS LIKE THIS...
DING
SHF
HOLDING AN ALL-NIGHT VIGIL, ARE WE?
Ribbit!
SENSEI!
YOU CAN CALL ME ERASER HEAD OUTSIDE OF SCHOOL.
ANY-WAY...
I WAS PLANNING TO TALK WITH YOU ALL ABOUT ENDING YOUR WORK STUDIES TODAY...
!!

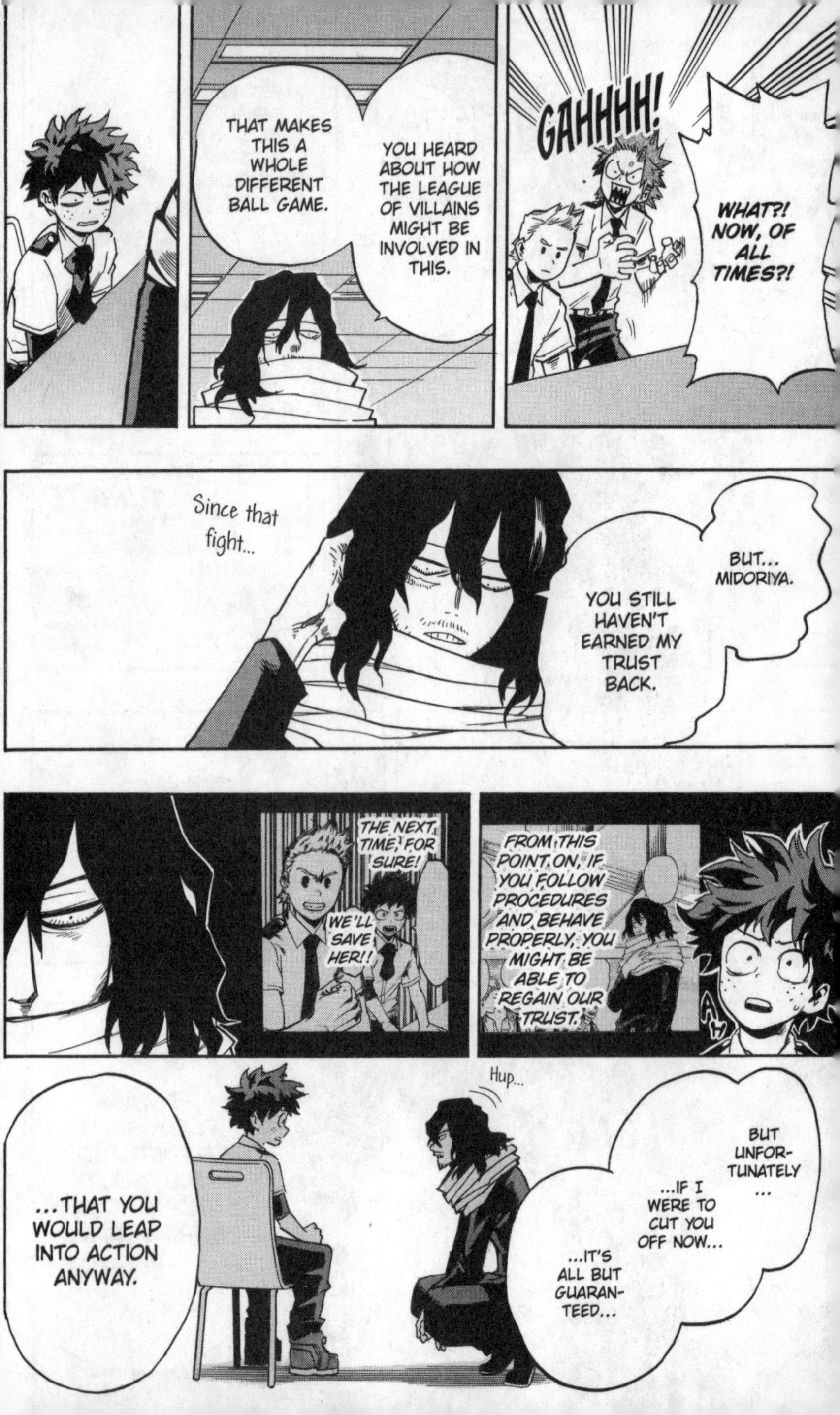
GAHHHH!
WHAT?! NOW, OF ALL TIMES?!
YOU HEARD ABOUT HOW THE LEAGUE OF VILLAINS MIGHT BE INVOLVED IN THIS.
THAT MAKES THIS A WHOLE DIFFERENT BALL GAME.
BUT... MIDORIYA.
YOU STILL HAVEN'T EARNED MY TRUST BACK.
Since that fight...
FROM THIS POINT ON, IF YOU FOLLOW PROCEDURES AND BEHAVE PROPERLY, YOU MIGHT BE ABLE TO REGAIN OUR TRUST.
AH
THE NEXT TIME, FOR SURE!
WE'LL SAVE HER!!
Hup...
BUT UNFORTUNATELY...
...IF I WERE TO CUT YOU OFF NOW...
...IT'S ALL BUT GUARANTEED...
...THAT YOU WOULD LEAP INTO ACTION ANYWAY.

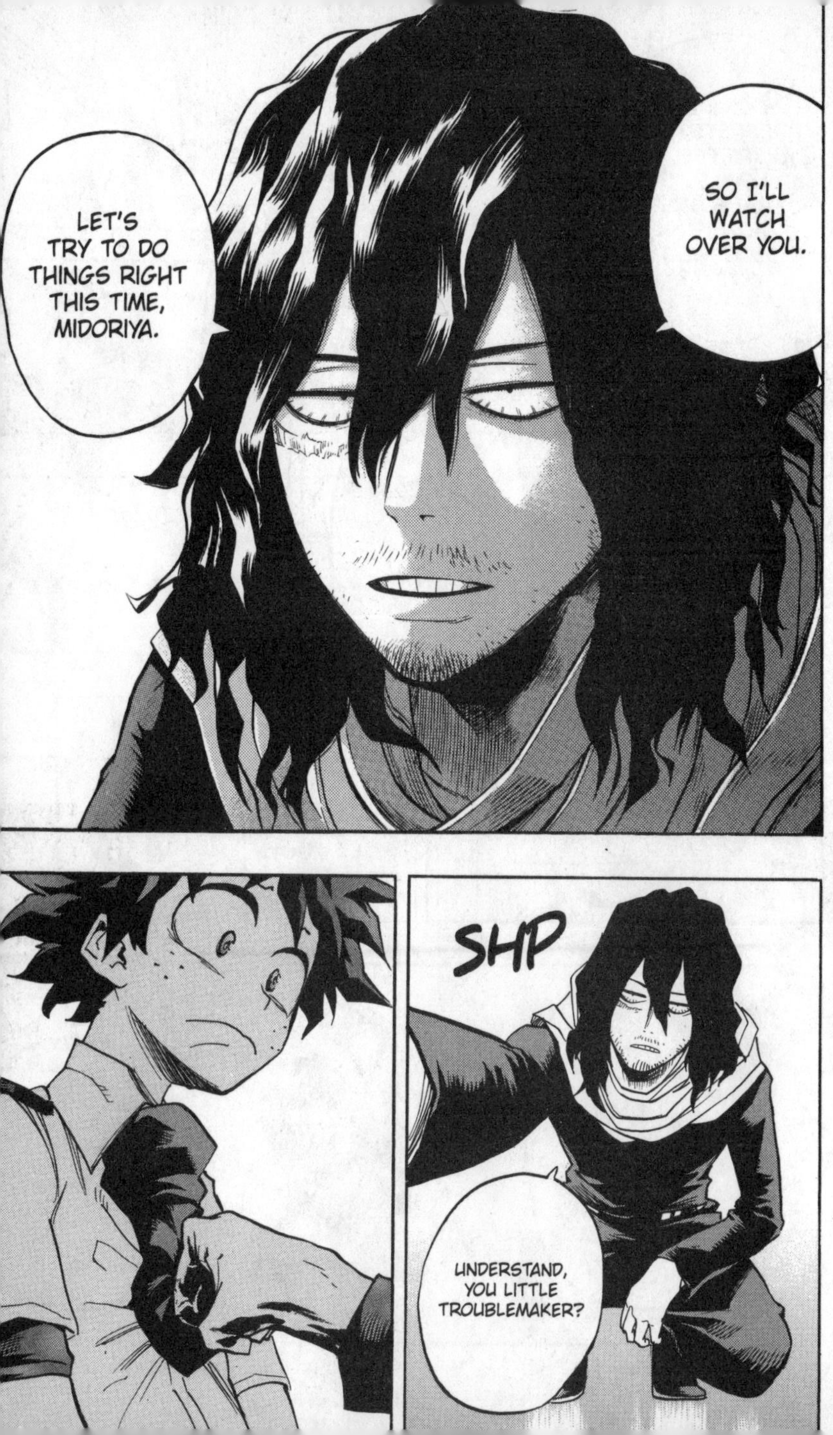
SO I'LL WATCH OVER YOU.
LET'S TRY TO DO THINGS RIGHT THIS TIME, MIDORIYA.
SHP
UNDERSTAND, YOU LITTLE TROUBLEMAKER?

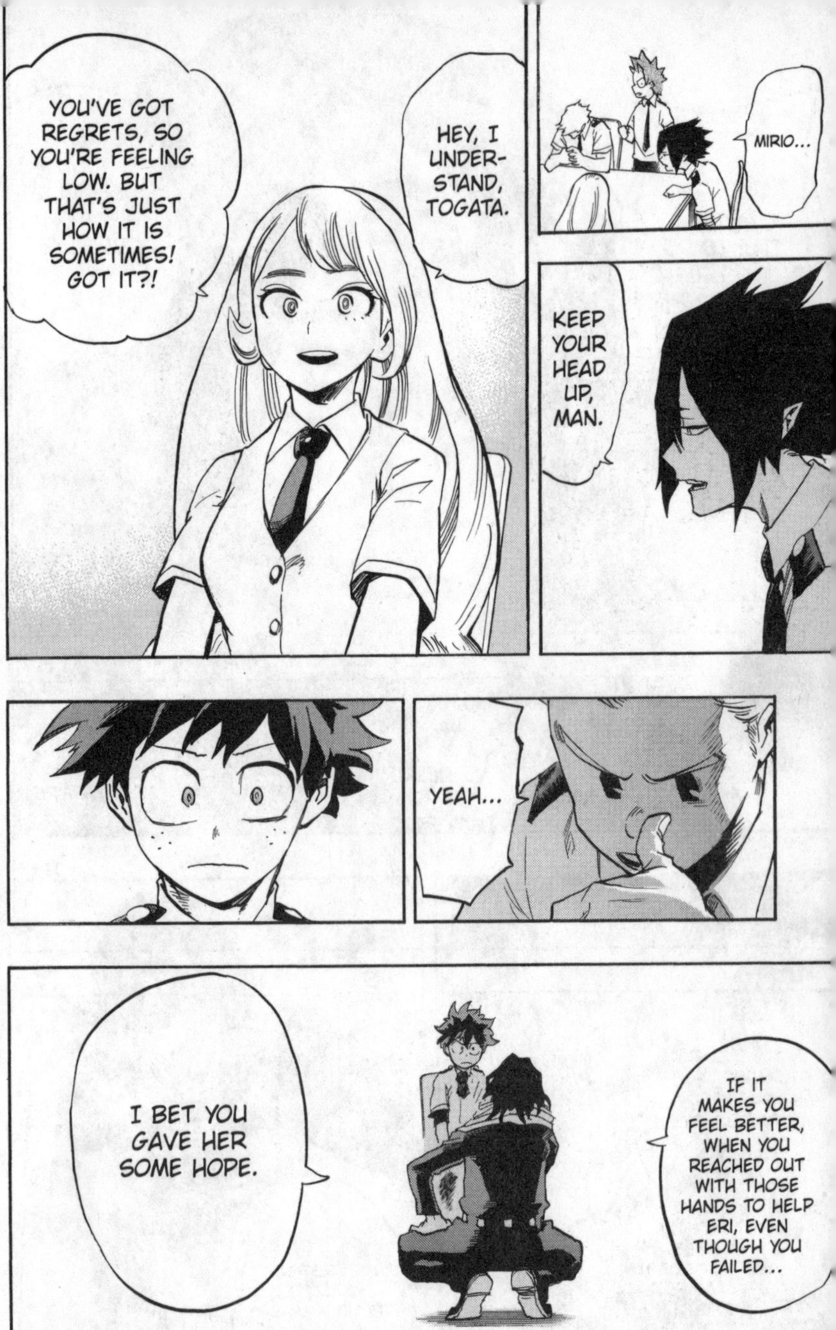
MIRIO...
KEEP YOUR HEAD UP, MAN.
HEY, I UNDER-STAND, TOGATA.
YOU'VE GOT REGRETS, SO YOU'RE FEELING LOW. BUT THAT'S JUST HOW IT IS SOMETIMES! GOT IT?!
YEAH...
IF IT MAKES YOU FEEL BETTER, WHEN YOU REACHED OUT WITH THOSE HANDS TO HELP ERI, EVEN THOUGH YOU FAILED...
I BET YOU GAVE HER SOME HOPE.

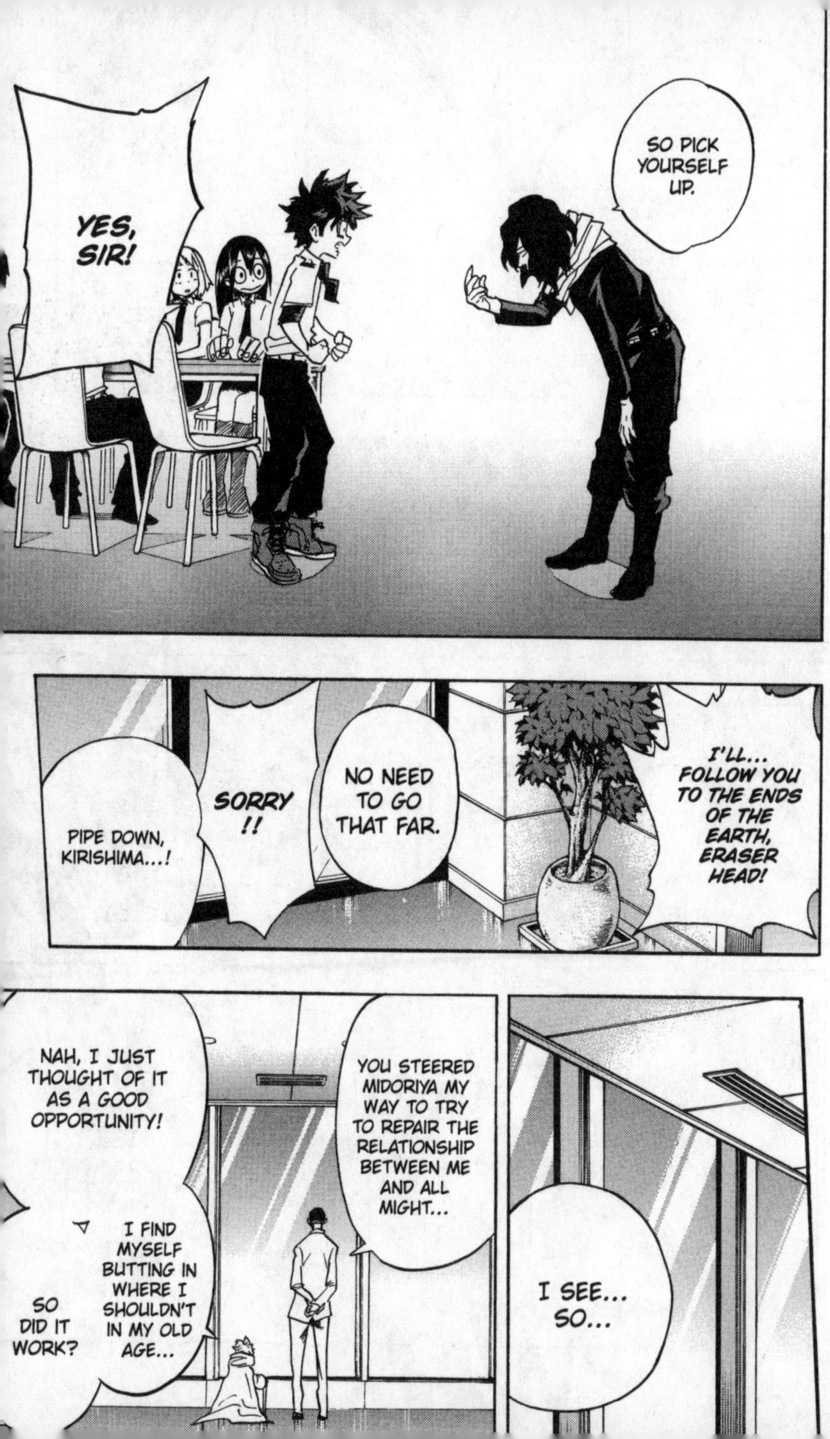
SO PICK YOURSELF UP.
YES, SIR!
I'LL... FOLLOW YOU TO THE ENDS OF THE EARTH, ERASER HEAD!
NO NEED TO GO THAT FAR.
SORRY !!
PIPE DOWN, KIRISHIMA...!
I SEE... SO...
YOU STEERED MIDORIYA MY WAY TO TRY TO REPAIR THE RELATIONSHIP BETWEEN ME AND ALL MIGHT...
NAH, I JUST THOUGHT OF IT AS A GOOD OPPORTUNITY!
I FIND MYSELF BUTTING IN WHERE I SHOULDN'T IN MY OLD AGE...
SO DID IT WORK?

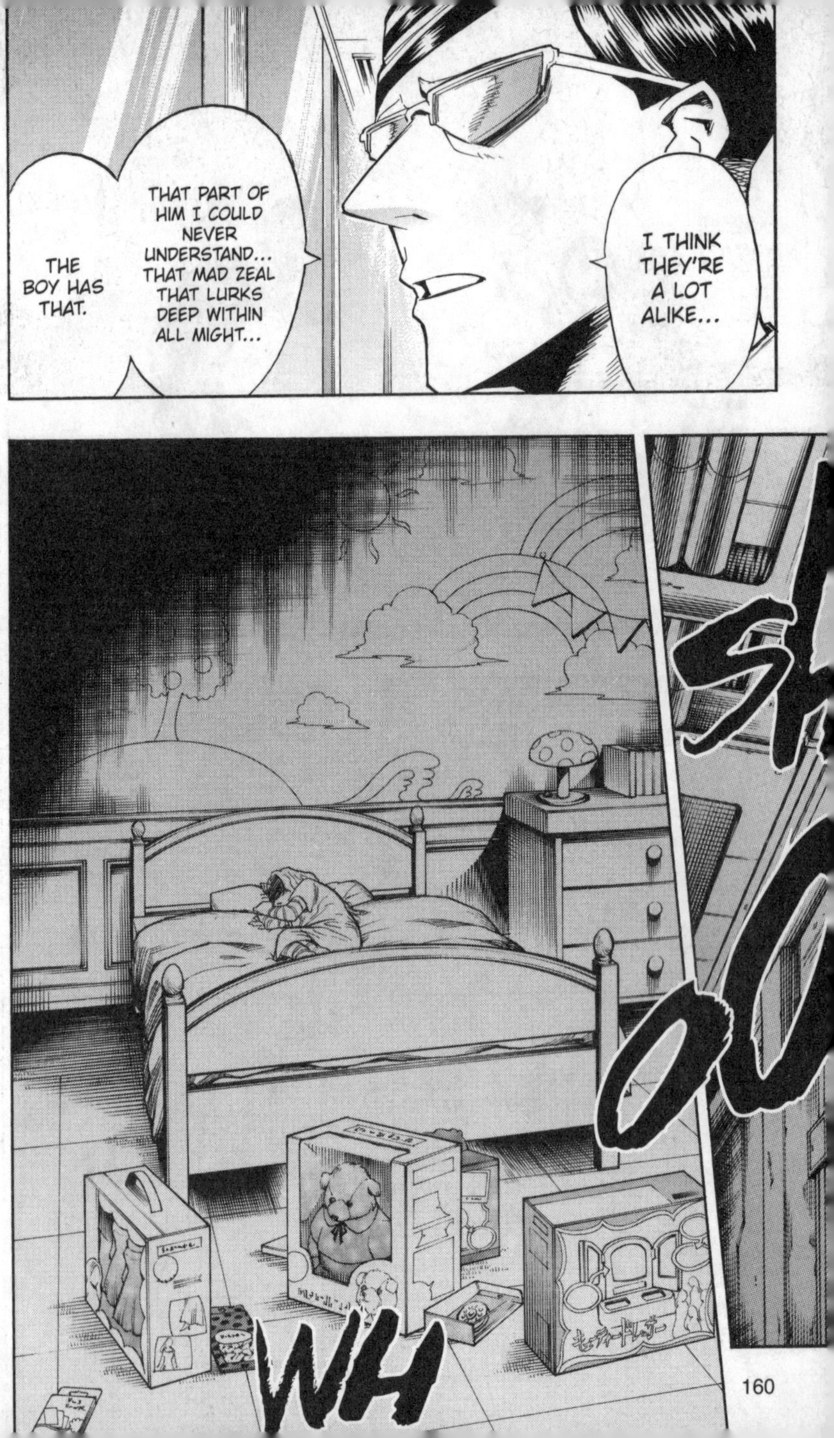
I THINK THEY'RE A LOT ALIKE...
THAT PART OF HIM I COULD NEVER UNDERSTAND... THAT MAD ZEAL THAT LURKS DEEP WITHIN ALL MIGHT...
THE BOY HAS THAT.
WH

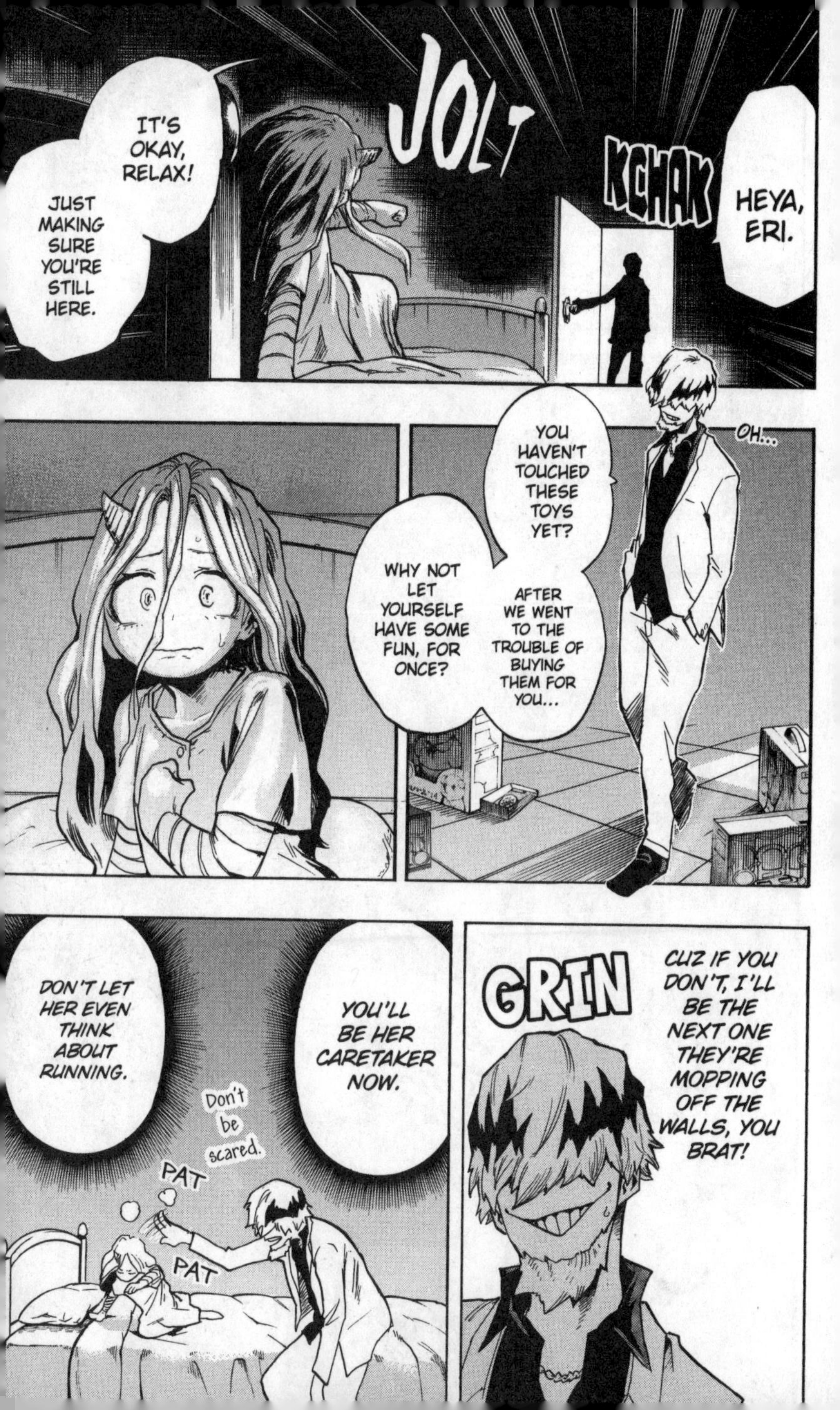
HEYA, ERI.
KCHAK
JOLT
IT'S OKAY, RELAX!
JUST MAKING SURE YOU'RE STILL HERE.
OH...
YOU HAVEN'T TOUCHED THESE TOYS YET?
AFTER WE WENT TO THE TROUBLE OF BUYING THEM FOR YOU...
WHY NOT LET YOURSELF HAVE SOME FUN, FOR ONCE?
CUZ IF YOU DON'T, I'LL BE THE NEXT ONE THEY'RE MOPPING OFF THE WALLS, YOU BRAT!
GRIN
YOU'LL BE HER CARETAKER NOW.
DON'T LET HER EVEN THINK ABOUT RUNNING.
Don't be scared.
PAT
PAT

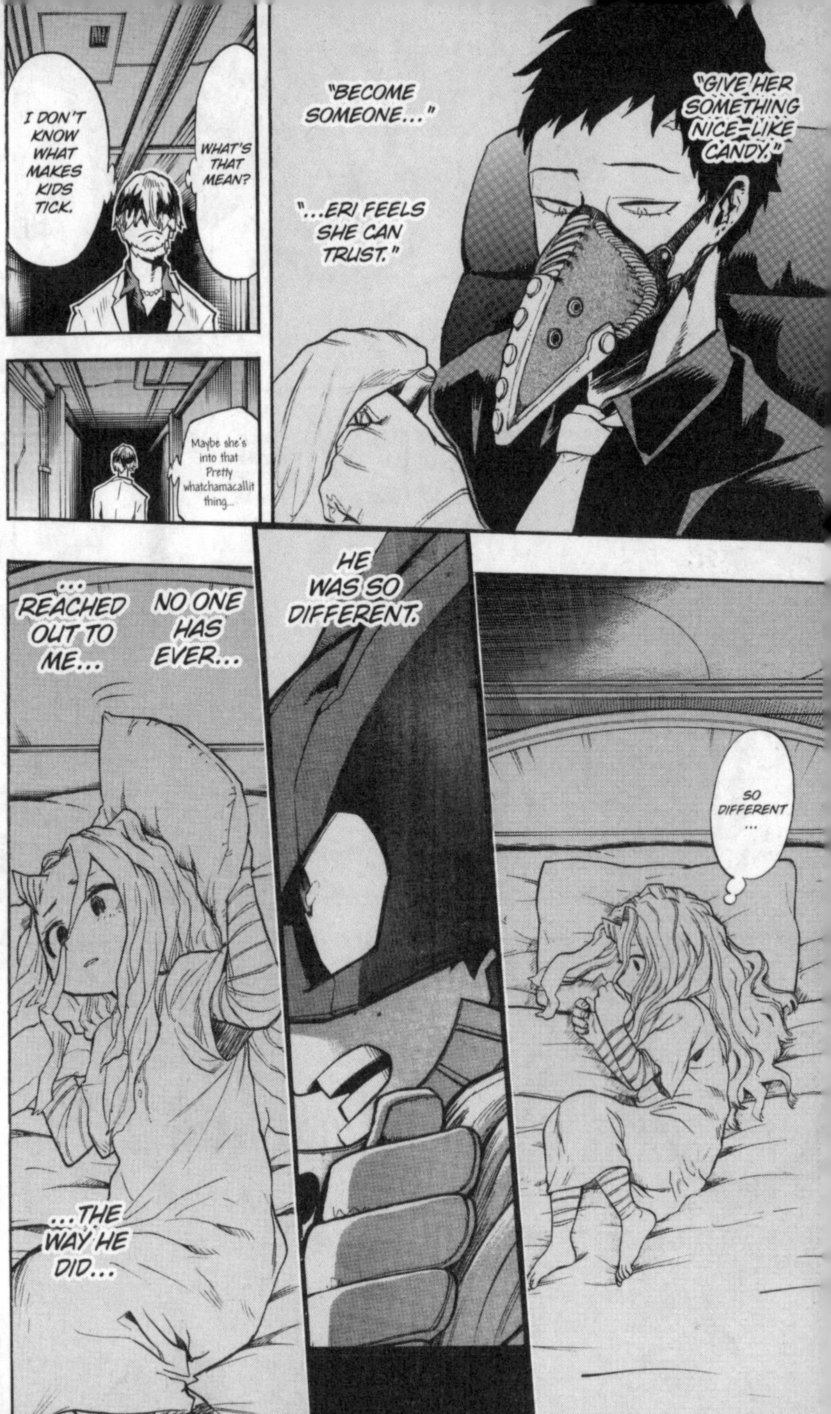
"GIVE HER SOMETHING NICE—LIKE CANDY."
"BECOME SOMEONE..."
"...ERI FEELS SHE CAN TRUST."
WHAT'S THAT MEAN?
I DON'T KNOW WHAT MAKES KIDS TICK.
Maybe she's into that Pretty whatchamacallit thing...
SO DIFFERENT ...
HE WAS SO DIFFERENT.
NO ONE HAS EVER...
...REACHED OUT TO ME...
...THE WAY HE DID...

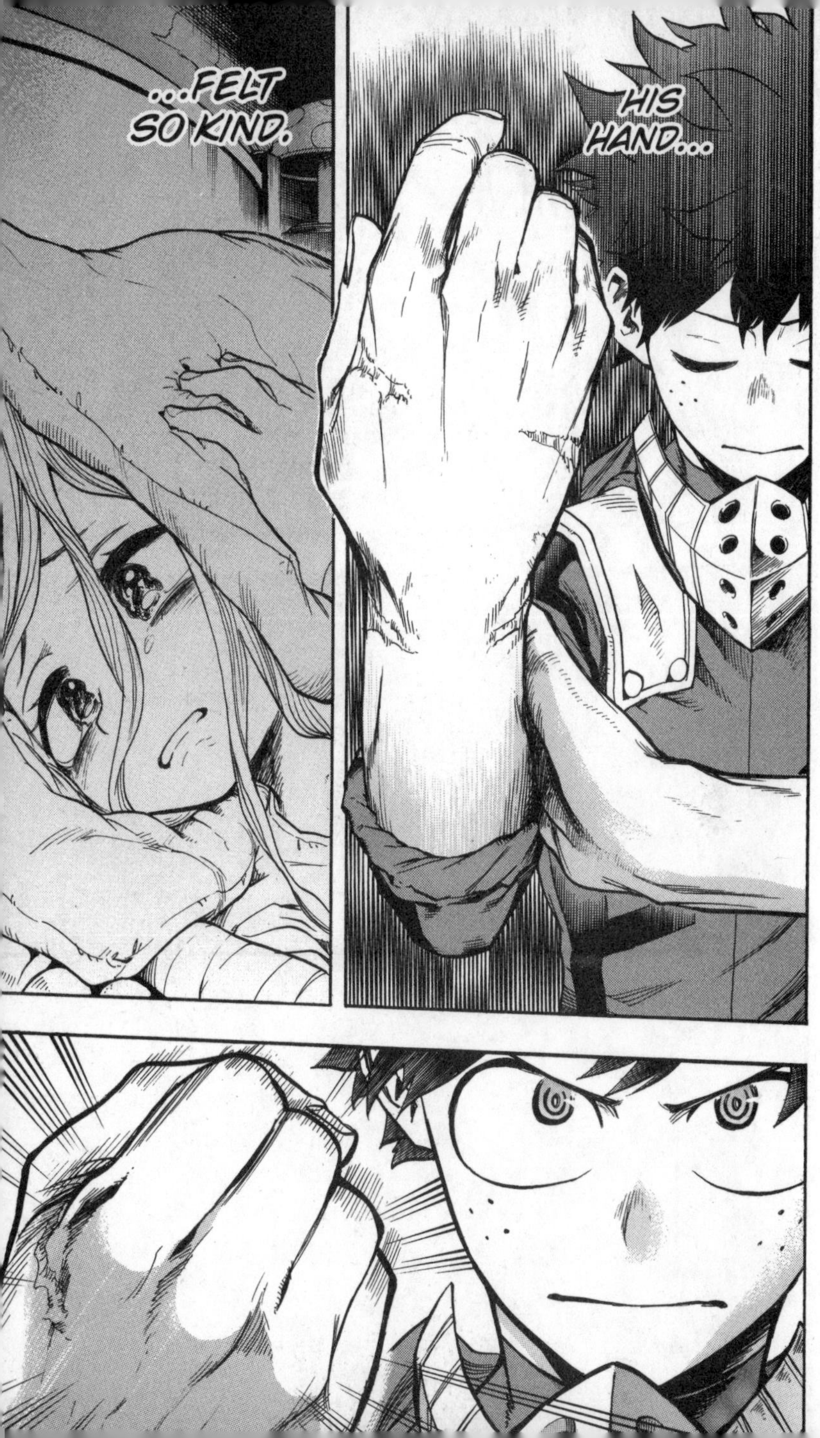
HIS HAND...
...FELT SO KIND.

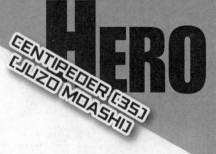

HERO

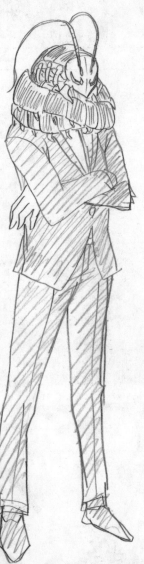

CENTIPEDER (35) (JUZO MOASHI)

STREET CLOTHES

Birthday: 6/4
Height: 205 cm
Favorite Thing: Fragrances

THE SUPPLEMENT
Like Bubble Girl, this is another character I chose from the submissions to the fan art contest. He's super-cool. A stylish gentleman!

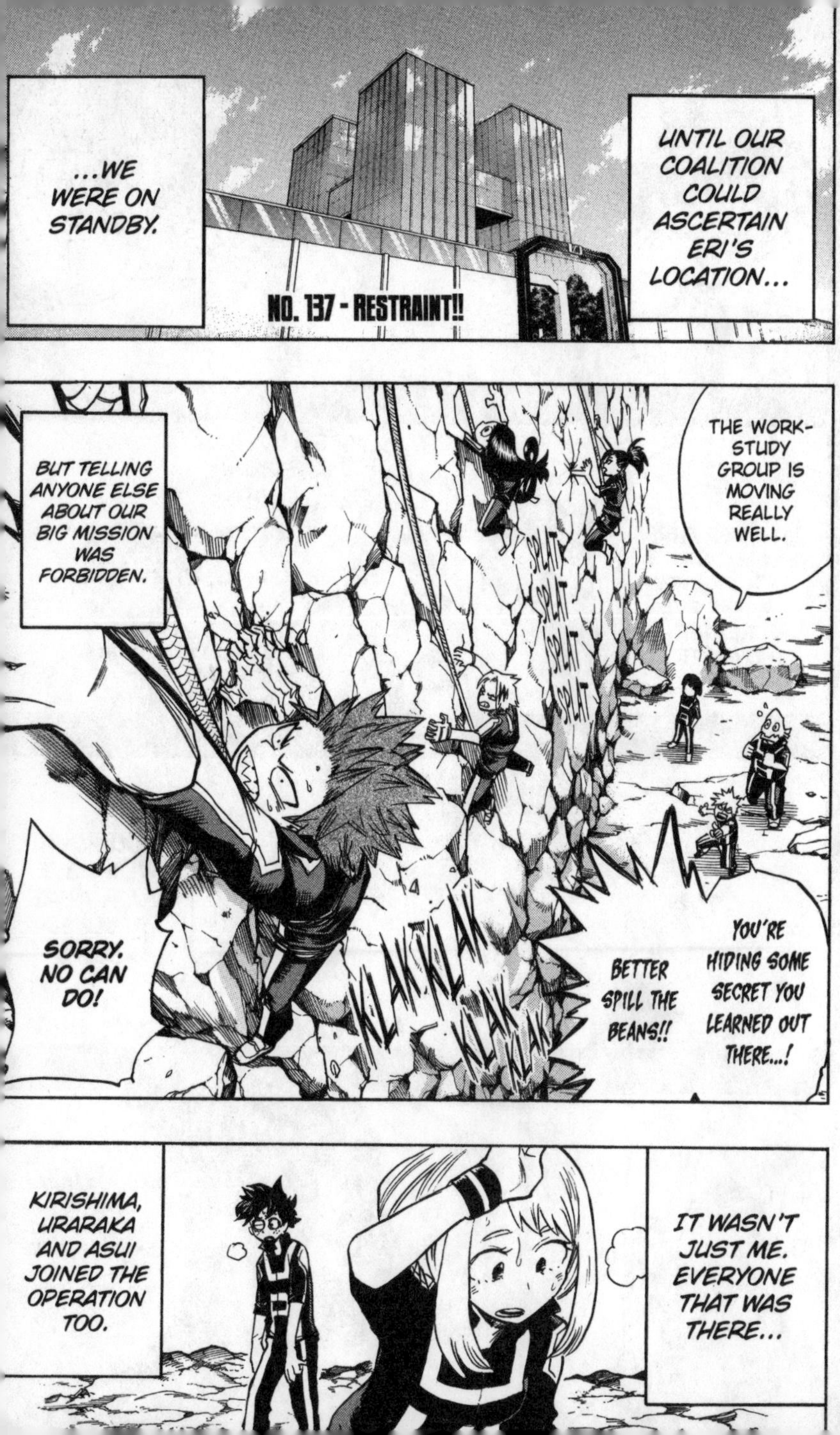
UNTIL OUR COALITION COULD ASCERTAIN ERI'S LOCATION...
...WE WERE ON STANDBY.
NO. 137 - RESTRAINT!!
THE WORK-STUDY GROUP IS MOVING REALLY WELL.
BUT TELLING ANYONE ELSE ABOUT OUR BIG MISSION WAS FORBIDDEN.
SPLAT SPLAT SPLAT SPLAT
YOU'RE HIDING SOME SECRET YOU LEARNED OUT THERE...!
BETTER SPILL THE BEANS!!
KLAK KLAK KLAK KLAK
SORRY. NO CAN DO!
IT WASN'T JUST ME. EVERYONE THAT WAS THERE...
KIRISHIMA, URARAKA AND ASUI JOINED THE OPERATION TOO.

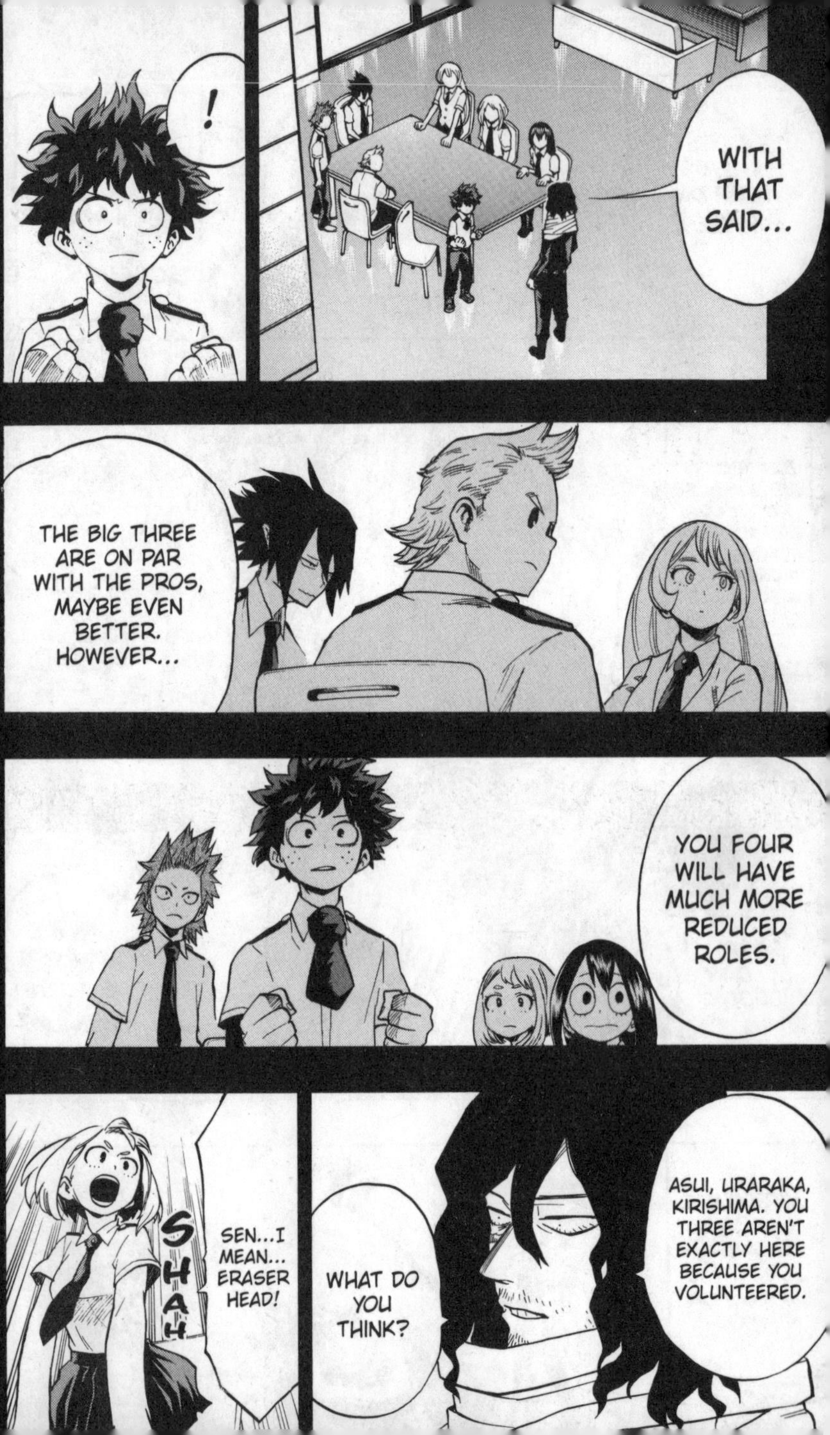
WITH THAT SAID...
!
THE BIG THREE ARE ON PAR WITH THE PROS, MAYBE EVEN BETTER. HOWEVER...
YOU FOUR WILL HAVE MUCH MORE REDUCED ROLES.
ASUI, URARAKA, KIRISHIMA. YOU THREE AREN'T EXACTLY HERE BECAUSE YOU VOLUNTEERED.
WHAT DO YOU THINK?
SEN...I MEAN... ERASER HEAD!
SHAH

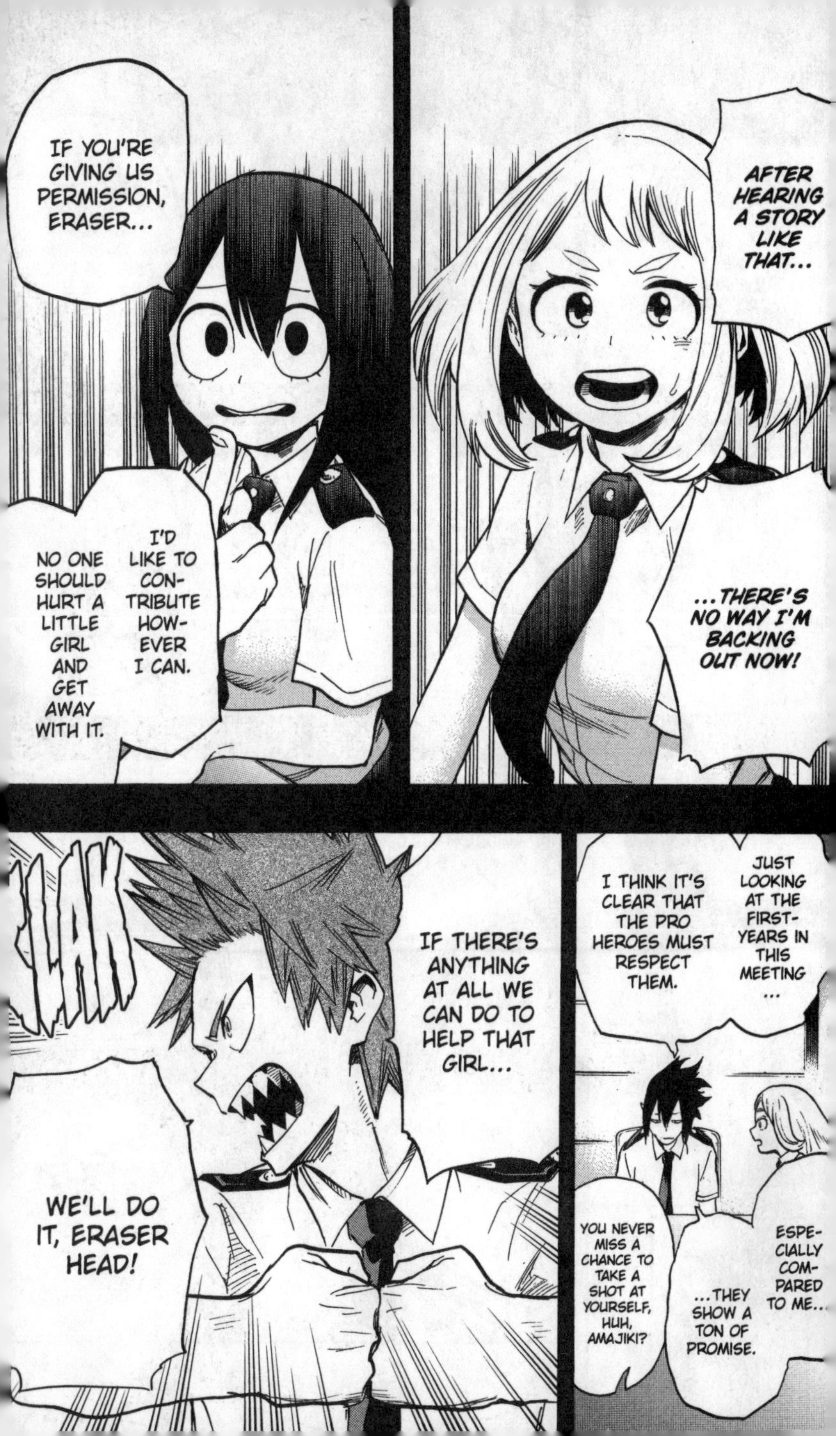
AFTER HEARING A STORY LIKE THAT...
...THERE'S NO WAY I'M BACKING OUT NOW!
IF YOU'RE GIVING US PERMISSION, ERASER...
I'D LIKE TO CONTRIBUTE HOWEVER I CAN.
NO ONE SHOULD HURT A LITTLE GIRL AND GET AWAY WITH IT.
JUST LOOKING AT THE FIRST-YEARS IN THIS MEETING...
I THINK IT'S CLEAR THAT THE PRO HEROES MUST RESPECT THEM.
ESPECIALLY COMPARED TO ME...
...THEY SHOW A TON OF PROMISE.
YOU NEVER MISS A CHANCE TO TAKE A SHOT AT YOURSELF, HUH, AMAJIKI?
IF THERE'S ANYTHING AT ALL WE CAN DO TO HELP THAT GIRL...
WE'LL DO IT, ERASER HEAD!

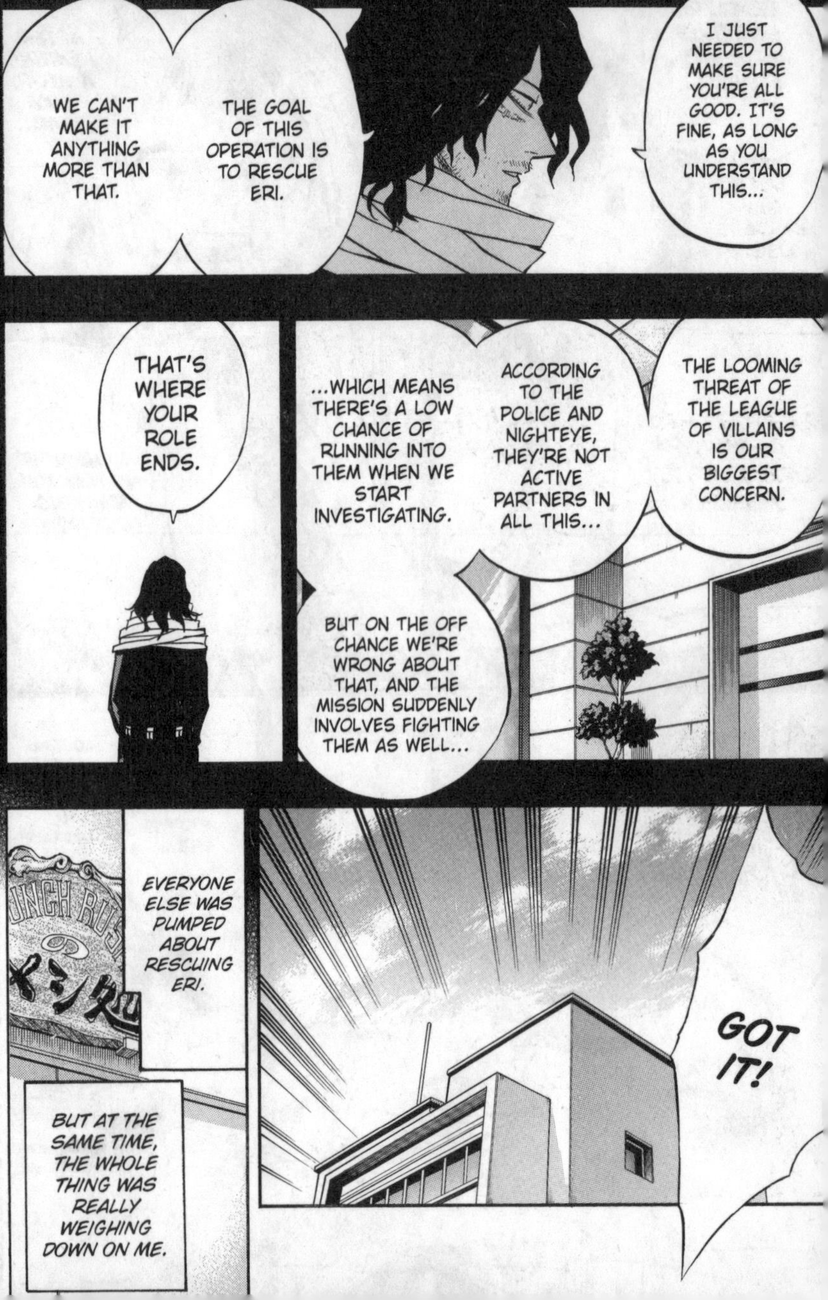

I JUST NEEDED TO MAKE SURE YOU'RE ALL GOOD. IT'S FINE, AS LONG AS YOU UNDERSTAND THIS...
THE GOAL OF THIS OPERATION IS TO RESCUE ERI.
WE CAN'T MAKE IT ANYTHING MORE THAN THAT.
THE LOOMING THREAT OF THE LEAGUE OF VILLAINS IS OUR BIGGEST CONCERN.
ACCORDING TO THE POLICE AND NIGHTEYE, THEY'RE NOT ACTIVE PARTNERS IN ALL THIS...
...WHICH MEANS THERE'S A LOW CHANCE OF RUNNING INTO THEM WHEN WE START INVESTIGATING.
BUT ON THE OFF CHANCE WE'RE WRONG ABOUT THAT, AND THE MISSION SUDDENLY INVOLVES FIGHTING THEM AS WELL...
THAT'S WHERE YOUR ROLE ENDS.
GOT IT!
EVERYONE ELSE WAS PUMPED ABOUT RESCUING ERI.
BUT AT THE SAME TIME, THE WHOLE THING WAS REALLY WEIGHING DOWN ON ME.

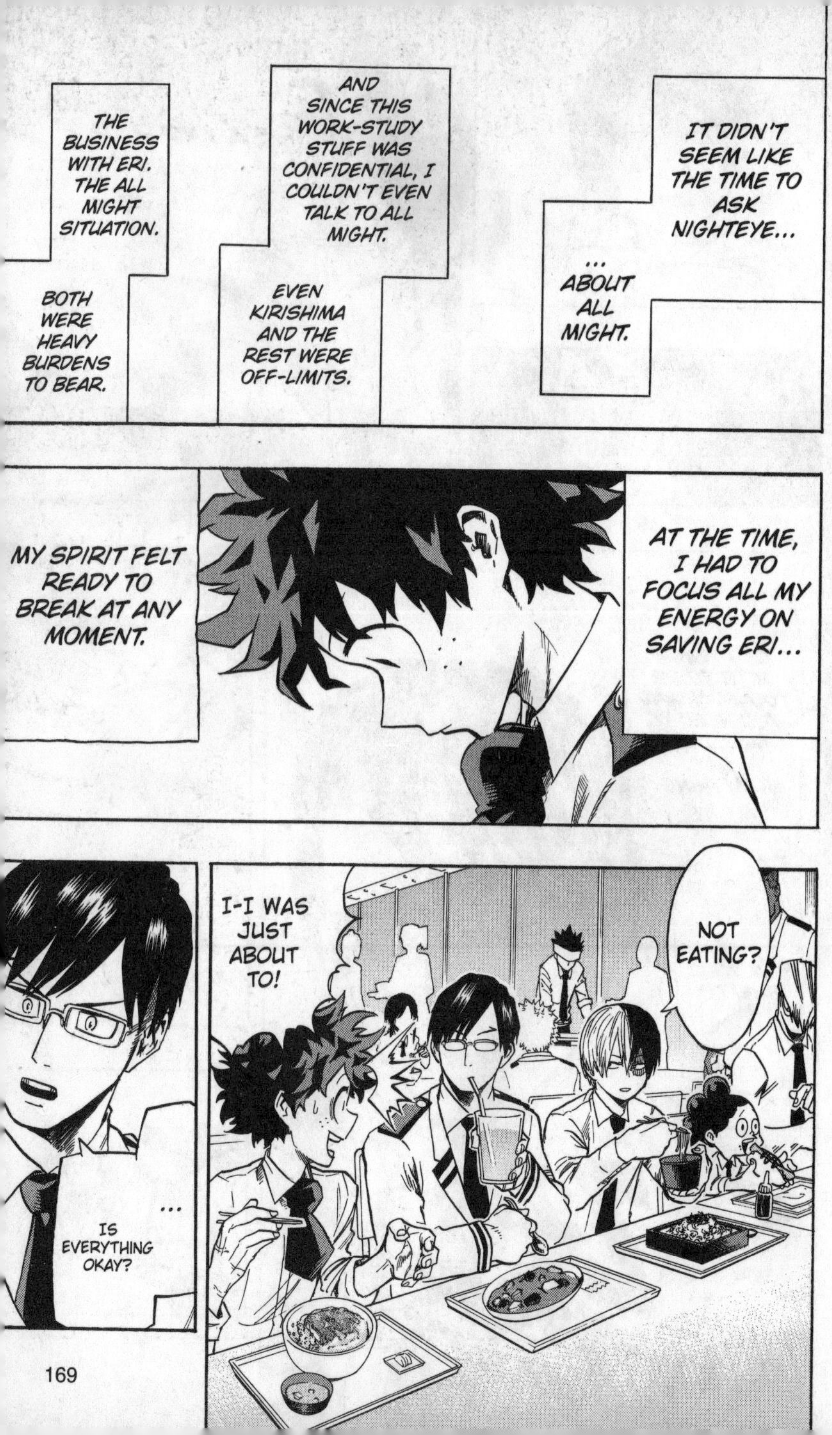
IT DIDN'T SEEM LIKE THE TIME TO ASK NIGHTEYE...
...ABOUT ALL MIGHT.
AND SINCE THIS WORK-STUDY STUFF WAS CONFIDENTIAL, I COULDN'T EVEN TALK TO ALL MIGHT.
EVEN KIRISHIMA AND THE REST WERE OFF-LIMITS.
THE BUSINESS WITH ERI. THE ALL MIGHT SITUATION.
BOTH WERE HEAVY BURDENS TO BEAR.
AT THE TIME, I HAD TO FOCUS ALL MY ENERGY ON SAVING ERI...
MY SPIRIT FELT READY TO BREAK AT ANY MOMENT.
NOT EATING?
I-I WAS JUST ABOUT TO!
... IS EVERYTHING OKAY?

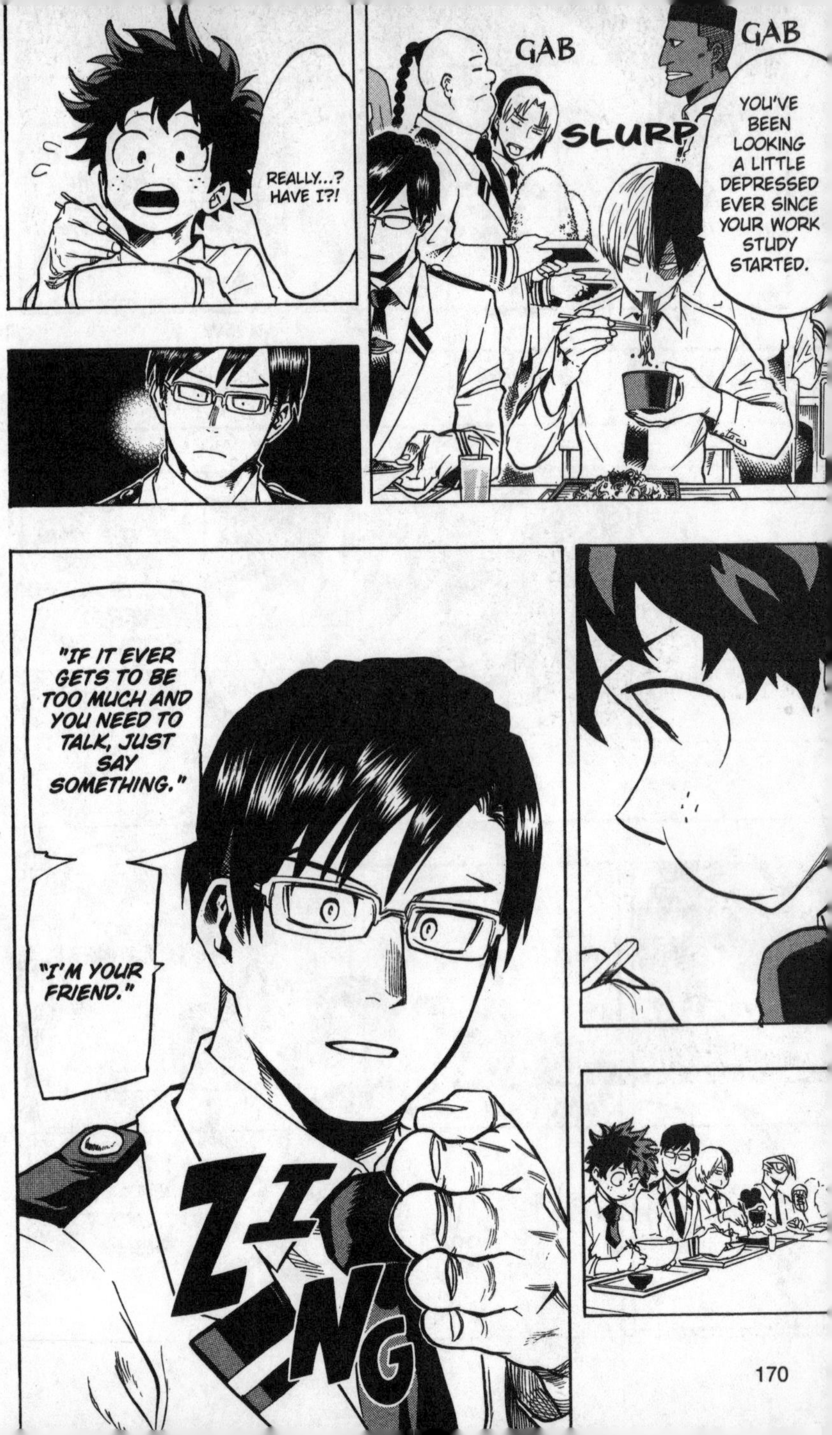
GAB
GAB
YOU'VE BEEN LOOKING A LITTLE DEPRESSED EVER SINCE YOUR WORK STUDY STARTED.
SLURP
REALLY...? HAVE I?!
"IF IT EVER GETS TO BE TOO MUCH AND YOU NEED TO TALK, JUST SAY SOMETHING."
"I'M YOUR FRIEND."
ZING

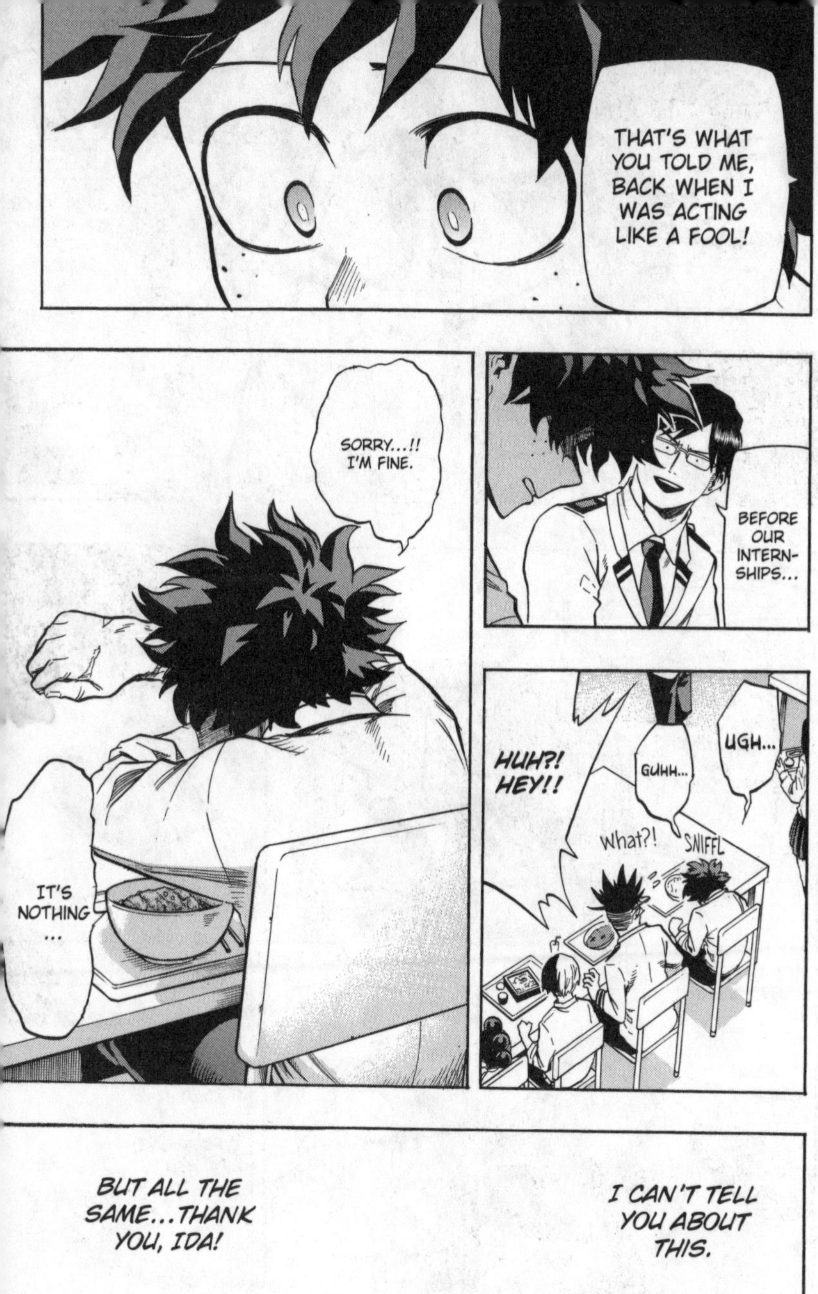
THAT'S WHAT YOU TOLD ME, BACK WHEN I WAS ACTING LIKE A FOOL!
BEFORE OUR INTERN-SHIPS...
UGH...
GUHH...
SNIFFL
What?!
HUH?! HEY!!
SORRY...!! I'M FINE.
IT'S NOTHING ...
I CAN'T TELL YOU ABOUT THIS.
BUT ALL THE SAME...THANK YOU, IDA!

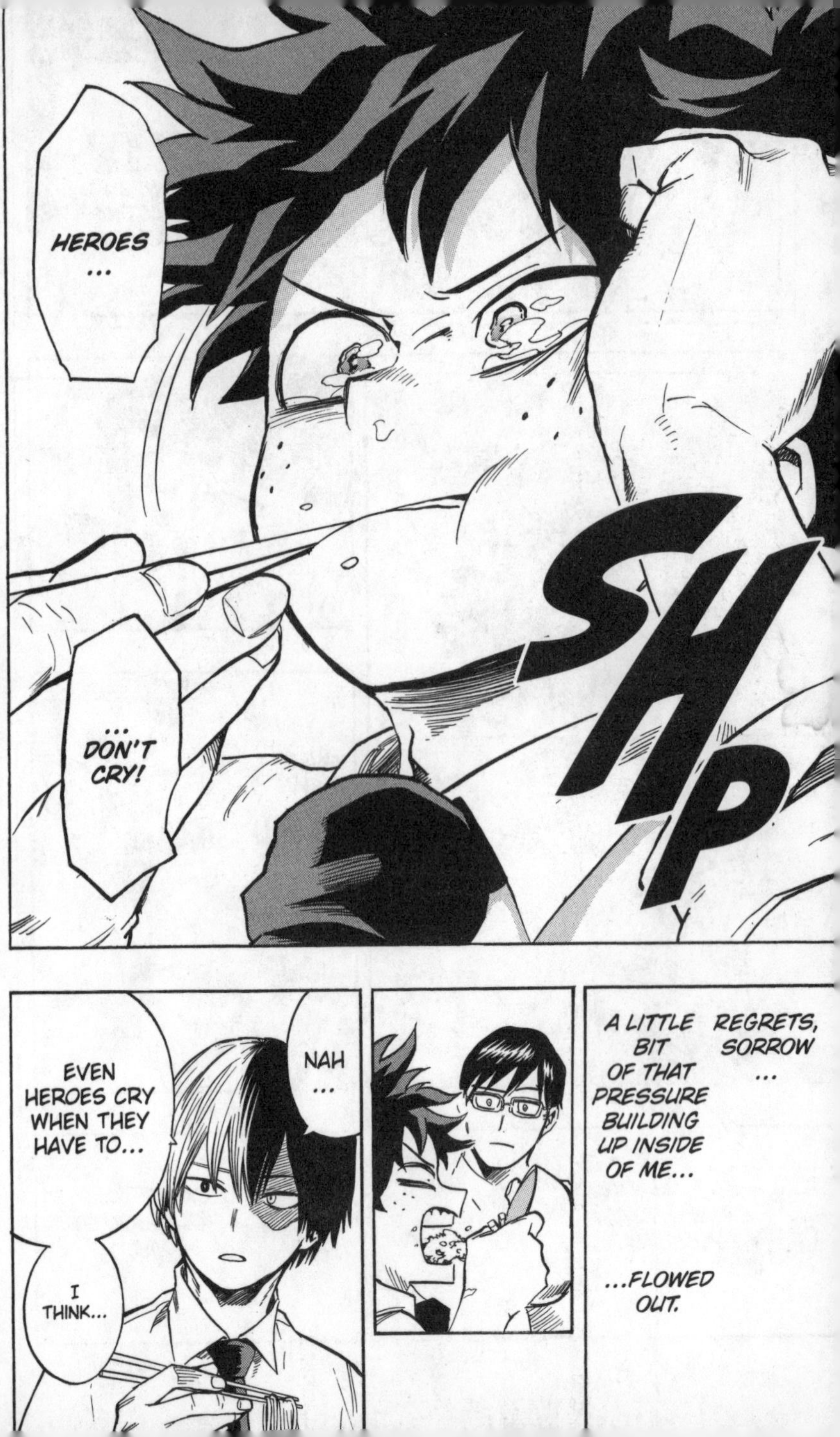
HEROES ...
... DON'T CRY!
SHP
REGRETS, SORROW ...
A LITTLE BIT OF THAT PRESSURE BUILDING UP INSIDE OF ME...
...FLOWED OUT.
NAH ...
EVEN HEROES CRY WHEN THEY HAVE TO...
I THINK...

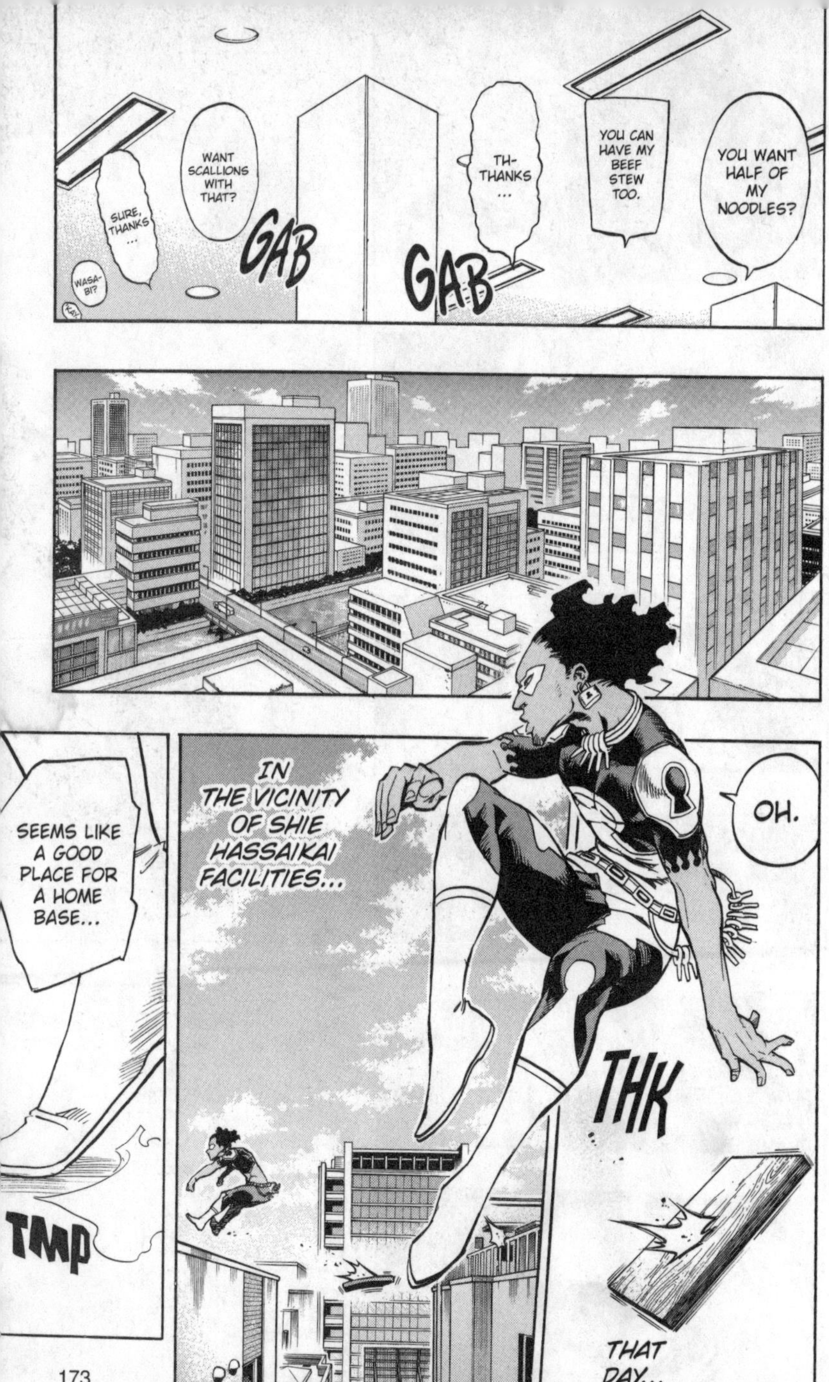
YOU WANT HALF OF MY NOODLES?
YOU CAN HAVE MY BEEF STEW TOO.
TH-THANKS...
GAB
WANT SCALLIONS WITH THAT?
GAB
SURE, THANKS...
WASA-BI?
OH.
IN THE VICINITY OF SHIE HASSAIKAI FACILITIES...
THK
THAT DAY...
SEEMS LIKE A GOOD PLACE FOR A HOME BASE...
TMP

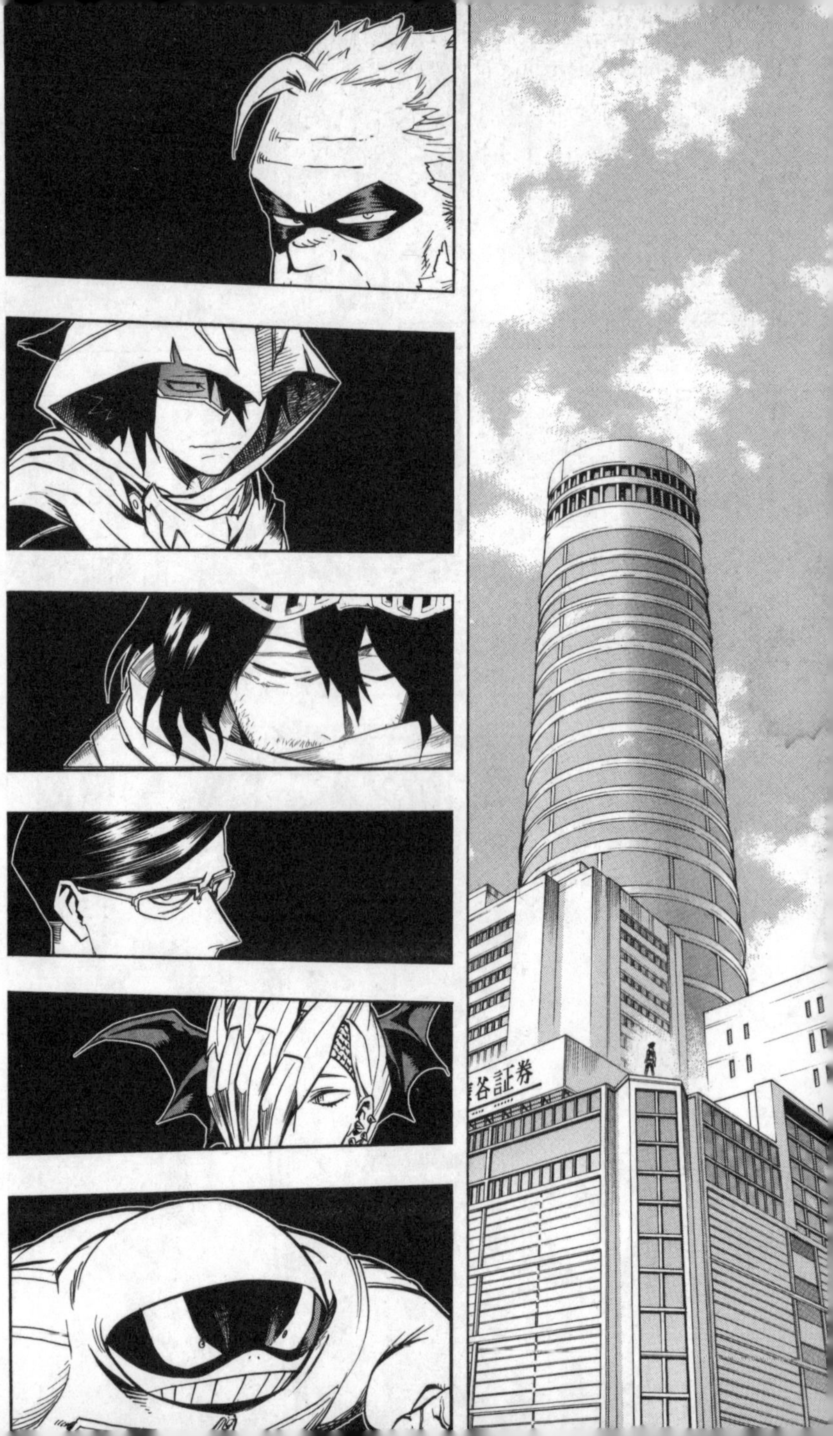
各証券

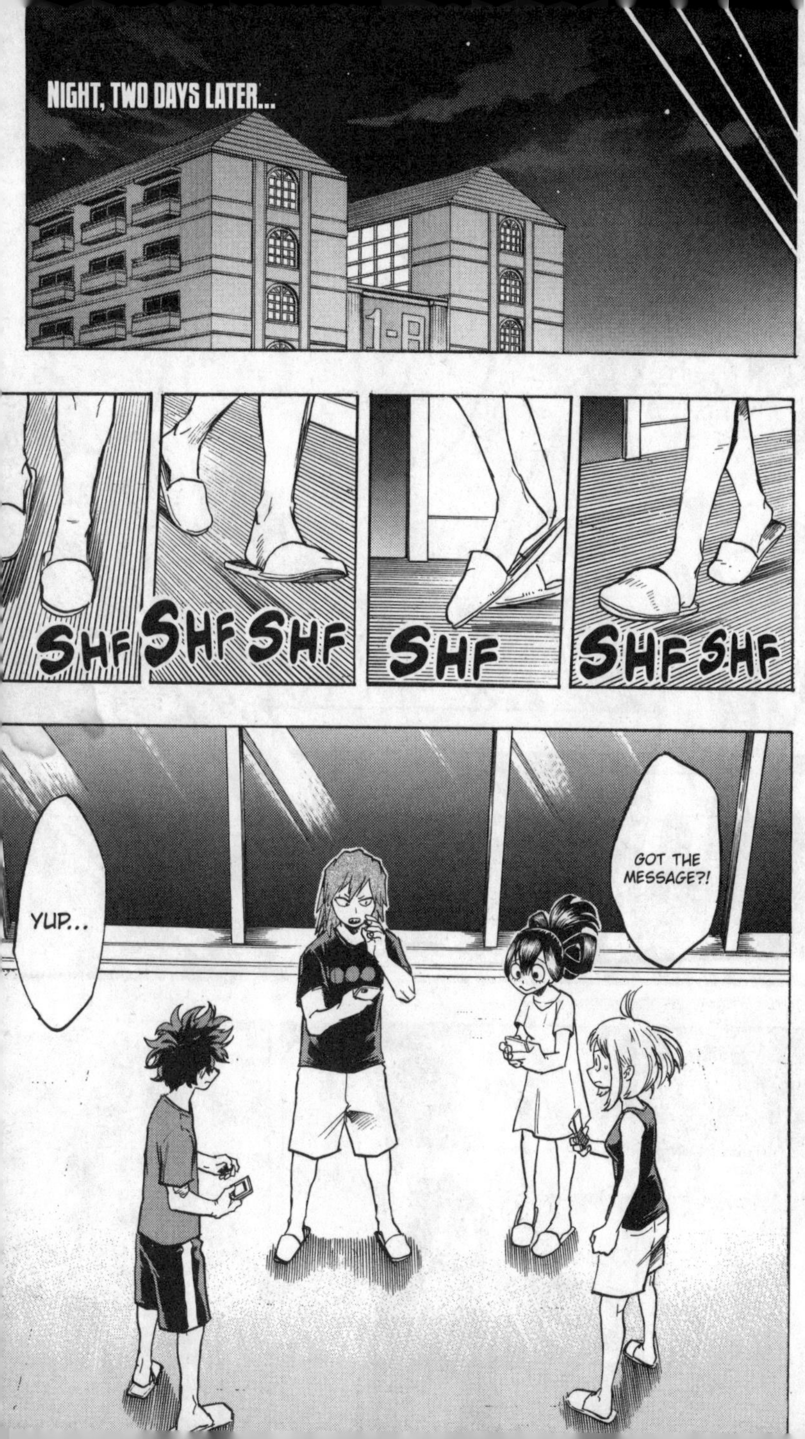

NIGHT, TWO DAYS LATER...
1-B
SHF SHF
SHF
SHF SHF
SHF
GOT THE MESSAGE?!
YUP...
...

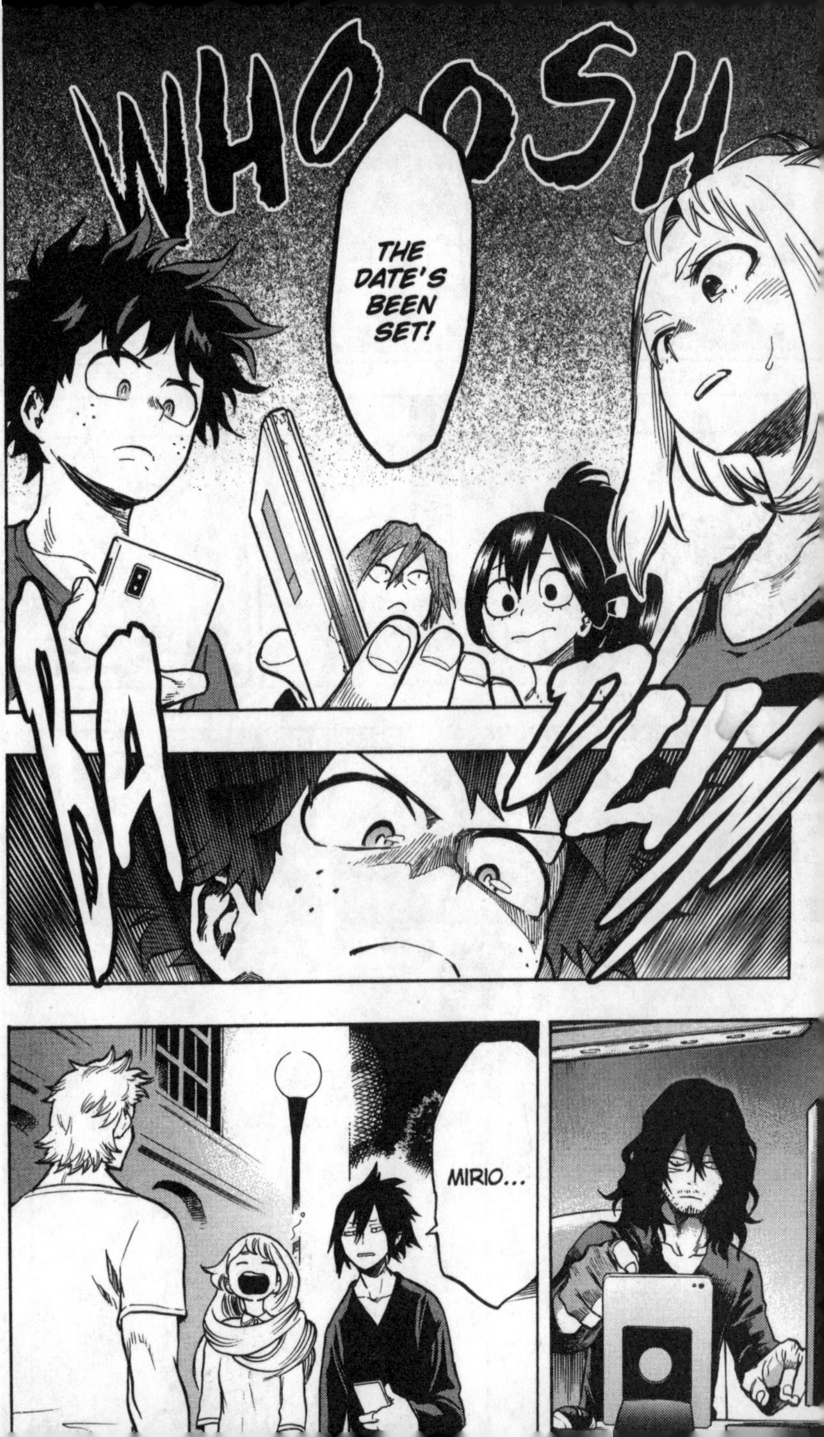
WHOOSH
THE DATE'S BEEN SET!
BA
DUM
MIRIO...

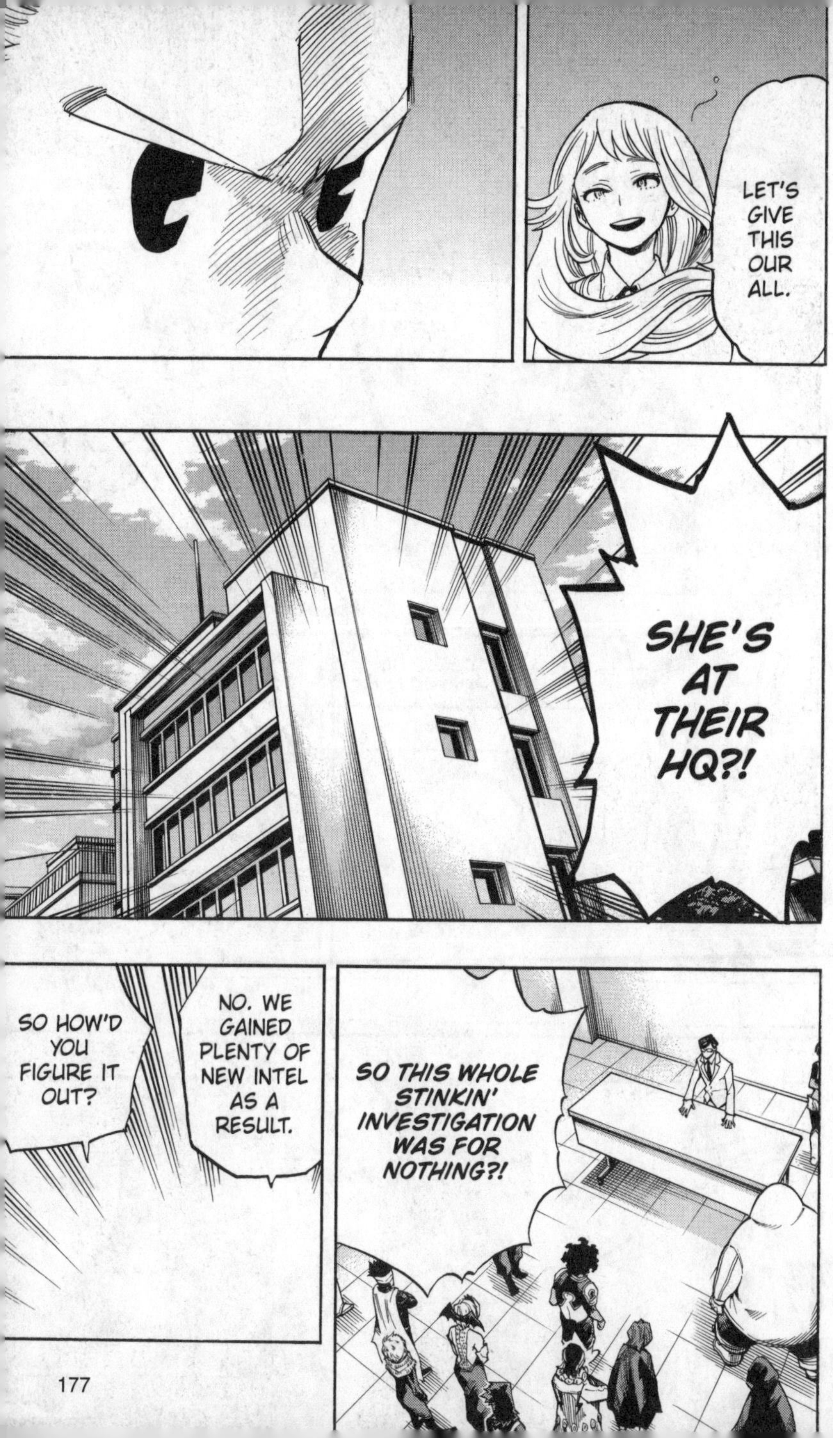
LET'S GIVE THIS OUR ALL.
SHE'S AT THEIR HQ?!
SO THIS WHOLE STINKIN' INVESTIGATION WAS FOR NOTHING?!
NO. WE GAINED PLENTY OF NEW INTEL AS A RESULT.
SO HOW'D YOU FIGURE IT OUT?

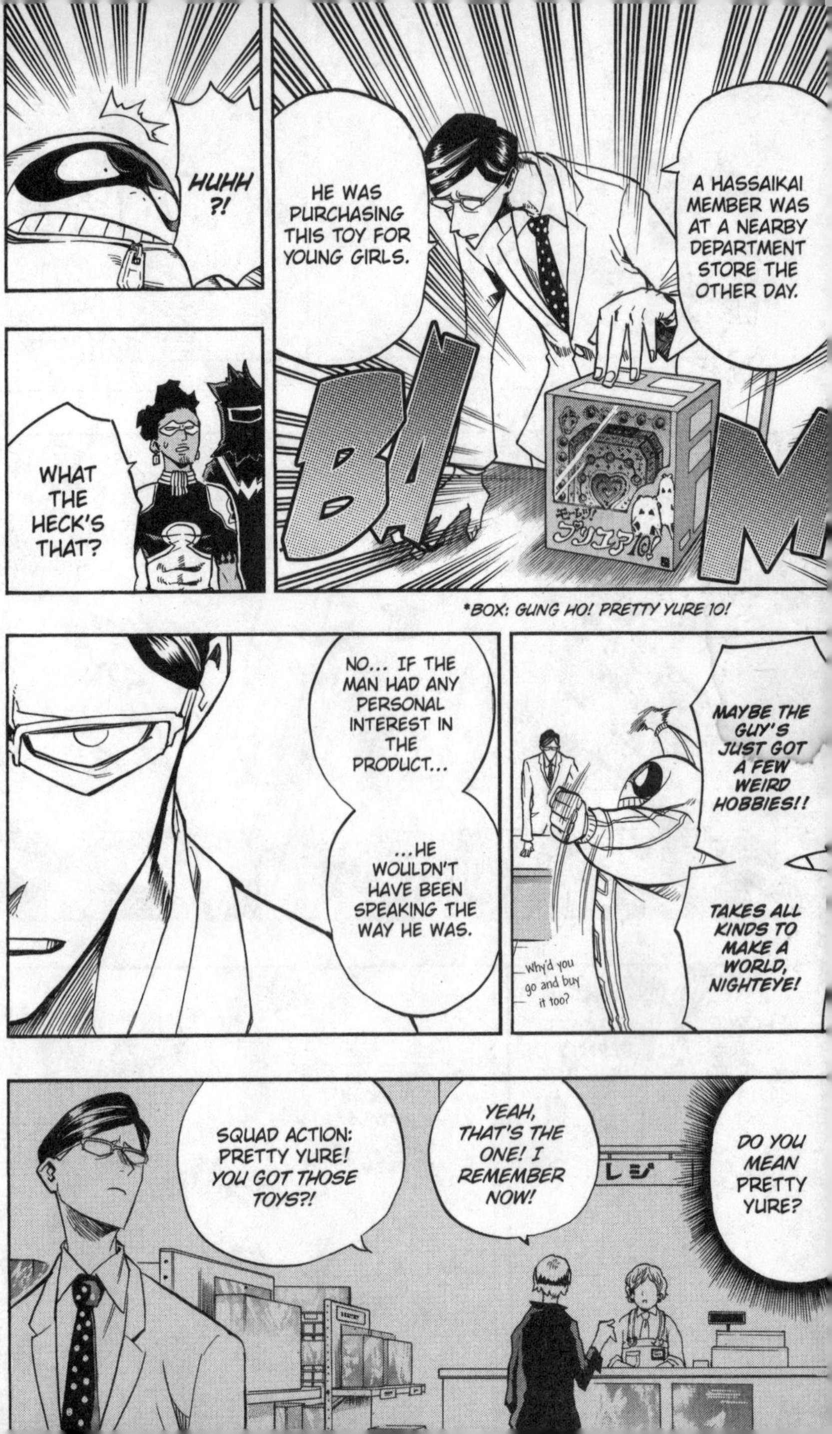
A HASSAIKAI MEMBER WAS AT A NEARBY DEPARTMENT STORE THE OTHER DAY.
HE WAS PURCHASING THIS TOY FOR YOUNG GIRLS.
BAM
HUHH ?!
WHAT THE HECK'S THAT?
*BOX: GUNG HO! PRETTY YURE 10!
MAYBE THE GUY'S JUST GOT A FEW WEIRD HOBBIES!!
TAKES ALL KINDS TO MAKE A WORLD, NIGHTEYE!
Why'd you go and buy it too?
NO... IF THE MAN HAD ANY PERSONAL INTEREST IN THE PRODUCT...
...HE WOULDN'T HAVE BEEN SPEAKING THE WAY HE WAS.
DO YOU MEAN PRETTY YURE?
レジ
YEAH, THAT'S THE ONE! I REMEMBER NOW!
SQUAD ACTION: PRETTY YURE! YOU GOT THOSE TOYS?!

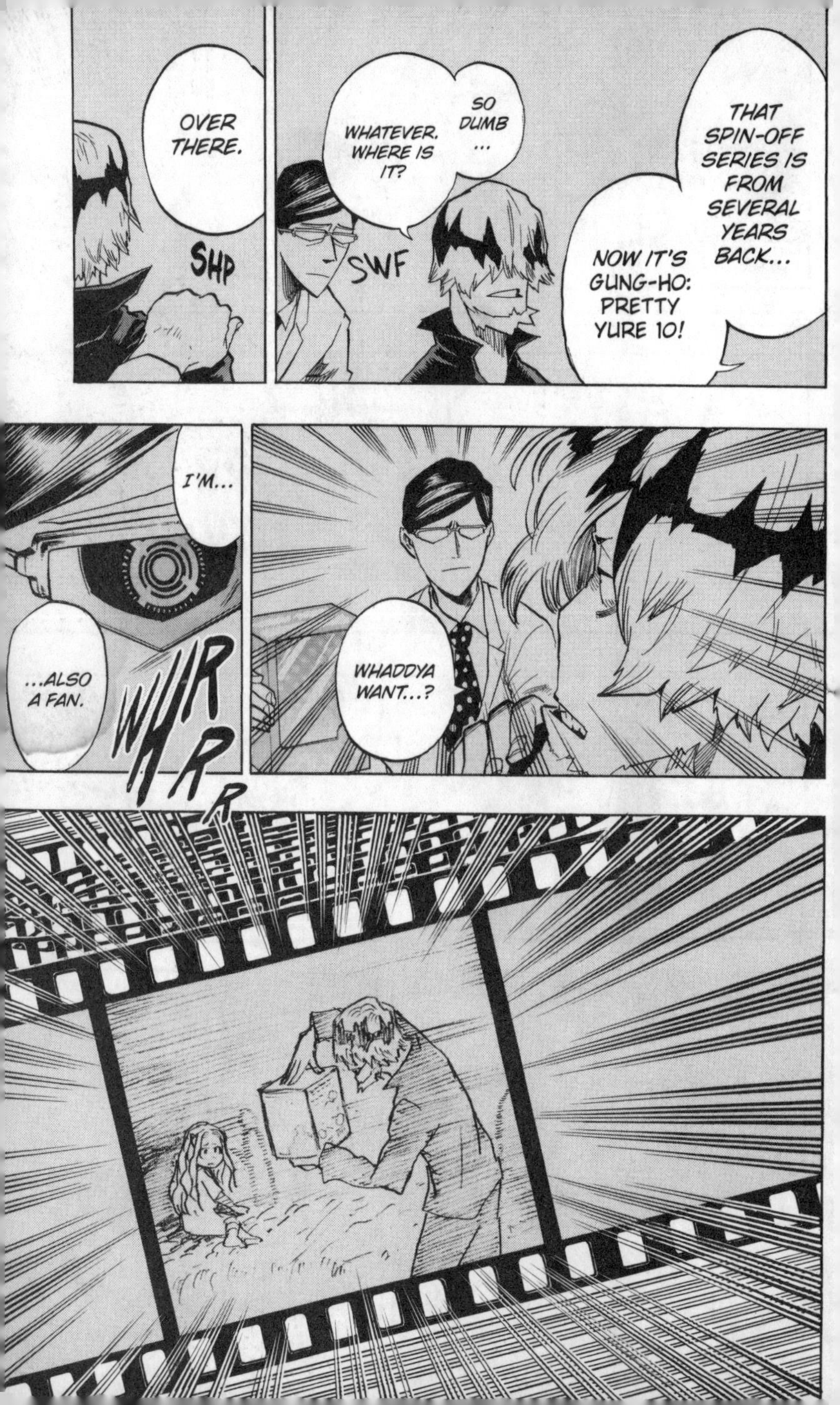
THAT SPIN-OFF SERIES IS FROM SEVERAL YEARS BACK...
NOW IT'S GUNG-HO: PRETTY YURE 10!
SO DUMB...
WHATEVER. WHERE IS IT?
SWF
OVER THERE.
SHP
WHADDYA WANT...?
I'M...
...ALSO A FAN.
WHRRR

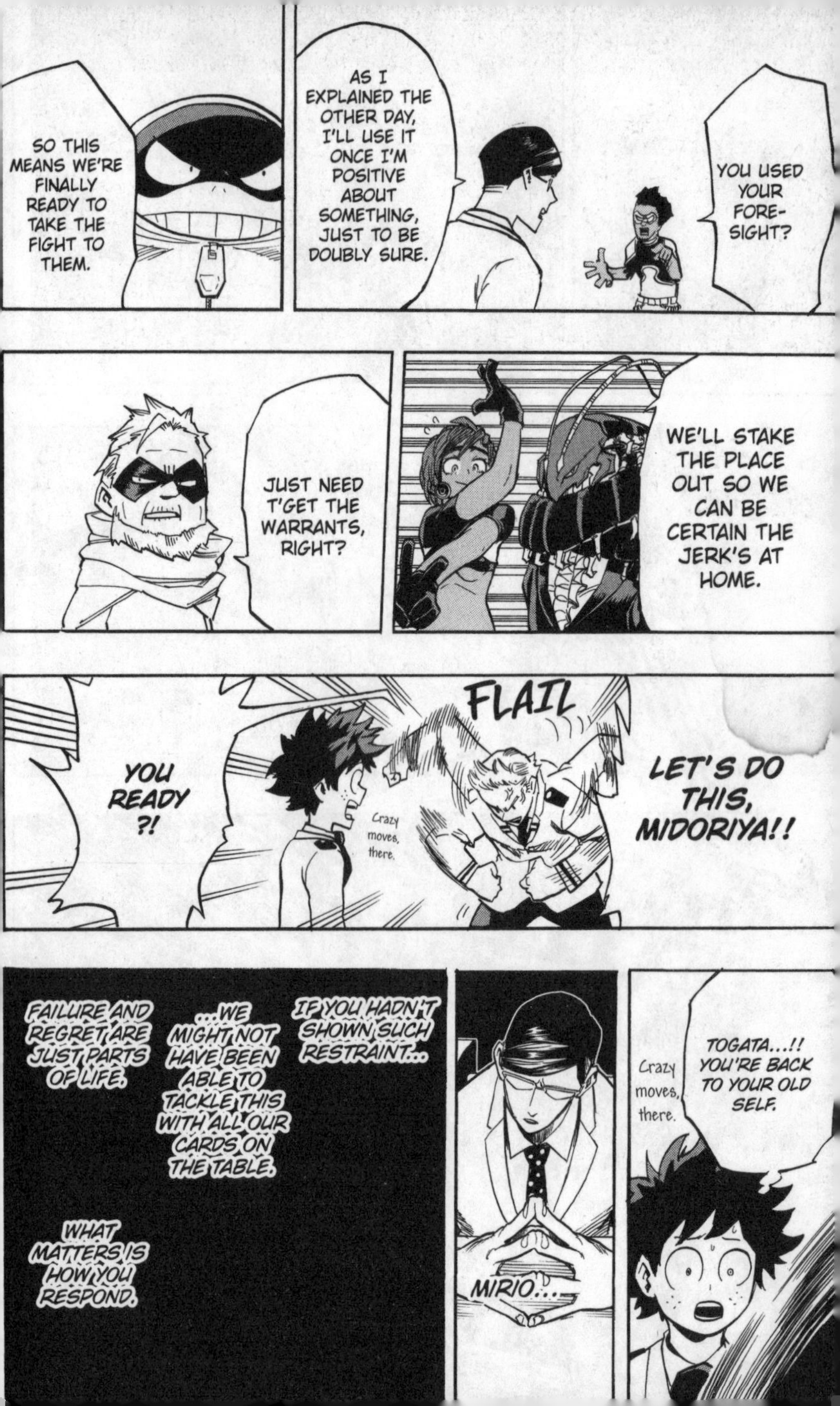
YOU USED YOUR FORE-SIGHT?
AS I EXPLAINED THE OTHER DAY, I'LL USE IT ONCE I'M POSITIVE ABOUT SOMETHING, JUST TO BE DOUBLY SURE.
SO THIS MEANS WE'RE FINALLY READY TO TAKE THE FIGHT TO THEM.
WE'LL STAKE THE PLACE OUT SO WE CAN BE CERTAIN THE JERK'S AT HOME.
JUST NEED T'GET THE WARRANTS, RIGHT?
FLAIL
LET'S DO THIS, MIDORIYA!!
Crazy moves, there.
YOU READY?!
TOGATA...!! YOU'RE BACK TO YOUR OLD SELF.
Crazy moves, there.
MIRIO...
IF YOU HADN'T SHOWN SUCH RESTRAINT...
...WE MIGHT NOT HAVE BEEN ABLE TO TACKLE THIS WITH ALL OUR CARDS ON THE TABLE.
FAILURE AND REGRET ARE JUST PARTS OF LIFE.
WHAT MATTERS IS HOW YOU RESPOND.

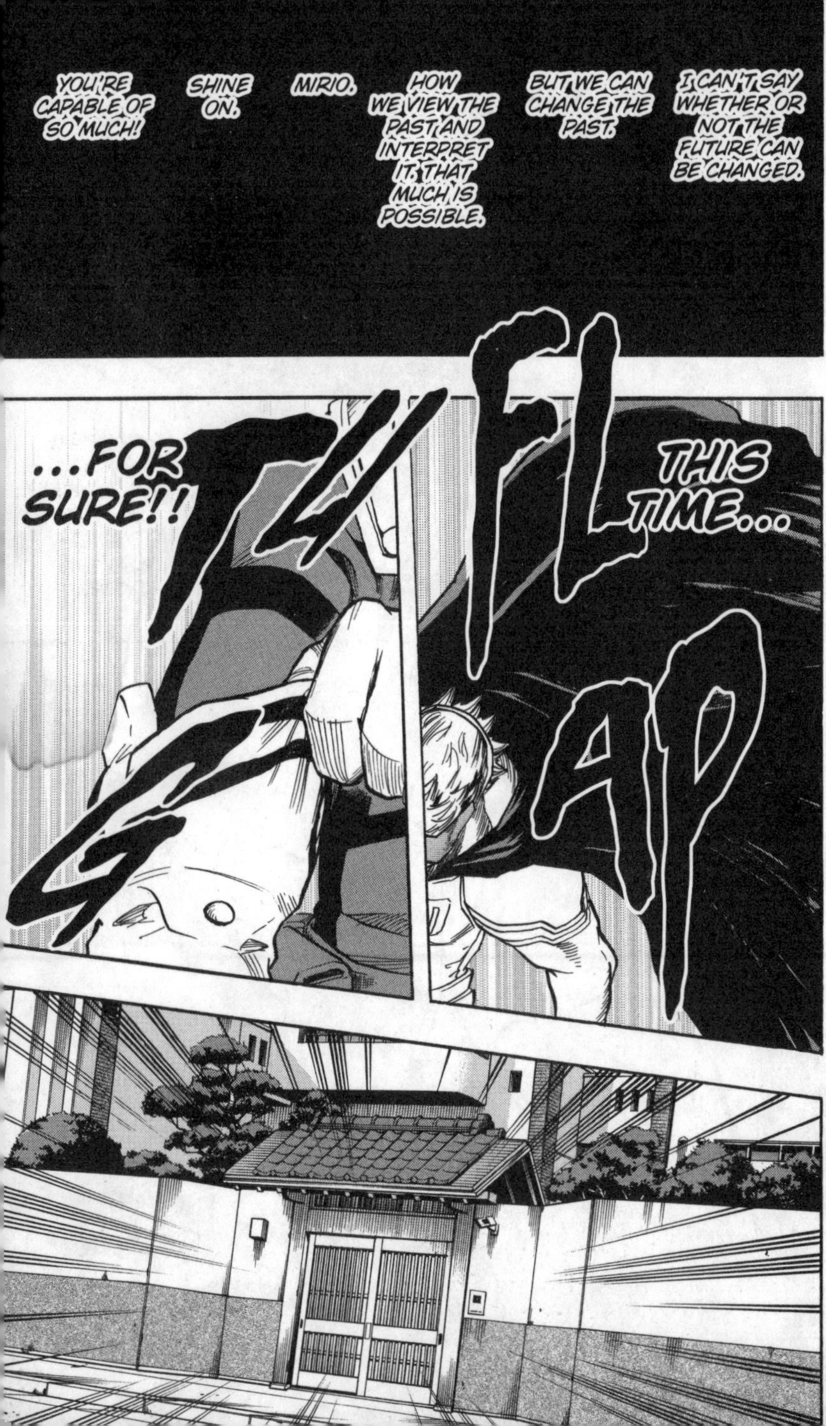
I CAN'T SAY WHETHER OR NOT THE FUTURE CAN BE CHANGED.
BUT WE CAN CHANGE THE PAST.
HOW WE VIEW THE PAST AND INTERPRET IT. THAT MUCH IS POSSIBLE.
MIRIO.
SHINE ON.
YOU'RE CAPABLE OF SO MUCH!
THIS TIME...
FLAP
...FOR SURE!!

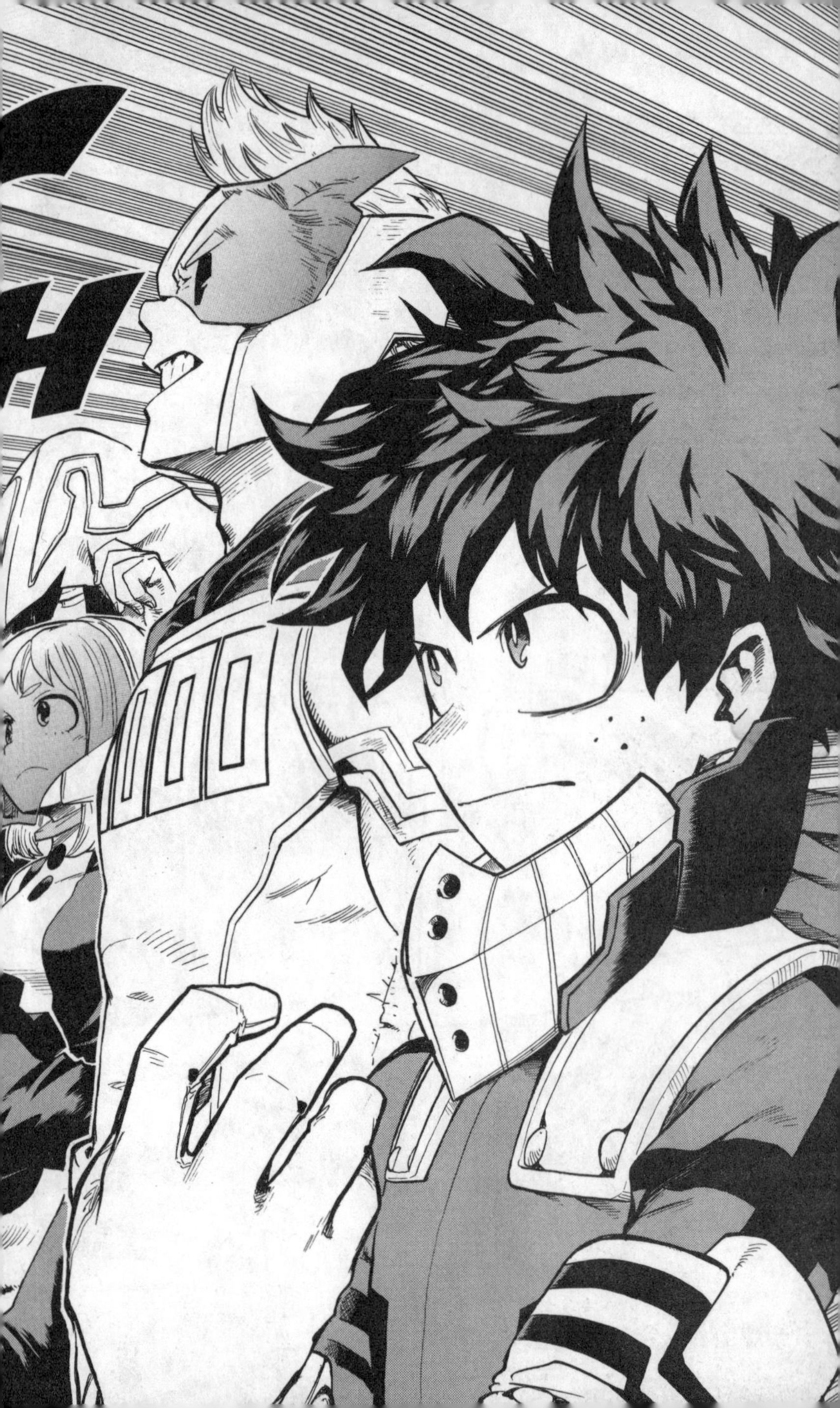

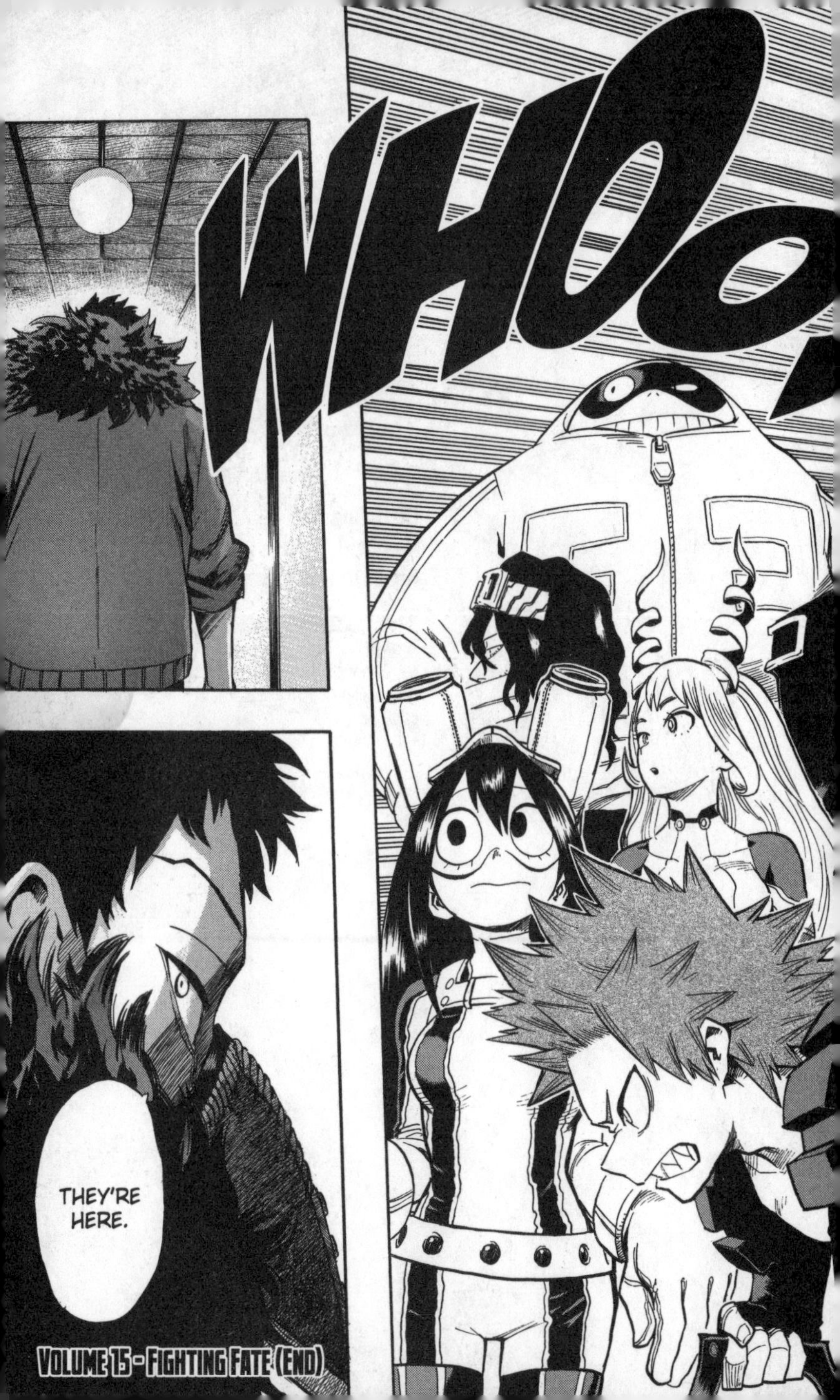
WHOO
THEY'RE HERE.
VOLUME 15 - FIGHTING FATE (END)

HERO
ROCK LOCK [32] [KEN TAKAGI]

STREET CLOTHES

Birthday: 6/9
Height: 173 cm
Favorite Thing: Bicycles

THE SUPPLEMENT
A married man. He's got a dirty mouth, but he's a good guy deep down. Also has a cool face.

HERO

KESAGIRI MAN

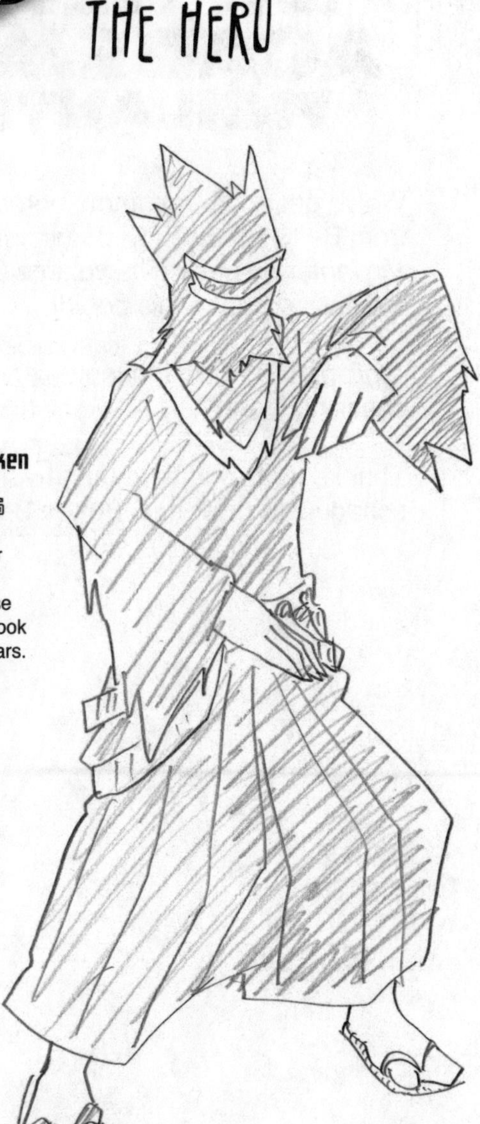
THE HERO

Birthday: 4/4
Height: 175 cm
Favorite Thing: Fried chicken

BEHIND THE SCENES
Part of his design was repurposed from some older work of mine. His head, specifically. I frequently reuse old assets, such as sketchbook doodles from my college years.

MY HERO ACADEMIA: VIGILANTES

We've got another commemorative illustration from Betten Sensei, whose spin-off series, *Vigilantes,* is getting its volume 2 release at the same time as this book!!

Vigilantes is really fun, so I highly recommend checking it out!!

Thanks for taking time out of your busy schedule to draw this, Betten Sensei!!

SOMEONE THINKS I'M CUTE? SCORE!

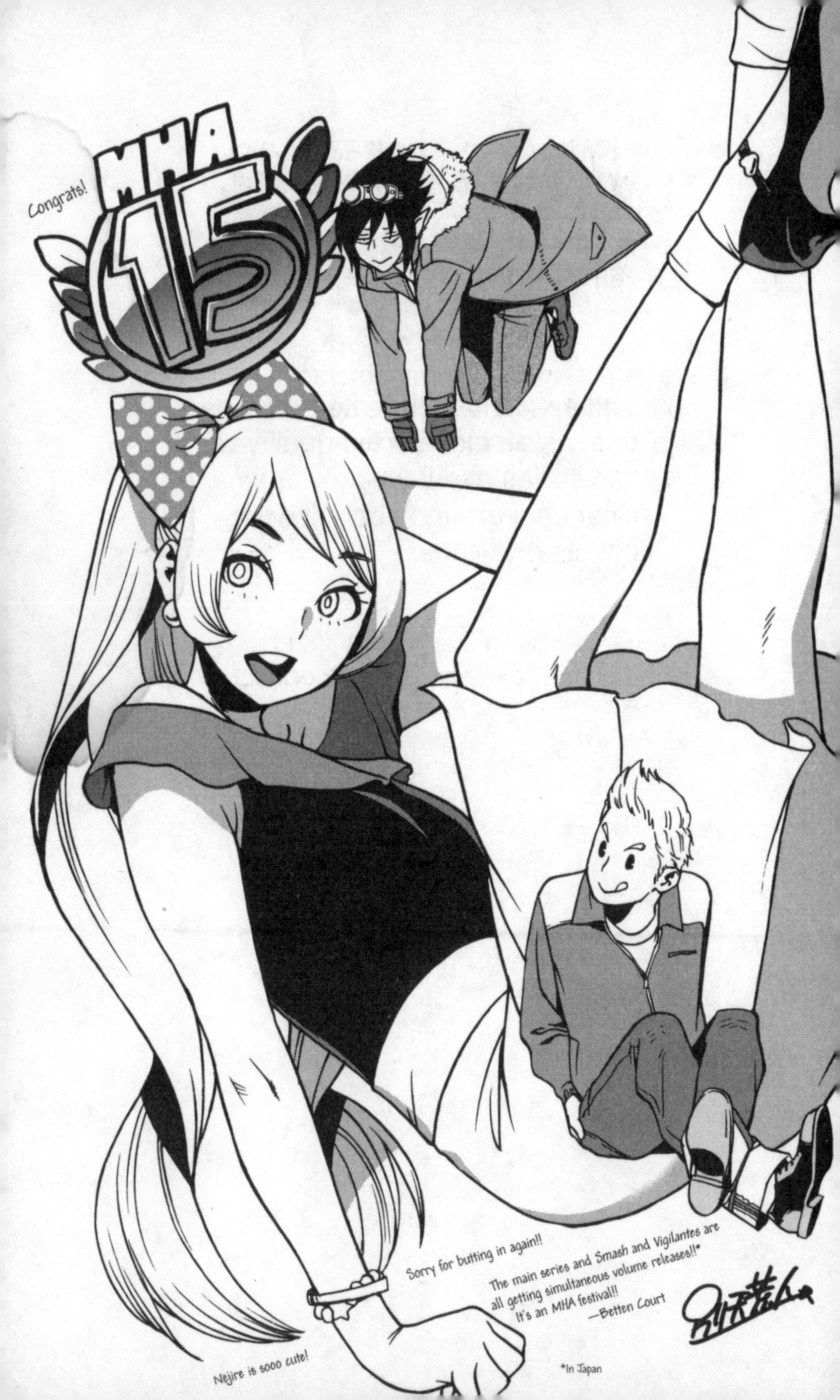
Congrats!
MHA
15
Sorry for butting in again!!
The main series and Smash and Vigilantes are all getting simultaneous volume releases!!*
It's an MHA festival!!
—Betten Court
Nejire is sooo cute!
*In Japan

MY HERO ACADEMIA STAFF

The awesomely talented members of my staff elevate the quality of this series every week with their killer backgrounds and special effects drawings.

SORRY THAT INKING MY HAIR IS SUCH A PAIN IN THE BUTT!!

Q: If you could have any Quirk that's been shown in the story, which would you choose?

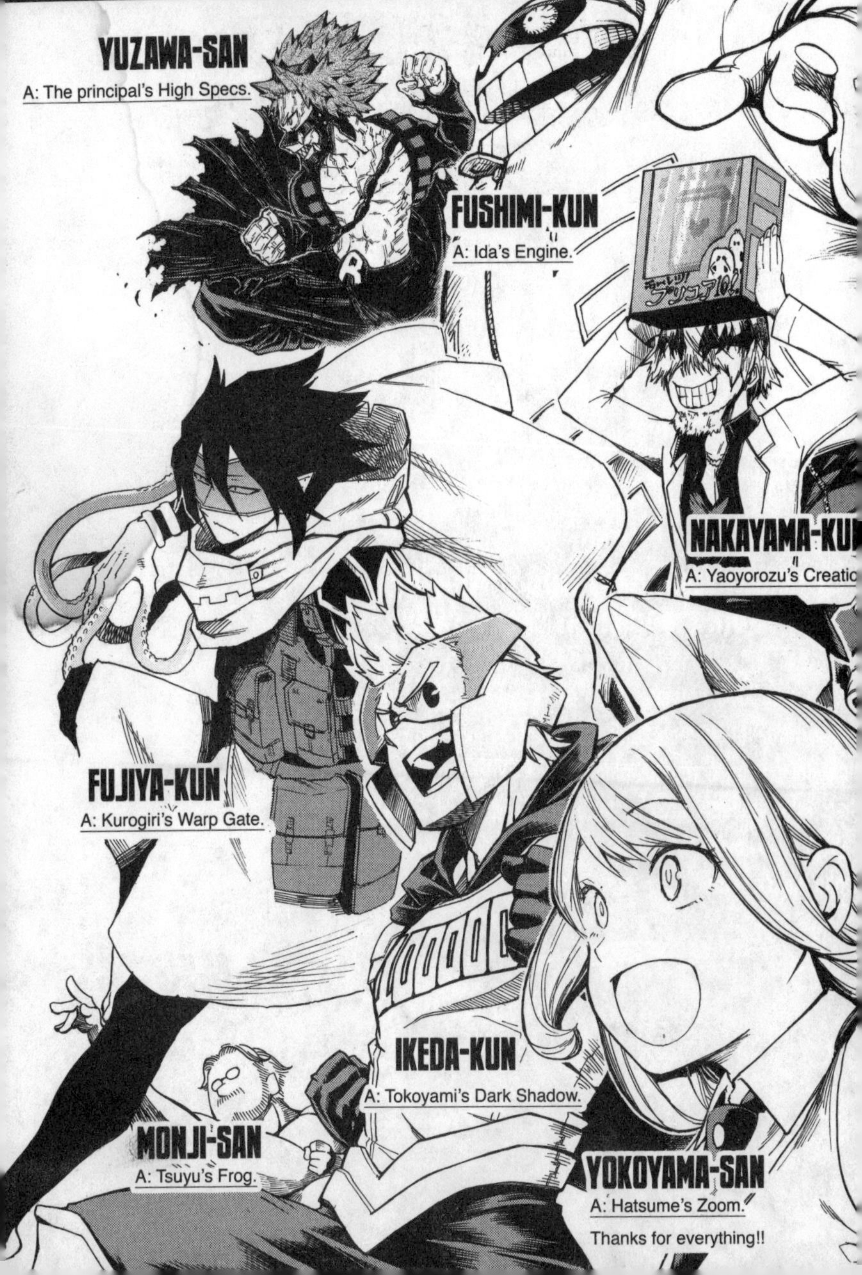
YUZAWA-SAN
A: The principal's High Specs.
FUSHIMI-KUN
A: Ida's Engine.
NAKAYAMA-KU
A: Yaoyorozu's Creatio
FUJIYA-KUN
A: Kurogiri's Warp Gate.
IKEDA-KUN
A: Tokoyami's Dark Shadow.
MONJI-SAN
A: Tsuyu's Frog.
YOKOYAMA-SAN
A: Hatsume's Zoom.
Thanks for everything!!

ASTRA
LOST IN SPACE

CAN EIGHT TEENAGERS FIND THEIR WAY HOME FROM 5,000 LIGHT-YEARS AWAY?

t's the year 2063, and interstellar space travel has become he norm. Eight students from Caird High School and one hild set out on a routine planet camp excursion. While here, the students are mysteriously transported 5,000 ight-years away to the middle of nowhere! Will they ever make it back home?!

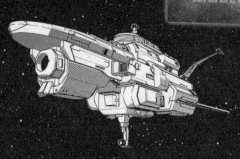

ASTRA
LOST IN SPACE

Story and Art by KENTA SHINOHARA